T0199248

Recurrent Neural Networks

The text discusses recurrent neural networks for prediction and offers new insights into the learning algorithms, architectures, and stability of recurrent neural networks. It discusses important topics including recurrent and folding networks, long short-term memory (LSTM) networks, gated recurrent unit neural networks, language modeling, neural network model, activation function, feed-forward network, learning algorithm, neural turning machines, and approximation ability. The text discusses diverse applications in areas including air pollutant modeling and prediction, attractor discovery and chaos, ECG signal processing, and speech processing. Case studies are interspersed throughout the book for better understanding.

FEATURES

- Covers computational analysis and understanding of natural languages
- Discusses applications of recurrent neural network in e-Healthcare
- Provides case studies in every chapter with respect to real-world scenarios
- Examines open issues with natural language, health care, multimedia (Audio/ Video), transportation, stock market, and logistics

The text is primarily written for undergraduate and graduate students, researchers, and industry professionals in the fields of electrical, electronics and communication, and computer engineering/information technology.

Recurrent Neural Networks

Concepts and Applications

Edited by
Amit Kumar Tyagi
Ajith Abraham

3 CB

07 - 18

CRC Press
Taylor & Francis Group
Boca Raton London New York

CRC Press is an imprint of the
Taylor & Francis Group, an **informa** business

First edition published 2023
by CRC Press
6000 Broken Sound Parkway NW, Suite 300, Boca Raton, FL 33487-2742

and by CRC Press
4 Park Square, Milton Park, Abingdon, Oxon, OX14 4RN

CRC Press is an imprint of Taylor & Francis Group, LLC

ISBN: 978-1-032-08164-9 (hbk)
ISBN: 978-1-032-31056-5 (pbk)
ISBN: 978-1-003-30782-2 (ebk)

DOI: 10.1201/9781003307822

Typeset in Times
by SPi Technologies India Pvt Ltd (Straive)

Access the Support Material: https://www.routledge.com/9781032081649

Contents

SECTION I   Introduction

SECTION II   Process and Methods

SECTION III   Applications

SECTION IV Post–COVID-19 Futuristic Scenarios–Based Applications: Issues and Challenges

Preface

The key component in forecasting demand and consumption of resources in a health care and other useful network like supply chain management, transportation, and natural processing, this book completes one step in providing an accurate prediction of real-valued time series. Indeed, both service interruptions and resource waste can be reduced with the implementation of an effective forecasting system. Significant research has thus been devoted to the design and development of methodologies for different applications' forecasting over the past decades. A class of mathematical models, called recurrent neural networks, are nowadays gaining renewed interest among researchers, and they are replacing many practical implementations of the forecasting systems, previously based mostly on statistical methods. Despite the undeniable expressive power of these architectures, their recurrent nature complicates their understanding and poses challenges in the training procedures. Although recently different kinds of recurrent neural networks have been successfully applied in fields like natural language processing or text translation (or text analysis, image captioning, sentiment analysis and machine translation) and a systematic evaluation of their performance in multimedia (also transportation, i.e., for online and offline activity), the context of load forecasting is still lacking. Also, there is a huge need for intelligent interactive multimedia system (for health care applications) and forecasting system for stock market that could work on recurrent neural network. This book offers a comparative study of the problem of real-world applications' forecast by using different classes of state-of-the-art recurrent neural networks. The authors provide a general overview of the most important architectures and define guidelines for configuring the recurrent networks to predict real-valued time series. Also discussed are several future possibilities with many applications for future researcher to empower their knowledge. The contributors test the reviewed models on controlled synthetic tasks and on real-world datasets, covering important practical case studies. It is our hope that this collection of essay can become a useful resource for data scientists in academia and industry to keep up to date with the latest developments in the field of deep learning and prediction.

In general, a neural network is a network or circuit of neurons, or in a modern sense, an artificial neural network composed of artificial neurons or nodes. Deep learning and supervised sequence labeling represent a vital area of machine learning, encompassing tasks such as machine translation, speech, handwriting, text recognition, etc. Recurrent neural networks are powerful sequence learning tools, i.e., robust to input noise and distortion and able to exploit long-range contextual information that would seem ideally suited to such problems. However, their role in large-scale sequence labeling systems has so far been auxiliary. The goal of this book is to provide a complete framework for classifying and transcribing sequential data with recurrent neural networks.

The MathWorks, Inc.
3 Apple Hill Drive
Natick, MA, 01760-2098 USA
Tel: 508-647-7000
Fax: 508-647-7001
E-mail: info@mathworks.com
Web: www.mathworks.com

Editors

Amit Kumar Tyagi, PhD, is Assistant Professor (Senior Grade) and Senior Researcher at the School of Computer Science and Engineering, Vellore Institute of Technology (VIT), Chennai Campus, Chennai, Tamilnadu, India. His current research focuses on machine learning with big data, blockchain technology, data science, cyber physical systems, smart and secure computing, and privacy. He has contributed to several projects such as AARIN and P3-Block to address some of the open issues related to the privacy breaches in vehicular applications (such as parking) and medical cyber physical systems. He earned a PhD at Pondicherry Central University, India. He is a member of the IEEE.

Ajith Abraham, PhD, is Director of Machine Intelligence Research Labs (MIR Labs), a not-for-profit scientific network for innovation and research excellence connecting industry and academia. As an investigator and co-investigator, he has won research grants worth over US$100 million from Australia, the United States, the European Union, Italy, the Czech Republic, France, Malaysia, and China. His research focuses on real-world problems in the fields of machine intelligence, cyber-physical systems, Internet of Things, network security, sensor networks, Web intelligence, Web services, and data mining. He is Chair of the IEEE Systems Man and Cybernetics Society Technical Committee on Soft Computing. He is the editor-in-chief of *Engineering Applications of Artificial Intelligence* and serves or has served on the editorial board of several international journals. He earned a PhD in computer science at Monash University, Melbourne, Australia.

Contributors

V. Abinash
School of Computer Science and
Engineering
Vellore Institute of Technology
Chennai, Tamil Nadu, India

Aditya Agarwal
MIT-World Peace University
Pune, Maharashtra, India

Zuhra Al-Barmani
Department of Computer Science
Faculty of Science for Women (SCIW)
University of Babylon
Babylon, Iraq

Samaher Al-Janabi
Department of Computer Science
Faculty of Science for Women (SCIW)
University of Babylon
Babylon, Iraq

G. AL-Taleby
University of Babylon
Babylon, Iraq

Ayad Alkaim
Department of Computer Science
Faculty of Science for Women (SCIW)
University of Babylon
Babylon, Iraq

Harish Chandra Arora
CSIR-Central Building Research
Institute
Roorkee, Uttarakhand, India

K. Aswani
Department of Applied Electronics
Noorul Islam Center for Higher Education
Kumaracoil, Tamil Nadu, India

Partha Sarathi Barma
Department of Computer Science and
Engineering
NSHM Knowledge Campus Durgapur
Durgapur, West Bengal, India

J. Bhuvana
Department of Computer Science and
Engineering
Sri Sivasubramaniya Nadar College of
Engineering
Chennai, Tamil Nadu, India

Debashreet Das
Department of Computer Science and
Engineering
Karunya Institute of Technology and
Sciences
Coimbatore, Tamil Nadu, India

Kusumika Krori Dutta
Department of Electrical and
Electronics Engineering
M.S. Ramaiah Institute of Technology
Bangalore, Karnataka, India

Romit Ganjoo
MIT-World Peace University
Pune, Maharashtra, India

Raj Ghamsani
Dwarkadas Jivanlal Sanghvi College of
Engineering
Mumbai, Maharashtra, India

Kanupriya Goswami
Department of Physics
Keshav Mahavidyalaya
University of Delhi
Pitam Pura, Delhi, India

Richa Gupta
Department of Computer Science
University of Delhi
Pitam Pura, Delhi, India

Shivesh Jha
Dwarkadas Jivanlal Sanghvi College of
    Engineering
Mumbai, Maharashtra, India

Vinita Jindal
Department of Computer Science
Keshav Mahavidyalaya
University of Delhi
Pitam Pura, Delhi, India

G. Kadhum
Department of Computer Science
Faculty of Science for Women (SCIW)
University of Babylon
Babylon, Iraq

Nishant Raj Kapoor
CSIR-Central Building Research
    Institute
Roorkee, Uttarakhand, India

A. Kathirvel
Department of Computer Science and
    Engineering
Karunya Institute of Technology and
    Sciences
Coimbatore, Tamil Nadu, India

Suchitra Khojewe
MIT-World Peace University
Pune, Maharashtra, India

Stewart Kirubakaran
Department of Computer Science and
    Engineering
Karunya Institute of Technology and
    Sciences
Coimbatore, Tamil Nadu, India

Aman Kumar
CSIR-Central Building Research
    Institute
Roorkee, Uttarakhand, India

Ashok Kumar
CSIR-Central Building Research
    Institute
Roorkee, Uttarakhand, India

R. Maheswari
School of Computer Science and
    Engineering
Vellore Institute of Technology
Chennai, Tamil Nadu, India

S. Maheswari
School of Computer Science and
    Engineering
Vellore Institute of Technology
Chennai, Tamil Nadu, India

Saibal Majumder
Department of Computer Science and
    Engineering
NSHM Knowledge Campus Durgapur
Durgapur, West Bengal, India

Bijoy Kumar Mandal
Department of Computer Science and
    Engineering
NSHM Knowledge Campus Durgapur
Durgapur, West Bengal, India

S. Meghanth
School of Computer Science and
    Engineering
Vellore Institute of Technology
Chennai, Tamil Nadu, India

D. Menaka
Department of Applied Electronics
Noorul Islam Center for Higher Education
Kumaracoil, Tamil Nadu, India

Ofaletse Mphale
Department of Computer Science
University of Botswana
Gaborone, Botswana

Aswin Murali
School of Computer Science and
    Engineering
Vellore Institute of Technology
Chennai, Tamil Nadu, India

A. Muralidhar
School of Computer Science and
    Engineering
Vellore Institute of Technology
Chennai, Tamil Nadu, India

Deebul Nair
University of Applied Sciences
Germany

Kashinadh S. Nair
School of Computer Science and
    Engineering
Vellore Institute of Technology
Chennai, Tamil Nadu, India

V. Lakshmi Narasimhan
Department of Computer Science
University of Botswana
Gaborone, Botswana

S. Naveneethan
Department of Computer Science and
    Engineering
SRM Institute of Science and
    Technology
Chengalpattu, Tamil Nadu, India

V. M. Nisha
School of Computer Science and
    Engineering
Vellore Institute of Technology
Chennai, Tamil Nadu, India

Harsh Panchal
MIT-World Peace University
Pune, Maharashtra, India

V. Pattabiraman
School of Computer Science and
    Engineering
Vellore Institute of Technology
Chennai, Tamil Nadu, India

Paul G. Ploeger
University of Applied Sciences
Germany

S. Poornima
M.S. Ramaiah Institute of Technology
Bangalore, Karnataka, India

Sakshi Purwar
School of Computer Science and
    Engineering
Vellore Institute of Technology
Chennai, Tamil Nadu, India

Ratnavel Rajalakshmi
School of Computer Science and
    Engineering
Vellore Institute of Technology
Chennai, Tamil Nadu, India

P. Rakesh
School of Computer Science and
    Engineering
Vellore Institute of Technology
Chennai, Tamil Nadu, India

V. Ramchander
School of Computer Science and
    Engineering
Vellore Institute of Technology
Chennai, Tamil Nadu, India

Richa
School of Computer Science and
    Engineering
Vellore Institute of Technology
Chennai, Tamil Nadu, India

Yakub Kayode Saheed
School of Information Technology and
    Computing
American University of Nigeria
Yola, Nigeria

S. A. Sajidha
School of Computer Science and
    Engineering
Vellore Institute of Technology
Chennai, Tamil Nadu, India

Preet Sanghavi
Dwarkadas Jivanlal Sanghvi College of
    Engineering
Mumbai, Maharashtra, India

Sanay Shah
Dwarkadas Jivanlal Sanghvi College of
    Engineering
Mumbai, Maharashtra, India

Arpana Sharma
Department of Mathematics
Keshav Mahavidyalaya
University of Delhi
Pitam Pura, Delhi, India

Ramit Sharma
University of Applied Sciences
Germany

Narendra M. Shekokar
Dwarkadas Jivanlal Sanghvi College of
    Engineering
Mumbai, Maharashtra, India

Abhinav Basil Shinow
School of Computer Science and
    Engineering
Vellore Institute of Technology
Chennai, Tamil Nadu, India

M. Subramaniam
Department of Computer Science and
    Engineering
Sree Vidyanikethan Engineering
    College
Tirupati, Andhra Pradesh, India

Amit Kumar Tyagi
School of Computer Science and
    Engineering
Vellore Institute of Technology
Chennai, Tamil Nadu, India

Section I

Introduction

1 A Road Map to Artificial Neural Network

Arpana Sharma, Kanupriya Goswami and Vinita Jindal
Keshav Mahavidyalaya, University of Delhi, Delhi, India

Richa Gupta
University of Delhi, Delhi, India

CONTENTS

1.1 INTRODUCTION

Artificial neural network (ANN) is a biologically inspired learning algorithm designed to process information in the same way as the human brain. ANN is a versatile and powerful mathematical tool that can handle many complex tasks such as classification problems, time series, and function approximation. The greatest ability of an ANN is to improve its performance by learning through its previous experiences. ANN has the ability to work as a function approximator and is capable of handling noisy data. It is capable of working with various training algorithms, and the nonlinear nature makes it very efficient in computing problems where the usual methods fail. ANN can draw precise information from data and is able to handle complex nonlinear relationships in the data, which makes it useful for solving multidimensional problems. This chapter describes the basics of ANN and discusses its applicability in various fields.

The work in the field of ANN started in the late twentieth century, when in 1943 McCulloch and Pitts [1] introduced the first computational model of a neuron inspired by the human brain. Their research showed that arithmetic and logical computations

DOI: 10.1201/9781003307822-2

3

can be carried out efficiently by an interconnected network of neurons. Later, Norbet Wiener and von Neumann [2, 3] presented the architecture of a computer analogue to the human brain. In 1949, Hebb [4] described the relationship between brain activity and complex psychological phenomena. The year 1951 witnessed the first neuro-computer called "The Snark" created by Marvin Minsky. This system was never practically implemented because it failed to justify the basis of computations.

In 1958, Frank Rosenblatt developed the first "Perceptron" [5], based on McCulloch and Pitts' work, and introduced the concept of weights. His work was later instrumental in the formation of neural networks. In 1959, Bernard Widrow and Hoff developed models called "ADALINE & MADALINE", which are acronyms coming from ADAptive Linear Neuron or Element and Multiple ADAptive LInear Neuron, respectively. MADALINE was the first artificial neural network (ANN) that was used to solve real-world problems, and ADALINE introduced a new learning mechanism that still remains relevant today. Taking the work further in this field, Widrow and Hoff in 1962 developed a learning procedure where the model examines the value of error before the weights are adjusted. In 1969, Minsky and Papert published a book titled *Perceptrons* [6], which focused on the limitations of neural networks. According to their work, neural networks were incapable of computing logical functions such as XOR. This led to the loss of interest in this field.

The 1970s saw the progression in research on artificial neural networks in various fields such as pattern recognition, biological modeling, and signal processing, to name a few. Many research papers were published during this time [7–11], and all this contributed to a major surge in the field of neural networks. The most important contribution in this era was that of Paul Webros, who documented the application of back-propagation within artificial neural networks in his work. In 1982, John Hopfield, a physicist, published two papers [12, 13] on ANNs in which he described that using bidirectional lines in these machines would give them more strength. In the same year, Reilly and Cooper introduced the concept of a "hybrid network" with multiple layers, where each layer had a different method to solve a problem. Also in 1982, in a joint US–Japan conference on neural networks, Japan announced the fifth generation of neural networks, which led the United States to increase funding for this field, and the research in this area further accelerated.

In 1986, with the publication of "PDP" books edited by Rumelhart and McClelland [14], the field saw the beginning of explosive growth. In 1987, the IEEE International Conference on Neural Networks was held in San Diego, which was the first open conference on ANN. In 1988, the INNS (International Neural Network Society) launched a journal titled *Neural Networks*. In 1989, Yann LeCun et al. at the AT&T Bell Labs published a paper [15] on the use of constraints in back-propagation, illustrating its integration into the neural network architecture for training. They used a large dataset from the United States Postal Service and showed that ANN could recognize the handwritten zip codes. The past two decades saw much development in the field of ANNs, with many research papers published and many kinds of ANNs studied. ANN is comprised of interconnected units called neurons, which are arranged in layers. Each neuron linearly combines its inputs by summing up the products of its weights and biases, which is then transformed by an activation function. ANN generates output by feed-forward data flow, based on the minimization of error by optimization, and updates the network parameters by back-propagation of errors during each training epoch.

This work formed a basis for use of ANN in various commercial fields. Nowadays, ANNs are used in several fields such as science, industry, finance, medicine, and others, some of which shall be discussed later in this chapter. Artificial neural networks are indeed the most promising technological development and can handle almost any computational task in various fields with ease and precision. The advantage of using ANN in any complex problem lies in their ability to be universal approximators, meaning ANN can predict an optimal solution even in the absence of an exact solution. The field of ANN is still evolving, and researchers are coming up with new variations to compute the solutions for real-time complex problems. The next section discusses the inspiration behind the origin of artificial neural networks.

1.2 BIOLOGICAL INSPIRATION OF ARTIFICIAL NEURAL NETWORK

ANNs, also known as NNs, are biologically inspired from the neurons of the human brain and consist of artificial neurons configured to perform specialized computational tasks. The basic model of ANN is like a biological neuron, which is depicted in Figure 1.1. The human brain is composed of billions of neurons that form a highly complex system due to a massive interconnection of units working in parallel along with other neurons. These neurons receive signals from about 10,000 other neurons.

The structure of a neuron comprises four main parts: soma or the cell body, a synaptic terminal, and two offshoots from soma called dendrites and axons. The cell body is the main part of the cell and contains the nucleus. The role of the dendrites is to receive signals from other neurons, and that of axon is the conduction of these signals. The signals, called the action potentials, are received at the dendrite and transmitted along the axon. When the sum of these input signals is sufficiently large to activate the neuron, it transmits the signal to other neurons whose dendrites are connected at the axon terminals. The point where one neuron is interconnected with other neurons is called the *synaptic terminal*. The neuron fires only if the signal received exceeds a certain threshold level.

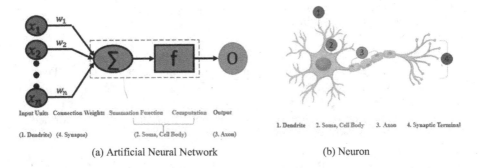

FIGURE 1.1 Basic model of an artificial neural network and a neuron. (a) Artificial neural network. (b) Neuron.

TABLE 1.1

Similarities and Differences in ANN and BNN

Artificial Neural Network (ANN)	Biological Neural Network (BNN)

ANN has the following components:
  1. Nodes
  2. Input
  3. Output
  4. Weights
	BNN has the following structure:
	  1. Soma – the cell body
	  2. Dendrites
	  3. Axon
	  4. Synapses

The ANN is made up of an arrangement of neurons and has three layers called the input layer, the hidden layer, and the output layer.	In BNN, the signals are received at dendrites and transmitted to soma for processing. The output signal is then sent down to synapses for further transmission to other neurons.
ANN can have 10–10^4 neurons.	BNN has 10^{11} neurons.
ANN needs properly formatted and structured data.	BNN can handle ambiguity and can learn from disorganized and unstructured data.
ANN learns from experience to improve its accuracy level.	BNN learns from experience to improve its performance level.
The response time of ANN is in nanoseconds.	The response time of BNN is in milliseconds.
Connections between neurons in ANN is precisely specified.	Random and massive connectivity is seen between neurons in BNN.

The ANN, however, works on the principle of the human brain, although in reality, to date, ANN has not been able to match the working of the complex human brain. The ANNs are good at solving those problems which are difficult for a computer to solve using standard techniques, such as pattern recognition and predictive analysis. Table 1.1 lists the similarities and differences between an ANN and a biological neural network (BNN) [16]. The next section describes the architecture of neural networks.

1.3   THE ARCHITECTURE OF ARTIFICIAL NEURAL NETWORK

The architecture of ANN consists of many layers of artificial neurons called nodes, which are arranged in layers as depicted in Figure 1.2.

The three layers of ANN are:

1. Input Layer: This layer receives data that must be processed by the network.
2. Hidden Layer(s): This layer is between the input layer and output layer and may consist of more than one layer. This layer processes information received from the input layer.
3. Output Layer: This layer gives the final output based on the transformed information received from the hidden layer.

The input layer of the ANN receives data in the form of patterns and images. The inputs are designated by $x_1, x_2, x_3, \dots x_n$ for n number of inputs. A weight w_{ij} is associated with each input, and the weights represent the strength of the connection between

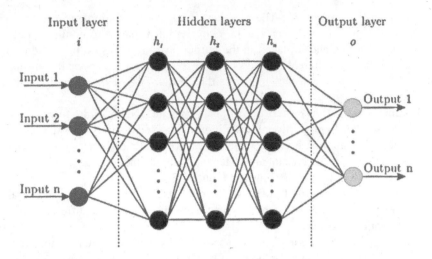

FIGURE 1.2 Architecture of artificial neural network.

neurons inside the ANN. The weighted inputs are all summed up by the neuron. If the weighted sum is zero, bias is added to make output non-zero. The bias always has the weight and input equal to 1. This weighted output is then passed through a function called *activation* or *transfer function*.

If b_0 is the bias, then output (O) of the ANN is given in Equation (1.1).

$$\text{Output}\left(\text{O}\right) = f\left[b_0 + \sum_{j=1}^{n} w_{ij}\, x_j\right] \tag{1.1}$$

where f is the activation function.

A neuron produces an output only if its input signal exceeds the threshold value in a short period. If θ_k is the threshold value, then for a neuron to produce an output, the condition is given in Equation (1.2).

$$b_0 + \sum_{j=1}^{n} w_{ij}\, x_j \geq \theta_k \tag{1.2}$$

1.4 ACTIVATION FUNCTIONS FOR ARTIFICIAL NEURAL NETWORK

An activation function (AF) in an ANN defines the transfer of the weighted sum of input and biases into an output using some gradient. The AF changes the linear input signal into a nonlinear output signal, which improves the learning process, especially for computations of higher order. The AF performs different computations such as classifications or predictions. The position of AF is also important in a network. If placed after the hidden layer, the AF converts linear data into nonlinear one for further propagation, and if placed in the output layer, it works on predictions. The choice of AF across different domains of tasks is also important, since it controls the output of the network and thus improves the results. The AFs may be divided into two types:

1. **Linear Activation Function:** A linear AF in an ANN is of the form $y = A_x$ where output is proportional to the input. This kind of AF is not suitable for binary activation. A network with a linear AF cannot use back-propagation, as its derivative is constant and independent of the input. The graphical representation of this AF is shown in Figure 1.3.

2. **Nonlinear Activation Function:** The nonlinear AFs are widely used neural networks. This kind of AF helps process a range of data. The different kinds of nonlinear AFs are:

   a. **Sigmoid Function**: This is a S-shaped nonlinear differentiable real function that transfers the input between 0 and 1 and is mostly used in feed-forward NN. The sigmoid function is given by:

$$f(x) = \frac{1}{\left(1 + e^{-x}\right)}$$

The sigmoid function is also known as logistic function or squashing function [17, 18]. The sigmoid function is usually used in models for predicting probability-based output and in other domains such as binary classification problems and regression tasks. However, the sigmoid function has disadvantages of slow convergence and gradient saturation. Also, since the output is not zero-centered, the gradients propagate in different directions [17].

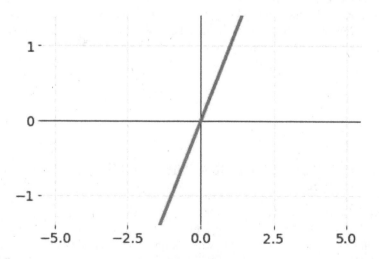

FIGURE 1.3   Linear activation function.

b. **Tanh or Hyperbolic Tangent Function**: The hyperbolic tangent function known as tanh function is a nonlinear, S-shaped, zero-centred function whose range is from −1 to +1. The tanh function is defined by:

$$f(x) = \frac{e^x - e^{-x}}{\left(e^x + e^{-x}\right)}$$

The tanh function has a zero-centered output that facilitates the back-propagation process. It also gives a better training performance for multiple-layer neural networks [17–19] and is usually utilized in models for speech recognition and language processing [17, 20, 21]. This AF suffers from a vanishing gradient problem.

c. **Rectified Linear Unit Function (ReLU)**: ReLU is a widely used faster AF proposed by Nair and Hinton in 2010 [17, 22], ranges from 0 to ∞, and allows for back-propagation. It has a much better performance compared to tanh and sigmoid activation function in deep learning and rectifies the problem of vanishing gradient. Due to its simple mathematical form, the models with ReLU have an enhanced computation speed [17, 23]. The function is defined as

$$f(x) = \begin{cases} x \text{ if } x \geq 0 \\ 0 \text{ if } x < 0 \end{cases}$$

The **main** limitation of this AF is the dying ReLU problem, which is a kind of vanishing gradient and refers to a condition when ReLU neurons become inactive, leading to zero output for any input. This problem decreases the ability of the network to train the data properly.

d. **Leaky ReLU Function**: The leaky ReLU AF, proposed in 2013 [17, 21], solves the dying ReLU problem by introducing a small negative slope to ReLU. This enables back-propagation keeping the weights alive during the entire process even for negative input values and eliminating the problem of dead neurons. The leaky ReLu is defined as:

$$f(x) = \begin{cases} x \text{ if } x > 0 \\ 0.01x \text{ if } x \leq 0 \end{cases}$$

This AF **has** a limitation in the sense that the smaller gradient makes the learning more time consuming.

e. **Parametric ReLU function (PReLU)**: The parametric ReLU function, also known as PReLU, proposed by He et al. in 2015 [17, 24], solves the problem of vanishing gradient for the negative input values. This AF has a slope in the negative part of the graph as a function of parameter a_i, called a negative slope controlling parameter. The function PReLU is defined as:

$$f(x_i) = \begin{cases} x_i \text{ if } x_i > 0 \\ a_i \, x_i \text{ if } x_i \leq 0 \end{cases}$$

f. **Exponential Linear Unit (ELU)**: Exponential linear unit, also known as ELU, proposed by Cevert et al. in 2015 [17], makes the convergence faster and reduces the problem of vanishing gradients. The function is defined as

$$f(x) = \begin{cases} x \text{ if } x > 0 \\ \alpha\left(e^x - 1\right) \text{ if } x \leq 0 \end{cases}$$

where $\alpha \geq 0$.

g. **Swish Function**: The swish activation function was founded by Google [17, 25]. This AF is a smooth, self-gating, and non-monotonic function that performs better than ReLU on deep learning models, especially on the tasks of machine translation and image classification. This function is defined as:

$$f(x) = x \times \text{sigmoid}(x) = \frac{x}{\left(1 + e^{-x}\right)}$$

h. **Softplus Function**: This AF is an alternative to ReLU and was proposed by Dugas et al. in 2001 [17, 26]. This function is defined as:

$$f(x) = \log\left(1 + e^x\right)$$

The softplus AF has a smooth derivative and has nonvanishing gradient properties, which enhances the performance in deep networks.

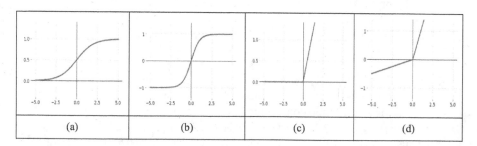

| (a) | (b) | (c) | (d) |

FIGURE 1.4 Nonlinear activation functions: (a) sigmoid, (b) tanh, (c) ReLU, (d) leaky ReLU.

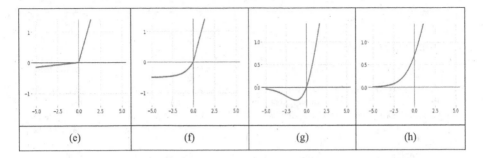

| (e) | (f) | (g) | (h) |

FIGURE 1.5   Nonlinear activation functions: (e) PReLU, (f) ELU, (g) swish, (h) softplus.

All the above-mentioned nonlinear activation functions are shown graphically in Figures 1.4 and 1.5.

1.5   TYPES OF ARTIFICIAL NEURAL NETWORK

We present the overview of different kinds of artificial neural networks discussed in this chapter in Figure 1.6 and detailed below in a tabular form in Table 1.2.

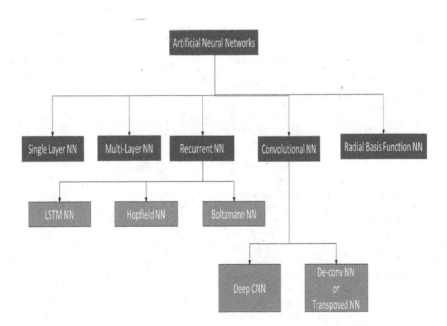

FIGURE 1.6   Types of artificial neural networks.

TABLE 1.2

Different Types of Artificial Neural Networks

Description	Advantage	Limitation	Application
Multi-Layer Perceptrons (MLPs): It is a group of perceptrons arranged in layers. It can be subcategorized as a feed-forward neural network, processing inputs only in the forward direction, deep neural network, with multiple interconnections between neurons. These networks are also known as universal function approximators, as they can learn any nonlinear function.	MLPs are built to learn weights that can map inputs values with output values. This process is achieved with the help of AFs already discussed in this chapter.	1. It requires converting 2D data to 1D for image classification problems. This leads to a loss in spatial features of an image. 2. The performance of these ANNs for very large images may not be good. 3. They often suffer from the problem of vanishing and exploding gradient, which exists with back-propagation. 4. They cannot deal with sequential data.	MLPs are useful in applications having data in tabular form, text, or images.
Recurrent Neural Network (RNN): A looping constraint placed over the hidden layer of ANN turns the network into RNN. This helps in capturing the sequential information in the input data.	1. It allows parameter sharing across different time steps. This has an advantage of fewer parameters during the training phase and hence decreases the computational cost. 2. It can be used to extend the pixel effectiveness through convolution layers.	1. They suffer from the problem of vanishing and exploding gradient, which exists with back-propagation. 2. Training RNN could be a difficult task.	RNN is useful in time series data, audio data, text data, sentiment classification, image captioning, and language translation.
Convolutional Neural Network (CNN): CNNs are extensively used in video and image processing projects. They work by convolving the image with a filter to extract features from the image.	1. CNN can extract the features automatically by learning. 2. CNN utilizes the spatial features from an image. 3. CNN uses parameter sharing.	1. They are comparatively complex to design and maintain. 2. The speed of CNN is comparatively slow usually due to the higher number of hidden layers and input data.	Applications of CNN include image processing, machine translation, computer vision, and speech recognition.

(Continued)

TABLE 1.2 (*Continued*)
Different Types of Artificial Neural Networks

Description	Advantage	Limitation	Application
Long Short-Term Memory (LSTM): LSTM networks are the advanced version of RNN that uses special neurons that include a "memory cell" to store information for longer periods.	It overcomes the problem of vanishing and exploding gradients.	1. LSTMs face the problem of moving the data from cell to cell in evaluation. 2. The learning process is quite time consuming due to the need for high memory bandwidth of cells. 3. LSTMs are affected by random weight initialization like the feed-forward NN. 4. LSTMs are vulnerable to overfitting.	LSTM is used in gesture recognition, speech recognition, text prediction, and speech processing.
Hopfield Neural Network (HNN): A Hopfield neural network is a single-layered RNN in which the neurons are entirely connected. HNN has cyclic and recursive characteristics. It combines storage and binary systems. HNNs are divided into discrete and continuous types.	It is good for solving optimization problems.	1. The memorizing capacity is severely limited. 2. There is a limitation to the percentage variation allowed in the training patterns and testing patterns. 3. The network takes an unusually long time for training the model.	HNN is widely used in many domains like AI, machine learning, associative memory, pattern recognition, optimized calculation, VLSI, and parallel realization of optical devices.
Deconvolutional Neural Network (DCNN): Deconvolutional networks aim at finding features that may not have been previously identified by CNN. DCNN is reverse engineering of the CNN and is useful in scientific and engineering fields.	DCNN helps in image restoration.	They suffer from a checkered board effect. The main cause of this is uneven overlap at some parts of the image causing artifacts.	DCNN Is applied in image synthesis and analysis, to enlarge the images, in semantic segmentation.

1.6 TRAINING ALGORITHMS FOR ARTIFICIAL NEURAL NETWORK

The process of learning in an ANN involves the training of the network by adjusting the weights and biases—that is, network parameters—until the desired output is achieved. This process of training the network is performed by algorithms known as training algorithms and shown in Figure 1.7.

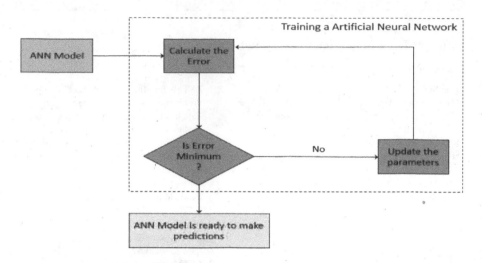

FIGURE 1.7   Training process in ANN.

Gradient Descent Algorithm: Gradient descent is the most common first-order iterative optimization algorithm, which is used to train ANN by minimizing the error between the predicted and actual output. This algorithm updates the network parameters in the direction of the negative gradient of the cost function for network parameters. This first-order technique is used to improve the learning of the network and is used in the supervised mode of learning. In this method, the functions must be differentiable and convex.

Working of Gradient Descent Algorithm: The working of a network is based on minimizing the error. The error is quantified by the cost function, which measures the performance of the network. To calculate the cost function, we need a hypothesis function $h\theta(x)$ and input parameters θ_0 "and" θ_1.

$$\text{Cost Function} = J(\theta_0, \theta_1) = \frac{1}{2n} \sum_{i=1}^{m} \left(h_\theta(x_i) - y^{(i)} \right)^2 \tag{1.3}$$

The aim of the gradient descent is to minimize the error, which is achieved by taking the gradient of the cost function and then moving in the direction of the negative gradient. Then, the input parameters are updated until convergence is reached. The equation to update the parameters is given by:

$$\theta_{j+1} = \theta_j - \eta \frac{\partial}{\partial \theta} J(\theta_0, \theta_1) \tag{1.4}$$

where η is the learning rate

This important parameter η has a strong influence on the performance of the network, as it controls the step size and determines how quickly the model adapts to the problem. Since the network layers are interconnected, the gradient of the cost function of the previous layers is related to the gradient of the cost function of the next layer. This leads to the propagation of the loss in the backward direction and is known as back-propagation. Back-propagation is the core of the training in a neural network. As can be seen, the parameters are updated based on the error calculated, in each previous epoch, and this helps compute the gradient of the function. We summarize the steps of the gradient descent algorithm below.

1. Initialization of input parameters.
2. Choosing a learning rate η.
3. Normalization of data.
4. On each iteration, computation of the partial derivative of the cost function with respect to network parameters.
5. Update the parameters as given by Equation (1.4).
6. Repeat the above steps 4 and 5 util the convergence is reached.

Types of gradient descent methods:

i. **Batch Gradient Descent**: This kind of gradient descent considers all the points in the training data to compute the error and updates the model only after all the training points have been evaluated. This gradient descent is computationally efficient and produces a stable convergence but can take a long time to process all the datasets. In a batch gradient descent, the input parameters θ are updated as:

$$\theta = \theta - \eta \nabla_\theta E\left(x,y;\theta\right)$$

ii. **Stochastic Gradient Descent**: This kind of gradient descent considers each point of the dataset for running an epoch and updates the parameters one at a time. This makes the method computationally less efficient as compared to batch descent, and the frequent updates result in a faster global minimum. In a stochastic gradient descent, the input parameters θ are updated as:

$$\theta = \theta - \eta \nabla_\theta E\left(x^i,y^i;\theta\right)$$

iii. **Mini-batch Gradient Descent:** This kind of gradient descent involves the splitting of the training dataset into small batch sizes, and updates are performed on those batches. This gradient descent is a fine balance between the batch gradient descent and the stochastic gradient descent in terms of speed of SGD and computational efficiency of batch gradient descent. In a mini-batch gradient descent with batch size b, the input parameters θ are updated as:

$$\theta = \theta - \eta \nabla_\theta E\left(x^{(i:i+b)}, y^{(i:i+b)};\theta\right)$$

1.7 APPLICATIONS OF ARTIFICIAL NEURAL NETWORK

i. Science:

    (a) **Biometrics:** ANNs have generalized the learning process in biometrics. It has been able to achieve enhanced accuracy for biometric recognition and hence to develop an efficient biometric system. This has been possible by using CNN, which works well for classification problems. CNN has been successfully deployed in many biometrics like fingerprint, iris, finger-vein, face, etc. The CNN has an advantage over conventional approaches for its ability to extract features, reduce dimensionality, and classify the data. Another ANN, capsule network, has gained attention recently. It has a high learning capacity and the ability to be trained with a limited number of samples compared to the CNN. This network was tested with 99% accuracy on the face95 and CASIA-Iris-Thousand databases [27, 28].

    (b) **Crime Detection:** Multitask cascade neural network is a powerful tool for the recognition and identification of criminals through face detection. This helps in retrieving the information of identified criminals stored in the database [29].

    (c) **Management Fraud:** Management fraud is a crucial issue faced by auditing professionals. The networks developed for this application can distinguish between genuine and fake companies with improved accuracy [30].

ii. Industry:

    (a) **Automation**:

        1. **Driverless Cars:** CNN has been used in the domain of intelligent video analytics. This technique is useful in controlling driverless cars and for the implementation of obstacle detection using an IoT device [31, 32].

        2. **Robotics:** Many scientific research and engineering applications are based on the technique of robot manipulators. ANNs featuring high-speed parallel distributed processing has gained recognition as a powerful tool for real-time processing. It has been successfully applied in the control of robot manipulators [33].

        3. **Sensor Systems:** The recursive architecture of the neural network is used for different purposes of surveillance applications in areas like military, health, and environment etc. This network is used to predict the state of a node of a sensor, which can be used in a hostile environment, such as floods, earthquakes, battlefields, etc. [34].

    (b) **Chemical Industry:** ANN has been used in the chemical industry to generate the steam methane reformer performance data. This is based on the simulation of deterministic and stochastic data depending on major variables. The ANN model predicts the outputs—that is, pressure, mole fraction, velocity, and temperature—with high accuracy and reduces the computational time. ANN has also been able to simulate potable water quality properties, that is, dissolved oxygen, total dissolved solids, total hardness, alkalinity, and turbidity [35].

   (c) **Additive Manufacturing:** In the modern industrial paradigm, additive manufacturing, also known as 3-D printing, is a promising digital approach that fabricates objects layer by layer from three-dimensional computer-aided design models to complex shapes. ANN algorithm is applied to various aspects of additive manufacturing whole chain, including quality evaluation, model design, and in situ monitoring [36].

   (d) **Petrochemical Industry**: CNN designed as a three-layer structure for this application helps achieve better capability and stability in the petrochemical industry [37].

   (e) **Petroleum Industry**: ANNs are used in this area to decide to reduce non-productive time and cost. The applications of ANNs in this field are categorized into four groups: explorations, drilling, production, and reservoir engineering [38].

   (f) **Pharmaceutical Industry**: Recurrent neural network is most suited in this field for model predictive control applications, applied to enable this aim by providing superior regulation of critical quality attributes [39].

   (g) **Aircraft Designing**: Long short-term memory recurrent neural network (LSTM-RNN) model has been used in this area to automatically classify common defects occurring in materials like debonding, adhesive pooling, and liquid ingress [40].

iii. **Finance**:

Stock Market: ANNs are used in predicting stock market developments. Further, convolutional neural networks have been used to predict the fluctuations of the stock index and to improve the model performance [41, 42].

iv. **Medicine**:

   (a) **Cardiovascular Diseases:** ANN is useful in predicting the occurrence of coronary artery disease, diagnosis of acute myocardial infarction, and estimation of mortality risk following cardiac surgery based on classification of a dataset. This helps in the immediate diagnosis and treatment of the patients [43].

   (b) **Neurosciences:** ANN is applied to building a technique for the determination of cancer and detection of brain MRI through an image classifier. This is based on the Deep Wavelet Autoencoder along with the image decomposition property of wavelet transform [44].

   (c) **Radiology**: ANNs are widely used in the analysis of medical images such as tumor detection in ultrasonograms, X-ray spectral reconstruction, determination of skeletal age from X-ray images and brain maturation, etc. ANN also plays an important role in the detection, for example, that of breast cancer. This technique requires raw image data only and shows promising results when applied to glaucoma detection [45].

   (d) **COVID**: A multilayer ANN can be applied to forecast the GDP figures of countries affected severely due to the ongoing COVID-19 pandemic [16]. CNN model was developed to test the sensitivity of RT-PCR with high accuracy. A deep convolutional NN design is tailored for the screening and detection of COVID-19 cases through chest radiography [46, 47].

v. **Environment**:

(a) **Humidity prediction:** Prediction of the surrounding environment can be done with the help of ANN model. The trained data collected from the surrounding environment were used to predict the temperature with 100% accuracy [48].

(b) **Air Pollution Detection:** ANN in this area is developed to detect air quality [49].

(c) **Prediction of Landslide Susceptibility:** The problem of landslide prediction is very common in mountain regions across the world. To overcome this problem, ANN can be used to predict landslide suscepti-bility of a particular area. It is optimized with particle swarm optimiza-tion to achieve the most reliable maps of landslide susceptibility [50].

1.8 CONCLUSION

This chapter collates the existing work on ANNs to give researchers an insight into this interesting and useful area. ANN emulates a human brain–creating networks that can learn and predict on their own, making them computationally efficient. ANN can act as universal approximators for many complex real-life problems—the COVID-19 pandemic, for example—and predict their solutions. In this chapter we have pre-sented a detailed description of ANN, its architecture, training algorithm, activa-tion functions, types of ANN, and its applications in various fields such as science, industry, medicine, finance, and environment. The research in the field of ANN can advance by formulating more algorithms and learning techniques that would make them an appropriate choice for numerous applications across various domains.

REFERENCES

[1] Cowan, Jack D. "Discussion: McCulloch-Pitts and related neural nets from 1943 to 1989." *Bulletin of Mathematical Biology* 52, no. 1–2 (1990): 73–97.

[2] Neumann, John Von. *The general and logical theory of automata*. Vol. 5. Berlin: Taylor & Francis (1951).

[3] Neumann, John Von. "Probabilistic logics and the synthesis of reliable organisms from unreliable components." In *Automata Studies. (AM-34)*, Vol. 34, pp. 43–98. Princeton, NJ: Princeton University Press, (2016.

[4] Hebb, Donald O. "The first stage of perception: Growth of the assembly." *The Organization of Behavior* 4 (1949): 60–78.

[5] Rosenblatt, Frank. "The perceptron: A probabilistic model for information storage and organization in the brain." *Psychological Review* 65, no. 6 (1958): 386.

[6] Minsky, M. L., and Papert, S. A. *Perceptrons: An introduction to computational geom-etry*. Cambridge, MA: The MIT Press (1969) (expanded edition, 1988).

[7] Amari, Shunichi. "A theory of adaptive pattern classifiers." *IEEE Transactions on Electronic Computers* 3 (1967): 299–307.

[8] Fukushima, Kunihiko. "Visual feature extraction by a multilayered network of analog threshold elements." *IEEE Transactions on Systems Science and Cybernetics* 5, no. 4 (1969): 322–333.

[9] Grossberg, Stephen. "Embedding fields: A theory of learning with physiological implications." *Journal of Mathematical Psychology* 6, no. 2 (1969): 209–239.

[10] Klopf, A. Harry, and Earl Gose. "An evolutionary pattern recognition network." *IEEE Transactions on Systems Science and Cybernetics* 5, no. 3 (1969): 247–250.

[11] Yadav, Neha, Anupam Yadav, and Manoj Kumar. *An introduction to neural network methods for differential equations.* Berlin: Springer, 2015.

[12] Hopfield, John J. "Neural networks and physical systems with emergent collective computational abilities." *Proceedings of the National Academy of Sciences* 79, no. 8 (1982): 2554–2558.

[13] Hopfield, John J. "Neurons with graded response have collective computational properties like those of two-state neurons." *Proceedings of the National Academy of Sciences* 81, no. 10 (1984): 3088–3092.

[14] McClelland, James L., David E. Rumelhart, and PDP Research Group. *Parallel distributed processing.* Vol. 2. Cambridge, MA: MIT press (1986).

[15] LeCun, Yann, Bernhard Boser, John S. Denker, Donnie Henderson, Richard E. Howard, Wayne Hubbard, and Lawrence D. Jackel. "Backpropagation applied to handwritten zip code recognition." *Neural Computation* 1, no. 4 (1989): 541–551.

[16] Eluyode, O. S., and Dipo Theophilus Akomolafe. "Comparative study of biological and artificial neural networks." *European Journal of Applied Engineering and Scientific Research* 2, no. 1 (2013): 36–46.

[17] Nwankpa, Chigozie, Winifred Ijomah, Anthony Gachagan, and Stephen Marshall. "Activation functions: Comparison of trends in practice and research for deep learning." In *2nd International Conference on Computational Sciences and Technology*, pp. 124–133, (2021).

[18] Karlik, Bekir, and A. Vehbi Olgac. "Performance analysis of various activation functions in generalized MLP architectures of neural networks." *International Journal of Artificial Intelligence and Expert Systems* 1, no. 4 (2011): 111–122.

[19] Neal, Radford M. "Connectionist learning of belief networks." *Artificial Intelligence* 56, no. 1 (1992): 71–113.

[20] Dauphin, Yann N., Angela Fan, Michael Auli, and David Grangier. "Language modeling with gated convolutional networks." In *International conference on machine learning, PMLR*, pp. 933–941, (2017).

[21] Maas, Andrew L., Awni Y. Hannun, and Andrew Y. Ng. "Rectifier nonlinearities improve neural network acoustic models." In *Proc. ICML*, Vol. 30, No. 1, p. 3, (2013).

[22] Nair, Vinod, and Geoffrey E. Hinton. "Rectified linear units improve restricted Boltzmann machines." In *Icml* (2010).

[23] Zeiler, Matthew D., M. Ranzato, Rajat Monga, Min Mao, Kun Yang, Quoc Viet Le, Patrick Nguyen et al. "On rectified linear units for speech processing." In *2013 IEEE International Conference on Acoustics, Speech and Signal Processing*, pp. 3517–3521. IEEE (2013).

[24] K. He, Kaiming, Xiangyu Zhang, Shaoqing Ren, and Jian Sun. "Delving deep into rectifiers: Surpassing human-level performance on imagenet classification." In *Proceedings of the IEEE international conference on computer vision*, pp. 1026–1034. 2015.

[25] Ramachandran, Prajit, Barret Zoph, and Quoc V. Le. "Searching for activation functions." *ICLR workshop* (2018).

[26] Dugas, Charles, Yoshua Bengio, François Bélisle, Claude Nadeau, and René Garcia. "Incorporating second-order functional knowledge for better option pricing." *Advances in neural information processing systems*, pp. 472–478, (2001).

[27] Radzi, Syafeeza Ahmad, Mohamed Khalil Hani, and Rabia Bakhteri. "Finger-vein biometric identification using convolutional neural network." *Turkish Journal of Electrical Engineering & Computer Sciences* 24, no. 3 (2016): 1863–1878.

[28] Jacob, I. Jeena. "Capsule network based biometric recognition system." *Journal of Artificial Intelligence* 1, no. 02 (2019): 83–94.

[29] Bykov, A. D., V. I. Voronov, L. I. Voronova, and I. A. Zharov. "Web application development for biometric identification system based on neural network face recognition." In *2020 Systems of Signals Generating and Processing in the Field of on Board Communications*, pp. 1–6. IEEE, 2020.

[30] Fanning, Kurt, Kenneth O. Cogger, and Rajendra Srivastava. "Detection of management fraud: A neural network approach." *Intelligent Systems in Accounting, Finance and Management* 4, no. 2 (1995): 113–126.

[31] Alheeti, Khattab M. Ali, Anna Gruebler, and Klaus D. McDonald-Maier. "An intrusion detection system against malicious attacks on the communication network of driverless cars." In *2015 12th Annual IEEE Consumer Communications and Networking Conference (CCNC)*, pp. 916–921. IEEE, 2015.

[32] Bechtel, Michael G., Elise McEllhiney, Minje Kim, and Heechul Yun. "Deeppicar: A low-cost deep neural network-based autonomous car." In *2018 IEEE 24th international conference on embedded and real-time computing systems and applications (RTCSA)*, pp. 11–21. IEEE, 2018.

[33] Jiang, Yiming, Chenguang Yang, Jing Na, Guang Li, Yanan Li, and Junpei Zhong. "A brief review of neural networks based learning and control and their applications for robots." *Complexity* 2017 (2017): doi: 10.1155/2017/1895897.

[34] Atiga, Jamila, Nour Elhouda Mbarki, Ridha Ejbali, and Mourad Zaied. "Faulty node detection in wireless sensor networks using a recurrent neural network." In *Tenth International Conference on Machine Vision (ICMV 2017)*, Vol. 10696, p. 106962P. International Society for Optics and Photonics (2018).

[35] Vo, Nguyen Dat, Dong Hoon Oh, Suk-Hoon Hong, Min Oh, and Chang-Ha Lee. "Combined approach using mathematical modelling and artificial neural network for chemical industries: Steam methane reformer." *Applied Energy* 255 (2019): 113809.

[36] Qi, Xinbo, Guofeng Chen, Yong Li, Xuan Cheng, and Changpeng Li. "Applying neural-network-based machine learning to additive manufacturing: Current applications, challenges, and future perspectives." *Engineering* 5, no. 4 (2019): 721–729.

[37] Geng, Zhiqiang, Yanhui Zhang, Chengfei Li, Yongming Han, Yunfei Cui, and Bin Yu. "Energy optimization and prediction modeling of petrochemical industries: An improved convolutional neural network based on cross-feature." *Energy* 194 (2020): 116851.

[38] Rahmanifard, Hamid, and Tatyana Plaksina. "Application of artificial intelligence techniques in the petroleum industry: A review." *Artificial Intelligence Review* 52, no. 4 (2019): 2295–2318.

[39] Wu, Jia, Wei Luo, Xuekai Wang, Chaoguo Sun, and Hui Li. "A new application of WT-ANN method to control the preparation process of metformin hydrochloride tablets by near infrared spectroscopy compared to PLS." *Journal of Pharmaceutical and Biomedical Analysis* 80 (2013): 186–191.

[40] Hu, Caiqi, Yuxia Duan, Shicai Liu, Yiqian Yan, Ning Tao, Ahmad Osman, Clemente Ibarra-Castanedo, Stefano Sfarra, Dapeng Chen, and Cunlin Zhang. "LSTM-RNN-based defect classification in honeycomb structures using infrared thermography." *Infrared Physics & Technology* 102 (2019): 103032.

[41] Zhang, Dehua, and Sha Lou. "The application research of neural network and BP algorithm in stock price pattern classification and prediction." *Future Generation Computer Systems* 115 (2021): 872–879.

[42] Chung, Hyejung, and Kyung-shik Shin. "Genetic algorithm-optimized multi-channel convolutional neural network for stock market prediction." *Neural Computing and Applications* 32, no. 12 (2020): 7897–7914.

[43] Malav, Amita, Kalyani Kadam, and Pooja Kamat. "Prediction of heart disease using k-means and artificial neural network as Hybrid Approach to Improve Accuracy." *International Journal of Engineering and Technology* 9, no. 4 (2017): 3081–3085.

[44] Mallick, Pradeep Kumar, Seuc Ho Ryu, Sandeep Kumar Satapathy, Shruti Mishra, Gia Nhu Nguyen, and Prayag Tiwari. "Brain MRI image classification for cancer detection using deep wavelet autoencoder-based deep neural network." *IEEE Access* 7 (2019): 46278–46287.

[45] Ting, Fung Fung, Yen Jun Tan, and Kok Swee Sim. "Convolutional neural network improvement for breast cancer classification." *Expert Systems with Applications* 120 (2019): 103–115.

[46] Bhardwaj, Prashant, and Amanpreet Kaur. "A novel and efficient deep learning approach for COVID-19 detection using X-ray imaging modality." *International Journal of Imaging Systems and Technology* 31, no. 4 (2021): 1775–1791.

[47] Wang, Linda, Zhong Qiu Lin, and Alexander Wong. "Covid-net: A tailored deep convolutional neural network design for detection of covid-19 cases from chest x-ray images." *Scientific Reports* 10, no. 1 (2020): 1–12.

[48] Al-Shawwa, Mohammed O., Abd Al-Rahman Al-Absi, Saji Abu Hassanein, Khaled Abu Baraka, and Samy S. Abu-Naser. "Predicting temperature or humidity in the surrounding environment using artificial neural network." *International Journal of Academic Pedagogical Research (IJAPR)* 2, no. 9 (2018): 1–6.

[49] Cabaneros, Sheen Mclean, John Kaiser Calautit, and Ben Richard Hughes. "A review of artificial neural network models for ambient air pollution prediction." *Environmental Modelling & Software* 119 (2019): 285–304.

[50] Moayedi, Hossein, Mohammad Mehrabi, Mansour Mosallanezhad, Ahmad Safuan A. Rashid, Biswajeet Pradhan. "Modification of landslide susceptibility mapping using optimized PSO-ANN technique." *Engineering with Computers* 35, no. 3 (2019): 967–984.

2 Applications of Recurrent Neural Network

Overview and Case Studies

Kusumika Krori Dutta and S. Poornima
M.S. Ramaiah Institute of Technology, Bangalore, India

Ramit Sharma, Deebul Nair and Paul G. Ploeger
University of Applied Sciences, Germany

CONTENTS

DOI: 10.1201/9781003307822-3

2.1 INTRODUCTION

The growth of the deep learning (DL) methods for processing sequential and symbolic data leads to numerous applications in various fields. RNN has become a state-of-art model to classify sequential data. It is a standard ANN with feedback to obtain activations from its immediate inputs after correlating with its predecessor. Its vanishing and exploding gradient issues are well handled using its architecture development as long short-term memory (LSTM) and gated recurrent units (GRU). The development timeline of RNN [1–15] since its evolution as shown in Figure 2.1a might admire the industrial or commercial users such as Amazon, Apple, Facebook, and Microsoft employing it in their products. The architecture of the recurrent neural network shown in Figure 2.1b is one of the most popular methods of computer vision

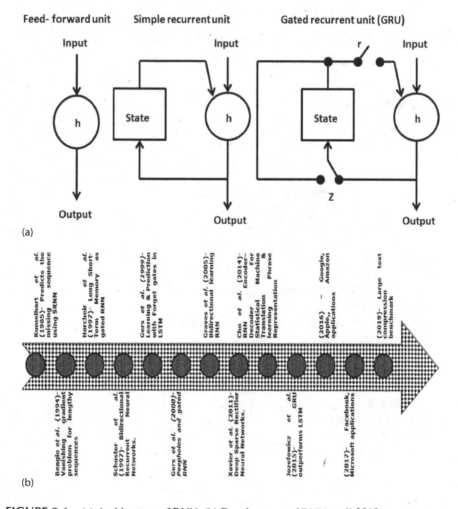

FIGURE 2.1   (a) Architecture of RNN. (b) Development of RNN until 2019.

applications. Its plenarily connective architecture [16–24] provides storage and many advantages over other architectures.

To model time series sequences, RNN was proposed during the 1980s [25–27]. These networks are not only fully connected but allow time delay connection for even hidden layer units, which is unlike multilayer perceptron techniques. This time delay feature of fully connected architecture makes it the most powerful architecture, as it can store past information and correlate the same with present data. It uses linear and softmax activations in the output layer for real and discrete data predictions, respectively. The time series data consists of various and huge quantity of time stamps along with short or long-term dependency. But the main problem arises during training, because as it advances into deeper layers, the network faces vanishing exploding gradient issues [28]. Though the length of time series gives prediction or forecasting challenges, LSTM and GRU models have excellent practical applications. A few applications of RNN and its variants developed and proposed as per literature are given in Table 2.1.

TABLE 2.1
Applications of RNN

SRNN	BRNN	LSTM	GRU	CNN+RNN
Sequential dependent time series, image captioning, sentiment analysis, text and biological data, machine translation, frame-level video analysis, visual question answering	Recognition of speech, audio and handwriting, bioinformatics	Robotics, prediction of homology and subcellular localization of proteins, medical care pathways, traffic forecast, all kinds of time series applications and business management processes, drug design, recognition of speech, handwriting and human action, rhythm learning, music composition, grammar learning, sign language translation, semantic parsing	Forecasting river water levels and batch productions, road traffic flow, prediction of dissolved oxygen gas, financial sequence	Object detection, labeling images and videos, fake news detection, hand gesture or any human activity recognition, abnormal flow detection in smart grid, EEG analysis for Parkinson's disease

The RNN, CNN, and deep belief networks (DBN)-based DL techniques outperformed EEG classification tasks compared to autoencoder and multilayer perceptron models. The EEG data used to analyze emotion recognition, seizure detection, sleep scoring, and mental pressures are formulated as inputs and classified at the output layer with respect to its characterization. Similarly, society needs digitally semantic interpretation of natural language processing (NLP) data that helps information extraction, categorization, translation or grading, and spam detection applications. The DL techniques efficiently encode long sentences. For large-sized inputs, the attention mechanism interprets precisely without missing the textual entailment relations among the inputs.

Two different applications of RNN are discussed from the basics of architecture, training, and performance. The comparison of various models in each study highlights the role of RNN and its analysis. It will be easy for a beginner to understand the discussed cases from its evolution. The chapter is organized to understand EEG signal classification starting from DL architectures, methodology used, and finally analyzed with a number of units and layers. The second part of this chapter explains RTE analysis with respect to the decomposable attention model. Initially, the section describes how the DA model has been chosen from performance comparison among symmetric attention, LSTM, and GRU models. The consequent sections explain the recognition of general text and active-passive voice pairs as neutral, contradiction, and entailment using the DA model. The summary of both the case studies highlights the role of RNN.

2.1.1 EEG Signal Analysis on Seizure Detection

EEG is the most commonly used electrophysiological test to record electrochemical reactions of the brain. The encephalon activities are recorded as a 1D signal using different electrodes in 10–20 patterns connected at different positions of the encephalon. The interpretation of 1D signals of 16 or 32 channels is very consequential and relegates different activities of encephalon to various diagnostic purposes. Sometimes it is difficult to understand the difference between replication of salubrious encephalon area and replication of diseased encephalon area with the presence of noises and artifacts (physical forms of kineticism). It requires expertise to diagnose, and the possibility of misdiagnosis due to human error cannot be ruled out. Improving accuracy at the diagnostic level is very important as this ensures correct treatment. With advancements in the field of DL, many researchers started working toward automatic diagnostic systems. To aid automatic detection, in this section various recurrent neural networks models are developed for multiclass systems to classify EEG signals with different physiological and pathological encephalon states. This section also discusses comparisons among simple recurrent neural networks (SRNN), LSTM, and GRU.

2.1.1.1 Types of Recurrent Neural Networks

Various RNNs are mainly categorized based on input-output interconnection and its different architectural features. In this case study, categorization on the basis of architectural differences is considered. The three main types are: (i) simple RNN,

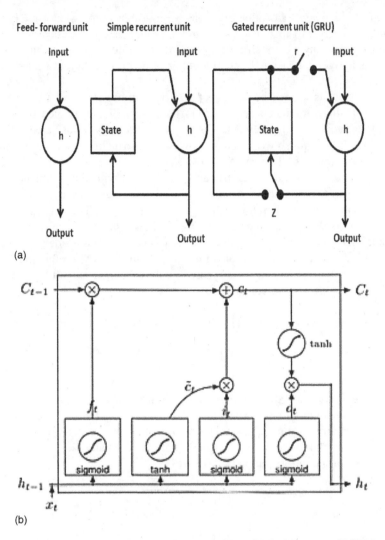

FIGURE 2.2 (a) Architecture of simple RNN and GRU. (b) Architecture of LSTM cell.

(ii) LSTMs, (iii) GRUs. Figure 2.2 shows architectures of simple RNN and GRUs, respectively. Equations (2.1) and (2.2) represents computation of hidden layer and output layer vectors, respectively

$$h_t = F\left(W_{ih}u_t + W_{hh}h_{t-1} + b_h\right) \qquad (2.1)$$

$$y_t = W_{h0}h_t + b_0 \qquad (2.2)$$

Here u represents input sequence $u = \{u_1, u_2, \dots u_T\}$, h represents hidden vector sequence $h = \{h_1, h_2, \dots h_T\}$, W represents weight matrix, b represents bias, F

represents hidden layer activation functions, y represents output vector $y = \{y_1, y_2, \ldots y_T\}$, and t varies from 1 to T. Though the input, hidden, and output layers are considered to have the same vector size, i.e., 1 to T, they are not required to have the same size; as each layer can take a different number of neurons, different vector sizes are possible.

Simple RNN is trained by back-propagation through time (BPTT), which has issues of vanishing gradient in deeper layers, because of which simple RNN is unable to train long sequences. To overcome this, in place of a RNN cell, a gated cell is used as in Figure 2.2a, which provides control over the information stored in memory.

Among the three, LSTMs are the most advantageous architecture, as (a) it can learn from raw time series data, (b) can process data with long sequences (up to 200–400 steps), (c) can handle sequences of different sizes without any preprocessing, and (d) provide solution to vanishing gradient problem. The main disadvantage of LSTMs is its dependence on each neuron and each layer for the long term. The horizontal line shown in Figure 2.2b of the LSTM cell at the top side (C_t) represents the cell state, which plays a vital role in its architecture. LSTM prefers to remove or insert information into cell state using three gates: (a) forget gate, (b) gate with sigmoid layer, and (c) final output gate.

(a) Forget gate: This gate helps in removing the information from cell state

$$h_t = \sigma\left(W_f\left[h_{t-1}, u_t\right] + b_f\right) \qquad (2.3)$$

where σ represents the sigmoid function in the above equation.

(b) Gate with sigmoid layer: The main function of this gate is decision-making about weight update sequence. The storage of the new updated weight value is done at tanh by creating a vector. Equations (2.4) and (2.5) represent the mathematical interpretation of this gate.

$$i_{t=} = \sigma\left(W_i.\left[h_{t-1}, u_t\right] + b_i\right) \qquad (2.4)$$

$$\hat{C}_t = \tanh\left(W_c.\left[h_{t-1}, u_t\right] + b_c\right) \qquad (2.5)$$

Using Equations (2.1)–(2.3), the cell state (C_t) is updated as shown in Equation (2.6).

$$C_t = h_t * C_{t-1} + i_{t*}\hat{C}_t \qquad (2.6)$$

(c) Final Output Gate: The output is calculated considering the updated cell state and a sigmoid layer, after which this gate decides the final output among the cell states based on Equations (2.7) and (2.8).

$$O_t = \sigma\left(W_0 \cdot \left[h_{t-1}, u_t\right] + b_0\right) \qquad (2.7)$$

$$h_t = O_t * \tanh\left(C_t\right) \qquad (2.8)$$

where σ: logistic sigmoid function makes O_t in range (0,1); tanh: hyperbolic tangent function varies between -1 and 1; W_i's: weight matrix; h_{t-1}: past hidden state; b_i's: bias vector; u_t: input vector.

In case of GRUs, it uses one gate fewer in comparison to LSTMs, so it is a slightly simpler architecture compared to LSTMs. Using all three architectures, the EEG dataset has been trained, described in the next section.

2.1.1.2 EEG Dataset

This study uses an EEG dataset [29], which has five different categorical data: (a) EEG of patients with network disorder, (b) EEG of patients with tumor, (c) EEG of a healthy person, (d) EEG recorded with eyes closed, and (e) EEG recorded with eyes open. This dataset is a preprocessed, multivariate time series, structured, and unbiased. It has the following features:

(1) Bandwidth: 0.5 Hz to 85 Hz
(2) Sampling rate: 173.61 Hz
(3) Each recording duration: 23.6 seconds
(4) Each time series data sample into 4,097 points
(5) Data point per second: 178
(6) Number of subjects: 500
(7) Number of categories: 5

Since it has 178 data points per second and five categories, so the input vector is set as 178 and the output vector as 5, i.e., the architect should classify five class systems. The full dataset is divided into 70% and 30% where 70% of randomly picked data are used for training the networks and the remainder is used for testing and validation of the performance of the architecture used.

2.1.1.3 Methodology Implemented

Multiclass classification of the above-mentioned EEG dataset is performed using simple RNN, GRU, and LSTM models. Since RNN is a supervised learning method, all the different categories of EEG datasets are labeled according to its classes. In the case of simple RNN, the classification is done with the help of softmax. Figure 2.3 shows the flow of the LSTM method used. In this model, the first layer ReLU and second layer sigmoid activations are used, and also two other layers are considered: (1) dropout layer and (2) dense layer, which helps avoid overfitting. For modeling these architectures, Keras library [30] and TensorFlow backend are chosen. A learning rate of 0.01 is chosen with RMSprop optimizer; 16 batch size is utilized and tried out for 100 epochs.

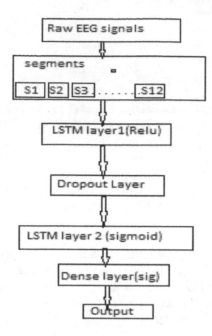

FIGURE 2.3   Proposed LSTM model.

To begin with, all three different architectures are tested keeping a single layer but units vary from 1 to 1,024. This provides the unit-wise performance of each architecture. After that, one particular unit (which provides good performance) is fixed and gradually layers are changed to note the time complexity of all three architectures, where in layer 1 and layer 2, 64 and 32 numbers of hidden units used, and output size considered as (172,64) and (64,1) with 1720 and 64 parameters, respectively. In a fully connected layer, 50 hidden units (1,50) output size and 50 parameters are considered.

2.1.1.4   Result

It has been observed that with one unit, the percentage of accuracy achieved is 27.4, 36.6, and 38.9 for simple RNN, LSTM, and GRU, respectively. Figure 2.4 shows the unit-wise performance of all three architectures. It is clear from this figure that after 32 units the accuracy is almost constant for GRU architecture, and LSTM shows little improvement, while simple RNN increases very slowly but shows maximum accuracy of only 53% with 1,024 units, whereas GRU and LSTM show 68% and 71% accuracy, respectively, for a single layer and 32 units. Therefore, 32 units are fixed while the number of layers is altered. Table 2.2 shows the accuracy and time taken by all three architectures for multilayer systems. For this trial the batch size 1,024 is considered, conducted over 300 epochs.

It can be seen that the time required to train the system increases with the number of layers increased. LSTM architecture shows the best results (78.16% accuracy) for four-layer 32 units.

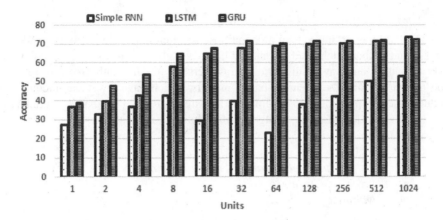

FIGURE 2.4 Unit versus accuracy in the percentage of all the methods.

TABLE 2.2
Accuracy and Time Consumption of Multilayer Network with 32 Units

Layers	Accuracy (%)			Time (s)		
	SRNN	LSTM	GRU	SRNN	LSTM	GRU
1	14.44	68.03	67.97	187.2	489.34	408.53
2	45.34	69.14	73.08	371.0	977.76	800.39
3	50.589	70.46	72.14	556.7	1,471.5	1,222.7
4	51.478	78.16	70.97	741.2	1,956.1	1,635.6
5	52.723	70.37	70.01	923.1	2,453.2	2,057.4

2.1.2 RECOGNIZING TEXTUAL ENTAILMENT

Entailment is the directional relationship between a given pair of sentences, such that if the first sentence referred to as text is true, then the second sentence referred to as hypothesis must also be true. Hence, recognizing textual entailment (RTE) is the task to classify the directional relationship between text and hypothesis into three different categories, namely entailment, contradiction, and neutral. RTE is used in applications like machine translation evaluation, relation extraction, automatic short answer grading, and text summarization. Over the years, researchers have tried to solve the problem of RTE in several ways, but major success has been obtained by the application of deep learning. Hence, in this case, a survey of DL-based models used in the field of RTE is done.

2.1.2.1 Architecture

Based on the survey, four deep learning–based models, namely decomposable attention, asymmetric attention, LSTM, and GRU, were selected. A comparative evaluation of these models was carried out with respect to the performance, time for training, and a number of trainable parameters.

2.1.2.1.1   Decomposable Attention Model

In [31], Parikh et al. introduced a decomposable attention model, also claimed that LSTM and CNN models used for natural language inference (NLI) are computationally expensive and have millions of parameters. Hence the authors came up with the notion of using the attention-based models, which have fewer parameters and reduces the computational cost significantly. Attention-based mechanisms are based on the idea that for NLI it is enough to align bits of the local text substructure and aggregate this information.

- *John is in the airport, but because of the storm and heavy rain, the plane has been delayed, and he has to wait.*
- *John is waiting.*
- *The weather is sunny.*

The first sentence is quite complex, and it is very challenging to create a compact representation that elaborates its entire meaning. It is quite easy to reach a conclusion that the second sentence entails the first one by aligning "John" with "John" and "has to wait" with "waiting." It is seen that the sentence "The weather is sunny" contradicts the first sentence, when we align "storm and heavy rain" with "sunny" and recognize that they are incompatible. This intuition has been used to make a simpler model for NLI, which has fewer parameters. The authors claim that this model performs better than the existing complex architectures. The model uses a soft attention mechanism, and the entire process can be divided into three steps:

- Attend
- Compare
- Aggregate

(i) *Attend*

In this step, the unnormalized attention weight e_{ij} is calculated, which is expressed as

$$e_{ij} = F(a)^T F(b) \qquad (2.9)$$

where $F(a)$ and $F(b)$ are the attention weights obtained by feeding text embedding (a) and hypothesis embedding (b) to feed-forward neural network (FFNN). The unnormalized attention weights are then normalized as follows:

$$\beta_i := \sum_{j-1}^{l_b} \frac{\exp(e_{ij})}{\sum_{k=1}^{l_b} \exp(e_{ik})} \bar{b}_j \ \& \ \alpha_i := \sum_{j=1}^{l_a} \frac{\exp(e_{ij})}{\sum_{k=1}^{l_a} \exp(e_{kj})} \bar{a}_i \qquad (2.10)$$

(ii) *Compare*

The aligned phrases are compared separately in this step. The text embedding is concatenated with β_i and fed to the FFNN to get the comparison vector v_1. Similarly, hypothesis embedding is concatenated with α_j and fed to the FFNN to get the comparison vector v_2.

(iii) *Aggregate*

The summation of the comparison vectors is calculated as follows:

$$v_1 = \sum_{i=1}^{l_a} v_1, i \,\&\, v_2 = \sum_{j=1}^{l_b} v_2, j \tag{2.11}$$

Here, v_1 and v_2 are concatenated and fed to the FFNN to obtain the final result.

2.1.2.1.2 Asymmetric Attention Model

This model is also based on Parikh et al. [31] and example notebooks of Spacy [32]. This model intends to demonstrate that to classify entailment, only the strength of the association that exists between hypothesis and text is required. This model eliminates the consideration of text to hypothesis vectors from the computation. This elimination of text to hypothesis vector reduces the parameter count considerably and enhances the model by reducing the training time. The preliminary calculations are done until we achieve the attention weights being the same as the previous model. In the previous model, they had the dot product between the normalized attention weights and text embedding (a_j) to get α_j and hypothesis embedding with attention weights to obtain β_i. But in this model, they only calculate α_j and not β_i. The concatenation of α_j with hypothesis embedding b gives the comparison vector v_2. The vector v_2 is fed to the FFNN, to calculate the summation of comparison vectors. This summation of comparison vectors is fed to the FFNN whose output is sent to the softmax layer to obtain the classification.

2.1.2.2 LSTM

This LSTM model was based on the blog "Textual Entailment with TensorFlow" [33]. This implementation has the drawback that the output was not stable. To avoid this anomaly, Bi-LSTM layers were increased from 64 to 200 [34], and three dense layers are added with a softmax function after the Bi-LSTM layers, hence the output of the model became stable. The model uses Global Vectors for Word Representation (GloVe) [35, 36] embeddings of 300 dimensions to convert text and hypothesis sentences to text and hypothesis embeddings. The text and hypothesis embeddings are then concatenated and fed to 200 layers of Bi-LSTM networks. The output of the Bi-LSTM networks is fed to three dense layers and then finally to softmax activation function to get the final output.

2.1.2.3 GRU

The overall architecture of this model is the same as the LSTM model. The only difference is that this model uses GRU instead of LSTM.

2.1.2.4 Evaluation

The three activation functions, namely tanh, ReLU, and sigmoid, are evaluated on a decomposable attention model to analyze the impact of activation function on the performance of models. The four different models, namely the decomposable attention model, asymmetric attention model, LSTM, and GRU, are evaluated with respect to the accuracy, training time, and complexity of models. The datasets like SNLI, MultiNLI, and SCITAIL are evaluated respectively in the decomposable attention model. The sentences are fed to a decomposable attention model, whose results are recorded and the sentences are analyzed to get a deep understanding of the model. The parameters used for evaluation are given in Table 2.3

2.1.3 DATASET

The corpus or dataset used in this study are:

- 570,000 sentences from Stanford Natural Language Inference (SNLI) corpus [37]
- 393,000 sentences from Multi-Genre Natural Language Inference (MultiNLI) corpus [38]
- 27,026 sentences from SCITAIL: A Textual Entailment Dataset from Science Question Answering [39]

2.1.4 EVALUATION OF MODELS

In this experiment, the accuracy of the decomposable attention model, asymmetric attention model, LSTM, as well as GRU model is compared. In Figure 2.5, it is observed that the training accuracy of the LSTM model is 94% and the testing accuracy is only 75%. So, considering testing accuracies, it is found that the decomposable attention model is the best, i.e., it gives an accuracy of 86%. The asymmetric attention model gives an accuracy of 81%. LSTM model gives an accuracy of 75%, and GRU gives an accuracy of 74%. Hence from this evaluation, it is concluded that decomposable attention is the best model among these four different models when testing accuracy is taken into account. LSTM model performs better than GRU.

In Figures 2.6 and 2.7, DA refers to the decomposable attention model and AA refers to the asymmetric attention model. Figure 2.6 shows the various models with their trainable parameters. LSTM model has the highest number of parameters, followed by GRU decomposable attention and asymmetric attention model. From this

---

TABLE 2.3
Parameters of Evaluation

Maximum Sequence Length	Hidden Size	Batch Size	Learning Rate	Embedding Dimension
50	200	1024	0.0001	300

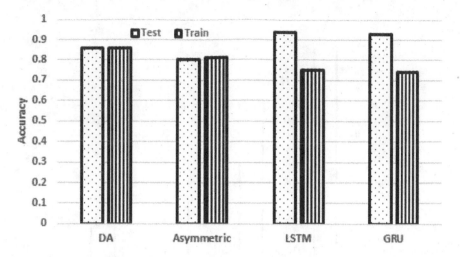

FIGURE 2.5   Accuracy of different models.

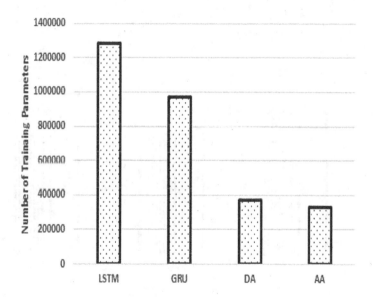

FIGURE 2.6   Trainable parameters.

experiment, it is found that attention-based models have a few parameters, unlike the LSTM model. Though the LSTM model taken into consideration is the simplest possible model, the number of training parameters is very high compared to the decomposable attention model. The training time and parameters for the models are directly proportional to each other. Thus, the training time for the LSTM model has the highest training time and the asymmetric model has the least.

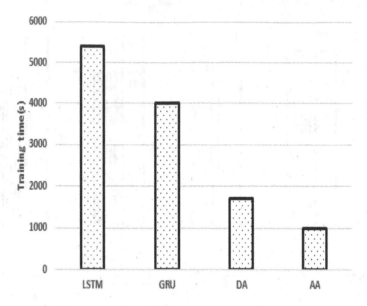

FIGURE 2.7 Training time.

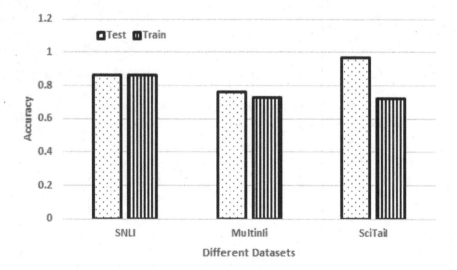

FIGURE 2.8 Analysis with different datasets.

Decomposable attention model executes better than the LSTM model by using fewer parameters. The asymmetric attention model has fewer parameters than the decomposable attention model. However, the performance of the decomposable attention model is better than the asymmetric attention model. It is inferred from previous experiments that the DA model performs better than other models. Hence, this model was taken into consideration for training SNLI, MultiNLI, and SciTail datasets.

As seen in Figure 2.8, the training accuracy and testing accuracy obtained for the SNLI dataset are 86%. The training accuracy obtained using the MultiNLI dataset is 76%, and the testing accuracy obtained is 73%. The training accuracy for the SciTail dataset is 97%, and the testing accuracy is only 72%. Hence, considering testing accuracy, it is found that the DA model performs best with the SNLI dataset. The SNLI dataset has the highest number of training sentences, which could be the reason that the model gives the highest accuracy when trained. In the case of the MultiNLI dataset, the training accuracy is more than the testing accuracy. The number of sentences in the MultiNLI dataset is less than that of SNLI, and the accuracy is also less. In the case of the SciTail dataset, the training accuracy being higher than the testing accuracy clearly shows that the model suffers from the problem of overfitting.

2.1.5 ANALYSIS OF SENTENCES

An analysis with general descriptive and active-passive sentences helped understand the performance of the chosen DA model.

2.1.5.1 General Sentences

In Table 2.4, the sentences "A woman with a green headscarf, blue shirt, and a very big grin." and "The woman is young." are given and correctly classified as neutral. Because there is no relation between the sentences, the word "young" has no relationship with the other words of the sentence. In the same way, for the sentence "The woman has been shot.", the word "shot" has no relation with the sentences

TABLE 2.4
Analysis of Sentences for SNLI Dataset

Number	Sentence Pairs	Known Value	Predicted Value
1	1. A woman with a green headscarf, blue shirt, and a very big grin. 2. The woman is young.	Neutral	Neutral
2	1. A woman with a green headscarf, blue shirt, and a very big grin. 2. The woman is very happy.	Entailment	Entailment
3	1. A woman with a green headscarf, blue shirt, and a very big grin. 2. The woman has been shot.	Contradiction	Neutral
4	1. The two young girls are dressed as fairies, and green are playing in the leaves outdoors. 2. Girls are playing outdoors.	Entailment	Entailment
5	1. The two young girls are dressed as fairies, and are playing in the leaves outdoors. 2. Two girls play dress-up indoors.	Contradiction	Contradiction
6	1. The two young girls are dressed as fairies, and are playing in the leaves outdoors. 2. The two girls play in the Autumn.	Entailment	Neutral

above; hence, it is wrongly classified as neutral. As explained in the description of the model, the model first aligns, then compares, and then aggregates to give the prediction. Hence in the first sentence of fourth row, "playing" is aligned with "playing," and "outdoors" with "outdoors," therefore it is classified as entailment, whereas in the fifth row, the word "outdoors" is aligned with "indoors," and since the words are contradictory, the sentences are classified as a contradiction. Similarly, "outdoors" has no relationship with "Autumn." Consequently, the model classifies it as neutral, even though it is labeled as entailment.

2.1.5.2 Active-Passive Sentences

There are some active-passive sentence pairs in the SNLI and MultiNLI datasets. A list of active-passive sentences taken from the Your Dictionary website [40] is also analyzed using the DA model. All the sentences were correctly classified. In Table 2.5, "Harry" is aligned with "Harry," "ate" with "eaten," "six shrimp" with "six shrimp," "at dinner" with "At dinner," hence the sentences were classified as entailment. Similarly in the rest of the sentences as well, the words are aligned respectively.

Since in active-passive sentences only a few extra words are added and the arrangement of words is different but the sentences are similar, the sentences are correctly classified by the model.

2.1.6 INFERENCE

The decomposable attention, asymmetric attention, LSTM, and GRU models are tested using the SNLI dataset. It was found that the DA model has the best training accuracy among the four models with fewer parameters and time compared to LSTM and GRU models. Though asymmetric attention models have less training parameters and training time compared to DA models, the accuracy of the asymmetric attention model is less than that of the DA model. The DA model has been trained on SNLI, MultiNLI, and SciTail datasets. It was found that the model trained on the SNLI dataset has the highest accuracy among others, as it has the highest number of

---

TABLE 2.5
Active-Passive Sentences [40]

Number	Sentence Pairs	Known Value	Predicted Value
1	1. Harry ate six shrimp at dinner. 2. At dinner, six shrimp were eaten by Harry.	Entailment	Entailment
2	1. Beautiful giraffes roam the savannah. 2. The savannah is roamed by beautiful giraffes.	Entailment	Entailment
3	1. Sue changed the flat tire. 2. The flat tire was changed by Sue.	Entailment	Entailment
4	1. We are going to watch a movie tonight. 2. A movie is going to be watched by us tonight.	Entailment	Entailment
5	1. I ran the obstacle course in record time. 2. The obstacle course was run by me in record time.	Entailment	Entailment

training sentences. The various sentences have been analyzed using the DA model, and it was found that when the sentences are similar (active-passive sentence pairs), the model is classified correctly.

2.2 CONCLUSION

The case studies of RNN and attention-based models were discussed from its requirement to development levels. The general conclusions and future work of individual cases are summarized as follows:

2.2.1 EEG ANALYSIS

- *Using three different techniques, a multiclass classification of EEG signal (five classes) is performed. In this study, units considered from 1 to 1,024 and up to 100 epochs, the training done, and also layers considered from 1 to 5 with 32 cells and trained for 300 epochs to get a conception about precision and to know each variant of RNN takes how much time for training networks. It can be applied toward the precision and time consumption for different sized batches with dissimilar epochs to fine-tune an opportune network provided that the network should not be overfitted.*
- ➤ A study can be done on the same dataset using different optimizers and more layers. These algorithms can be tried out with different datasets for various multiclass classifications.

2.2.2 RTE ANALYSIS

- *Attention models perform better than LSTM and GRU models. Decomposable attention model has fewer parameters, less training time, and better accuracy than LSTM and GRU. The number of sentences in the training dataset has a considerable impact on the overall accuracy of the model. The key idea is that when the sentences are aligned and when it finds a proper relation, it classifies it, but in some cases the sentences are complex, and this strategy of aligning and predicting fails, and the model is not able to make correct predictions.*
- ➤ It is found that the DA model has the best accuracy with fewer training parameters than LSTM and GRU. So, this model can be used to improve the performance of many applications of RTE like automatic short answer grading, machine translation evaluation, relation extraction, text summarization, etc.

These cases being examples of RNN and attention-based models will enable the reader to involve themselves to explore the various variants, combinations, or training parameters of the DL model using different datasets of their choice.

REFERENCES

1. Rumelhart, D. E., Hinton, G. E., and Williams, R. J. (eds.) (1986). Learning internal representations by error propagation. *Parallel distributed processing: explorations in the microstructure of cognition, vol. 1: Foundations.* MIT Press, Cambridge, MA, pp. 318–362.

2. Schuster, Mike, and Paliwal, Kuldip. (1997). Bidirectional recurrent neural networks, *IEEE Transactions on Signal Processing*, **45**, No. 11, 2673–2681. doi:10.1109/78.650093.

3. Hochreiter, S., and Schmidhuber, J. (1997). Long short-term memory. *Neural Computation*, **9**, No. 8, 1735–1780.

4. Glorot, Xavier, Bordes, Antoine, and Bengio, Yoshua. (2011). Deep sparse rectifier neural networks, *Proceedings of the Fourteenth International Conference on Artificial Intelligence and Statistics, PMLR* 15, pp. 315–323.

5. Bengio, Y., Simard, P., and Frasconi, P. (1994). Learning long-term dependencies with gradient descent is difficult. *IEEE Transactions on Neural Networks*, **5**, No. 2, 157–166.

6. Glorot, Xavier, Bordes, Antoine, Bengio, Yoshua, (2011). Deep sparse rectifier neural networks, *Proceedings of the Fourteenth International Conference on Artificial Intelligence and Statistics, PMLR*, April 11–13, 2011, Fort Lauderdale, FL, USA 15, pp. 315–323.

7. Graves, A., and Schmidhuber, J. (2005). Frame wise phoneme classification with bidirectional LSTM and other neural network architectures. *Neural Networks.* **18**, No. 5–6, 602–610.

8. Cho, Kyunghyun, van Merriënboer, Bart and Caglar Gulcehre, et al. (2014). *Learning Phrase Representations using RNN Encoder-Decoder for Statistical Machine Translation.* doi:10.3115/v1/D14-1179.

9. Rafal Jozefowicz et al. (2015) An empirical exploration of recurrent network architectures, *Proceedings of the 32nd International Conference on Machine Learning*, Lille, France. JMLR: W&CP volume 37.

10. Wu, Yonghui et al. (2016), Google's Neural Machine Translation System: Bridging the Gap between Human and Machine Translation, https://arxiv.org/abs/1609.08144.

11. Can global semantic context improve neural language models? - https://machinelearning.apple.com/research/can-global-semantic-context-improve-neural-language-models

12. Vogels, Werner. (2016). Bringing the Magic of Amazon AI and Alexa to Apps on AWS.– All Things Distributed. www.allthingsdistributed.com. 30 November 2016.

13. Ong, Thuy. Facebook's translations are now powered completely by AI. www.allthingsdistributed.com.

14. Haridy, Rich (August 21, 2017). Microsoft's speech recognition system is now as good as a human. newatlas.com

15. Bellard, Fabrice (2019). Lossless Data Compression with Neural Networks. https://bellard.org/nncp/nncp.pdf.

16. Hochreiter, Sepp, and Schmidhuber, Jurgen (1997). Long short-term memory. *Neural Computation*, **9**, No. 8, pp. 1735–1780.

17. Cho, KyungHyun, Bengio, Yoshua, Chung, Junyoung, and Gulcehre, Caglar (2014). Empirical evaluation of gated recurrent neural networks on sequence modeling. arXiv:1412.3555v1 [cs.NE], pp. 1–9.

18. El-Khoribi, Reda A., Alhagry, Salma, and Fahmy, Aly Aly. (2017). Emotion recognition as ed on EEG using LSTM recurrent neural network. *International Journal of Advanced Computer Science and Applications*, **8**, No. 10, 355–358.

19. Krizhevsky, Alex, Sutskever, Ilya, and Hinton, Geoffrey E. (2012). Image net classification with deep convolutional neural networks. In *Advances in Neural Information Processing Systems.*

20. Gers, F., Schraudolph, N., and Schmidhuber, J. (2002). Learning precise timing with LSTM recurrent networks. *Journal of Machine Learning Research*, 3, 115–143.
21. Graves, A., and Schmidhuber, J. (June/July 2005). Framewise Phoneme classification with bidirectional LSTM and other neural network architectures. *Neural Networks*, 18, No. 5–6, 602–610.
22. Graves, A., Fernandez, S., Gomez, F., and Schmidhuber, J. (2006). Connectionist temporal classification: labelling unsegmented sequence data with recurrent neural networks. In *ICML*, Pittsburgh, USA.
23. Graves, A., Mohamed, A., and Hinton, G. (May 2013). Speech recognition with deep recurrent neural networks. In *Proc ICASSP 2013*, Vancouver, Canada.
24. Jaeger, H. (2012). Long short-term memory in echo state networks: Details of a simulation study. Technical Report, Jacobs University Bremen, 2012.
25. Rumelhart, D. E., Hinton, G. E., and Williams, R. J. (1986). Learning representations by backpropagating errors. *Nature*, 323, No. 6088, 533–536.
26. Werbos, P. J. (1988). Generalization of backpropagation with application to a recurrent gas market model. *Neural Networks*, **1**, No. 4, 339–356.
27. Elman, J. (1990). Finding structure in time. *Cognitive Science*, **14**, No. 2, 179–211.
28. Bengio, Y., Simard, P., and Frasconi, P. (1994). Learning long-term dependencies with gradient descent is difficult. *IEEE Transactions on Neural Networks*, **5**, No. 2, 157–166.
29. Rieke, C., Mormann, F., David, P., Elger, C. E., Andrzejak, R. G., and Lehnertz K. (2001). Indications of nonlinear deterministic and finite dimensional structures in time series of brain electrical activity: Dependence on recording region and brain state. *Physical Review E*, 64, 061907-1–061907-8.
30. Chollet, Francois et al. *Keras*. https://github.com/fchollet/keras.2015
31. Parikh, Ankur P., Täckström, Oscar, Das, Dipanjan, and Uszkorei, Jakob. (2016). A decomposable attention model for natural language inference. In arxiv.org.
32. Spacy. https://github.com/free-variation/spaCy/tree/master/examples.
33. Oreilly. https://www.oreilly.com/learning/textual-entailment-with-tensorflow.
34. Sharma, Ramit, Ploeger, Paul G., and Nair, Deebul. (2018). Recognizing textual entailment: A comprehensive evaluation of the existing state of the art techniques. In *R&D Report hbrs*.
35. Pennington, Jeffrey, Socher, Richard, and Manning, Christopher D. (2014). Glove: Global vectors for word representation. In *Conference on Empirical Methods in Natural Language Processing (EMNLP)*.
36. Bahdanau, Dzmitry, Cho, Kyunghyun, and Bengio, Yoshua. (2015). Neural machine translation by jointly learning to align and translate. In *ICLR*.
37. Bowman, Samuel R., Angeli, Gabor, Potts, Christopher, and Manning, Christopher D. (2015). A large annotated corpus for learning natural language inference. In *Cornell University Library*.
38. Williams, Adina, Nangia, Nikita, and Bowman, Samuel. (2018). A broad-coverage challenge corpus for sentence understanding through inference. In *Proceedings of the 2018 Conference of the North American Chapter of the Association for Computational Linguistics: Human Language Technologies, Volume 1 (Long Papers)*, pp. 1112–1122. Association for Computational Linguistics.
39. Khot, Tushar, Sabharwal, Ashish, and Clark, Peter. (2018). SciTail: A textual entailment dataset from science question answering. In *AAAI*.
40. Machine Learning Mastery. https://examples.yourdictionary.com/examples-of-active-and-passive-voice.html.

3 Image to Text Processing Using Convolution Neural Networks

V. Pattabiraman and R. Maheswari
Vellore Institute of Technology, Chennai, India

CONTENTS

3.1 INTRODUCTION

In the early stages of internet technologies, captcha consisted of only simple characters and numbers. But in modern-day internet, captcha consists of a variety of distortion and noises incorporated with it, such as overlapping characters, multicolor verification letters, and a variety of textured, twisted, and misshaped letters. Consequently, the difficulty in identifying characters in a captcha image has also increased. This chapter covers the efforts to engineer an end-to-end neural network model to accomplish captcha recognition [1, 2]. It also presents convolutional neural network with a strong capability to extract features from an image and recurrent neural network to find a sequence between the characters. Captcha technology is used to discriminate between humans and robots. For websites, captcha technology is used to avoid automated harmful programming attacks [3, 4]. Captcha technology has become popular as the internet has grown [5]. The results show that the proposed model accomplishes a significant accuracy in recognition of captcha compared to traditional models that are discussed in the later part of the chapter.

3.1.1 CONVOLUTIONAL NEURAL NETWORKS

Convolution neural network (CNN) is a deep learning technique widely used in computer vision, object detection, and image recognition tasks. Therefore, the CNN can

DOI: 10.1201/9781003307822-4

be applied to develop a handwritten digit recognition system. To train CNN requires a huge dataset of images, which must be preprocessed before training the model. The main advantage of the convolution neural network is that it can extract features automatically by considering the correlation of pixels. In general, convolution neural network consists of the convolution layer, ReLU layer, pooling layer, and fully connected layer [6]. The weed detection model is being built with multilayer CNN that has four convolution layers and four max-pooling layers alternatively. After extracting the feature map in the network, one flattening layer is applied, then two dense layers, using a dropout method [7]. The flattening layer is used to convert the feature map to a one-dimensional stack, as the fully connected layer can process only one-dimension data. The dense layer consists of a fully connected network in which each neuron in one layer is connected to the neurons in the next layer. The dropout of 0.5 is applied to activate only 50% of neurons in the layer, and it will transfer only those features to the next layer that have high probability value. The multilayer CNN enhances the model to extract more robust features [8]. In the convolution layer, the convolution operation is applied that acts as a filter on the given data and extracts the features from the input data, and it summarizes the features that are necessary to classify or to detect objects. The features extracted from a two-dimensional array are collectively called a feature map. Max pooling and average pooling are the two types of pooling layers. In max-pooling the values that are maximum in the filter are selected, whereas on average, pooling the values from the filter is evaluated to mean value and the value is said to be average [9]. The result of the pooling layer provides the maximum capability features that are used for classifying. In a fully connected layer, the output of the pooling layer is converted into a one-dimensional stack that computes the class score, and then finally the given data class is categorized. VggNet transformer is also known as OxfordNet. This model consists of only a convolution layer and a max-pooling layer. This architecture can be divided into five divisions. The first division contains two convolutional layers and one pooling layer. The number of filters used in convolutional layers is 64 in this division. The second division also contains two convolutional and one pooling layer. The number of filters used in convolutional layers is 128 in this division. The third division consists of three convolutional layers and a pooling layer. The number of filters used in convolutional layers is 256 in this division. The fourth and fifth divisions also consist of three convolutional layers and a pooling layer [10]. The number of filters applied in the division is 512 for the convolutional layer. The size of the filter for all convolutional layers in all division is same, which is 3*3. The size of the filter for all max-pooling layer in all division is same, which is 2*2. Finally, three dense layers are connected to the final division. The ReLU activation function is applied on every convolutional layer. LeNet is incorporated with three different types of layers, which are convolutional layers, average pooling layers, and fully connected layers. This model contains two pairs of convolutional layer and average pooling layers, then finally trailed by two flattening layer. The first layer is convolutional layer, which has six feature maps or filters having a size of 5*5, and the stride is one. The second layer is an average pooling layer, also known as sampling layer, which has one filter having a size of 2*2, and the stride is two. The third layer is again a convolutional layer. This time it has 16 filter maps having a size of 5*5, and a stride is one. The fourth layer of this model is again an average pooling layer, which has 16 filter maps having a size of 2*2, and again the stride is two. The fifth and sixth layers of this model are flattening layers, also known as a fully connected layer. The final layer is an output layer with five softmax layers for multi-classification. Tanh activation function is applied as the activation function in an convolution layer. Softmax activation function is applied as the activation function in an output layer [11]. This model won the ImageNet classification challenge in 2012. This model is an updated architecture of LeNet. AlexNet is deeper compared to LeNet. A rectified linear unit is applied as the activation function in AlexNet, which enumerates nonlinearity. This is the main difference between AlexNet and LeNet. AlexNet contains eight divisions in which the first five division are convolutional layers and the last three divisions are fully connected layers. The first division is a convolutional layer that consists of 96 filters having a size of 11*11, and the stride is four. The second division is a maxpooling layer that has one filter with a size of 3*3, and the stride is two. The third division is a convolutional layer that consists of 256 filters with a size of 5*5. The stride is one and the padding is two [12]. The fourth division is again a maxpooling layer that consists of one filter with a size of 3*3, and the stride is two. The fifth and sixth divisions are convolutional layer that consists of 384 numbers of filters with a size of 3*3. The stride is one and the padding is one. The seventh division is also a convolutional layer that consists of 256 filters with a size of 3*3. The stride is one and the padding is one. The final layer is a maxpooling layer with a filter size of 3*3. Dropout is applied at the final stage, which helps reduce the overfitting problem. Dropout rate is 0.5 in this model. ReLU activation function is applied as the activation function in a convolution layer. Softmax activation function is applied as activation function in an output layer [13].

3.2 LITERATURE SURVEY

Yujin Shu and Yongjin Xu used different types of CNN for extracting the features from the captcha image and used the optimized gated recurrent unit of long short-term memory network to predict the output characters. In their work, there are four types of datasets used for training the models, such as water ripple images, shadow images, fisheye, and finally crawled images from websites. The crawled images from the websites are used for testing the models. The work also proposed different combinations of convolution and recurrent neural networks and compared them with respect to the results for each dataset types. The disadvantage of this research work is that the length of predicted output is very small, and accuracy of the model is substandard [14]. YuHu, Li Chen, and Jun Cheng compared the performance of different types of CNN such as LENET and VGGNET. This work proposed the VGGNET-based convolutional neural networks that contain reduced size filters and more convolutional layers in the network. By doing that, the authors proclaimed that the performance of this proposed model outsmarted the other convolutional-based neural network–based models. For datasets, authors used Python script to generate a captcha image with five characters. Each character was arbitrarily chosen from the list of 10 digits and 26 characters. The dataset contained only unique images because of reliability of the model [15]. Yuxiang Jiang and Haiwei Dong proposed two models for captcha recognition. The first model is a deep convolutional neural network, and the second model is a convolutional recurrent neural network. The datasets are captcha style images that contain arithmetic operations. The authors conclude convolutional recurrent neural networks outperformed the deep convolutional neural networks because of their greater capability in capturing the contextual information [16]. Chen Rui, Yang Jing, Hu Rong-gui, and Huang Shu-guang established the two-dimensional neural networks for captcha recognition. The dataset used in their work was created by a captcha-generating program. The research work proposed a novel method of adding the connectionist temporal classification layer at the output of the recurrent neural network. This work explained the conceptualization of the connectionist temporal classification layer [17]. It proposed an optical character recognition system for scanning documents. The proposed system consists of three blocks such as a segmenter, switcher, and multiple recognizers for different languages. Synthetic word–based images are used to train segmenter block. Real-world images are used to train switcher. Segmented blocks consist of multiple convolutional layers and bidirectional long short-term memory layers. The switchers block consists of convolutional layers, maxpooling layers, and three fully connected layers. Each recognizers block uniformly consists of average pooling layers, convolutional layers, and softmax as the lost function but varied by size and number of filters. The proposed model performed well in predicting the English, Chinese, and Korean language characters [18]. Rahul Palekar, Sushant U. Parab, and Dhrumil P. Parikh proposed a method to extract text from license plates using opencv library and tesseract. Image-processing techniques like blurring, contouring, thresholding, and RGB-grey, are used to process the input images. Tesseract is used to extract a text from the processed image. Neuro-fuzzy logic technique is used for optimizing an output image from the tesseract. Live images are used as the dataset [19].

3.3 METHODOLOGY

3.3.1 Recurrent Neural Networks

A recurrent neural network (RNN) is an appropriate neural network method for sequential data input. Recurrent neural networks are used in sequence processing of data, which stores prior information. Sequence data are all around us, like text, audio, video, and stock market prizes. The problems in feed-forward when it comes to sequencing data is that it only accepts a fixed length of input vector as its input. Thus it raises the problem when it tries to predict the next word for a phrase that has seven or sometimes ten words. So, the proposed model needs to handle variable inputs, which paves the way to handling this problem by using a fixed input window. By doing that, however, it limits the information to predict the next word, or the system loses long-term dependencies. In certain types of problems this plays an important role. So, RNNs come as the better solution to hold variable-length sequences and trail long-term dependencies. It maintains information in order and shares parameters across the sequence. In feed-forward neural networks, data will propagate in one direction only. Recurrent neural networks have these loops in them, which allows information to persist over time. Thus at some time step denoted by T, Rnn takes input denoted as xt and at the time step T computes output denoted as ct. In addition

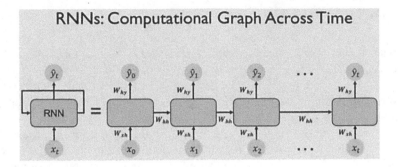

FIGURE 3.1 Recurrent neural network.

to the output it computes internal state update denoted by ht. Internal state update passes the information at the current time step to the next time step of the network. In a RNN block, the two separate weight vectors are multiplied by the input of the current state and internal state update from the previous state. Then these two vectors are added and passed to nonlinearity function. This is the internal update state of the current time step. The third weight vector is multiplied by the internal state to compute the output of the current time step of the network. Figure 3.1 shows the process of RNN discussed here. The RNN has one downside: the vanishing gradient problem. The gated cells are used to tackle this problem. Different types of gated cell architectures are used. Long short-term memory cell (LSTM) is one of the gated cell types. Long short-term memory is a more complex recurrent unit. It maintains a separate cell state for each time step. It can track more effectively long-term dependencies in the data by controlling what information is ignored and what information is used to update the internal state. The key building block behind long short-term memory is called a gate. The gate works to enable a long short-term memory to have the ability to selectively add or remove information to the cell state. Long short-term memory contains four gates: forget, store, update, output. In the forget gate, it resolves which information is important and which information is irrelevant in a cell state and throws away the irrelevant history. In the store stage, it resolves what chunk of new information is relevant and stores that chunk of information in a cell state. In the update gate, by using the information from forget and store gate, it selectively updates its cell gate [20]. In the output gate, it resolves what chunk of information stored in the cell state to send to the next time step in the network as input. Long short-term memory allows the back-propagation through time with uninterrupted gradient flow. There are two contradictory types of lstm in deep learning. The first model is one-directional lstm, and the second model is bidirectional lstm. The difference between one-directional lstm (normal lstm) and bidirectional lstm is that one-directional lstm passes the input in one direction, specifically left to right, but bidirectional lstm passes the input in both directions. Bidirectional predicts an output only when it receives all time step inputs, but normal lstm predicts the outputs at each time step it receives an input. Bidirectional lstms are very complicated compared to normal lstm. Bidirectional lstms are used in this work to predict the final output.

3.4   IMPLEMENTATION

The dataset contains 1,040 images. Each image in the dataset is in a PNG format. Width and height of every image in the dataset is 200 by 50. The label of each image is the same as the characters appearing in the image. Each image contains five characters. Figure 3.2 shows the collage of 16 input images along with their label. Combinations of uppercase and lowercase alphabet characters and ten digits are used in a captcha image. The dataset is split into training and testing data at a ratio of 9:1. The size of each image in a dataset is different, but the input layer in our neural network accepts only fixed-size images, which means the scaling process has to be performed. This problem is solved using the resize tensorflow method. Then the image is converted into an array by tensorflow library. The label of each image contains alphabet characters. So, the alphabets are converted into numbers by a char_to_num method, and at the final stage, to show the predicted character, a num_to_char tensorflow method is used. The training images and testing images are converted into dataset objects. Dataset object in keras is the way of representing the image. Thus, the image can be passed as the input vector to the neural network. The end-to-end neural network model is implemented using the keras framework. Python programming language is used. In preprocessing step, the size of each image is scaled into 200*50. Then it is given to the input layer. In this work the CNN is used to extract the features from an image. The transformers used in this work are LeNet, AlexNet, and VGG-NET. The transformer consists of two convolutional layers and two maxpooling layers with same filter map size but different in number of filters used. At the final stage, all the extract features are flattened by the dense layer and passed as the input to long short-term memory-based recurrent neural network.

The total number of parameters trained in this model is 432,596. In the first convolution layer 320 parameters are learned, and in the second convolution layer around 10,000 parameters are learned. After the dense layer, around 50,000 parameters are learned. The first bidirectional lstm learned around 100,000 parameters, and then the second bidirectional lstm also learned around 100,000 parameters.

Figure 3.3 shows the summary of the LeNet model, and Table 3.1 demonstrates the various features of the image.

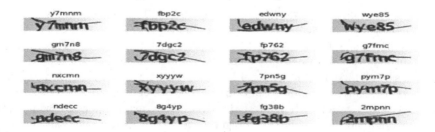

FIGURE 3.2   Input image for LeNet model.

```
Layer (type)                    Output Shape              Param #
===================================================================
image (InputLayer)              [(None, 200, 50, 1)]      0

Conv1 (Conv2D)                  (None, 200, 50, 32)       320

pool1 (MaxPooling2D)            (None, 100, 25, 32)       0

Conv2 (Conv2D)                  (None, 100, 25, 64)       18496

pool2 (MaxPooling2D)            (None, 50, 12, 64)        0

reshape (Reshape)               (None, 50, 768)           0

dense1 (Dense)                  (None, 50, 64)            49216

dropout (Dropout)               (None, 50, 64)            0

bidirectional (Bidirectional    (None, 50, 256)           197632

bidirectional_1 (Bidirection    (None, 50, 128)           164352

dense2 (Dense)                  (None, 50, 20)            2580
===================================================================
Total params: 432,596
Trainable params: 432,596
Non-trainable params: 0
```

FIGURE 3.3   Summary of LeNet and Bilstm model.

TABLE 3.1
Features of the Image

Features of the Image	Description
Size	200*50
Number of channels	Three

3.5   RESULTS AND DISCUSSION

After the training phase and the validation phase, the VggNet model achieved the accuracy of 98%. The LeNet model achieved the accuracy of 72.9%. The AlexNet model achieved the accuracy of 85.5%. The LeNet model achieved the lowest accuracy because of its simple architecture. Table 3.2 shows the performance comparison of models below, and Figure 3.4 shows the graphical representation of accuracy

TABLE 3.2

Performance Comparison of Different Models

Method	Accuracy of Recognition
LeNet based	72.91%
AlexNet based	85.5%
VggNet based	98%

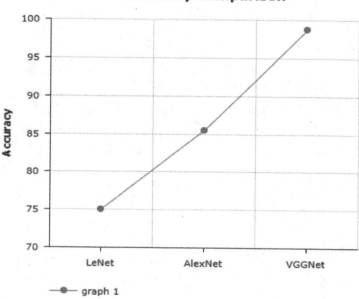

FIGURE 3.4 Accuracy comparison.

comparisons. AlexNet performed better than LeNet, but VggNet outperformed all of them. VGGNet performed very well in this dataset, which has only 1,000 images. The system used an Adam optimizer to train the model. Adam is the best optimizer in the deep learning field. If one wants to train the neural network in less time and more efficiently, then Adam is the optimizer of choice. The model predicted the output of five-character letter composition of numbers and alphabet characters. Predicted labels are attached with each input image. Figure 3.5 shows the predicted outputs. The predicted result was to extract the text from an image, which was executed perfectly and obtained good results.

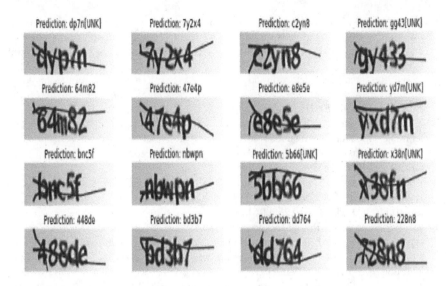

FIGURE 3.5 Predicted results.

3.6 CONCLUSION

In this work, the system recognized the captcha using convolutional recurrent neural network. There are different times of captcha that are being used in this advanced internet world. But the system has discussed text-based captcha recognition. Thus, the system helps understand the challenges faced in captcha recognition by referring to different proposed methods. The future works can be carried out to produce results in different types of captcha and extracting a captcha from a more distorted image with good accuracy. The advances in captcha recognition and major techniques have been covered in this work and highlighted the latest trend.

REFERENCES

1 A. Rusu and V. Govindaraju, "Handwritten CAPTCHA: using the difference in the abilities of humans and machines in reading handwritten words," *Ninth International Workshop on Frontiers in Handwriting Recognition*, 2004, pp. 226–231, doi:10.1109/IWFHR.2004.54.

2 J. Yan and A. S. El Ahmad, "CAPTCHA security: a case study," *IEEE Security & Privacy*, vol. 7, no. 4, pp. 22–28, July–Aug. 2009, doi:10.1109/MSP.2009.84.

3 P. M. Manwatkar and S. H. Yadav, "Text recognition from images," *2015 International Conference on Innovations in Information, Embedded and Communication Systems (ICIIECS)*, 2015, pp. 1–6, doi:10.1109/ICIIECS.2015.7193210.

4 P. M. Manwatkar and K. R. Singh, "A technical review on text recognition from images," *2015 IEEE 9th International Conference on Intelligent Systems and Control (ISCO)*, 2015, pp. 1–5, doi:10.1109/ISCO.2015.7282362.

5 K. M. Yindumathi, S. S. Chaudhari, and R. Aparna, "Analysis of image classification for text extraction from bills and invoices," *2020 11th International Conference on Computing, Communication and Networking Technologies (ICCCNT)*, 2020, pp. 1–6, doi:10.1109/ICCCNT49239.2020.9225564.

6 T. C. Wei, U. U. Sheikh, and A. A. A. Rahman, "Improved optical character recognition with deep neural network," *2018 IEEE 14th International Colloquium on Signal Processing & Its Applications (CSPA)*, 2018, pp. 245–249, doi:10.1109/CSPA.2018.8368720.

7 Y. He, "Research on text detection and recognition based on OCR recognition technology," *2020 IEEE 3rd International Conference on Information Systems and Computer Aided Education (ICISCAE)*, 2020, pp. 132–140, doi:10.1109/ICISCAE51034.2020.9236870.

8 Z. Zhao, M. Jiang, S. Guo, Z. Wang, F. Chao, and K. C. Tan, "Improving deep learning based optical character recognition via neural architecture search," *2020 IEEE Congress on Evolutionary Computation (CEC)*, 2020, pp. 1–7, doi:10.1109/CEC48606.2020.9185798.

9 J. Chen, X. Luo, Y. Liu, J. Wang, and Y. Ma, "Selective learning confusion class for text-based CAPTCHA recognition," *IEEE Access*, vol. 7, pp. 22246–22259, 2019, doi:10.1109/ACCESS.2019.2899044.

10 C. Rui, Y. Jing, H. Rong-Gui, and H. Shu-Guang, "A novel LSTM-RNN decoding algorithm in CAPTCHA recognition," *2013 Third International Conference on Instrumentation, Measurement, Computer, Communication and Control*, 2013, pp. 766–771, doi:10.1109/IMCCC.2013.171.

11 T. Zhang, H. Zheng, and L. Zhang, "Verification CAPTCHA based on deep learning," *2018 37th Chinese Control Conference (CCC)*, 2018, pp. 9056–9060, doi:10.23919/ChiCC.2018.8482847.

12 E. Diao, J. Ding, and V. Tarokh, "Restricted recurrent neural networks," *2019 IEEE International Conference on Big Data (Big Data)*, 2019, pp. 56–63, doi:10.1109/BigData47090.2019.9006257.

13 S. Albawi, T. A. Mohammed, and S. Al-Zawi, "Understanding of a convolutional neural network," *2017 International Conference on Engineering and Technology (ICET)*, 2017, pp. 1–6, doi:10.1109/ICEngTechnol.2017.8308186.

14 Y. Shu and Y. Xu, "End-to-End Captcha recognition using deep CNN-RNN network," *2019 IEEE 3rd Advanced Information Management, Communicates, Electronic and Automation Control Conference (IMCEC)*, 2019, pp. 54–58, doi:10.1109/IMCEC46724.2019.8983895.

15 Y. Hu, L. Chen, and J. Cheng, "A Captcha recognition technology based on deep learning," *2018 13th IEEE Conference on Industrial Electronics and Applications (ICIEA)*, 2018, pp. 617–620, doi:10.1109/ICIEA.2018.8397789.

16 H. Zhan, S. Lyu, and Y. Lu, "Handwritten digit string recognition using convolutional neural network," *2018 24th International Conference on Pattern Recognition (ICPR)*, 2018, pp. 3729–3734, doi:10.1109/ICPR.2018.8546100.

17 J. Park, E. Lee, Y. Kim, I. Kang, H. I. Koo, and N. I. Cho, "Multi-lingual optical character recognition system using the reinforcement learning of character segmenter," *IEEE Access*, vol. 8, pp. 174437–174448, 2020, doi:10.1109/ACCESS.2020.3025769.

18 C. J. Chen, Y. W. Wang, and W. P. Fang, "A study on Captcha recognition," *2014 Tenth International Conference on Intelligent Information Hiding and Multimedia Signal Processing*, 2014, pp. 395–398, doi:10.1109/IIH-MSP.2014.105.

19 Y. Jiang, H. Dong, and A. El Saddik, "Baidu meizu deep learning competition: Arithmetic operation recognition using end-to-end learning OCR technologies," *IEEE Access*, vol. 6, pp. 60128–60136, 2018, doi:10.1109/ACCESS.2018.2876035.

20 R. R. Palekar, S. U. Parab, D. P. Parikh, and V. N. Kamble, "Real time license plate detection using openCV and tesseract," *2017 International Conference on Communication and Signal Processing (ICCSP)*, 2017, pp. 2111–2115, doi:10.1109/ICCSP.2017.8286778.

4 Fuzzy Orienteering Problem Using Genetic Search

Partha Sarathi Barma, Saibal Majumder and Bijoy Kumar Mandal

NSHM Knowledge Campus Durgapur, Durgapur, India

CONTENTS

4.1 INTRODUCTION

The objective of the traveling salesman problem (TSP) problem is to find the minimal route in terms of distance or time that cover all the cities. There are several variations of TSP problems. One such variation is known as reward-gathering TSP (PC-TSP) or orienteering problem (OP) [1]. In OP, there is a deadline of distance traveled, and within that the salesman has to maximize the reward points, sometimes called score. Generally, OP has two parts. One is to find the cities to cover, and the next one is to find the Hamiltonian path that covers those cities. That is, the first part is like the

DOI: 10.1201/9781003307822-5

knapsack problem (KP), and the second part is the TSP. No algorithm exists that can solve the problem in polynomial time.

In the earlier days, the OP was solved using the exact solution methods by applying mathematical models like dynamic programming, branch and bound algorithm, and binary integer programming to explore the superior solution as described in Sevkli and Sevilgen [2]. All the methods based on the exact solution will be time consuming and practically infeasible. That is why most of the cases are based on some heuristic approach. Moreover, finding a good heuristic is also not such an easy task, as described in Gendreau et al. [3].

Some of the heuristic methods like greedy insertion, sweep-based insertion, path improvement, random insertion, and ant colony optimization were also described in Sevkli and Sevilgen [2]. Wang et al. [4] solved OP using an artificial neural network. Chao et al. [5] demonstrated the application of applied deterministic simulated annealing to the OP to obtain superior solutions. Cai et al. [6] employed the tabu search method to determine the approximate solutions of the OP. Tsiligirides [7] developed a stochastic algorithm for the OP. A genetic algorithm with an adaptive penalty function for OP is described in Tasgetiren [8]. Sevkli and Erdogan Sevilgen [2] have used particle swarm optimization to solve the OP.

The first application of OP can be observed in Tsiligirides [8] for the case of the TSP, but the salesperson has insufficient time to visit the cities, and they have to maximize their sales. Another area of application is the home fuel delivery problem, as described in Golden et al. [9]. Thomadsen and Stidsen [10] applied the OP in the single-ring design problem when building telecommunication networks. The latest area of application is the mobile tourist guide, as described in Souffriau et al. [11]. The OP also has application in vehicle routing and production scheduling as described in Golden et al. [9]. Furthermore, the application of evolutionary algorithms can be observed in some recent studies [12–16]. This paper applies the fuzzy chance constraint approach using the genetic algorithm to orienteering problems. Here it applies fuzziness in the maximum distance. The main contribution of this article is as follows.

- A fuzzy orienteering problem is constructed considering the maximum time limit as linear fuzzy number.
- Chance-constrained programming technique is used for the fuzzy model.
- Genetic algorithm is employed to solve the model.

The rest of the article is arranged as follows. In Section 4.2, the concept of chance-constrained programming is discussed. The proposed model of the orienteering problem is presented in Section 4.3. An improved version of the genetic algorithm is discussed in Section 4.4. The result and its discussions are provided in Section 4.5. The conclusion of the study is presented in Section 4.6.

4.2 CHANCE-CONSTRAINED PROGRAMMING

Fuzzy constraints can be represented by possibility measure in an optimistic way and can be managed by chance constraint programming method [17]. Hence the constraint $\left(\tilde{A} \geq \tilde{B} \right)$ can be written as $\text{Pos}\left(\tilde{A} \geq \tilde{B} \right) \geq \alpha$, which represents that the constraint will satisfy with a chance α, where $0< \alpha \leq 1$ and will be the choice of the decision-maker. Let us assume $\tilde{A}$ and $\tilde{B}$ be two fuzzy sets having membership functions $\mu_{\tilde{A}}(x)$ and $\mu_{\tilde{B}}(x)$ respectively, then following the studies of Liu and Iwamura [18] and Dubios and Prade [19], the possibility of $\left(\tilde{A} * \tilde{B}\right)$ is represented as $\text{Pos}\left(\tilde{A} * \tilde{B}\right)$ and given by $\text{Pos}\left(\tilde{A} \geq \tilde{B}\right) = \sup\left\{\min\left(\mu_{\tilde{A}}(x), \mu_{\tilde{B}}(y)\right), x, y \in \Re, x * y\right\}$, where $*$ indicates any relation $<, >, =, \geq, \leq$. If there is no fuzzy parameter in the objective function, then possibility-based constraints can be converted to their corresponding deterministic equivalence as per the predetermined confidence level. The below-mentioned lemma can be employed to determine the solution to the orienteering problem described in our study.

Lemma 1: If $\tilde{A}$ be a linear fuzzy number given by the membership function $\mu_{\tilde{A}}(x)$ defined as

$$\mu_{\tilde{A}}(x) = 1 \text{ if } x \leq a_1, a_1 \geq 0$$
$$= \frac{a_2 - x}{a_2 - a_1} \text{ if } a_1 \leq x \leq a_2$$
$$= 0 \text{ otherwise,}$$

where $a_1 \geq 0$.

Then $\text{Pos}\left(\tilde{A} \geq b\right) \geq \alpha$, where b is a crisp value if and only if $\frac{a_2 - b}{a_2 - a_1} \geq \alpha, 0 \leq \alpha \leq 1$.

Proof: It is clear from the Figure 4.1 that

$$\text{Pos}\left(\tilde{A} \geq b\right) = \begin{cases} 1, x \leq a_1 \\ \frac{a_2 - b}{a_2 - a_1}, a_1 \leq x \leq a_2 \\ 0, \text{otherwise.} \end{cases}$$

Since $0 \leq \alpha \leq 1$, then $\text{Pos}\left(\tilde{A} \geq b\right) \geq \alpha$ iff $\frac{a_2 - b}{a_2 - a_1} \geq \alpha$.

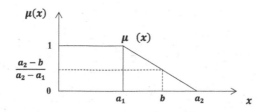

FIGURE 4.1 Ranking fuzzy number with a crisp number.

4.3 THE ORIENTEERING PROBLEM

The orienteering problem can be defined using a connected network $G = \{V, A\}$ where $V = \{v_1, v_2, \ldots, v_n\}$ is the set of cities i having score S_i and $A = \{(v_i, v_j) : i \neq j, \forall i, j = 1, 2\ldots, n\}$ is the set of arcs. The beginning city (v_1) and terminal city (v_n) are considered as fixed. The path length between i^{th} city and j^{th} city or the travel duration between city i^{th} to city j^{th} for every pair of cities are available in advance. Not all the cities are required to be visited, rather a deadline of distance or time, T_{max} will be given and within that deadline the salesperson must visit some cities to maximize the score. Here the scores are additive in nature and the salespersons should visit a city exactly once. The main goal in OP is to find the maximal path by following the above-mentioned conditions. So, the solution of OP is the process of finding a Hamiltonian path $G'(\subset G)$, which contains starting (v_1) and terminating (v_n) vertex, and the length of the path must not exceed T_{max}, with the aim to maximize the total score.

4.3.1 DETERMINISTIC MODEL

Using the notation mentioned in above section, OP can be modeled as a linear integer programming problem. The decision variables OP is binary and defined as: $x_{ij} = 1$ if j^{th} vertex is visited immediately after i^{th} vertex, and $x_{ij} = 0$ otherwise.

$$\max \sum_{i=2}^{N-1} \sum_{j=2}^{N} S_i x_{ij} \tag{4.1}$$

subject to constraints

$$\sum_{j=2}^{N} x_{1j} = \sum_{i=1}^{N-1} x_{iN} = 1 \tag{4.2}$$

$$\sum_{i=1}^{N-1} x_{ik} = \sum_{j=2}^{N} x_{kj} \leq 1; \forall k = 2,3,\ldots,N-1 \tag{4.3}$$

$$\sum_{i=2}^{N-1} \sum_{j=2}^{N} t_{ij} x_{ij} \leq T_{max} \tag{4.4}$$

$$2 \leq u_i \leq N, \forall i = 2,\ldots,N \tag{4.5a}$$

$$u_i - u_j + 1 \leq (N-1)(1 - x_{ij}), \forall i \neq 1, \forall j \neq 1 \tag{4.5b}$$

$$x_{ij} \in \{0,1\}; \forall i, j = 1,\ldots,N \tag{4.6}$$

The objective function (4.1) is employed to maximize the accumulated score. The first constraint (4.2) determine that a path exists from v_1 to v_N. The second constraint (4.3) is used to ensure that the vertices visited no more than once. The third constraint ((4.4) impose the limited time or distance budget. Finally, the constraint (4.5a) and (4.5b) are used to prevent sub tours. These sub-tour removal constraint is used by following Miller et al. [15].

4.3.2 FUZZY MODEL

When the maximum distance $\tilde{T}_{\max}$ is fuzzy, then the constraint ((4.4) will be

$$\sum_{i=1}^{N-1}\sum_{j=2}^{N} t_{ij}x_{ij} \leq \tilde{T}_{\max} \tag{4.7a}$$

Now using the chance constraints method and possibility theory the constraint (4.7a) can be written as

$$\text{Pos}\left(\tilde{T}_{\max} \geq \sum_{i=1}^{N-1}\sum_{j=2}^{N} t_{ij}x_{ij}\right) \geq \alpha, 0 \leq \alpha \leq 1 \tag{4.7b}$$

The imprecise constraint (4.7b) can be converted to deterministic one using the aforementioned lemma 1. Therefore, using the lemma constraints (4.7b) reduces to

$$\frac{a_2 - \sum_{i=1}^{N-1}\sum_{j=2}^{N} t_{ij}x_{ij}}{a_1 - a_2} > \alpha, \quad 0 \leq \alpha \leq 1 \tag{4.7c}$$

4.4 THE PROPOSED METHOD

This study uses the concept of fuzzy chance-constrained programming along with a genetic algorithm to solve the orienteering problem. Here, it applies fuzziness in the maximum distance [20]. Subsequently, we present the genetic operators of the proposed genetic algorithm, which is presented in the last subsection.

4.4.1 ENCODING SCHEME

This study uses an integer sequence {1, 2, 5, 12, 9, 7, 3, 11, 6, 4, 10, 8, 27} of 27 diverse cities, where city 1 is considered as the first (beginning), and the last (terminal) city is considered to be the city 27, representing the destination city. The numbers between 1 and 27 represent different cities as per the sequence number from the Table 4.1. An example of chromosomes with their total score, distance and $T_{\max}$ are

TABLE 4.1
The Geographical Coordinates of 27 Diverse Cities of China and Their Related Score

Sl. No	Name of the City	Longitude	Latitude	Score	Sl. No	Name of the City	Longitude	Latitude	Score
1	Beijing	116.4	39.91	35	15	Wuhan	114.3	30.55	26
2	Tianjin	117.18	39.16	27	16	Changsha	113	28.2	23
3	Jinan	117	36.67	25	17	Guangzhou	113.15	23.15	27
4	Qingdao	120.33	36.06	23	18	Dalian	121.6	38.92	25
5	Shijiazhuang	114.5	38.05	19	19	Guilin	110.29	25.28	22
6	Taiyuan	112.58	37.87	21	20	Xi' an	108.92	34.28	28
7	Huhehaote	111.7	40.87	22	21	Yinchuan	106.27	38.48	22
8	Zhengzhou	113.6	34.75	21	22	Lanzhou	103.8	36.03	24
9	Huangshan	118.29	29.73	16	23	Chengdu	104.07	30.66	24
10	Nanjing	118.75	32.04	29	24	Guiyang	106.7	26.59	22
11	Shanghai	121.45	31.22	27	25	Kunming	102.8	25.05	29
12	Hangzhou	120.15	30.25	30	26	Shenyang	123.4	41.8	24
13	Nanchang	115.88	28.35	23	27	Haikou	110.35	20.02	22
14	Fuzhou	119.3	26.1	23	—	—	—	—	—

TABLE 4.2
Encoding Rule Used in the Genetic Algorithm for the Proposed Model

Chromosome	Total Score	Distance	T_{max}
{1, 2, 3, 10, 12, 9, 14, 16, 18, 17, 27}	35 + 27 + 25 + 29 + 30 + 16 + 23 + 23 + 22 + 27 + 22 = 279	3682	4000

given in the Table 4.2. To calculate the path length among two cities, we have used the Haversine formula [21].

4.4.2 FITNESS FUNCTION

The objective of the OP is to maximize the accumulated score collected from the served cities while satisfying the constraint of maximum time or distance T_{max}. Here the fitness of a chromosome is evaluated by accumulation the score of every city, which embraces the beginning city and the terminal city as well. For instance, for the chromosome {1, 2, 3, 10, 12, 9, 14, 16, 18, 17, 27} the fitness value is 279.

4.4.3 SELECTION

Tournament selection is implemented in this study. In tournament selection, potential parents are selected, and a comparison is made to decide the parent. High selection pressure will give a better parent, but the chance of getting the same parent also increases. The best individual from the tournament is the one with the highest fitness, the winner of the individuals.

4.4.4 CROSSOVER

It is the method of producing a child chromosome from the selected parents. This paper proposes a random crossover technique. It is designed with randomly selected cities to explore more diversity in the solutions. Here two offspring will be generated from the parent chromosomes P_1 and P_2, respectively. The steps of developing the Offspring1 are described below.

Step 1: Generate a random number i within the range from 2 to one less than the length of P_2. Generate two more random numbers m, n within the range from 2 to one less than the length of P_1.

Step 2: Copy the numbers from the second position of P_2 up to the ith position in a temporary variable X. Copy the numbers from m^{th} position of P_1 up to the nth position in X from the $(i + 1)^{th}$ position if it is not already present in X.

Step 3: Copy the remaining numbers from the left except the first and last one from P_2 in X from next free position if it is not already present in X.

Step 4: From the parent chromosomes, generate a child chromosome Offspring1 with 1 as the beginning city and 27 as the termination city and the central position progressively include one after another number from X gradually from the end of the beginning city such that the cumulative weighted path length of the chromosome does not exceed T_{max}.

4.4.5 MUTATION

A mutation operator is used to maintain the population diversity. It also prevents premature convergence, i.e., it prevents the algorithm to stuck in local optima. Here, we have presented a randomized technique of the mutation. The mutation technique is applied to a newly generated offspring after crossover. Here, the mutation will follow the distance constraint while adding as many cities as possible. The steps of the mutation process are presented as follows.

Step 1: For chromosome M, determine its length L, where L is the number of cities in M. Create a copy of M in N.

Step 2: Generate a random number within the range 2 to one less than the total number of cities, i.e., 26 that is not present in M and assign it on a temporary variable $NEWCITY1$. Generate a random number with in the range 2 to $(L - 1)$ and assign it on a temporary variable I. Replace the city present in the ith position of M with $NEWCITY_1$.

Step 3: Generate a random number within the range 2 to one less than the total number of cities, i.e., 26 that is not present in M and allocate it on a temporary variable $NEWCITY2$. Insert the $NEWCITY_2$ just before the destination city in M.

Step 4: With respect to the total distance, determine the superior solution in terms of the arrangement of the cities with starting and terminating cities in the beginning and final position respectively from the chromosomes M.

Step 5: Find the distance D of the sequence Q. If D is less than the T_{max}, then return Q else return N.

4.4.6 Probability of Crossover and Mutation

The crossover and mutation probabilities are the important parameter of the genetic algorithm. Crossover probability (p_c) describes the rate of crossover to be performed. Mutation probability (p_m) gives the rate of mutations to be performed. High mutation probability may lead to divergence of the algorithm, whereas low mutation probability will lead to slow convergence. As proposed by Srinivas and Lalit [22], we have used the adaptive probability for the genetic operators, crossover, and mutation in this discussion.

4.4.7 The Proposed Genetic Algorithm

The following section describes the steps of the algorithm.

Step 1: Parameter initialization: population size (P_SZ), maximum generation (MX_GN), adaptive crossover probability (p_c), mutation probability (p_m), maximum cities (NOD).

Step 2: By using the using natural number encoding method, a population that follows the distance constraint $\tilde{T}_{max}$ is randomly generated.

Step 3: Consider Gn_count = 1. Accordingly, if Gn_count ≤ MX_GN, navigate to Step 4, otherwise navigate to Step 10.

Step 4: Determine the fitness value of each chromosome of the population and essentially preserve the elitist chromosome of that generational population.

Step 5: Employ tournament selection method to select two chromosomes.

Step 6: Evaluate p_c and perform the crossover on the selected parents to produce the corresponding offspring.

Step 7: Evaluate p_m and perform the mutation on the offspring generated in Step 6.

Step 8: With respect to the fitness values of the parent and offspring chromosomes after Step 7, the new population is generated.

Step 9: The newly formed population becomes the current population and increases the generation count (Gn_count) by 1.

Step 10: Determine the superior chromosome from each generation and eventually select the best chromosome among them, which becomes the solution of the problem with its maximum score V.

4.5   RESULT AND DISCUSSION

The necessary results related to the proposed genetic algorithm are presented in the subsequent subsections.

4.5.1 Data

As far as the execution of our proposed algorithm is concerned, we have used MATLAB® 2012b on an x64-based computation platform having Intel® Core™

i3-7100U CPU @ 2.40GHz and installed with Windows 10 Professional. In order to assess the performance of the proposed method, different levels of α value are compared for the same set of parameters. Here the value 1 for α is the crisp method, and any other value of α signifies the different levels of fuzziness in maximum distance. The algorithm has been tested on the data sets present in Table 4.1 [4]. The chance of visiting a city is high if the score is high. The Haversine formula [21] is employed to determine the distance matrix.

4.5.2 PARAMETERS OF PROPOSED ALGORITHM

P_SZ and MX_GN used in this paper are 1000 and 25, respectively. The maximum distance T_{max} after independent runs on different levels of α at 1, 0.8, and 0.6 value are given in the Tables 4.3, 4.4, and 4.5, respectively. The parameters for finding adaptive crossover and mutation probability are k_1, $k_2 \in [0.8, 1]$ and k_3, $k_4 \in [0.01, 0.1]$. The NOD considered in this paper is 27.

TABLE 4.3
Result of Algorithm When α = 1, i.e., the Deterministic Model

Run No.	Maximum Distance T_{max} (km)	Total Score	Path
1	4000	342	1, 2, 5, 6, 3, 4, 10, 11, 12, 9, 13, 16, 18, 27
2	5000	400	1, 2, 5, 6, 8, 3, 4, 11, 12, 10, 15, 13, 16, 18, 17, 27
3	6000	450	1, 2, 5, 6, 7, 19, 8, 3, 4, 11, 12, 10, 15, 13, 16, 18, 17, 27
4	7000	512	1, 2, 5, 6, 7, 20, 21, 19, 8, 3, 4, 11, 12, 9, 10, 15, 13, 16, 18, 17, 27
5	8000	545	1, 2, 5, 6, 7, 20, 21, 19, 8, 3, 4, 26, 25, 11, 12, 10, 15, 13, 16, 18, 17, 27

TABLE 4.4
Result of the Algorithm When α = 0.8 of the Proposed Fuzzy Model

Run No	Total Distance T_{max} (km)	Path Length	Total Score	Path
1	4000	4024	347	1, 2, 5, 3, 4, 11, 12, 10, 9, 13, 15, 16, 18, 27
2	5000	5015	416	1, 2, 5, 6, 8, 3, 4, 11, 12, 9, 10, 15, 13, 16, 18, 17, 27
3	6000	6094	459	1, 2, 5, 6, 7, 20, 21, 19, 8, 3, 4, 10, 12, 9, 13 16, 18, 17, 27
4	7000	6820	512	1, 2, 5, 6, 7, 20, 21, 19, 8, 3, 4, 11, 12, 9, 10, 15, 13, 16, 18, 17, 27
5	8000	8068	547	1, 2, 5, 6, 7, 20, 21, 19, 8, 3, 4, 11, 12, 10, 15 13, 16, 17, 18, 23, 24 27

TABLE 4.5

Result of the Algorithm When $\alpha = 0.6$ of the Proposed Fizzy Model

Run No	Total Distance T_{max} (km)	Path Length	Total Score	Path
1	4000	4172	358	1, 2, 5, 3, 4, 11, 12, 10, 15, 13, 16, 18, 17, 27
2	5000	5015	416	1, 2, 5, 6, 8, 3, 4, 11, 12, 9, 10, 15, 13, 16, 18, 17, 27
3	6000	6094	459	1, 2, 5, 6, 7, 20, 21, 19, 8, 3, 4, 10, 12, 9, 13 16, 18, 17, 27
4	7000	7185	514	1, 2, 5, 6, 7, 20, 21, 19, 8, 3, 4, 26, 11, 12, 9 10, 15, 16, 18, 17, 27
5	8000	8153	561	1, 2, 5, 6, 7, 20, 21, 19, 8, 3, 4, 11, 12, 10, 15 13, 16, 17, 18, 23, 24, 27

4.5.3 RESULTS

Based on different data and parameters, the algorithm shows the following results.

The effectiveness of the proposed algorithm, i.e., the implementation of fuzziness of the maximum distance, can be easily described with the help of the data of run number 2 of Tables 4.3 and 4.5. When the value of α is equal to 1, that is the crisp model, the total score is 400, whereas if we allow maximum distance to be fuzzy with α value of 0.8, the total score will be 416. So, by travelling an extra 15 km, the total score can be increased by 16. Figures 4.2 and 4.3 depict respectively the surface plot and convergence plot for the second independent execution of the genetic algorithm on the proposed problem.

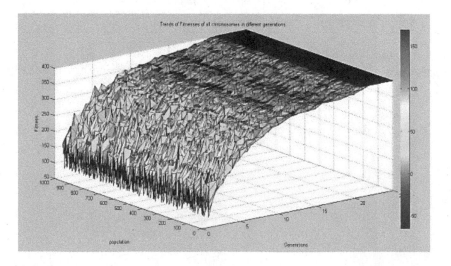

FIGURE 4.2 Generation vs. fitness surface plot of all chromosomes for the independent execution #2 of Table 4.3.

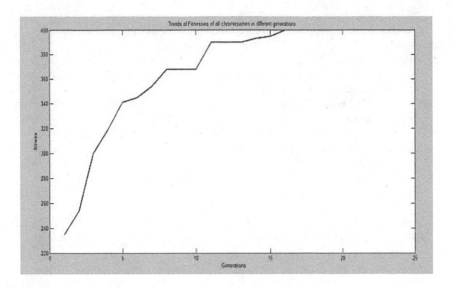

FIGURE 4.3 Generation vs. maximum fitness for the independent execution #2 of Table 4.3.

4.6 CONCLUSION AND FUTURE SCOPE

Gendreau et al. [3] discussed some complications of designing good heuristics for orienteering problems. The score corresponding to the vertex is not dependent on time or distance to reach it and sometimes produces contradictory results. The OP is one of the problems to select vertices to be covered in the final solution. Therefore, simple structure and improvement heuristics may lead to undesirable results, as the solution space is not well explored.

In future, we will extend the proposed algorithm to address the round-trip problems. Furthermore, we will extend the proposed model to the multi-objective domain under the paradigm of rough set and uncertainty theory. We will develop suitable multi-objective evolutionary algorithms to solve the problem.

REFERENCES

1 Golden, Bruce L., Larry Levy, Rakesh Vohra. "The orienteering problem." *Naval Research Logistics* 34, no. 3 (1987): 307–318.
2 Sevkli, Zülal, and F. Erdogan Sevilgen. "Variable neighborhood search for the orienteering problem." In: Levi A., Savaş E., Yenigün H., Balcısoy S., Saygın Y. (Eds) *Computer and Information Sciences – ISCIS 2006*. ISCIS 2006. Lecture Notes in Computer Science, vol 4263. Springer, Berlin, Heidelberg (2006): 134–143.
3 Gendreau, Michel, Gilbert Laporte, and Frédéric Semet. "A tabu search heuristic for the undirected selective travelling salesman problem." *European Journal of Operational Research* 106 (1998): 539–545.
4 Wang, Xia, Bruce L. Golden, and Edward A. Wasil. "Using a genetic algorithm to solve the generalization orienteering problem." *The Vehicle Routing Problem: Latest Advances and New Challenges*. Cham: Springer Science+Business Media, LLC, 2008: 263–273.

5   Chao, I-Ming, Bruce L. Golden, and Edward A. Wasil. "A fast and effective heuristic for the orienteering problem." *European Journal of Operational Research* 88, no. 3 (1996): 475–489.

6   Cai, Qing, Maoguo Gong, Bo Shen, Lijia Ma, and Licheng Jiao. "Discrete particle swarm optimization for identifying community structures in signed social networks." *Neural Networks* 58 (2014): 4–13.

7   Tsiligirides, T. "Heuristics methods applied to orienteering." *Journal of the Operational Research Society* 35, no. 9 (2017): 797–809.

8   Tasgetiren, Mahmet F. "A genetic algorithm with an adaptive penalty function for orienteering problem." *Journal of Economic and Social Research* 4, no. 2 (2000): 1–26.

9   Golden, B., A. Assad, and R. Dahl. "Analysis of a large-scale vehicle routing problem with inventory component." *Large Scale Systems* 7 (1984): 181–190.

10 Thomadsen, Tommy, and Thomas Stidsen. *The Quadratic Selective Travelling Salesman Problem.* Denmark: Technical University of Denmark, 2003.

11 Souffriau, Wouter, Pieter Vansteenwegen, Joris Vertommen, Greet Vanden Berghe, and Dirk Van Oudheusden. "A personalised tourist trip design algorithm for mobile tourist guides." *Applied Artificial Intelligence* 22, no. 10 (2008): 964–985.

12 Majumder, Saibal. 2019. "Some network optimization models under diverse environments." PhD diss., National institute of Technology Durgapur. https://arxiv.org/abs/2103.08327.

13 Majumder, Saibal, Samarjit Kar, and Tandra Pal. "Uncertain multi-objective chinese postman problem." *Soft Computing* 23 (2019a): 11557–11572.

14 Majumder, Saibal, Samarjit Kar, and Tandra Pal. "Rough-fuzzy quadratic minimum spanning tree problem." *Expert Systems* 36, no. 2 (2019b): e12364.

15 Miller, C.E., A.W. Tucker and R. A. Zemlin. "Integer programming formulations and travelling salesman problems." *Journal of the ACM* 7, no. 4 (1960): 326–329.

16 Sevkli, Zülal, and F. Erdogan Sevilgen. "Discrete particle swarm optimization for the orienteering problem." *Proceedings of International Symposium on Innovation in Intelligent Systems and Applications*, Istanbul, (2007): 185–190.

17 Charnes, A., and W.W. Cooper. "Chance-constrained programming." *Management Science* 6, no. 1 (1959): 73–79.

18 Liu, Baoding, and Kakuzo Iwamura. "A note on chance-constrained programming with fuzzy co-efficients." *Fuzzy Sets and Systems* 100, no. 1–3 (1998): 229–233.

19 Dubios, Didier, and Henri Prade. "Ranking fuzzy numbers in the setting of possibility theory." *Information Sciences* 30, no. 3 (1983): 183–224.

20 Wang, Qiwen, Xiaoyun Sun, Bruce L. Golden, and Jiyou Jia. "Using artificial neural networks to solve the orienteering problem." *Annals of Operations Research* 61 (1995): 111–120.

21 Gardiner, Ben, Waseem Ahmad, and Travis Cooper. *Collision Avoidance Techniques for unmanned Aerial Vehicles.* Auburn, AL: Auburn University, 2011.

22 Srinivas, M. K., and Lalit M. Patnaik. "Adaptive probabilities of crossover and mutation in genetic algorithms." *IEEE Transactions on Systems Man and Cybernetics* 24, no. 4 (1994): 656–667.

5 A Comparative Analysis of Stock Value Prediction Using Machine Learning Technique

V. Ramchander and Richa

Vellore Institute of Technology, Chennai, India

CONTENTS

DOI: 10.1201/9781003307822-6

5.1 INTRODUCTION

Artificial neural network (ANN) is a biologically inspired learning algorithm designed to process information in the same way as the human brain. ANN is a versatile and powerful mathematical tool, which can handle many complex tasks such as classification problems, time series, and function approximation. The greatest ability of an ANN is to improve its performance by learning through its previous experiences. ANN has the ability to work as a function approximator and is capable of handling noisy data. It is capable of working with various training algorithms, and its nonlinear nature makes it very efficient in computing problems where usual methods fail. ANN can draw precise information from data as well as is able to handle complex nonlinear relationships in the data, which makes it useful to solve multidimensional problems. This chapter describes the basics of ANN and discusses the applicability of ANN in various fields.

5.1.1 STOCK MARKET

Stock market is one of the most profitable, yet volatile, parts of the financial sector. It deals with millions of transactions every day that involve stocks amounting to billions of dollars US. Stock market, in recent times, due to advancement of news delivery and communication technology, has proved very volatile and capable of drastic change within minutes of a particular news. Stock exchanges are the main institutes of the global stock market, which are often regulated by the government of the country in which they are located. These stock exchanges are where the stocks are listed for public trading. Examples of stock exchanges include the New York Stock Exchange (NYSE) [1], the National Stock Exchange (NSE) [2], and the Bombay Stock Exchange (BSE) [3].

Stock traders usually employ a variety of trading techniques to try and maximize their profit. One of the major ways of trading stock is investing in stock of companies for the long term. Investors tend to buy stock at a low price, often early in the development of a company, and wait for years for the stock to grow in value, generating very high returns. This kind of stock trading tends to work best when invested in a diversified portfolio—that is, being invested in variety of stocks to minimize the risk of complete loss. The disadvantage of this method is a long waiting period; also, diversification often reduces the profits. That is why many traders and hedge fund companies try to focus on day-to-day trading.

Day-to-day stock trading is a form of stock trading that focuses on holding stocks (positions) for a short term and maximizing profit within the day. Day-to-day stock trading mainly involves the method of pattern recognition and predictions of sudden rise or fall of stock value. The traders do not diversify their portfolio, but rather invest in one particular stock that they expect to increase in value within the short time, mostly within a day. The traders use various technology, data, graphs, news, and social media to try and predict the future value of a particular stock and thereby maximize the profit.

The growth of the computer technology and internet has fundamentally changed the workings of almost all the fields. One such field that it had massive effect on is the media and news industry. Generally, news takes a day or two to reach the public, but with online news websites and online public forums such as (among many others) Twitter, Facebook, and Reddit, news from halfway around the world reaches the public within seconds of publication. Social media has become so mainstream that people are able to get news directly from persons involved by following them on various social media platforms. Twitter is mainly used by various prominent persons and companies to convey important information about various important topics. Like any other fields, the stock market has also been drastically changed in its way of working by the recent massive development of online communication. Social media in particular have changed how traders get vital information for their job. Twitter has changed the stock trading in two major ways, particularly for day-to-day stock traders. One: the traders must now be alert 24/7 for sudden and important tweets or other announcements from a company, prominent personality, or the government that can have a drastic positive or negative impact on a particular stock and thereby must react immediately to it. Two: various traders across the world have the ability to form groups and communicate with each other and work together. They tend to discuss the various aspects and information available about a stock to take a general stand on the movement of the stock, whether all holding, buying, or selling a particular stock. This tends to move the stock price in the direction desired by the group. Therefore, the job description of a day-to-day stock trader has changed, from being able to predict the future trends to now including various other aspects of being able to use and obtain useful information from social media on the stocks. It also requires a constant 24/7 awareness of the news from around of the world, and how it will affect the stock.

5.1.2 DEEP LEARNING

Deep learning is a subfield of artificial intelligence, which involves the usage of various algorithms for the development of a model able to recognize a pattern in the given data and thus be able to classify or predict for new data [4]. Deep learning is used in various fields, from bank security to medical diagnosis, to help improve the accuracy and speed of decision-making. Deep learning models have been proven to perform very well in recognizing a time series pattern that predicts future value of the required variable [5, 6]. They tend to find the patterns that are difficult for the human brain to analyze, and therefore perform better in certain circumstances.

5.1.3 OBJECTIVE

The expertise and work done by stock traders involves major tasks, which can be aided by the use of the currently available technologies. The chapter aims to develop different machine learning models for the prediction of stock value in the short term [7].

Nowadays it becomes essential to deal with exponential data by using machine learning approaches. In this chapter we have used a few techniques of machine learning, specifically RNN, LSTM, and DL, to handle and predict the required deals with the stock data. The chapter aims to give information to traders about the stocks, their predicted trends and analysis of the news currently circulating about the stock or company, and to help them make better decisions in managing their portfolio or to manage the risk in day-trading of the stocks.

5.2 LITERATURE REVIEW

Various machine learning approaches exist that are used in stock market prediction [8]. They have focused mainly on regression and LSTM technique that predicts the stock value with the factors such as low, high, and volume, along with open and close. Decision-making about the market as moving into a positive or negative direction with the help of different attributes [9] has used historical market data. They have included various factors and techniques to compare and found the best predicting model. Another attempt to improve the accuracy in prediction [10] has combined RNN with informative input variables. They have used LSTM with stock basic trading data to discuss stock prediction models. They have used various evaluation criteria to analyze the performance of different models.

Deep learning enables the system to maintain the multiple layers of learning to multiple levels of abstraction. In order to continue with the interest of deep learning and comparing with LSTM, bidirectional and stacked LSTM prediction model has been proposed [11]. This provides a breakthrough in improving the object detection and recognition, speech recognition, and, similar to many other fields [7], has implemented and compared two different machine learning algorithms for the prediction of stock values based on the trend of the stock. The authors have obtained the dataset required for the training and testing of models from the historical data available on the Yahoo! Finance website. They have retrieved data in the CSV format, with the open, close, high, low, and volume features given priority, and kept 20% of the data available for testing the models. They have implemented two models, namely regression and long short-term memory (LSTM), and trained and tested these models. The regression model tried to form a linear equation using the features as independent variables and the prediction as the dependent variable. The LSTM is an advancement of recurring neural networks (RNN), which try to form a connection between the past values of the prediction value and the current value; this follows a hypothesis that the current value of the stock is dependent on its historical performance. The R-square confidence metric was used to score the regression model, while the root mean square error was calculated for the LSTM model. Sharma et al. [7] have tried the hypothesis of predicting the next day's closing stock value using recurring neural networks and informative input features. They have proposed and implemented a long short-term memory model, which is an advanced RNN model for the prediction. They have used the data of the Standard and Poor (S&P 500) and NASDAQ historical values for the training and testing of the models. The features of the dataset include various stock market variables, such as the high price which is the highest price of a stock during a given trading day; the low price, which is the lowest price of a stock in the given trading day; and the open and close prices, which represent the price of the stock in the opening and closing times of the exchange, respectively. They also included the adjusted price (AD), which depicts the effect of the company actions on the stock price. Using this data, they prepared a simple LSTM model, which the architecture of an input layer, single LSTM hidden layer, and an output layer. ReLU activation function for the activation of the neuron is used with the threshold at zero. They have also used the Adam optimizer, which is efficient in computations, has low memory requirements, and is invariant to diagonal rescaling of the gradients. Therefore, it is optimal for problems such as the stock trend, which deal with huge amounts of data and parameters. This model was trained and tested on the data gathered, and metrics such as mean absolute error (MAE), root mean square error (RMSE), mean absolute percentage error (MAPE), and average mean absolute percentage error (AMAPE) were calculated and analyzed. The authors have reached the conclusion that the general trend of the stock market can be predicted using the LSTM model within acceptable error percentage.

Singh et al. [10] have compared and analyzed various proposed methods for the prediction of stock market trends. They have proposed new features and variables important in increasing the performance and accuracy of the available models. They argued that stock traders regularly include analysis of the public sentiments, government initiatives, and other important events such as disasters or elections as external factors while evaluating their market positions. Thus, they must also be considered by the model in predicting the trend. They have analyzed the results of different techniques and compared them across different metrics and features used in it. They have compared classification techniques, regression models, ensemble techniques, evolutionary models, deep learning methods, and hybrid methods. In classification techniques, they have compared support vector machine (SVM) and multi-source multiple instance learning (MMI). In regression models, they have compared linear regression with an artificial neural network, the multi-layer perceptron (MLP). In ensemble techniques, they have compared a random forest model with boosted decision tree model, which gave a better performance than SVM and linear regression. The evolutionary techniques of generic algorithm and particle swarm optimization (PSO) were compared, and the PSO proved to perform better than other models under certain circumstances of the market. Some hybrid models, such as support vector regression and artificial neural network, were also compared, along with deep learning models such as convolutional neural networks and LSTM. It was concluded the hybrid models provide more accurate results but represent a computationally intensive process.

5.3 METHODOLOGY AND ANALYSIS

Three different models are implemented, analyzed, and compared in this chapter. Those are the basic deep neural network (DNN), the recurrent neural network (RNN), and the long short-term memory model (LSTM). These models will be used for the prediction of the stock market trends. The tweets have been imported from Twitter for the sentiment analysis using Python.

5.3.1 DEEP NEURAL NETWORK

The output layer is presented in Figure 5.1. DNNs are generally feed-forward networks, where data usually flows in one direction, from the input layer to the output layer [8]. The DNN calculates the output by performing matrix vector multiplication of the input sequence, and the edge weights are added with the bias of each neuron.

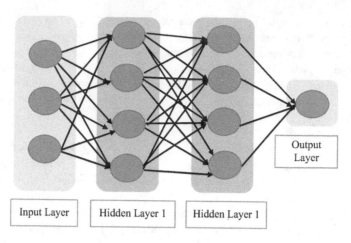

Input Layer   Hidden Layer 1   Hidden Layer 1   Output Layer

FIGURE 5.1 Deep learning.

5.3.1.1 Input Layer

The input layer is common to all neural networks and is the first layer in the network. It is designed to match the number of features in the input sequence. It takes the initial data for calculation from the user or external source and passes it on as a vector to the next layer, the first hidden layer, for the computation.

5.3.1.2 Hidden Layers

The layers between the input layer and the output layer are known as the hidden layers. The neurons in this layer contain values known as bias; the edge weights are multiplied with the input values and added with the buyers of the neuron, and the value calculated and forwarded to the activation function. If the value satisfies the activation function, the neuron is activated and the output value is passed to the next layer. The number of layers in the hidden layer part of the neural network can vary from one to any number, and every layer can be of any type—examples include Dense, SimpleRNN, and LSTM, among others [12, 13].

5.3.1.3 Activation Function

The activation function is the main function of a neuron responsible for calculating the output based on the given inputs. There are various types of activation function that are useful in different situations. The activation functions decide whether the neurons should be activated, that is, whether the output of the neuron should be passed down to the next layer. Some of the common activation functions are rectified linear activation (RELU) [14], hyperbolic tangent (Tanh) [15], and logistic activation [16].

5.3.1.4 Neuron Weights

Every neuron contains a trainable parameter known as weight; the weight value, with the bias, is used in calculation of the output by the activation function. On initialization of the neural network, the neuron weights are assigned random values. During training, the weight values are changed to match the output with the actual value.

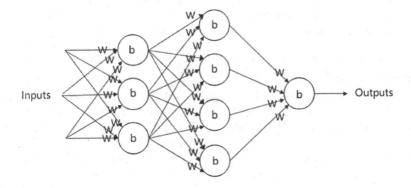

FIGURE 5.2 Weights and biases in artificial neural network.

The value of the weight affects the scale in which the input affects the output: the smaller the weight value, the smaller the influence of the input on the output value. As shown in Figure 5.2, the weights are represented by W and the bias by B.

5.3.1.5 Output Layer

The output layer is the final layer of an artificial neural network. The value calculated by the output neurons is expected to match the actual values during training. The number of neurons in the output layer should match the number of expected outputs per input sequence. Deep neural networks are robust and can usually overcome the errors in the data. For example, small errors in the training data do not affect the outcome, as seen in machine learning models. Deep neural networks are usually fast in the calculation of the target variable. It requires a lot of computational power, and they usually carry out processes in parallel, therefore requiring a lot of parallel processors to speed up the calculations.

5.3.2 Recurrent Neural Network (RNN)

Recurrent neural network is a special type of artificial neural network that considers the output of the previous step in calculation of the output of the present step. RNN is mainly used in predicting statements where to predict the next word, the previous words in the statement need to be considered. RNNs usually have a parameter called memory, which remembers the information about the previously calculated outputs, which are then used with the new inputs to perform the same task [17].

A decision taken by the recurrent network at time T-1 affects the decision that will be taken at time T. So recurrent networks can be thought to have two sets of data: the present input sequence and the recent past output. Recurrent networks defer from feed-forward networks by the presence of a lookback edge that makes the output of the previous sequence considered for the current sequence. This is sometimes referred to as a memory, that is, recurrent networks are thought to have stored the output in their memory for further calculations. The information of the sequences is stored in the recurrent networks' hidden state, where it exists for a long time, affecting the calculations of the next sequences. The recurrent network is trying to find a correlation between the different inputs and their corresponding outputs such as a series of events; these are known as long-term dependency events.

5.3.2.1 Back-Propagation through Time

Back-propagation through time (BPTT) is the technique used in the recurrent neural networks to update the weights of the neurons during the training phase [18]. The goal of BPTT is to minimize the error of the output. BPTT is usually applied to time series data, which typically have shown the dependence of the present value on the previous historical values. Some of the disadvantages of adding BPTT include the need for a huge amount of computational power and a high number of iterations to update the values of the rates; this, in turn, tends to make the model too noisy or overfit.

Truncated BPTT is an advancement of the BPTT algorithm to reduce the impact of the memory parameter but still keep it significant [19]. In this method the input in the process specifies that time and the parameters are updated only after a fixed number of time steps. Truncated BPTT uses two parameters to determine the influence of memory parameters, namely K1 and K2. K1 specifies the number of forward pass time steps before an update to the parameters of the networks such as weights and bias. This influences the speed of the training process and the number of times the weights are updated. To specify the total number of time steps for the BPTT algorithm, it must be large enough to allow the network to learn properly but yet be small enough to avoid overfitting, thus reducing time and computational requirements.

5.3.2.2 Problems in RNN

One of the most common problems in RNN is the vanishing gradient problem, as during the back-propagation algorithm, the weights are updated proportional to the partial derivative of the error and the current weight during every iteration of the back-propagation algorithm. When the gradient becomes too small, it affects the change to the weight, thus preventing further training of the network. In the worst-case scenario, the gradient becomes too small to have any meaningful effect on the change of the weights, and this scenario is known as the vanishing gradient problem. The reverse of the vanishing gradient problem is when the gradient of error becomes too high and thus affects the weight too much. This scenario causes the model to become unstable and overfit for a particular training dataset. This scenario is known as gradient explosion problem. The gradient explosion problem can be overcome by using activation functions such as sigmoid function, a ReLU function that prevents the gradient value from reaching a value higher than a set limit.

5.3.3 Long Short-Term Memory Models (LSTM)

Long short-term memory networks is an upgrade of the recurrent neural networks, which is still capable of handling sequential time series data but can overcome the vanishing gradient problems experienced in recurrent neural networks. LSTM neurons also work similarly to RNN neurons but have three gates, which makes the model more efficient than the RNN model [14].

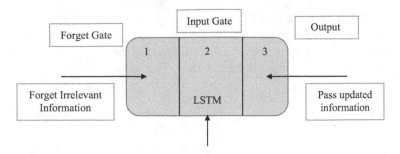

FIGURE 5.3 Long short-term memory model.

As seen in Figure 5.3, an LSTM neuron is made of three gates: the forget gate, the input gate, and the output gate. Like any RNN neuron, the LSTM neuron gets input from the sequence as well as the previous output for its calculations, but the forget gate now determines whether the output sequence is required for this calculation and thus discards unwanted historical sequences.

The input sequence is fed to the input gate after being filtered by the forget gate, and calculations are performed by the activation function. The calculated value is then passed down to the output gate and forwarded to the other layers. This method helps overcome the vanishing gradient problem.

Some features of LSTM are as follows:

1. The constant error back-propagation in LSTM allows for them to understand complex sequences and time series data efficiently.
2. LSTM networks usually handle noise in the data very well, as they tend not to overcompensate to fit the data.
3. LSTM has a huge number of parameters that can be edited, such as input bias, output bias, and learning rate, that allows the model to be altered easily for the given task.
4. Even though LSTMs can handle gradient vanishing problems, they do not completely eliminate the problem; they are also prone it.
5. LSTM models require huge computational resources and time to be trained for real-world applications such as speech recognition and time series predictions.
6. LSTM models do usually overfit the training data.

5.3.4 Activation Functions

An activation function is the most important function of a neuron, as it basically calculates the output of the neuron based on the input given, including the weights and the bias. Depending on the output value, the activation function determines whether or not the neuron is to be activated. There are various types of activation functions that pass the output after modification to the next layer.

5.3.4.1   Rectified Linear Unit Function

The rectified linear unit function (ReLU) is an activation function that helps in reducing the vanishing gradient problem in many networks. The ReLU function works by giving a 0 if the value calculated is negative and giving the value itself if the calculated value is positive. It is one of the most common and useful activation functions available.

$$f(x) = 0 \ \text{for} \ x < 0$$
$$= x \ \text{for} \ x \geq 0$$

5.4   EXPERIMENTATION AND RESULTS

This subsection provides an insight into the experimentation and evaluation of the work.

5.4.1   Data Collection

This chapter has used the data about the NIFTY50 stock prices and various other features corresponding to the stocks for training of the neural networks [20]. It includes the information on stocks, including features like open price, close price, high price, low price, and volume traded, collected from the National Stock Exchange for the 2007–2020 time period. It contains 50 CSV-format files, each containing 3200-plus rows of data (Figures 5.4(a) and 5.4(b)).

Based on the research and analysis done, only certain features from the dataset were considered for the training and development of the model. The features that selected for consideration were:

- High Price
- Low Price
- Open Price
- Close Price

These features were used against the date of the trade to create a timeline series values of each feature.

In obtaining tweets using the Twitter API, tweets from major news magazines like *Economics Times* and *Forbes India* were given priority. If they have not tweeted anything about the required company, then tweets from stock traders were extracted.

Only certain details about the tweets were extracted from the search query and written to a CSV file for preprocessing. The extracted features were:

- Username/Screen Name
- Text of the tweet
- Date of the tweet creation

A new column, "Media," was added, to categorize the source of the tweet.

	Date	Open	High	Low	Close
0	2007-11-27	770.00	1050.00	770.0	962.90
1	2007-11-28	984.00	990.00	874.0	893.90
2	2007-11-29	909.00	914.75	841.0	884.20
3	2007-11-30	890.00	958.00	890.0	921.55
4	2007-12-03	939.75	995.00	922.0	969.30

(a)

	Name	Text	Date	Media
0	EconomicTimes	Dr Harsh Vardhan addresses media on the curren...	2021-05-17 08:54:39	1
1	EconomicTimes	Amid #Covid19 cases continuing to show an upwa...	2021-05-17 08:47:33	1
2	EconomicTimes	India reports 2,81,386 new #COVID19 cases, 3,7...	2021-05-17 05:21:19	1
3	EconomicTimes	With full rituals, portals of Kedarnath temple...	2021-05-17 04:52:50	1
4	EconomicTimes	Delhi Police arrests Navneet Kalra in oxygen c...	2021-05-17 04:15:00	1

(b)

FIGURE 5.4 (a) A snapshot of the sample data NIFTY50 stock prices. (b). A snapshot of the sample data NIFTY50 stock prices.

5.4.2 DATA PREPROCESSING

The stock data were all in the same scale, with all prices in Indian rupees; they also did not require much cleaning because they were obtained from a government data source. One of the issues with the dataset is the fact that the stock is closed, and the stock prices are not available for those days. The data was converted into a matrix with values for the previous 30 days, making the features and the current day value the target value.

Data from Twitter was extracted and stored in a CSV file, and the text needed to be cleaned: unwanted special characters, hashtags, and emojis needed to be removed. This was done using the regular expressions in Python. After cleaning, the text was added as a new column to the data frame, so that the original text could still be displayed if required later.

5.4.3 ANALYSIS OF VARIOUS MODELS ON STOCK DATA

We have considered three models for the analysis of stock data and visualization in terms of train loss and validation loss.

5.4.3.1   DNN Model

We used the DNN model to analyze the stock data in terms of train loss and validation loss. The following epoch versus loss graph is presented in Figures 5.5 and 5.6. The graph shows that as the number of iterations increases with time, the loss decreases.

5.4.3.2   RNN Model

The RNN model is applied on the various layers to various neurons distributions. For the analysis of RNN on stock data, the ReLU activation function has been used. The mean squared error is captured and compared on various epochs. The model loss

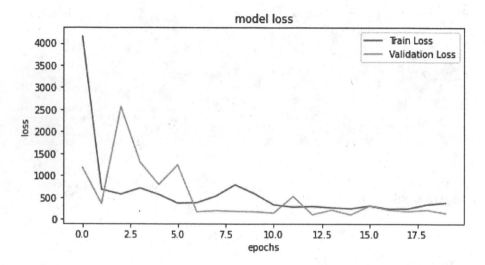

FIGURE 5.5   Model loss visualization.

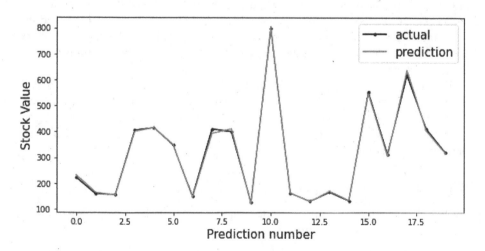

FIGURE 5.6   Prediction comparison for actual and predicted using DNN model.

is compared between train and test loss for varying epochs. Now, we can find result analysis of our implementation in Figures 5.7–5.12.

5.4.3.3 LSTM Model

The LSTM is compared by using the activation function ReLU and is analyzed for mean squared error. The layer is varying from 0 to 5, and the number of neurons also varies after a certain interval. The loss is compared for train versus test for the LSTM model for varying epochs.

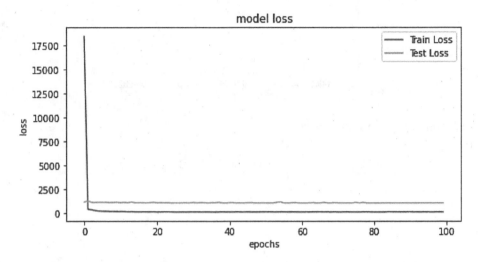

FIGURE 5.7   Train versus test loss analysis for RNN.

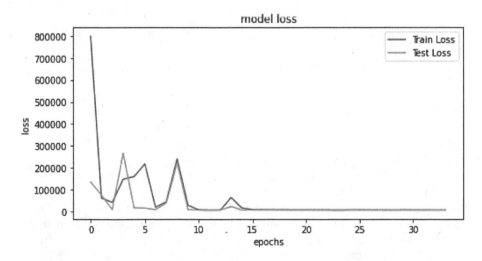

FIGURE 5.8   Loss comparison for train and test for LSTM model loss.

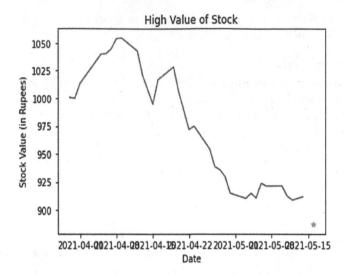

FIGURE 5.9 High stock price model.

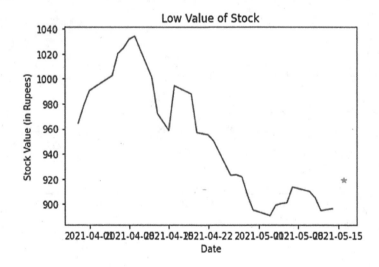

FIGURE 5.10 Low stock price model.

On comparing the various models, i.e., DNN, RNN, and LSTM, the metric R-Square score [21, 22], loss values, and graphs [23] (see Table 5.1).

This clearly shows the DNN model performs best for the given dataset.

High stock price is the highest price that the stock value reaches on a particular trade day. Low stock price is the lowest value that the model reaches in one day of trading. If the closing value of the stock is higher than the opening value, then the company has profited in that one day of trading.

The graph in Figure 5.13 is known as a candlestick graph, and is one of the most commonly used by stock traders to gain insight into the stock trend, mainly because

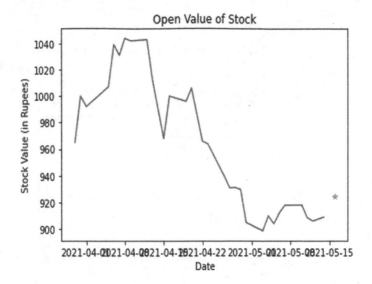

FIGURE 5.11 Open stock price model.

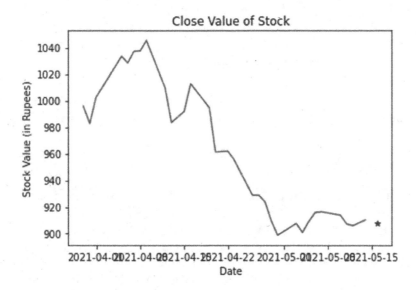

FIGURE 5.12 Close stock price model.

of the amount of data that can be represented in a simple graph. Each bar represents a particular stock trading day. A green candle indicates that the day was profitable to the company, as the closing price of the stock was greater than opening price of the stock; the bigger the candle, the bigger the profit for the day.

A red candle indicates that the day was a loss for the company, as the closing price of the stock was less than opening price of the stock; the bigger the candle, the bigger the loss on that day.

TABLE 5.1

Comparison between DNN, RNN and LSTM Models

	R2_Score	MSE
DNN	0.988915049384684	1827.8611648731048
RNN	−2.4785824494561974	573603.4366616679
LSTM	0.8555950455047183	23811.762225849863

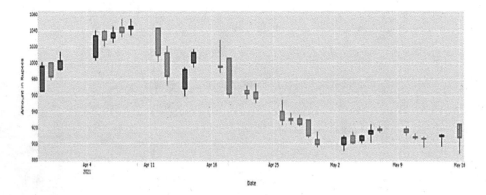

FIGURE 5.13 Candlestick graph of the predicted values.

The stick on either side of the candle depicts the highest and lowest price of the stock on that day. The longer the stick, it depicts the bigger the difference between the high and low prices.

5.5 CONCLUSION

In this chapter, we have provided a comparison between DNN, RNN, and LSTM methods in terms of stock data analysis for trend prediction. In the train and test loss graph of the RNN and LSTM models, they did not train well after the first few epochs, thus making the rest of the epochs training hard to result. The R-square of the RNN model proved it was one that most succeptible to the vanishing gradient problem with a final R-square score on the test data being −2.47. As expected, LSTM model did overcome the vanishing gradient problem better than the RNN model, but still did suffer a litter bit. The LSTM model had a R-square of 0.855 and mean square error value of 23811.76 on the test data set, while DNN model had a R-square score of 0.988 and mean square error of 1827.86 across a test data set of more than 3000 rows in the dataset. In this work it is observed that the DNN model with only dense layers performed better than the LSTM and RNN models tested for a given dataset. In the future, various algorithms can be tried to figure out the best model and more architecture with different optimizations and activation functions.

REFERENCES

[1] https://www.nyse.com/index
[2] https://www.nseindia.com/
[3] https://www.bseindia.com/
[4] Goodfellow, Ian, Yoshua Bengio, and Aaron Courville. "Deep learning. MIT Press, 2016," *Conference on information and communication systems (ICICS)*, pp. 151–156. IEEE, 2018.
[5] Chowdhury, Gobinda G. "Natural language processing." *Annual Review of Information Science and Technology* 37, no. 1 (2003): 51–89.
[6] Feldman, Ronen. "Techniques and applications for sentiment analysis." *Communications of the ACM* 56, no. 4 (2013): 82–89.
[7] Sharma, Ashish, Dinesh Bhuriya, and Upendra Singh. "Survey of stock market prediction using machine learning approach." In *2017 International Conference of Electronics, Communication and Aerospace Technology (ICECA)*, vol. 2, pp. 506–509. IEEE, 2017.
[8] Singh, Sukhman, Tarun Kumar Madan, Jitendra Kumar, and Ashutosh Kumar Singh. "Stock market forecasting using machine learning: Today and tomorrow." In *2019 2nd International Conference on Intelligent Computing, Instrumentation and Control Technologies (ICICICT)*, vol. 1, pp. 738–745. IEEE, 2019.
[9] Raza, Kamran. "Prediction of Stock Market performance by using machine learning techniques." In *2017 International Conference on Innovations in Electrical Engineering and Computational Technologies (ICIEECT)*, pp. 1–1. IEEE, 2017.
[10] Gao, Tingwei, Yueting Chai, and Yi Liu. "Applying long short term momory neural networks for predicting stock closing price." In *2017 8th IEEE International Conference on Software Engineering and Service Science (ICSESS)*, pp. 575–578. IEEE, 2017.
[11] Althelaya, Khaled A., El-Sayed M. El-Alfy, and Salahadin Mohammed. "Evaluation of bidirectional LSTM for short-and long-term stock market prediction." In *2018 9th International Conference on Information and Communication Systems (ICICS)*, pp. 151–156. IEEE, 2018.
[12] Miikkulainen, Risto, Jason Liang, Elliot Meyerson, Aditya Rawal, Daniel Fink, Olivier Francon, Bala Raju et al. "Evolving deep neural networks." In *Artificial Intelligence in the Age of Neural Networks and Brain Computing*, pp. 293–312. Academic Press, 2019.
[13] Koutnik, Jan, Klaus Greff, Faustino Gomez, and Juergen Schmidhuber. "A clockwork rnn." In *International Conference on Machine Learning*, pp. 1863–1871. PMLR, 2014.
[14] Greff, Klaus, Rupesh K. Srivastava, Jan Koutník, Bas R. Steunebrink, and Jürgen Schmidhuber. "LSTM: A search space odyssey." *IEEE Transactions on Neural Networks and Learning Systems* 28, no. 10 (2016): 2222–2232.
[15] Jin, Xiaojie, Chunyan Xu, Jiashi Feng, Yunchao Wei, Junjun Xiong, and Shuicheng Yan. "Deep learning with s-shaped rectified linear activation units." In *Proceedings of the AAAI Conference on Artificial Intelligence*, vol. 30, no. 1, 2016.
[16] Namin, Ashkan Hosseinzadeh, Karl Leboeuf, Roberto Muscedere, Huapeng Wu, and Majid Ahmadi. "Efficient hardware implementation of the hyperbolic tangent sigmoid function." In *2009 IEEE International Symposium on Circuits and Systems*, pp. 2117–2120. IEEE, 2009.
[17] Chen, Zhixiang, Feilong Cao, and Jinjie Hu. "Approximation by network operators with logistic activation functions." *Applied Mathematics and Computation* 256 (2015): 565–571.
[18] Zaremba, Wojciech, Ilya Sutskever, and Oriol Vinyals. "Recurrent neural network regularization." arXiv preprint arXiv:1409.2329 (2014).

[19] Ahmad, Abdul Manan, Saliza Ismail, and D. F. Samaon. "Recurrent neural network with backpropagation through time for speech recognition." In *IEEE International Symposium on Communications and Information Technology, 2004*. ISCIT 2004, vol. 1, pp. 98–102. IEEE, 2004.

[20] keras.io/api.

[21] Israeli, Osnat. "A Shapley-based decomposition of the R-square of a linear regression." *The Journal of Economic Inequality* 5, no. 2 (2007): 199–212.

[22] Akita, Ryo, Akira Yoshihara, Takashi Matsubara, and Kuniaki Uehara. "Deep learning for stock prediction using numerical and textual information." In *2016 IEEE/ACIS 15th International Conference on Computer and Information Science (ICIS)*, pp. 1–6. IEEE, 2016.

[23] Cohen, Alon, Tamir Hazan, and Tomer Koren. "Online learning with feedback graphs without the graphs." In *International Conference on Machine Learning*, pp. 811–819. PMLR, 2016.

Section II

Process and Methods

6 Developing Hybrid Machine Learning Techniques to Forecast the Water Quality Index (DWM-Bat & DMARS)

Samaher Al-Janabi, Ayad Alkaim and
Zuhra Al-Barmani
University of Babylon, Babylon, Iraq

CONTENTS

6.1   INTRODUCTION

Water is considered the most important resource to continuous life in the world; without water there is no life. The sources of water are divided into two types: surface and groundwater. In general, surface water is available in lakes, rivers, and reservoirs, while ground water lies beneath the surface of the land, where it flows through and fills the openings in the rock formations [1]. The water supply crisis is a harsh truth not only on a national level but also on a worldwide scale. The recent Global Risks report from the World Economic Forum lists the water supply issue as one of the world's top five risks to occur over the next decade. Based on the current population numbers and models for water use, there is a solid sign that most African countries will exceed the limits of their usable water resources by as early as 2025 [2, 3]. The forecasted increase in the temperature resulting from climate change will place additional demands on overused water resources in the form of droughts. An increase in population is associated with an increase in urbanization and industrial and agricultural practices. These human impacts, in turn, contribute to a reduction in water quality as a result of eutrophication, salt accumulation, acid mineral, and fecal pollution. Finally, more than 70% of the earth's surface is covered by water [4–6]. In addition to being the most basic requirement for the survival of all life on Earth, it promotes aquatic life and other ecosystems. Any irresponsible behavior on the part of humanity affects all other beneficiaries [7, 8]. There is, therefore, a need to protect water bodies from premeditated pollution. The main water challenges are increasing water demand, water scarcity, water pollution, inadequate access to safety, sanitation, water hygiene, and the impact of climate change on water. There is endemic pollution of all bodies of water due to irresponsible human use. Pollutants may end in the water by direct or indirect application. This is the second most common type of environmental pollution after air pollution. And the quality of water depends on the ecosystem as well as on human use, such as sewage, industrial pollution, wastewater, and, more importantly, the overuse of water, which leads to a decrease in its supply. Water quality is monitored by measurements taken at the original location and by assessment of local water samples [9], so achieving low costs and high efficiency in wastewater treatment plants is a popular challenge in developing countries [10]. Consequentially, water is necessary for survival and is a key part of our food, energy systems, and manufacturing. It also sustains the ecosystems and climates on which our natural and built world depends. Today, between a rapidly growing population and a changing climate, we are putting more pressure on water resource than ever before, which is why water risks are increasing worldwide.

Data [11, 12] is considered the most valuable commodity in the world, so everything around us is data that need to be analyzed in one or another way in order to extract important information\knowledge from it. Data analytics are classified into two types: (a) statistical, operation research\mathmetics-based methods, and (b) intelligent based on computation intelligent techniques (AI, machine learning, ANN, fuzzy logic, and evaluation computation). Big data analytics uses both statistical and intelligent methods, so in this chapter we focus on the big data analytics. In general, intelligence data mining [13, 14] is a reasoning system that can approximate incomplete information. Where it merges computational intelligence techniques is in the search for solutions to the complex real-world problems to find their solution based on the prior requisites and data-mining techniques that extract knowledge from large amounts of data. This allows to obtain not only the result but also its interpretation. Finally, data mining plays a central role in knowledge discovery. Forecasting modeling [12, 14, 15] is a process used in predictive analysis to create a statistical model for future behaviors. Predictive analytics is the field of intelligent data mining, which is concerned with forecasting probabilities and trends. These include multi-techniques such as Chi-squared automatic interaction detection (CHAID), exchange Chi-squared automatic interaction detection (ECHAID), random forest regression and classification (RFRC), multivariate adaptive regression splines (MARS), and boosted tree classifiers and regression (BTCR) [14]. On the other hand, intelligence techniques (IT) is concerned with intelligent behavior, i.e., things that make us seem intelligent. Following this thinking process, the main objective is to assess the impact of the use of AI-based tools on the development of intelligent prediction models.

Optimization is the finding of the best values dependent on the type of objective function for the problem identified. Generally, the problem of maximizing some functions and minimizing others relative to some set often represents a range of options available in a given situation. Its function is to compare the different options for determining which may be the "best" ones. From popular examples for optimization, these are: minimal cost, maximum profit, minimal mistake, optimum design, optimal management, and variation principles. It has three key elements, which are decision variables, objective and constrictions. An optimization algorithm distinguishes a procedure that is performed iteratively by comparing different solutions until an optimum or reasonable solution is found. There are many types of optimization, namely continuous optimization, bound constrained optimization, constrained optimization, derivative-free optimization, discrete optimization, global optimization, linear programming, and nondifferentiable optimization. As a consequence, optimization is the process of achieving the best result under certain circumstances. Optimization is divided into maximization/minimization, single variable/multi-variables, with/without constrains. There are two types of objective function optimization, a single objective function and a multiple objective function. In single-objective optimization, the decision to accept or decline solutions is based on the objective function value and there is only one search space, while a feature of multi-objective optimization involves potential conflicting objectives. There is therefore a trade-off between objectives, i.e., the improvement achieved for a single objective can only be achieved by making concessions to another objective. There is no optimal solution for all m objective functions at the same time. As a result, multiple-objective functions under a set of constrains are specified.

Water quality (WQ) [3, 15–17] is determined by analyzing the physicochemical characteristics and composite algae and invertebrates and taking into account the embedded geography of the study area [18]. There is no pure water available for overall use in the natural environment; all water can contain some contaminants, usually in the form of suspended solids, micro-organisms [19], and dissolve substances. Raw state is not usually appropriate for potable water. The following factors of water quality are important in the water treatment: (a) it must not pose a health risk due to chemical or microbiological contamination; (b) it must be esthetically pleasing [20]; and (c) it must not have harmful effects on either the distribution system or the consumer equipment. Consumer health is the most important factor to consider in the treatment of water. In addition, the customer is also entitled to a water of esthetically acceptable quality [4, 21]. The main goal of water treatment is to produce uncontaminated water by removing undesirable elements from the water source during the treatment process chosen. The selection of the water treatment process is determined by the quality of the source water as well as the intended purpose of the treated water [22–24]. The process can either remove pollutants or change the nature of the source water by adding chemicals.

Water treatment [25–27] procedures are combined to form a process for the production of drinking water that meets national drinking water quality standards. The main issues for water quality are: (a) eutrophication, (b) microbial contamination, (c) salinity, (d) modified flow regime, (e) and radioactivity [28]. Water treatment processes include conventional water treatment processes and advanced treatment processes [29–31].

Finally, physical, biological, and chemical characteristics of water can be used to predict water quality [32, 33]. The water treatment technology is used to remove harmful contaminants from water before it is distributed to homes or used for other activities. It is important to carry out an evaluation of the quality of water in order to ensure water quality and sustainable development. Clean, safe freshwater is essential for all living organisms, but decreasing water quality has become a worldwide issue in the household, industrial, and agricultural use. So, a day-to-day assessment of water resource policy is needed [17, 34, 35].

6.2   LITERATURE SURVEY

The issue of water quality prediction is one of the key issues directly related to people's lives and the continuation of healthful life generally. The goal of this search is to find a modern predictive way to deal with this type of extensive data and works within the range of data series. So, in this part of the thesis, this research will try to review works of previous searchers in same area and compare the works with seven key points.

Ahmed suggests a method for predicting dissolved oxygen (DO) in the Surma River using two artificial neural network (ANN) models, namely a feed-forward neural network (FFNN) and a radial basis function neural network (RBFNN). It was observed that FFNN obtained better performance than RBFNN, but the overall performance of both models was satisfactory in predicting DO. These models can be used for water management and treatment systems. This work is similar to the research work in terms of prediction but uses intelligence data-mining algorithm. The research is different in that it uses evaluation measures and in data use in prediction.

Heddam and Kisi [9] propose the comparison of least square support vector machine (LSSVM), model tree (M5T), and multivariate adaptive regression splines (MARS) models for the forecasting of daily DO concentration using water quality variables from three station in the United States. Six various scenarios having different input combinations have been developed and compared. Based on the results obtained, it was found that the DO concentration could be successfully predicted using the three models and the best model among all others differs from one station to another station. This work is similar to my research work in terms of prediction and use MARS algorithm, while the difference is in the use of evaluation measure.

Isiyaka et al. suggested the artificial neural network (ANN) model and multivariate statistical tools to investigate WQ. The hierarchical agglomerative cluster (HAC) analysis helped cluster the monitoring site in two, and the principal component analysis (PCA) was used to identify pollution sources such as surface runoff, anthropogenic, and rock weathering, in which the latter was the maximum contributor of pollution. A sensitivity test was used to detect the most sensitive variables to pollution. All techniques combined with the ANN model have increased overall performance. This research work differs from that work through the use of clustering techniques and the use of another evaluation measure, similar to problem research and sensitive variables to pollution but out of consideration for weather.

Bui et al. evaluated the effectiveness of 4 standalone (random forest [RF], M5P, random tree [RT], and reduced error pruning tree [REPT]) and 12 hybrid data-mining algorithms (hybrids of the standalones with bagging [BA], CV parameter selection [CVPS], and randomizable filtered classification [RFC]) for forecasting monthly Water Quality Index (WQI) in the wet environment of northern Iran. The goal was to develop and suggest new algorithms not only for the prediction of WQI but also for other areas of water science in regions with very narrow distributions of water quality gauging stations. The modeling process showed that the fecal coliform concentration was the key element of WQI. This work is similar with research work presented here in terms of predication but using intelligence data mining algorithm, while the research is different in its evaluation measure.

Safari suggested models for predictive incipient deposition were generalized by including a cross-section shape factor in the model parameters. Data were collected from channels for five different cross-section shapes, namely trapezoidal, circular, U-shaped, rectangular, and V-bottom, which are used for modeling. Two machine learning models—multivariate adaptive regression splines (MARS) and random forest (RF)—and an empirical multi nonlinear regression (MNLR) model are developed. The precision of standalone models is improving by hybridization the MARS and RF models with the MNLR equation to produce robust MARS-MNLR and RF-MNLR models. And the explicit formulations proposed may be used as practical tools for channel design. This research is similar to that work in using prediction and MARS algorithm, while different by using evaluation measure, and this research include of a cross-section shape factor into the model parameters.

Banda [36] proposed developing a universal water quality model for South African river catchments. And as part of the study, review work attempts to outline the objectives of establishing water quality monitoring tools, their classification, and the basic procedure of developing WQIs. This research work is similar to that work by goal.

6.3 BUILDING IM12CP-WQI

Building an effectiveness prediction model includes four stages: the first stage is dataset preprocessing that includes data collection, split season, normalizing the dataset, and correlation; the second stage consists of applying Bat algorithm to find the best of weight for each concentration, number of base model "M" of that MARS; the third stage includes building a prediction model called IM12CP-WQI to find the predicted values of 12 concentrations. The final stage is the evaluation of the results based on three measures (R2, NSE, and D) and five cross-validations (Figure 6.1).

6.3.1 DESCRIPTION OF DATASET

A dataset contains 120 samples, each of which has 12 concentrations related to two seasons in the Iraq region. These 12 concentrations cause water pollution in rivers, and their designators, used to compute the WQI based on their percentage increasing or decreasing, are PH, TDS, turbidity, TH, TA, Ca, Mg, K, Na, Cl, NO_3, and SO_4. That dataset is related to winter and summer seasons.

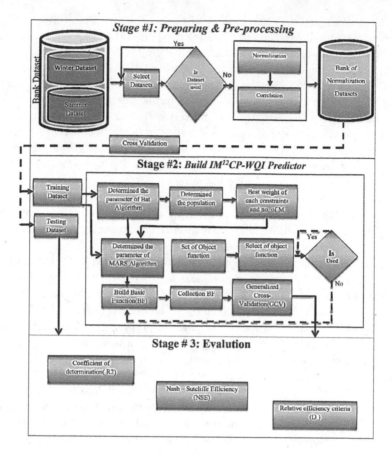

FIGURE 6.1   Block diagram of *IM12CP-WQI*.

6.3.2   Results of IM12CP-WQI

This section shows the results for each stage in IM12CP-WQI, as well as the justification for all the results.

A. Collection of Dataset

At this stage, the dataset is used to test the proposed model taken from two seasons in a region of Iraq, as explained previously.

B. Preprocessing

This stage consists of multiple steps, and each step handles one problem within the dataset.

Step #1: Normalization

The dataset is based on MinmaxScalar scales in the [0 and 1] range. This is a necessary step for the proposed predictor. Figures 6.2 and 6.3 show the result of normalization that is used on the original dataset and transforms

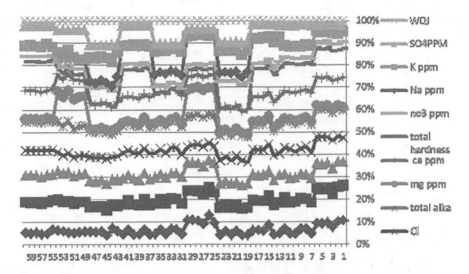

FIGURE 6.2   The visualizing of the winter dataset after normalization.

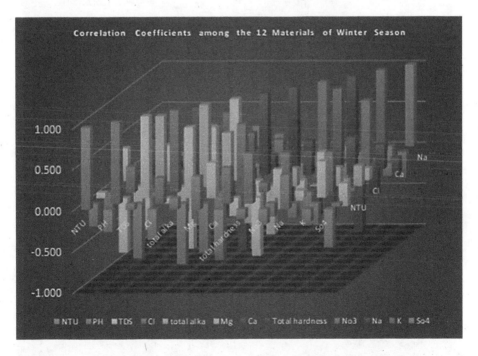

FIGURE 6.3   The visualizing of the summer season dataset after normalization.

each column of the dataset within the [0, 1] range because the activation function used requires that the values be within this range.

The main purpose of the normalization stage is to make all the values in the same range which save the natural of each feature in that dataset.

Step #3: The Correlations between Water Quality Parameters

Correlation coefficient is a statistical indicator that shows how correlated two or more variables are in relation to each other. Positive correlation refers to the degree to which these variables increase or decrease in parallel, while negative correlation means how often one variable increases with the decrease of the other variable. Figures 6.4 and 6.5 show the correlation coefficients. As shown in Tables 6.1 and 6.2.

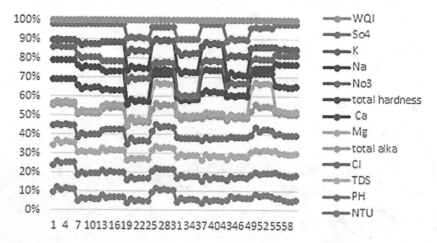

FIGURE 6.4   Correlation coefficients among the 12 materials of winter season.

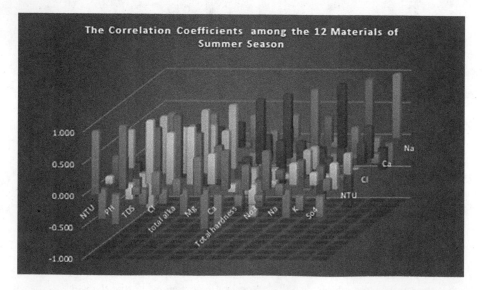

FIGURE 6.5   Correlation coefficients among the 12 materials of summer season.

TABLE 6.1
The Correlation Coefficients among the 12 Materials of Winter Season

	NTU	PH	TDS	Cl	Total Alka	Mg	Ca	Total Hardness	No3	Na	K	So4
NTU	1.000	-0.270	0.069	-0.371	0.137	0.402	-0.521	-0.115	-0.179	0.418	-0.153	-0.462
PH	-0.270	1.000	-0.661	0.314	-0.733	-0.593	0.439	0.608	-0.157	-0.175	-0.249	-0.041
TDS	0.069	-0.661	1.000	-0.067	0.863	0.432	-0.223	-0.622	0.352	0.087	0.443	0.174
Cl	-0.371	0.314	-0.067	1.000	-0.323	-0.827	0.831	0.113	0.483	-0.409	0.487	0.049
Total Alka	0.137	-0.733	0.863	-0.323	1.000	0.653	-0.449	-0.584	0.223	0.014	0.232	0.250
Mg	0.402	-0.593	0.432	-0.827	0.653	1.000	-0.916	-0.347	-0.245	0.346	-0.313	0.149
Ca	-0.521	0.439	-0.223	0.831	-0.449	-0.916	1.000	0.172	0.290	-0.556	0.460	0.021
Total Hardness	-0.115	0.608	-0.622	0.113	-0.584	-0.347	0.172	1.000	-0.573	0.203	-0.768	0.298
No3	-0.179	-0.157	0.352	0.483	0.223	-0.245	0.290	-0.573	1.000	-0.410	0.770	-0.152
Na	0.418	-0.175	0.087	-0.409	0.014	0.346	-0.556	0.203	-0.410	1.000	-0.454	-0.241
K	-0.153	-0.249	0.443	0.487	0.232	-0.313	0.460	-0.768	0.770	-0.454	1.000	-0.317
So4	-0.462	-0.041	0.174	0.049	0.250	0.149	0.021	0.298	-0.152	-0.241	-0.317	1.000

TABLE 6.2

Correlation Coefficients among the 12 Materials of Summer Season

	NTU	PH	TDS	Cl	Total Alka	Mg	Ca	Total Hardness	No3	Na	K	So4
NTU	1.000	-0.488	0.121	0.365	0.254	0.596	-0.539	-0.197	-0.114	0.177	-0.250	-0.355
PH	-0.488	1.000	-0.262	-0.247	-0.420	-0.639	0.617	0.390	0.617	-0.457	0.025	0.186
TDS	0.121	-0.262	1.000	0.805	0.897	0.479	-0.143	-0.324	0.061	0.342	0.199	0.352
Cl	0.365	-0.247	0.805	1.000	0.722	0.530	-0.371	-0.458	0.157	0.312	0.217	0.086
Total Alka	0.254	-0.420	0.897	0.722	1.000	0.677	-0.346	-0.179	-0.092	0.385	-0.105	0.341
Mg	0.596	-0.639	0.479	0.530	0.677	1.000	-0.773	-0.310	-0.235	0.353	-0.331	0.018
Ca	-0.539	0.617	-0.143	-0.371	-0.346	-0.773	1.000	0.365	0.352	-0.596	0.230	0.342
Total Hardness	-0.197	0.390	-0.324	-0.458	-0.179	-0.310	0.365	1.000	-0.276	-0.258	-0.764	0.513
No3	-0.114	0.617	0.061	0.157	-0.092	-0.235	0.352	-0.276	1.000	-0.418	0.415	-0.175
Na	0.177	-0.457	0.342	0.312	0.385	0.353	-0.596	-0.258	-0.418	1.000	0.034	-0.349
K	-0.250	0.025	0.199	0.217	-0.105	-0.331	0.230	-0.764	0.415	0.034	1.000	-0.351
So4	-0.355	0.186	0.352	0.086	0.341	0.018	0.342	0.513	-0.175	-0.349	-0.351	1.000

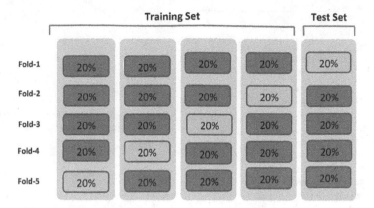

FIGURE 6.6   Five cross-validations.

Step #2: Split the Dataset into Training and Testing Based on Five Cross-Validations

Cross-validation is one of the best techniques for evaluating the performance of a given model. Because badly selected samples for training and testing negatively affects the performance, cross-validation has different methods for wisely selecting the best samples for training and testing a given model. This is shown in Figure 6.6.

C. Implementation of DWM–Bat Phase

Selecting the suitable parameters of any learning algorithm is considered one of the main challenges in science. MARS takes a very long time in implementation to produce a result, therefore this section shows how DWM–Bat solves this problem by finding the best structure from all the parameters to DMARS the main parameter of DWM–Bat shown in Table 6.3.

In other words, the determination of weights and the number of models (M) are essential parameters that fundamentally affect DMARS performance. In general, the MARS is based on the dynamic principle in selecting the parameters of it, therefore the main parameters of DMARS result from DWM–Bat.

By applying the DWM–Bat we get the best weight of each of the 12 contractions, as follow: W-PH = 0.247, W-NTU = 0.420, W-TDS = 0.004, W-Ca = 0.028, W-Mg = 0.042, W-Cl = 0.008, W-Na = 0.011, W-K = 0.175, W-SO4 = 0.008, W-NO3 = 0.042, W-CaCO3 = 0.011, and W-CaCO3 = 0.004, while the optimal number of M related to the winter dataset is 9 and to the summer dataset is 8.

D. Execution of DMARS Phase

DMARS is mainly based on the MARS algorithm, which is capable of handling the dynamic principle in selecting the parameters of it.

TABLE 6.3
The Parameters Utilized in DWM–Bat

Parameter	Value
Number of bats (swarm size) (NB)	720
Minimum (M)	2
Maximum (M)	12
Determine frequency(pulse_frequency)	Pulse_frequency=0*ones(*row_num,col_num*)
Loudness of pulse	1
Loudness decreasing factor(alpha)	0.995
Initial emission rate (init_emission_rate)	0.9
Emission rate increasing factor (gamma)	0.02
Bats initial velocity (init_vel)	0
Determine vector of initial velocity(velocity)	velocity=init_vel*ones(*row_num,col_num*)
Population size (row_num)	*60*
(col_num)	*12*
Minimum value of observed matrix (min_val)	*0.0200*
Maximum value of observed matrix (max_val)	*538*
Maximum number of iteration (max_iter)	*250*
Number of cells (n_var)	*n_var=row_num*col_num*
Lower bound (lb)	*lb=min_val*ones(row_num,col_num)*
Upper bound (ub)	*ub=max_val*ones(row_num,col_num)*
Position of bat (Pos)	*Pos=lb+rand((row_num,col_num)*(ub-lb)*

TABLE 6.4
The Parameters Utilized in MARS

Parameter	Description
Number of input variable (d)	$d = 12$
Datasets (x)	x = samples of winter season or samples of summer season
Number of columns (m)	$m = 13$
Number of row (n)	$n = 60$
Training data cases (Xtr,Ytr)	Xtr(i,:),Ytr(i), $i = 1,\ldots,n$
Vector of maximums for input variables (x_max)	x_max(winter) = [0.06, 7.55, 538, 42.60, 381.66, 417.424.88, 397.984, 15.32, 9.28, 457.20, 135.69, 94.27]
	x_max(summer) = [0.060, 7.470, 539, 24.850, 325, 417.760, 92, 447.424, 6.700, 3.800, 427.760, 137.945, 87.707]
Vector of minimums for input variables (x_min)	x_min(winter) = [0.02, 7.240, 363, 21.300, 300, 28.800, 36, 2.35, 1.859, 1.780, 0.89, 20.146, 12.233]
	x_min(summer) = [0.0200, 6.900, 390, 14.200, 235, 24, 33.600, 2.355, 1, 0.920, 0.630, 64.857, 11.449]
Size of dataset (x_size)	x_size(n,m)= x_size(60,12)

In this stage, forward the parameters result from DWM–Bat to DMARS that represents the weight of each material, and number of model (M) with the dataset of that seasons is generated from the best split of five cross-validations to represent training of DMARS (the main parameters of that algorithm are presented in Table 6.4). Then compute the prediction values based on the best split result from five cross-validations.

The main models are produced by replacing the core of MARS through different types of activation function: Linear kernel: polynomial kernel, rbf kernel, and sigmoid kernel, in addition to taking the best values resulting from DWM–Bat as explain below:

$$\text{Linear Kernel}: L\left(X_i, X_j\right) = X_i^T X_j \tag{6.1}$$

$$\text{Polynomial Kernel}: P\left(X_i, X_j\right) = \left(X_i^T X_j + \gamma\right)^d, \gamma > 0 \tag{6.2}$$

$$\text{RBF Kernel}: R\left(X_i, X_j\right) = \exp\left(-\gamma \|X_i^T - X_j\|\right)^2, \gamma > 0 \tag{6.3}$$

$$\text{Sigmoid Kernel}: S\left(X_i, X_j\right) = \tanh\left(\gamma X_i^T X_j + r\right), \gamma > 0 \tag{6.4}$$

Once evaluated, the results are as follow:
- Coefficient of determination (R^2)
  R^2 is known as the squared value of the Bravais Pearson correlation coefficient.

$$R^2 = \frac{\sum_i \left(Q_m(i) - \bar{Q}_m(i)\right)\left(Q_0(i) - \bar{Q}_0(i)\right)}{\sum_i \left(Q_m(i) - \bar{Q}_m(i)\right)^2 \sum_i \left(Q_0(i) - \bar{Q}_0(i)\right)^2} \tag{6.5}$$

The coefficient value would be in the range of 0 (no correlation) to 1 (perfect fit), and it explain by the modeling prediction the dispersion of the measured value. The reality is that quantifying the dispersion is one of the main drawbacks of R^2. A model that systematically over- or underpredicts will still yield good R^2 values close to 1.0, even though all predictions were in error.
- Nash–Sutcliffe efficiency (NSE)
  NSE was developed by Nash and Sutcliffe. NSE is described as 1 minus the sum of the absolute square differences between the expected and observed values, normalized during the period under investigation by the variance of the values observed. And it was broadly applied to access to hydrological models. It is also highly sensitive to the extreme value and could yield optimal results for the datasets containing extreme data [22]. It could be evaluated as:

$$\text{NSE} = 1 - \frac{\sum_{t=1}^{T} \left(Q_0(i) - Q_m(i)\right)^2}{\sum_{t=1}^{T} \left(Q_0(i) - \bar{Q}_0(i)\right)^2} \tag{6.6}$$

where, Q_0, Q_m, and $\bar{Q}_0(i)$ are the measured value, modeled value, and average measured value at the ith order observation, respectively. And T is the total number of samples. We used the absolute values to verify the difference between the values of calculated and modeled. Both coefficients of determination and Nash–Sutcliffe efficiency describe the difference between the calculated and modeled values for the absolute values. However, there might be an over- or underprediction due to higher or lower values, and the range of NSE lie between 1.0 (perfect fit) and $-\infty$. An efficiency of lower than zero indicates that the mean value of the observed time series would have been a better predictor than the model.

- Relative efficiency criteria d_{rel}:
  The criteria d describes the difference between observation and prediction by the absolute values. The result is that an over- or underprediction of higher values has a greater influence than those of lower values. To counteract these problems, we additionally applied the relative efficiency criteria (rel) to reduce the influence of the absolute differences between the observation value and modeled value during high values significantly.

$$d_{rel} = 1 - \frac{\sum_i \left(\dfrac{Q_0(i) - Q_m(i)}{Q_0(i)} \right)^2}{\sum_i \left(\dfrac{|Q_m(i) - \bar{Q}_0(i)| + |Q_m(i) - \bar{Q}_0(i)|}{\bar{Q}_0(i)} \right)^2} \tag{6.7}$$

The range of the relative efficiency criteria is also in the range from 0 to 1

- Index of agreement d:
  d was proposed by Willmot to resolve the insensitivity of NSE and R^2 to differences in the means and variances observed and forecasted. d represents the mean square error and the potential error and is defined as:

$$d = 1 - \frac{\sum_{i=1}^{n} (O_i - P_i)^2}{\sum_{i=1}^{n} \left(|P_i - \bar{O}| + |O_i - \bar{O}| \right)^2} \tag{6.8}$$

d is not sensitive to systematic model over- or underprediction. So, use the relative efficiency criteria d.

The importance of each concentration based on their relation with water quality index is $K = 0985$, Totalh $= 0.86$, No3 $= 0.761$, TDs $= 0.55$, Na $= 0.415$, PH $= 0.371$, TotalALka $= 0.37$, cl $= 0.362$ and CA $= 0.317$. It is explained in Figures 6.7 through 6.16.

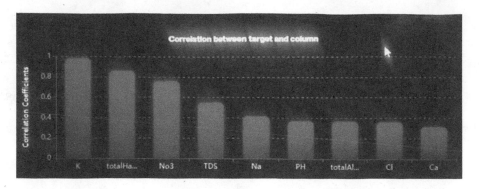

FIGURE 6.7   Correlation among WQI and each concentration based on IM12CP-WQI.

6.4   CONCLUSIONS AND RECOMMENDATION FOR FUTURE WORKS

Water quality index dataset is a sensitive data needed to improve the accuracy of techniques to extract a useful knowledge from it. In addition, the data used in this thesis were obtained from two seasons and contain 12 most important concentrations. The limitation of this dataset is in concentrations that cause water pollution, which are usually unknown to non-experts.

IM12CP-WQI is a development of MARS by BA used to determine the optimal weight for each concentration, number of base model "M" of that MAR. Also, the proposed model is used different types of activation functions (i.e., linear, polynormal, sigmoid, and RBF).

By applying the DWM–Bat, we get the best weight of each contraction as follow: *W-PH = 0.247, W-NTU = 0.420, W-TDS = 0.004, W-Ca = 0.028, W-Mg = 0.042, W-Cl = 0.008, W-Na = 0.011, W-K = 0.175, W-SO4 = 0.008, W-NO3 = 0.042, W-CaCO3 = 0.011, and W-CaCO3 = 0.004*, while the optimal number of M related to the winter dataset is 9 and to the summer dataset is 8. This stage increases the accuracy of results and reduces the time required to train the MARS algorithm.

This study proves the correlation between WQI, and the important concentration is *K = 0985, Totalh = 0.86, No3 = 0.761, TDs = 0.55, Na = 0.415, PH = 0.371, TotalALka = 0.37, CL = 0.362 and CA = 0.317* (Figures 6.7–6.16). This step focuses on determining the important constants, such as total hardness, that have a negative relation with WQI and TDs.

IM12CP-WQI discusses multiple challenges related of WQI, such as the weights for each water reservoir, which activation function is more suitable to build the predictor based on mathematical concept, and which measures are best used to evaluate the water quality as shown in Tables 6.5–6.9. IM12CP-WQI finds new predictors that improve the accuracy of the results by choosing the best weights and M through build DWM–Bat, then finding the optimal part of the dataset used in training/testing based on five cross-validations, and choosing the best activation function through built DMARS that replace the core of MARS by four types of functions (i.e., polynomial,

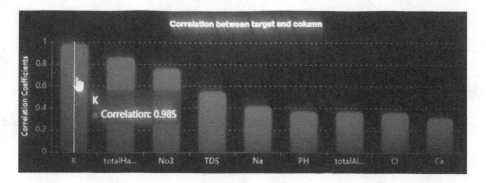

FIGURE 6.8   Correlation value between WQI and concentration of **K** based on IM12CP-WQI.

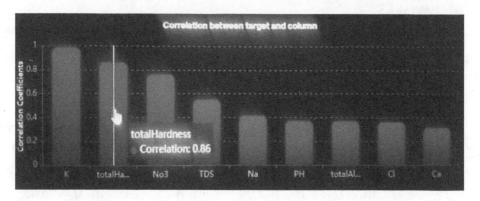

FIGURE 6.9   Correlation value between WQI and concentration of **total hardness** based on IM12CP-WQI.

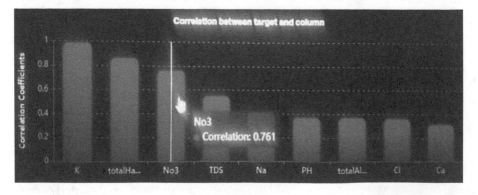

FIGURE 6.10   Correlation value between WQI and concentration of **NO₃** based on IM12CP-WQI.

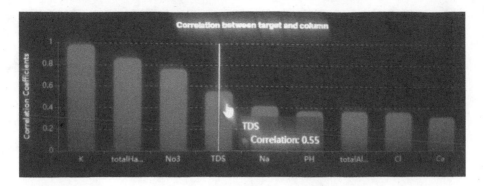

FIGURE 6.11 Correlation value between WQI and concentration of **TDS** based on IM12CP-WQI.

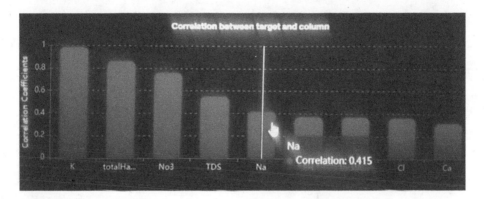

FIGURE 6.12 Correlation value between WQI and concentration of **Na** based on IM12CP-WQI.

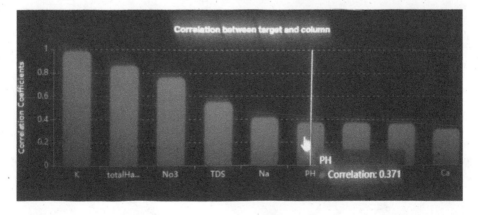

FIGURE 6.13 Correlation value between WQI and concentration of **PH** based on IM12CP-WQI.

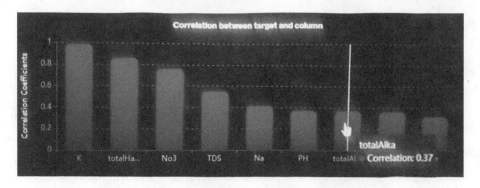

FIGURE 6.14 Correlation value between WQI and concentration of **TotalALka** based on IM12CP-WQI.

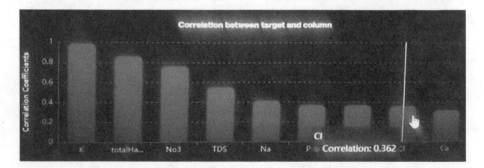

FIGURE 6.15 Correlation value between WQI and concentration of **CL** based on IM12CP-WQI.

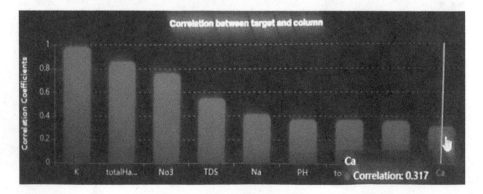

FIGURE 6.16 Correlation value between WQI and concentration of **Ca** based on IM[12]CP-WQI.

sigmoid, RFB, and linear). In addition, the final results are evaluated based on three measureas.

IM12CP-WQI provides a pragmatic model of water quality index for different seasons, showing that water quality with the QWI not exceeding 25 is suitable for drinking while QWI values between 25 and 50 makes it suitable for other forms of consumption such as agriculture, seafood farming, and industrial sector.

TABLE 6.5

Compute the Evaluation Measures of Traditional MARS-Based Five Cross Validation

MARS	R^2		NSE		d_{rel}	
	Train	Test	Train	Test	Train	Test
80–20	0.2242	0.7787	0.9922	0.9919	0.998	0.9979
60–40	0.2658	0.5419	0.9424	0.9251	0.9849	0.9795
50–50	0.3869	0.2408	0.7814	0.6614	0.9346	0.9234
40–60	0.4284	0.2886	0.9999	0.9999	1.0000	1.0000
20–80	0.2134	−0.0947	0	−0.0374	0	0.2515

TABLE 6.6

Compute the Evaluation Measures of MARS after Replay Core by Polynomial as Activation Function

Poly	R^2		NSE		d_{rel}	
	Train	Test	Train	Test	Train	Test
80–20	0.2884	1.1338	0.7545	0.8382	0.2080	0.9094
60–40	0.3961	0.6055	0.7595	0.7214	0.3141	0.5645
50–50	0.4045	0.4817	0.6386	0.6625	−1.5487	1.3020
40–60	0.6619	0.6053	0.5812	0.6272	−0.8451	−1.1077
20–80	0.1314	−0.0951	0	−4.5042e−04	1	0.9792

TABLE 6.7

Compute the Evaluation Measures of MARS after Replay Core by Sigmoid as Activation Function

Sigmoid	R^2		NSE		d_{rel}	
	Train	Test	Train	Test	Train	Test
80–20	0.2896	1.1987	0.7443	0.7735	0.0437	0.7603
60–40	0.4206	0.5808	0.6861	0.7910	−0.1189	0.7690
50–50	0.6778	0.7331	0.4327	0.5853	−2.3005	−0.7308
40–60	0.8307	0.4898	0.6256	0.6224	−0.3731	−1.2430
20–80	0.0213	−0.0370	0	−0.0459	1	−0.5379

TABLE 6.8
Compute the Evaluation Measures of MARS after Replay Core by RBF as Activation Function

RBF	R^2		NSE		d_{rel}	
	Train	Test	Train	Test	Train	Test
80–20	0.5034	4.2230	0.3472	0.2788	−4.0167	−0.5694
60–40	0.4080	0.4400	0.6365	0.7599	−1.9797	−0.3200
50–50	0.7765	0.6608	0.6962	0.7148	0.8723	0.9931
40–60	0.4596	0.2810	1.0000	0.9999	1	1.0000
20–80	0.0329	0.0175	0	−0.3232	1	−5.8051

TABLE 6.9
Compute the Evaluation Measures of $IM^{12}CP$-WQI

$IM^{12}CP$-WQI	R^2		NSE		d_{rel}	
	Train	Test	Train	Test	Train	Test
80–20	0.2189	0.8564	0.9999	0.9997	1.0000	0.9999
60–40	0.2819	0.4457	1.0000	0.9999	1.0000	1.0000
50–50	0.3386	0.3502	0.9999	0.9999	1.0000	1.0000
40–60	0.4119	0.2963	0.9999	0.9999	1.0000	1.0000
20–80	−0.1967	0.0942	0	−0.0666	0	0.2944

REFERENCES

1. A.A. Masrur Ahmed. 2017. Prediction of dissolved oxygen in Surma River by biochemical oxygen demand and chemical oxygen demand using the artificial neural networks (ANNs). *J. King Saud Univ. - Eng. Sci.* 29:151–158. doi:10.1016/j.jksues.
2. S. Heddam and O. Kisi. 2018. "Modelling daily dissolved oxygen concentration using least square support vector machine, multivariate adaptive regression splines and M5 model Tree," *Journal of Hydrology*. doi:10.1016/j.jhydrol.2018.02.061.
3. Senlin Zhu, Salim Heddam, Shiqiang Wu, Jiangyu Dai, and Benyou Jia. 2019. "Extreme learning machine-based prediction of daily water temperature for rivers," *Environmental Earth Sciences*, 78(6), 1–17, Springer. doi:10.1007/s12665-019-8202-7. S. Al-Janabi and I. Al-Shourbaji. 2016. "A Hybrid Image steganography method based on genetic algorithm," *2016 7th International Conference on Sciences of Electronics, Technologies of Information and Telecommunications (SETIT)*, Hammamet, pp. 398–404. doi:10.1109/SETIT.2016.7939903.
4. Jyoti Bansal and A.K. Dwivedi. 2018. "Assessment of ground water quality by using water quality index and physico chemical parameters: review Paper," *International Journal of Engineering Sciences & Research Technology*, 7:2, 170–174. doi:10.5281/zenodo.1165780.

5. Talent Diotrefe Banda and Muthukrishna Vellaisamy Kumarasamy. 2020. "Development of Water Quality Indices (WQIs): A Review," *Polish Journal of Environmental Studies*, 29:3. doi:10.15244/pjoes/110526.
6. Heddam S. 2021. "intelligent data analytics approaches for predicting dissolved oxygen concentration in river: Extremely randomized tree versus random forest, MLPNN and MLR," In Deo R., Samui P., Kisi O., and Yaseen Z. (Eds) *Intelligent Data Analytics for Decision-Support Systems in Hazard Mitigation*. Springer Transactions in Civil and Environmental Engineering. Springer, Singapore. doi:10.1007/978-981-15-5772-9_5.
7. Duie Tien Bui, Khabat Khosravi, John Tiefenbacher, Hoang Nguyen, and Nerantzis Kazakis. 2020. "Improving prediction of water quality indices using novel hybrid machine-learning algorithms," *Science of the Total Environment*, 721, 137612. doi:10.1016/j.scitotenv.2020.137612.
8. Mir Jafar Sadegh Safari. 2020, "Hybridization of multivariate adaptive regression splines and random forest models with an empirical equation for sediment deposition prediction in open channel flow," *Journal of Hydrology*, 590, 125392. doi:10.1016/j.jhydrol.2020.125392.
9. Priya Singh and Pankaj Deep Kaur. 2017. "Review on data mining techniques for prediction of water quality," *International Journal of Advanced Research in Computer Science*, 8:5, 396–401.
10. Y. Qiu, J. Li, X. Huang, and H. Shi. 2018. "A feasible data-driven mining system to optimize wastewater treatment process design and operation," *Water*, 10:1342. doi:10.3390/w10101342.
11. S. Al-Janabi, M. Mohammad, and A. Al-Sultan. 2020. "A new method for prediction of air pollution based on intelligent computation". *Soft Computer* 24, 661–680. doi:10.1007/s00500-019-04495-1.
12. S. H. Ali. 2012. "Miner for OACCR: Case of medical data analysis in knowledge discovery," In *IEEE, 2012 6th International Conference on Sciences of Electronics, Technologies of Information and Telecommunications (SETIT)*, Sousse, pp. 962–975. doi:10.1109/SETIT.2012.6482043.
13. Al-Janabi, S., Alkaim, A., Al-Janabi, E. et al. 2021. Intelligent forecaster of concentrations (PM2.5, PM10, NO2, CO, O3, SO2) caused air pollution (IFCsAP). *Neural Comput & Applic*, 33:14199–14229. doi:10.1007/s00521-021-06067-7
14. G. Madhu et al. 2010. "Hypothetical description for intelligent data mining," *(IJCSE) International Journal on Computer Science and Engineering*, 2:7, 2349–2352.
15. Hamza Ahmad Isiyaka, Adamu Mustapha, Hafizan Juahir, and Philip Phil-Eze. 2019. "Water quality modelling using artificial neural network and multivariate statistical techniques," *Model. Earth Syst. Environ*, 5:583–593. doi:10.1007/s40808-018-0551-9.
16. Sanju Mishra, Rafid Sagban, Ali Yakoob, and Niketa Gandhi. 2018. "Swarm intelligence in anomaly detection systems: an overview," *International Journal of Computers and Applications*. doi:10.1080/1206212X.2018.1521895.
17. Zhu Xuan. 2014. "Computational intelligence techniques and applications," *Computational Intelligence Techniques in Earth and Environmental Sciences*, pp. 3–26, Springer, Dordrecht. doi:10.1007/978-94-017-8642-3_1.
18. Lerios Jefferson L. and Villarica Mia V., 2019, "Pattern extraction of water quality prediction using machine learning algorithms of water reservoir," *International Journal of Mechanical Engineering and Robotics Research*, 8(6):992–997.
19. Weli Zahraa Naser Shah. 2020. "Data mining in cancer diagnosis and prediction:review about latest ten years," *CJAST*, 39(6):11–32, Article no. CJAST.55851. doi:10.9734/CJAST/2020/v39i630555.

20. M. Najafzadeh and A. Ghaemi. 2019. "Prediction of the five-day biochemical oxygen demand and chemical oxygen demand in natural streams using machine learning methods," *Environ Monit Assess* 191:380. doi:10.1007/s10661-019-7446-8.

21. W. Zhang and A.T.C. Goh. 2016. "Multivariate adaptive regression splines and neural network models for prediction of pile drivability," *Geoscience Frontiers*, 7:45–52. doi:10.1016/j.gsf.2014.10.003.

22. Hong Guo, Kwanho Jeon, Jiyeon Lim, Jeongwon Jo, Young Mo Kim, Jong-pyo Park, Joon Ha Kim, and Kyung Hwa Cho. 2015. "Prediction of effluent concentration in a wastewater treatment plant using machine learning models," *J. Environ. Sci., JES-00305*, 12. doi:10.1016/j.jes.2015.01.007.

23. P. Krause, D.P. Boyle, and F. Bäse. 2005. "Comparison of different efficiency criteria for hydrological model assessment," *Advances in Geosciences* 5:89–97. doi:10.5194/adgeo-5-89-2005.

24. Umair Ahmed, Rafia Mumtaz, Hirra Anwar, Asad A. Shah, Rabia Irfan, and José García-Nieto. 2019. "Efficient water quality prediction using supervised machine learning," *Water*, 11:2210. doi:10.3390/w11112210.

25. Nilanjan Dey and V. Rajinikanth. 2021. "Applications of Bat algorithm and its Variants," *Springer Tracts in Nature-Inspired Computing*, eBook ISBN 978-981-15-5097-3, Hardcover ISBN 978-981-15-5096-6, Series ISSN 2524-552X, Number of Pages XII, 172, Springer. doi:10.1007/978-981-15-5097-3.

26. Xiao-Xu Ma and Jie-Sheng Wang. 2018. "Optimized parameter settings of binary bat algorithm for solving function optimization problems," *Journal of Electrical and Computer Engineering*. 2018, 3847951. doi:10.1155/2018/3847951.

27. C.C. Aggarwal. 2020. "Optimization basics: a machine learning view," In *Linear Algebra and Optimization for Machine Learning*. Springer, Cham. doi:10.1007/978-3-030-40344-7_4.

28. Shiliang Sun, Zehui Cao, Han Zhu, and Jing Zhao. 2019. "A survey of optimization methods from a machine learning perspective," School of Computer Science and Technology, East China Normal University, 3663 North Zhongshan Road, Shanghai 200062, P. R. doi:10.1109/TCYB.2019.2950779.

29. Tushar Sharma. 2016. "BAT ALGORITHM: AN OPTIMIZATION TECHNIQUE," Electrical & Instrumentation Engineering Department Thapar University, Patiala Declared as Deemed-to-be-University u/s 3 of the UGC Act., 1956 Post Bag No. 32, PATIALA–147004 Punjab (INDIA). doi:10.13140/RG.2.2.13216.58884.

30. Chandra Shekhar, Shreekant Varshney, and Amit Kumar. 2020. "Optimal control of a service system with emergency vacation using bat algorithm," *Journal of Computational and Applied Mathematics*, 364, 112332. doi:10.1016/j.cam.2019.06.048.

31. X.S. Yang. 2013. "Optimization and metaheuristic algorithms in engineering, in: meta-heursitics in water," In X. S. Yang, A. H. Gandomi, S. Talatahari, and A. H. Alavi (Eds) *Geotechnical and Transport Engineering*, pp. 1–23, Elsevier, Amsterdam. doi:10.1016/B978-0-12-398296-4.00001-5.

32. Jhila Nasiri and Farzin Modarres Khiyabani. 2018. "A whale optimization algorithm (WOA) approach for clustering," *Cogent Mathematics & Statistics*, 5:1. doi:10.1080/25742558.2018.1483565.

33. S. Mirjalili and A. Lewis. 2016. "The whale optimization algorithm," *Advances in Engineering Software*, 95, 51–67. doi:10.1016/j.advengsoft.2016.01.008.

34. X.S. Yang. 2010. "A new metaheuristic bat-inspired algorithm," In González J.R., Pelta D.A., Cruz C., Terrazas G., and Krasnogor N. (Eds) *Nature Inspired Cooperative Strategies for Optimization (NICSO 2010)*. Studies in Computational Intelligence, vol 284, pp 65–74, Springer, Berlin, Heidelberg. doi:10.1007/978-3-642-12538-6_6.

35. N. Rana, M.S.A. Latiff, S.M. Abdulhamid, et al. 2020. "Whale optimization algorithm: a systematic review of contemporary applications, modifications and developments," *Neural Comput & Applic*. doi:10.1007/s00521-020-04849-z.

36. D. Banks, B.-M. Jun, J. Heo, N. Her, C.M. Park, and Y. Yoon. 2020. Selected advanced water treatment technologies for perfluoroalkyl and polyfluoroalkyl substances: A review, *Separation and Purification Technology*, 231:16, 115929. doi:10.1016/j.seppur.2019.115929.

7 Analysis of RNNs and Different ML and DL Classifiers on Speech-Based Emotion Recognition System Using Linear and Nonlinear Features

Shivesh Jha, Sanay Shah, Raj Ghamsani, Preet Sanghavi and Narendra M. Shekokar
Dwarkadas Jivanlal Sanghvi College of Engineering, Mumbai, India

CONTENTS

DOI: 10.1201/9781003307822-9

7.1   INTRODUCTION

Machine learning, also referred to as ML, is a popular field in computer science that carries out tasks without the separate need for programming. Many techniques are used to train the model on datasets and make predictions. The ML algorithm works by training models from a dataset. A dataset is a collection of inputs to the algorithm for which output is already known. The model is built by reading the dataset, predicting the output and comparing it with the known output, and making changes accordingly.

With high computing power and the advancement in the field of ML and deep learning, machines are able to achieve a high benchmark in performing tasks where human action or human intelligence is required. Communication with machines is getting popular these days; digital assistants like Alexa, Siri, Google Assistant, etc. are becoming ubiquitous. But none of these truly recognize our emotion and none of them react or respond in a way humans would do. There is a need for emotion recognition for machines to behave, act, and make human-like decisions. This is why the need for identifying human emotions has gained attention of many researchers.

Speech is the most viable way any human can express and explain feelings and problems. Speech is also considered as the most viable way for human–machine interaction. Hence speech is a widely used feature for emotion extraction by researchers over many years.

Speech emotion recognition is a process of extracting human emotions using speech as a parameter. Speech plays an important role in identifying the emotion of the speaker. Speech signals also have an advantage over text communication, as text is not an effective medium to express the emotional state of a person. For better and effective human–machine interaction (HMI), it is necessary to include emotions in the conversation. Human emotions can be classified as sad, happy, angry, fearful, or surprised. In our day-to-day life, we humans behave or react toward a particular situation based on our emotional state of mind. Machines lack the ability to make decisions based on emotions. Researchers also believe that emotion detection techniques can help people in building up their interpersonal skills.

Over the decades, various studies have been conducted in the field of SEC where the general pipeline includes feature extraction, dimensionality reduction, and emotion classification.

This rest of the chapter gives a brief analysis of various classifiers on speech-based emotion recognition system on linear and nonlinear features. The next section is focused on the methodology that included workflow, preprocessing, feature extraction, and audio features. Section 7.3 includes the description of various classifiers. Section 7.4 reports the dataset description and training process of all the classifiers studied in Section 7.3. Section 7.5 notes all the results and analyses. Section 7.6 closes the chapter with the conclusion and future directions in section 7.7.

7.2 METHODOLOGY

This section covers the methodology used by the authors in their work. It also discusses the features extracted from the audio signals.

7.2.1 WORKFLOW

Machine learning algorithms have been used to classify the emotions. The training data is first filtered for unwanted noises. Then the acoustic features using MFCC, Mel, Chroma, Contrast, and Tonnetz are extracted and converted into feature vectors that are passed to the classifier for training purposes. The workflow of the methodology used by the authors is shown in Figure 7.1. Preprocessing and feature

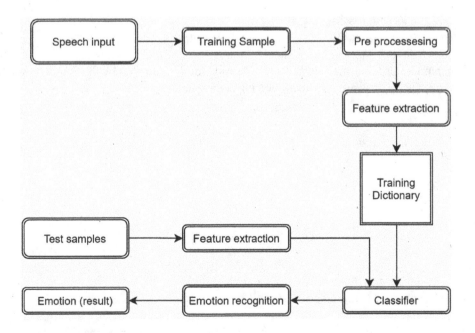

FIGURE 7.1   System flow chart.

extraction are the important modules in this architecture, and are discussed and explained in detail.

7.2.2 PREPROCESSING

Signal preprocessing, feature extraction, and classification are the typical steps in any speech-based emotion recognition system. The classification models are not directly applied to the audio files. First, pertinent features are extracted from the audio files, which account for a particular emotion. Before extracting the features, however, the audio should be processed and filtered for removing the noises that could hinder the model's ability to classify accurately. The data consisting of audio files is first split into training and testing data, and the training data is sent to the preprocessing module. Signal preprocessing consists of applying sound-related filters to original audio signals and splitting them into smaller fragments. The authors perform the following steps as discussed in Nema et al. [1] and Sahoo et al. [2] for processing and manipulating the audio signals before passing them for feature extraction.

7.2.2.1 Silence Removal

The human speech naturally contains many silent parts: for example, pre-utterances, post-utterances, and between-words silences. The silent signals are not important because they do not have any information. Moreover, these parts affect the accuracy of the model while classifying. The two methods used for silence removal are zero crossing rate (ZCR) and short time energy (STE).

7.2.2.2 Zero Crossing Rate

ZCR is the rate at which the sign of the signal changes from positive to zero and then negative or vice versa over the duration of the signal frame. In other words, it is the number of times the signal crosses the value of zero divided by the length of the frame. The ZCR is given by the following equation:

$$Z(i) = \frac{1}{2N} \sum_{n=1}^{N} \left| \text{sgn}\left[xi(n)\right] - \text{sgn}\left[xi(n-1)\right] \right|$$

Here, sgn( ) represents a sign function and it is given by

$$sgn\left[xi(n)\right] = \begin{cases} 1, xi(n) \geq 0 \\ -1, xi(n) < 0 \end{cases}$$

i stands for the frame number.
$xi(n)$ represents ith sample in frame i

ZCR is used to notice the silent and unvoiced speech signals. Signals detected as unvoiced by the ZCR method are then removed since they have no use and are futile.

7.2.2.3 Short Time Energy

The amplitude of an unvoiced speech segment is prodigiously less as compared to that of voiced segments. STE of a signal manifests this variation in the amplitude. Certain properties of a typical speech signal are tempestuous and vary with respect to time. For example, a considerable variation in the peak amplitude of the signal and a profound variation of the frequency within voiced regions of speech signal can be seen. The energy of a discrete time signal is given by $E = \sum_{m=-\infty}^{\infty} x^2(m)$ where $x(m)$ represents the data sequence. This quantity is not of much significance and use, since it does not provide sufficient information about the time dependent properties of the speech signal. The amplitude varies abjectly with time. In particular, the amplitude of a voiced signal is high as compared to that of an unvoiced one. The STE reflects this amplitude variation and is given as $E_n = \sum_{m=-\infty}^{\infty} \left[X(m).W(m-n) \right]^2$ where $W(n-m)$ is a limited time window sequence. Based on the value of E_n, the segment can be identified as voiced or unvoiced one. It can also be used to find the approximate time at which the voiced speech becomes unvoiced speech and vice versa.

7.2.2.4 Pre-emphasis

To augment higher frequencies, it is quite common to apply a pre-emphasis filter to the audio signal before starting the feature extraction process. This pre-emphasis filter offers a variety of advantages, including making the frequency spectrum balanced, as high frequencies often have smaller magnitudes than lower frequencies, and avoiding number-related issues during Fourier Transform calculation.

$$yt = xt - \alpha xt - 1$$

Here, α represents the pre-emphasis filter coefficient and its value is either 0.95 or 0.97.

7.2.2.5 Framing

The authors divide the audio stream into short-term windows termed *frames* after applying the pre-emphasis filter. Window sizes for speech processing typically vary from 20 to 50 milliseconds, with 40 to 50 percent overlap between two windows occurring simultaneously. One of the most frequent frame size choices is 25 milliseconds with 15 milliseconds overlap (10-millisecond window step). The main objective for this step is to avoid the loss of an audio signal's frequency contours over time owing to its volatile and turbulent character. Because the frequency characteristics of a signal vary with time, applying the Discrete Fourier Transform over the full sample isn't practical.

7.2.2.6 Windowing

The signal has been divided into fragments up to this point. A window function $w(n)$ having length N is then multiplied by the frame, where N is the frame's length. Windowing is the method of stressing and highlighting predefined aspects of a signal by multiplying a waveform of a voice signal segment by a temporal window of a specific shape. The voice signal is tapered to zero or near to zero at the beginning and end of each frame to eliminate discontinuity and hence minimize the mismatch. Windowing is applied to the voice signal to alleviate difficulties caused by signal shortening and truncation by smoothing the signal. The Hamming Window is the most common window. The window function $w(n)$ is as follows:

$$w(N) = 0.54 - 0.46\cos\frac{2\pi n}{N-1},\ 0 \le n \le N-1$$

7.2.3 FEATURE EXTRACTION

Now, the processed signal is sent to the feature extraction module for extracting the features. The feature extraction process is a prime step in a typical speech emotion recognition. The feature extraction process generates certain coefficient values of the acoustic features from the speech signal, and based on these coefficients the features are recognized. These features affect the accuracy of the classifier used for emotion recognition. It can be inferred from Garg et al. [3] that quantity and quality of the features are the factors enhancing the accuracy of the classifier. Their results varied when just MFCC coefficients were used as a feature vector and when a combination of MFCC, MEL, and CHROMA as a feature vector were used. The different types of sound features extracted from the feature extraction process are categorized as time domain features, frequency domain features, statistical features, deep features, and hybrid features as in Wang [4]. The speech signal is divided into frames/fragments ranging from 10 milliseconds to 30 milliseconds, since the feature extraction is dependent on the frame/fragment and not performed on the entire audio file but on the specific frames/segments individually.

7.2.4 AUDIO FEATURES

An audio file consists of various features that can be used to detect various aspects of speech. Many features among these are used to detect emotion from speech. The authors have used features from the following for detecting emotion from the audio. The features are explained below..

7.2.4.1 Chromagram

The chromagram adds the dimension of time to the chroma notion. The chromagram can be used to interpret properties about the distribution of a signal's energy across chroma and time, similar to how we use the spectrogram to infer features about a signal's energy distribution over frequency and time. When it comes to constructing the concept of a chromagram, there are two factors to consider, as mentioned by Shen et al. [5]. The first is the most difficult to define. The chromagram is a calculation of signal strength as a function of chroma and time, wherein chroma is a many-to-one mapping of frequency to the [0, 1] interval. As a result, the chromagram is a many-to-one mapping of signal strength at frequencies in the same chroma class, for example, $s(t,c)= G(s(!,JVf = 2c + h)$. The second problem is determining how to calculate the chromagram. Direct transforms of the original signal and transforms of a time-frequency picture of that signal, such as the spectrogram, can be distinguished. The form of the many-to-one function G becomes debatable when the practical constraint of creating a signal's time-frequency image through a lattice of points is considered.

7.2.4.2 Mel-Frequency Cepstrum (MFC)

MFC represents short-term power spectrum of sound. It is basically a linear cosine transform of a log power spectrum on a nonlinear mel scale of frequency. Mel-frequency cepstral coefficients (MFCCs) are the coefficients that are building blocks of Mel-frequency cepstral coefficient (MFC). They are a derivative of a type of audio clip cepstral representation. The main distinction between the cepstrum and the mel-frequency cepstrum is that the MFC's frequency bands are uniformly spaced on the mel scale, which more closely approximates the human auditory system's response than the normal spectrum's linearly spaced frequency bands. This frequency warping leads to a better representation of sound—for instance, in audio compression.

7.2.4.3 Mel-Frequency Cepstrum Coefficients (MFCC)

The most basic point to understand about speech is that the sounds generated by a human are filtered by the shape of the vocal tract including tongue, teeth, etc. This shape forms the basis of what sound is generated. A precise identification of shape will give an exact representation of the phenomenon fabricated. The vocal tract is presented in the envelope of the short power range, and this envelope is the primary job of MFCCs.

The formula for converting from frequency to Mel scale is:

$$M(F) = 1225\ln(1 + f/700)$$

To go from Mel's back to frequency:

$$M^{-1}(m) = 700(\exp(m/1125) - 1)$$

All the features are combined together, and a feature vector is created, which is nothing but a numpy array containing a series of numbers that represent the coefficients of the features. The training data will consist of an amalgam of the feature vector of all the audio files and a target variable, i.e., the label representing the emotion that is to be given to the classifiers, which are discussed in the next section.

7.3 CLASSIFICATION MODELS

In this section, the authors discuss multiple classifiers used in this chapter for comparing the results.

7.3.1 MLP Classifier

Similar to logistic regression, perceptron is a binary classification algorithm that classifies the input variable in just two classes. It is a very simple neural network model that classifies only into two categories: for example, 0:No and 1:Yes. Its architecture consists of a single node or neuron accepting a row of input variables and predicts the output, i.e., the label. Mathematically, it is expressed as:

$$y = \varphi\left(\sum_{i=1}^{n} w_i x_i + b\right) = \varphi\left(w^T x + b\right)$$

w = Weight vector,
x = Input Vector,
b = bias and φ is the non-linear activation function.

There are, however, many drawbacks in this simple perceptron classifier. It can only be used for binary classification and linear classification. It has just a single layer that represents a shallow neural network and restricted nonlinear classification.

The architecture as shown in Figure 7.2 consists of an input layer taking the input, the output layer making the decision or classification, and, in between, a random number of hidden layers that are the true computational engines of a multi-layer perceptron.

7.3.2   SVC

An SVM is a nonparametric supervised machine learning model. It advocates the kernel trick to map inputs to high-dimensional feature spaces for nonlinear classification

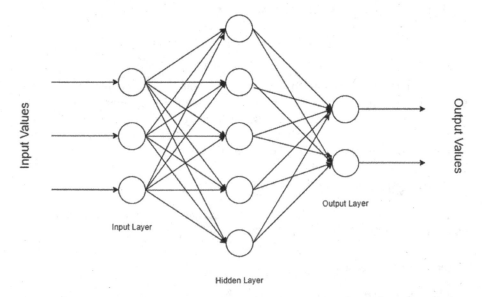

FIGURE 7.2   MLP architecture.

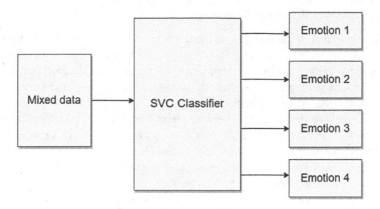

FIGURE 7.3 Architecture for SVC classifier.

and regression. SVMs generate a hyperplane or a set of hyperplanes in a high or infinite dimensional space, which is utilized for classification. The most basic way to use an SVC is with a linear kernel, which means the decision boundary is a straight line (or hyperplane in higher dimensions) (Figure 7.3).

7.3.3 RANDOM FOREST CLASSIFIER

The random forest (RF) consists of many individual decision-making trees, which work together. Each single tree produces a category prediction within the RF, and the class with the highest votes becomes a prediction for our model. A simple yet strong concept—the wisdom of the masses—works on RF. Trees protect each other from individual errors, which alleviates the overall accuracy of model. Few trees may be incorrect, but many trees are correct at the same time, so that the trees can move in the right direction as a group (Figure 7.4).

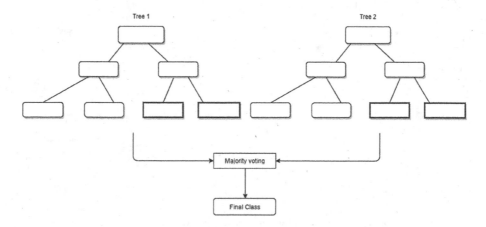

FIGURE 7.4 Architecture diagram for RFC.

7.3.4 Gradient-Boosting Classifier

In gradient boosting, decision trees are the weak learners. Decision trees can be imagined forming by iteratively asking questions to the data. To reduce the problem of overfitting, many decision trees are combined using the boosting methods. Boosting basically means getting a strong learner after combining sequentially many weak learners. Each tree focuses on improving the errors of the previous tree. Though it is a weak learner, combining all the weak learners together sequentially and focusing on the errors of previous trees results in a more accurate model. In a gradient-boosting algorithm, each new learner fits on the residuals from the previous weak learner. The aggregation of the results from each step by the final model results in a more accurate and efficient strong learner (Figure 7.5).

The overall parameters of this ensemble model are classified into three categories:

1. Tree-specific Parameters – Affect each individual tree of the model.
2. Boosting Parameters – Affect the boosting operation of the model.
3. Miscellaneous Parameters – Affect the overall functionality of the model.

7.3.5 K-Neighbors Classifier

In K-NN, the class of the object is decided based on majority votes by its neighbor. In K-NN classifier, the distance of the data point is calculated with every other known data point. Various distance metrics such as euclidean distance and manhattan distance are used to find the nearest data points. Among all the data points the nearest K-neighbor is selected and the data point is assigned the label similar to the majority of the K-selected data points. K-NN is a nonparametric model that makes it suitable for classification where input data has lot of preprocessing work (Figure 7.6).

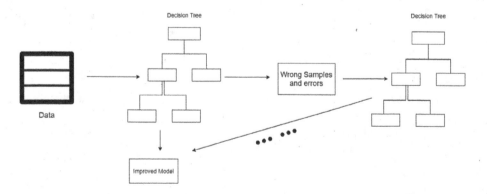

FIGURE 7.5 Architecture diagram for gradient-boosted trees.

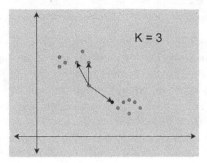

FIGURE 7.6 Working of KNN.

Input

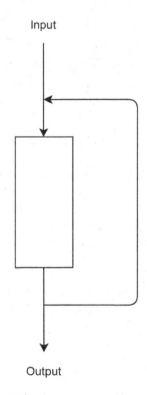

Output

FIGURE 7.7 Basic working of RNN.

7.3.6 Recurrent Neural Networks

RNN is one of the widely used sequence model in NLP [6–13]. In RNN, the output of the previous prediction is served with the newly fetched features to the model to achieve the final output. In RNN the sequence of the output is important. Hence, the model has two inputs, the present and the recent past, unlike any other neural network, which makes it special for language processing. RNN, along with LSTM, makes it simple for the model to remember the past predictions (Figure 7.7).

7.3.7   Bagging Classifier

It works as a meta-predictor ensemble that uses base models on every arbitrary sequence of the predefined dataset. Here X is the size of the database. Replacement of data entries is allowed while randomly drawing the data examples. Moreover, for each model, the training dataset is variable. The final training data can have original data more than once; however, the other data may be neglected completely. By using this technique (voting or averaging), variance is reduced. On the other hand, this reduction in overfitting can result in an increase in bias. The parameters used in our study are 100 estimators alongside the maximum depth of the base estimator ranging from 1 to 5 and the maximum number of samples have values ranging from 0.05 to 0.5.

7.4   EXPERIMENTATION

7.4.1   Dataset Description

The authors have used multiple datasets and combined them to get more training data. The more extensive extensive the data, the higher the accuracy. The datasets used by authors were EMODB and RAVDESS.

7.4.1.1   EMODB

The EMODB database is a freely available German database used by the authors in this chapter. Institute of Communication Science, Technical University, Berlin, Germany has created and maintained this dataset. The dataset consists of 535 utterances by 10 idiosyncratic professional speakers who are of different age groups and both genders. The dataset consists of the following emotions – Anger, Boredom, Anxiety, Happiness, Sadness, Disgust, Neutral.

Since the database is in German, the emotion labels are in German notations. The code of emotions is as follows:

Letter	Emotion in German	Emotion in English
W	Arger (Wut)	Anger
L	Langeweile	Boredom
E	Ekel	Disgust
A	Angst	Anxiety/Fear
F	Freude	Happiness
T	Trauer	Sadness
N	Neutral	Neutral

The database consists of a compendium of audio files according to a particular naming convention. The convention is as follows:

- Positions 1–2: speaker's assigned number
- Positions 3–5: code for text
- Position 6: emotion
- Position 7: if there are more than two versions, these are numbered a, b, c, and so on.

Example: The audio file from Speaker 03 speaking text a01 with the emotion "Angst" (Anxiety/Fear) would be 03a01Aa.wav.

Information about the speakers according to the age and sex: 03 represents 31 years old male, 08 represents 34 years female, 09 represents 21 years female, 10 represents 32 years male, 11 represents 26 years male, 12 represents 30 years male, 13 represents 32 years female, 14 represents 35 years female, 15 represents 25 years male, 16 represents 31 years female.

7.4.1.2 RAVDESS

A total of 7,356 files are present in the Ryerson Audio-Visual Database of Emotional Speech and Song (RAVDESS) as discussed in Livingstone et al., 2018 [14]. The size of this database is 24.8 GB. This database comprises 24 professional actors, 12 females and 12 males, in a neutral North American accent. The audio is of two types, speech and song. The emotions in speech are happy, calm, sad, fearful, angry, disgust, and surprise, and the song contains sad, happy, calm, fearful, and angry emotions. Every expression has two levels of emotional intensity, normal and strong, with a complementary neutral expression. All conditions are available in three modality formats i.e., Audio-only, Audio-Video, and Video-only (no sound). The authors in this chapter have used the audio only modality format since this chapter encompasses speech-based features. Out of the 7,356 total files, 2,452 files fall in the audio-only modality format. Each of the RAVDESS files has a different and unique name. The file name is a seven-part numerical identifier and each numerical part consists of two digits. For example, the filename 03-01-06-01-02-01-12.mp4 has Modality = 03 (Audio only), Vocal channel = 01 (Speech), Emotion = 06 (Fearful), Emotional, Intensity = 01 (normal), Statement = 02 (Dogs are sitting by the door), Repetition = 01 (1st repetition), Actor = 12 (Female, since 12 is an even number)

7.4.2 Training Process

The process of feature extraction included extracting features like mel, mfcc, chromogram, and torrentz from the training dataset. The dataset was divided into training and testing parts. The emotions used for classification were neutral, calm, happy, sad, angry, fear, disgust, and boredom. The training dataset was trained at different levels to analyze the results at different levels of training. Those levels were 1%, 10%, and 100%. All the models were then trained with the training dataset with optimal parameters to get the most accurate result. Parameter tuning of major parameters for models is discussed here. In the random forest classifier, the major factor is the number of trees/estimators. To find the best result, iteration from 10 to 100 number of trees with a gap of 30 trees was performed. The best result was obtained at 40 trees. For the KNN algorithm, the default value of nearest neighbors, i.e., 5, was used, which resulted in the most accurate result. In the gradient boosting classifier, the major parameter max_depth was tuned as 7 for the best result after testing for values 5 and 7. In the MLP classifier, the learning rate was kept adaptive for the best result after experimenting with constant and adaptive. Also, the max_iter parameter was found to be optimal at 500. In the Bagging classifier, the number of base estimators in the ensemble was tested from 10 to 70 with a gap of 20. The best result was obtained at

50 base estimators. In addition to this, other parameters for the mentioned models were tuned for the best result. For evaluating the accuracy of the models, the matrix used were accuracy score and f-score. The performance of models at different levels of training are discussed in the results section.

7.5   RESULTS

The accuracy of our model is mainly evaluated in terms of recognition accuracy. The original dataset with ground truth is compared with the results of the model. The evaluation is done on the grounds of various aforementioned feature extraction methods. We realize that an efficient emotion identifier can greatly help increase the relationship between a human and a supercomputer. In our study, we have mainly used two datasets, namely TESS and RAVEDESS. There are nine sentiments available, such as anger, boredom, anxiety/fear, happiness, sadness, calm, fear, disgust, neutral. In our work, we predict the input speech in the above emotions using different classification techniques after feature extraction. We have used different classifiers to classify the emotions. They include SVC, Random Forest Classifier, Gradient Boosting Classifier, KNeighborsClassifier, MLP classifier, and bagging classifier.

1. Gradient Boosting Classifier – To reduce the problem of overfitting, many decision trees are combined using the boosting methods. For 100 percent of the data, which amounts to 2,103 data samples, gradient boosting classifier achieved 94.769 percent validation score and 86.854 percent test score for 4.5642 s and 0.007 s, respectively.
2. KNN – The main factor in training a KNN classifier is commonly referred to as the number of closest values. Among all the data points the nearest K-neighbors are selected and the data point is assigned the label similar to the majority of the K-selected data points. K-NN is a nonparametric model that makes it suitable for classification where input data has lot of preprocessing work.
   For 100 percent of the data samples, that is 2103 data samples, the model achieved 93.20 percent validation score and 84.97 percent test score for 0.007 seconds and 0.004 seconds, respectively.
3. Bagging Classifier – This model is averaged based on its individual estimations using aggregation or selection methodologies to create an ultimate prediction. This is mainly used to decrease the variance of a decision tree or any other black-box estimator by involving irregularities in the development method after which an ensemble is created at the end. All base models in this type of a system are trained simultaneously, in which a training dataset is retrieved by arbitrarily picking up X amounts of data entries from the predefined original training database. For 100 percent of the data samples that total 2,103 data samples, the bagging classifier achieved a 92.1 percent accuracy for the validation set and 87.559 percent accuracy for the test set.

4. SVC – A precise separation is achieved by the hyperplane that has the largest distance to the nearest training data points of any class, since commonly the larger the margin, the lower the generalization error of the classifier. The decision function for a linearly separable problem has three samples on the margin boundaries called support vectors. The parameters used for tuning the SVC model were c, gamma, and kernel. Gamma high means more curvature. Gamma low means less curvature. C is the error term's penalty parameter. It monitors the trade between smooth decision limits and correctly classifies the training points. Here the main parameter is the number of degrees. For 100 percent of the data that amounts to 2,103 data samples, SVC achieved 93.8 percent validation score and 88.5 percent test score.

5. Random Forest Classifier – This classifier considers most of the selection by randomly picking data points, thereby making the most crucial factor as the number of estimators. The reasons for the brief work of the random forests is a huge number of relatively uncorrelated models working as a union will output each component model. A prominent factor is the low correlation between models. For 100 percent of the data that amounts to 2,103 data samples, Random Forest Classifier achieved 88.5 percent validation score and 84.5 perent test score.

6. MLP – The concepts of back-propagation and hidden layers were introduced later, which gave birth to MLP. The weights are adjusted and modified constantly to minimize the difference and the errors between the desired and actual outputs. This is the back-propagation technique. The nodes placed between the input and output layers represent the hidden layers that help in learning the complex functions. MLP is therefore a deep ANN that contains more than one perceptron. Out of all the classifiers, MLP is the best classifier with the test score as close to equal to 84.507 percent in 0.002 seconds and a 93 percent validation score in 2.7 seconds for a total of 2,103 data samples. The accuracy of all the classifiers is shown in the figure below.

7.5.1 RECURRENT NEURAL NETWORK (RNN)

One of the most intriguing results is how the skewness of the data affected the overall accuracy of RNN classifier. After training for just a few hours on 50 percent of the entire dataset (due to computational limits), RNN managed to achieve an accuracy of 0.75. In order to understand in greater depth as to how RNN behaved with respect to different emotions, the accuracy for angry was 92 percent, neutral was 82 percent, happy was 71 percent, and sad was 67%. This shows that with greater computational strength and increased data cleansing for each of the emotions, RNN has the potential to classify emotions with greater accuracy (Figures 7.8 and 7.9).

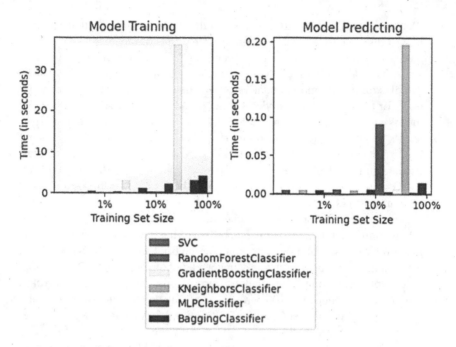

FIGURE 7.8 Comparison of training time for different test data sizes.

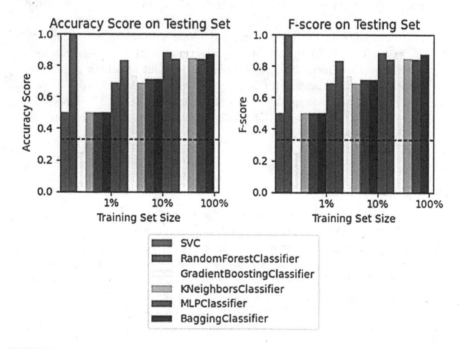

FIGURE 7.9 Accuracy and F-score against test data.

7.6 CONCLUSION

In this chapter, we have provided a detailed analysis of various classifiers over various datasets for recognizing emotions from speech. We have used various classification techniques to train our models over multiple datasets to classify speech signals into neutral, calm, happy, sad, angry, fear, disgust, and boredom.

After training and testing we can conclude that the MLP classifier has given the best result. MLP has achieved the test score equal to 84.507 percent in 0.002 seconds and a 93 percent validation score in 2.7 seconds for a total of 2,103 data samples. With more features and increased datasets, significant improvement can be seen in the performance of the models.

We hope our work helps the researchers trying to explore and experiment further on speech emotion recognition.

7.7 FUTURE DIRECTIONS

As the number of emotions considered for this research is limited, more emotions like rudeness, emotional sentiment, rage, and others can be inculcated in further research. Adding more emotions can help in creating even more efficient recommender systems. Moreover, building an AI bot that takes the input of the user after using a particular product can be beneficial for further development in product stages. Another flaw with our study is that the execution time increases as soon as the size of the file increases. Suitable methodologies can be used to tackle this problem by rigorous preprocessing methods to consider only the relevant part of a recording.

REFERENCES

[1] Nema, Bashar M. and Ahmed A. Abdul-Kareem. "Preprocessing signal for speech emotion recognition." *Al Mustansiriyah Journal of Science* 28, no. 3 (2018): 157–165.

[2] Sahoo, Tushar Ranjan and Sabyasachi Patra. "Silence removal and endpoint detection of speech signal for text independent speaker identification." *International Journal of Image, Graphics & Signal Processing* 6, no. 6 (2014).

[3] Garg, Utkarsh, Sachin Agarwal, Shubham Gupta, Ravi Dutt, and Dinesh Singh. "Prediction of Emotions from the Audio Speech Signals using MFCC, MEL and Chroma." In *2020 12th International Conference on Computational Intelligence and Communication Networks (CICN)*, pp. 87–91. IEEE, 2020.

[4] Wang, Chunyi. "Speech emotion recognition based on multi-feature and multi-lingual Fusion." *arXiv preprint arXiv:2001.05908* (2020).

[5] Shen, Peipei, Zhou Changjun, and Xiong Chen. "Automatic speech emotion recognition using support vector machine." In *Proceedings of 2011 International Conference on Electronic & Mechanical Engineering and Information Technology*, vol. 2, pp. 621–625. IEEE, 2011.

[6] Ibrahim, Y. A., Odiketa, J. C., and Ibiyemi, T. S.. "Preprocessing technique in automatic speech recognition for human computer interaction: An overview." *Ann. Comput. Sci. Ser.*, vol. XV, no. 1 (2017): 186–191.

[7] Lalitha, S., D. Geyasruti, R. Narayanan, and M. Shravani. "Emotion detection using MFCC and cepstrum features." *Procedia Computer Science* 70 (2015): 29–35.

[8] Kishore, KV Krishna and P. Krishna Satish. "Emotion recognition in speech using MFCC and wavelet features." In *2013 3rd IEEE International Advance Computing Conference (IACC)*, pp. 842–847. IEEE, 2013.

[9] Bedoya-Jaramillo, S., E. Belalcazar-Bolaños, T. Villa-Cañas, J. R. Orozco-Arroyave, J. D. Arias-Londoño, and J. F. Vargas-Bonilla. "Automatic emotion detection in speech using mel frequency cesptral coefficients." In *2012 XVII Symposium of Image, Signal Processing, and Artificial Vision (STSIVA)*, pp. 62–65. IEEE, 2012.

[10] Nithya, P. M. B. and S. Roopa, *"Speech emotion recognition using deep learning"*, *International Journal of Recent Technology and Engineering (IJRTE)*, 7, no. 4S, (2018): ISSN: 2277-3878.

[11] Utane, Akshay S. and S. L. Nalbalwar. "Emotion recognition through Speech." *International Journal of Applied Information Systems (IJAIS)* (2013): 5–8.

[12] Quatieri, Thomas F. *Discrete-time speech signal processing: Principles and practice.* Pearson Education India, 2006.

[13] Song, Mingli, Chun Chen, and Mingyu You. "Audio-visual based emotion recognition using tripled hidden Markov model." In *2004 IEEE International Conference on Acoustics, Speech, and Signal Processing*, vol. 5, pp. 5–877. IEEE, 2004.

[14] Livingstone S.R. and F.A. Russo. The Ryerson audio-visual database of emotional speech and song (RAVDESS): A dynamic, multimodal set of facial and vocal expressions in North American English. *PLoS One* 13(5) (2018): e0196391. https://doi.org/10.1371/journal.pone.0196391.

8 Web Service User Diagnostics with Deep Learning Architectures

S. Maheswari

Vellore Institute of Technology, Chennai, India

CONTENTS

8.1 INTRODUCTION

Deep learning could be explained as the current trend in the study of machine learning that applies high capacity and consistency by describing the world as a series of embedded ideas. Its determination falls in the creation of a neural network that pretends to be the human brain for mathematical learning. It exhibits the human brain

DOI: 10.1201/9781003307822-10

system to describe details such as images, sounds, and texts [1, 2]. Each deep learning architecture differs in parameters and hyperparameters. Fine-tuning the parameters inappropriate to the nature of the dataset will help in improving the performance of the model. Companies in the cloud domain, such as Amazon and Google, have developed custom web services that operate independently and together with third-party web services. They have not addressed the reason behind the nature of the web service performance at the end-user level. This has been the main motivation in considering how deep learning architectures can provide more insight with accurate user diagnostics.

8.2 CONVOLUTION NEURAL NETWORKS

A convolution neural network (CNN) is an artificial feed-forward neural network. It deals with the aerial data and the input size to be fixed. CNN is a kind of artificial neural network that has become a hotspot in the field of speech processing and image processing. Its load-sharing system structure makes it almost identical to a natural neural network, thus reducing complications in the network structure and limiting the count of load assigned. This advantage is more important when the network input is a multifaceted image, and the image can be directly used as the input of the network to avoid the critical data filtration and data reformation in the old identification or prediction-based algorithm. CNN is a multilayered sensor specifically designed to recognize two-dimensional shapes that are highly invariant to translation, scaling, tilting, and forms of deformation given [3].

CNN is the first truly successful learning algorithm for training multi-layer network structures as referred [3]. It reduces the number of features that require processing to facilitate an increase in the training performance of the given algorithm through aerial associations. As a deep learning architecture, CNN is expected to limit or decrease the data preprocessing requirements. Three important factors are native responsiveness, load sharing, and pooling. The most powerful part of CNN is learning feature hierarchies from large amounts of unlabeled data. CNN is quite encouraging for the system in the web services domain. Data as features can be single-variate or multivariate. The types of data include character, string, and numeric values. Each instance corresponds to a row that can be classified or predicted. However, non-numeric values "One Hot Encoding ML" is a solution for representation toward classification.

8.3 RECURRENT NEURAL NETWORKS

A recurrent neural network (RNN) handles the time-based data or the sequence of data. RNN is adopted for practicing the sequence data. In the earlier neural network model, features were from the first layer to the hidden layer to the output layer. The layers were fully connected, and there is no connection between the nodes between each layer.

8.4 IMPORTANCE OF DEEP LEARNING VERSUS MACHINE LEARNING

Deep learning is a recent advancement technique to improve the quality in many domain-specific regions such as image processing and text processing, as detailed by [4]. Different deep learning architectures can be used for the performance of operations involved in finding accuracy and false-positive rates. Then static and dynamic data can be analyzed. Static data analysis deals with the static data that have not been experimented with, whereas dynamic data deal with the experimented data that can be extracted based on the importance of features. In machine learning, algorithms like the random forest, Naive Bayes, and Support Vector Machine have employed the analysis of data for classification. The performance of the Random Forest and deep neural networks has been compared for the process of classification. The machine learning and deep learning methods are used in network analysis [5]. Machine learning techniques are mainly used for classification and regression-based analysis based on the training data. In machine learning, deep learning is a subdomain. Deep learning follows the behavior patterns of the human brain for perceptive learning. Deep learning techniques are applied to images, text, and other areas. Optimization-based problems are solved using deep belief networks layer by layer. Similarly, a CNN is an important architecture with multiple layers that use respective relationships for minimizing the size of the parameters to gain the performance of the learned data. The main points of distinction between machine learning and deep learning are based on the major characteristics of dependency in data, dependency in hardware, and feature extraction. The training phase of ML involves spending less time than DL. But in testing, DL performs faster than ML [6].

8.5   FEATURE EXTRACTION AND FEATURE ENGINEERING

Feature extraction [4] have been discussed based on static and dynamic analyses. Traditional machine learning algorithms such as Random Forest use sci-kit python libraries in this process. For deep neural network, it uses Keras framework and tensor flow as the back end. Different layers of 2, 4, and 7 have been used. The activation function of the exponential linear unit is used excluding the final layer. Authors [5] have indicated feature learning as the process of learning the domain data that are converted to understandable patterns as features for training the data. A machine learning model [7] has been implemented for federated industries. A deep neural network [8] has been suggested for detecting envy features. They used to filter 128, window size or weight as 1, and activation function as tanh for this envy process. Three CNN layers have been used for predicting accuracy. The features are learned and allow for the generation of new features through feature engineering.

8.6   MODEL REPRESENTATION AND GENERATION

Many models can be implemented for various types of applications. Each model is built based on the feature set. Here deep learning models of CNN and RNN are the possible models for the prediction of the efficiency of the output. In CNN the sequential data are difficult to preserve due to memory loss. But in RNN, the sequential data are preserved and used for processing the next procedure of applying data. A simple RNN model has some issues relating to the vanishing gradient problem. LSTM, GRU, and ResNet models are used for overcoming this issue. Deep learning architecture will provide the model as a weight matrix that preserves the information in the training data. This chapter maps the dataset as a row vector with padding for learning the model representation.

8.7   RELATED WORK

A survey has been done related to deep learning architectures, deep learning, and web services, deep learning performance evaluation.

8.7.1   DEEP LEARNING ARCHITECTURES

The set of web services [9] have been experimented from the programmable-web repository for the classification of web services using the Wide and Bi-LSTM model. The classification was deputed for similar functions. The services have been classified but not based on the user access patterns with web service states. With states, the status of the web service can be identified. Different variations in LSTM (FC LSTM) [10] have been designed for the measurement of the performance with respect to service description in the XML language. Tags were used to understand the functions using filtering. They adopted a context-oriented technique. This functional and context-based LSTM provided performance measures, namely f-measure and diversity in comparison with tag-LSTM, F-LSTM, and C-LSTM. In relevance to the nature of data used, CNN, LSTM, GRU, and RNN are appropriate for model validation. The parameters that are generally tuned are learning Rate, Number of epochs, Activation function, Layer level details, Optimizer, and Batch size.

8.8   DEEP LEARNING AND WEB SERVICES

Many deep learning and machine learning architectures have been used for the assessment of the performance evaluation of web services. There was a gap in the analysis of the web service behavior based on user satisfaction. The machine learning model [11] has been proposed for locating design defects. Authors [12] used stacked denoising auto encoders for feature extraction. A machine learning approach [13] has been proposed a for deep sources of the web. The sources were structured resources. Normally, classification is done for images and text. The existing works do not deal with the web service user classification based on the web service states. A deep neural network [14] have been presented for web service classification in 50 service categories. Serve-net adopts two-dimensional CNN and bidirectional LSTM for extracting the features of the past and future of text in various contexts. The model used basic machine learning models to advanced models of deep learning architectures for service classification. The classification was done with respect to the domain and the size of the services. The study has not concentrated on why the user is not having the same experience as a web service consumer. This limitation is the main motivation in analyzing deep learning architectures for web service user diagnostics.

8.9   DEEP LEARNING PERFORMANCE EVALUATION

Performance parameters [14] are proposed for Top-5 and Top-1 accuracy. They have been tested with all the possible machine learning models and compared based on the training and testing accuracy. Models such as LSTM, BI-LSTM, Naive Bayes, Support Vector Machine, CNN, and Random Forest were used for the assessment of the performance parameters. Web services [15] are analyzed for embedding a text with deep learning. Similarity between the methods of the service was found. Facebook, Twitter, and Hadoop functions were used for the comparison. Some effective measures of deep learning [16] have been suggested. They found the possibility of identifying measures of effectiveness to extend up to the measure of performance. The measure of effectiveness includes the efficiency of data by throughput, completeness in the aspect of problem illustration, and robustness in the aspect of security. Performance measures of efficiency in computation, speed of the operation, and assurance of learning a model were included. Precision is the measure used for information gain. Performance measures of execution time and accuracy are used [17]. Training and testing time were considered as execution time of the model. Despite the application of deep learning architecture in all the fields like image processing, text embedding the web service performance measurement of web service states has not been done. The deep neural network learning model helped obtain higher accuracy. The performance parameters used are accuracy and Log-loss of training and validation shown in Equation (8.1) and (8.2).

$$\text{Accuracy} = \frac{\text{Number of Correct Predictions}}{\text{Total Number of Predictions Made}} \tag{8.1}$$

$$H_p(q) = -\frac{1}{N}\sum_{i=1}^{N} y_i.\log\big(p(y_i)\big) + (1-y_i).\log\big(1-p(y_i)\big) \tag{8.2}$$

Machine learning performs analytics to predict the future based on current and historical data by data modeling and has the ability to process enormous volumes data. It uses various modeling techniques to analyze the data, visualize the trends, and help businesses make informed decisions. The basic machine learning models get better over time, but it still needs manual supervision to improve its predictions. If the machine learning algorithm provides an inaccurate prediction, the algorithm and the other parameters must be adjusted manually.

But deep learning has an artificial neural network, structures, and algorithms in multiple layers. It can process, analyze the labeled/unlabeled structured/unstructured data, and self-learn based on historic and current data. Deep learning can understand the change in the data stream and provide informed decisions by itself. Moreover, deep learning provides classifying the data with a probabilistic score for all the classes. In the nonlinear activation function, adaptive weight process together with the optimizers improves the learning with the reduction of error. Hence, the deep learning architectures CNN and its variants LSTM, RNN, and GRU are being tried with the web server user data. The research is unique, as there has been no deep learning architectures experimented with web service user data.

8.10   CNN AND WEB SERVICE DIAGNOSTICS

Convolution neural network is a deep learning algorithm that has the ability to take inputs as images and assign priorities to them, and that is to the weights and the biases to various features of the images and the text to indicate the differences between them or classify them. The amount of preprocessing required for training the model is much less than for the other algorithms available. The architecture of the CNN is very similar to the process and working of the human brain nodes, basically built on the reference to the human brain. There are three layers in the CNN: an input layer, a hidden layer, and an output layer. It has the ability to capture the low-level features of the images such as colors, edges, etc. Some layers are added to the CNN. These provide the ability to adapt to the high-level features of the images also. Two types of results are produced of which one increases the dimensionality while the other keeps it constant. This is achieved by applying the correct padding. Web service state logs with padding are modeled using CNN.

8.11   CONVOLUTION NEURAL NETWORK

Convolution neural network is one of the deep neural network models. It uses special convolution and pooling operations and performs parameter sharing. The main advantage of a CNN is that there is no need for human supervision; the model automatically detects the important features. The input is fed into the layers of convolution and pooling and then on to the fully connected layer.

Convolution layer: The convolution layer is the first layer in CNN. This layer mathematically merges two sets of information. The input is fed into the convolution filter, which then converts this into a feature map. The convolution filter is also called a kernel. A pooling layer is also there in this filter where element-wise matrix multiplication at each location is performed, and then the result is summed.

The resultant feature maintains the dimensionality of the input—for example, if the incoming input is of the dimension 32*32*3 and the given filter can be of size 5*5*3. The height, width, and depth should be mentioned in the filter, and the depth size should always be the same as that of the input depth size. The depth is normally the RGB factor of the input. Operations can be performed for maintaining the height and depth padding at the same levels.

Striding: The number of strides is the number of steps convolution filter moved on each step. The default value for the convolution filter is always 1. In the case of bigger strides, the resultant feature map becomes small due to a chance of skipping the potential locations that can happen.

Padding: Padding is performed for maintaining the same dimensionality as that of the input. Padding involves adding zero around the input. In some cases, it can also mean the addition of the edge values to the surrounding values.

Nonlinearity: Nonlinearity is another major component and is a necessary factor for the layer. It gives the system more power and strength. The major factors to be considered are that the nonlinear functions should be differentiable and have a degree more than 1, as well as curvature on plotting. ReLU is the general activation function used. The feature map also has the ReLU applied to it along with the filter.

Pooling: Pooling reduces the dimensionality of the input. This reduces the number of parameters, which shortens the training time and helps in reducing overfitting. Pooling also reduces the height and width and keeps the depth intact. This down-sampling is applied to each feature map independently. Pooling down samples on the feature map allows retention of important information without any loss. Pooling has no special parameters involved. The commonly used polling method is max pooling.

General pooling -> 2*2 window size with stride 2 and no padding
Convolution -> 3*3 window size, stride 1 and padding

Hyper Parameters: The major hyperparameters include filter size, filter count, stride, and padding. The filter can be set as 3*3 or 5*5 or 7*7. The filter size can also be set to 1*1. A filter count values are always the power of 2, mostly between 32 or 1024. The system can be more powerful by increasing the number of filters counts, although the number of parameters can be increased by increasing the count. The number of counts can be increased by moving deeper into the network. Stride value is usually set to 1 and padding is added.

Fully Connected Layer: The fully connected layer is the final layer in the CNN. After the convolution and pooling layer, the final vector is passed onto a fully connected layer. The fully connected layer expects the 1D vector and the incoming vector value is 3D, which is flattened to 1D. The final fully convolution layer stays over all the other layers that finally decide on the outcome of classification assigned the probability of the classification input image.

Dropout: Dropout is another feature on CNN that helps the system provide accurate results. In this feature, almost 50 percent of the neurons are dropped out at each iteration. This disables the existing 50 percent of the neurons from forcing the rest of the neurons to work independently to their level best and enhancing the working of the model. This CNN architecture is extended by fine-tuning the parameters in Table 8.2.

8.12   RECURRENT NEURAL NETWORK AND WEB SERVICES

8.12.1   RECURRENT NEURAL NETWORK

A recurrent neural network is a class of neural networks. Unlike other neural networks, this one remembers the past, and all its decisions are influenced by what it has learned from the past. RNN can take in one or more input vectors and can produce one or more output vectors. The output vector is fully influenced by hidden state representation. Hence, the same input can produce different outputs depending on the previous inputs in the series. The major application areas include language translation, classification, and image captioning. The incoming words are first transformed into machine-readable vectors, and then these vector values are processed in a one-by-one sequence.

The input and hidden state are mapped with a vector. These vectors then go through tanh activation. Now the output is the new hidden state or the memory of the network. Using tanh is meant to keep the values flowing through the network between −1 or 1.

Sigmoid is another one almost like the tanh and so, instead of from −1 to 1, sigmoid squishes the values between 0 and 1.

The major steps are as follows:

Step 1: The input is fed into the network at.
Step 2: The current state in RNN is a combination of the current input and its previous state ht.
Step 3: Hence, the next step ht becomes ht-1
Step 4: Move as many steps as possible forward and combine all the information from the previous states can be combined.
Step 5: Each time when each step is completed, the current final state is used for the calculation of the output yt.
Step 6: In the next step, the output is compared with the actual output, and an error is generated.
Step 7: After the error is calculated, the error is back-propagated to the network for updating the weights.

The RNN architecture is extended by fine-tuning the parameters as presented in Table 8.3. Hence,

8.13   LONG SHORT-TERM MEMORY AND WEB SERVICE STATE DIAGNOSTICS

8.13.1   LONG SHORT-TERM MEMORY

The above-mentioned RNN architecture suffers from short-term memory, as it suffers from the vanishing gradient problem during the back-propagation. While updating the gradient weights, the gradient shrinks as it back propagates through the network. Hence, many of the vectors are so small that they are not even considered after some more steps. This may be the cause of loss in some of the important data. Gradient update rule: In RNN, the layers with small gradient values stop learning. This usually occurs in the earlier layers. Hence, many useful features are lost after each iteration, RNNs can forget it.

LSTM is a solution for this. LSTM obtains an internal mechanism called the gates to regulate this information. This keeps relevant/important information alone for making predictions. LSTM consists of cell states and various gates. The cell states carry information in the sequence chain, making this the memory of the network that can keep small/shrinking values. Gates allow or decide which information is allowed on the cell state. LSTM contains three gates, namely the forget gate, the input gate, and the output gate.

Forget gate: Here the information from the previous hidden and the current input is passed through the sigmoid function, and the values become 0 and 1.
0 near to forget
1 near to keep
Input gate: This one updates the cell states. The previous and the current together pass through the sigmoid.

0 is not an important feature.

1 is not a very important feature.

Output gate: The gate that contains information on the previous input decides on what the next hidden state should be. This contains the information on the previous input.

The major steps are as follows:

Step 1: The previous hidden state and the current input value are passed on to the sigmoid function. The modified cell state is passed on to the tanh function.

Step 2: The sigmoid output and the tanh output are multiplied, and the product forms the hidden states' decision on which information must be kept in the hidden layer based on the above-mentioned results.

Step 3: The current output is now in the hidden state.

Step 4: Finally, the new cell state and the new hidden state are then carried over to the next step.

The web service user data ideally map as a vector string that can be classified using LSTM. The parameters are tuned and presented in tables.

8.14   GATED RECURRENT UNITS AND WEB SERVICE STATE DIAGNOSTICS

GRUs are almost like the LSTM but a bit newer than the LSTM. This has operations of a smaller number and is much faster to train than LSTM. Compared to LSTM, this does not have an output gate but has parameters of a smaller number than those of the LSTM. They have a hidden state but not a cell state.

The two gates here are the reset gate and the update gate.

The update gate is similar to the forget and input gates of the LSTM, and this can decide which of those can be added and which can be thrown away.

The reset gate decides on how much past information to forget. Every node in the convolution neural architecture [5] is not connected with each layer. So deep learning architecture provides the solution to connect the nodes in all the layers for better performance. The sequence of data LSTM is long short-term memory and GRU is gated recurrent unit. These two techniques are variants of the recurrent neural network. Traditional RNN uses the softmax function for prediction in the final layer and cross-entropy is used for computing the loss. The authors have suggested GRU-SVM for improved performance instead of the GRU–softmax model.

CNN [18] is used for feature extraction and the representation of input as a vector. CNN involves deep learning of neurons with convolution operation. It uses a kernel with the size s for feeding the input to the hidden layers. The activation function of ReLU can be used. Max pooling or average pooling can be used for reducing the dimensions of the data to feed for the nest layer as the input. CNN generates improved accuracy. It can be used in many application domains such as image processing, computer vision, and speech recognition. CNN is compared with SVM to check for accuracy in performance. Accuracy generated is based on the feature set.

A service recommendation model [19] has been introduced using a generative adversarial network for combining related services to the users in order to enable productive access to it. The preferred services are listed for the users based on the mashup data created. The dataset from programmable web is used for experimenting with the developed model. GRU is efficient as it provides feed-forward learning toward associating the features in the web service user log.

8.15   DATASET

The dataset in Table 8.1 used in this research work was collected from a custom-built web server on the C\# platform. The data was collected as the users logged in, and the time of the request to be processed was recorded along with its status code. The web service log contained six "6" labeled columns that were Time Spent on Discovery Invocation Time, Time Spent on Discovered State, Time Spent on Invoked State, Time Spent on Running State, Time Spent on Closed State, HTTP Status Code. The HTTP codes recorded were −200, 400, 404, 407, 500, 503, and 511.

The following steps were followed for obtaining the desired results. To start with, the complete dataset was divided into two parts, 75 percent for training and 25 percent for testing. The dataset with which the model is trained is known as the training dataset. The performance of the model was measured using the test dataset. The test

TABLE 8.1
Sample Dataset

Discovery Invocation Time	Time Spent on Discovered State	Time Covered on Invoked State	Time Spent on Running State	Time Spent on Halt State	Time Spent on Closed State	HTTP Status Code
0.0004	0.9471	0.101	0.8561	0.002	0.004	200
0.0004	0.992	0.12	0.8648	0.002	0.003	200
0.0003	1.0722	0.102	2.009	0.002	0.003	200
0.0003	0.994	0.101	0.8754	0.002	0.003	200
0.0003	1.0121	0	0	0	0	503
0.0003	0.9825	0.102	0.9579	0.002	0.003	200
0.0003	0.7372	0.101	0	0	0	404
0.0003	0.9533	0.1011	0	0	0	400
0.0003	0.9813	0.102	0.8647	0.002	0.003	200
0.0003	0.9693	0.102	0.8664	0.001	0.003	200
0.0003	0.9652	0.102	0.8625	0.002	0.003	200
0.0005	0.9652	0.102	0.8625	0.002	0.003	200
0.0003	1.0564	0.102	0.8796	0	0	407
0.0003	0.9562	0.101	0.8503	0.002	0.003	200
0	0.9581	0.102	0.8491	0.002	0.003	200
0.0004	0.9919	0.102	0.8491	0.002	0.003	200
0.0004	0.9443	0.102	0.8479	0.002	0.003	200
0.0004	0.7454	0.102	0.8722	0	0	511
0.0004	0.9979	0.101	1.0774	0.002	0.003	200
0.0004	0.7275	0.101	0.9696	0.0014	0.0025	200
0.0004	1.089	0.1011	0	0	0	500

set is what is commonly used in the evaluation of the competing models. "Label encoder" and "one hot encoder" were then applied for obtaining the features from the data. The "label encoder" simply arranges the data according to the respective labels and gives each of the labels a unique identifier. The "one hot encoder" converts the training dataset into a categorical one, which means that each label has its own column that will hold true value for the part of the data to which it belongs.

The model was created using the following parameters: The batch size = 2, the Number of epochs is 500, Validation Split is 0.25. The model was a sequential model to which Convolutional2D was added. Maximum pooling was used in the models. The optimizer used was "Adam Optimizer"; the activation function used was "ReLU". The learning rate of the model was 0.001 and the decay value was 1e-6. The seed value used was 1. The seed value defines how many columns or values are shifted at a time for the window adding the filters.

8.16   RESULTS AND DISCUSSION

The data was split into 70 percent for training and 30 percent for testing. The logs were handled with four architectures, namely convolution neural network (CNN), long short-term memory (LSTM), gated recurrent unit (GRU), and recurrent neural network (RNN). The architectures were analyzed for finding out their suitability for the web service user logs. Class imbalance is when the number of positive samples is smaller than the number of negative samples. In this case, the positive samples are higher than the negative samples. Hence, the class imbalance problem does not occur in the proposed contribution.

8.16.1   CONVOLUTION NEURAL NETWORK

The parameters for convolution neural network design are presented in Table 8.2.

TABLE 8.2
Parameters of CNN

Hyper Parameters	Purpose	Value (Units)
Filters	To specify the number of kernels in each layer	256, 128, 64, 32 (powers of 2)
Dropout	To specify how much information to forget and how much to remember	0.3 (optimal 0.1–0.6)
Activation	To define the output of each node	Softmax (works best for a multiclass problem)
Train_test_split	To separate the input data into train and test data	0.8, 0.2, i.e., 80%:20% (widely accepted optimal range)
Epochs	To specify the number of times to go through the training data	100 (after trial and error, found this to be suitable for chosen data set)
Batch size	To specify the number of training samples in one pass	12 (for the dataset used, it seems to be a reasonable value)
Kernel_size	Size of each kernel	1
Max Pooling	Pooling for one dimensional input	1

The performance is presented in the following figures.

Figure 8.1 shows the exponential increase in the training accuracy of the model followed by a fluctuation with a gradual increase till its stopping value. Figure 8.2 shows the overall increase in CNN accuracy for the validation data set with timely depressions indicating the model making mistakes but with a gradual learning of mistakes. Figure 8.3 exhibits the consistent lower losses suffered by the following the 20th epoch, indicating the efficient generalization of the model. Figure 8.4 displays the consistent lower loss suffered by the model following the 20th epoch indicating

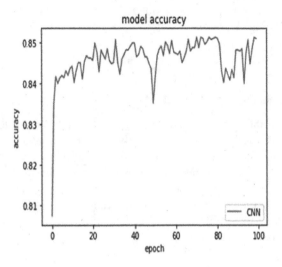

FIGURE 8.1   Model accuracy.

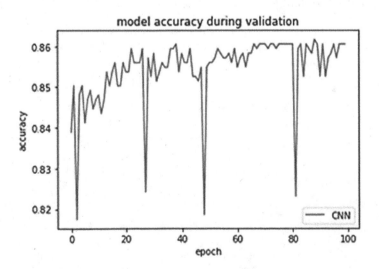

FIGURE 8.2   Model accuracy during validation.

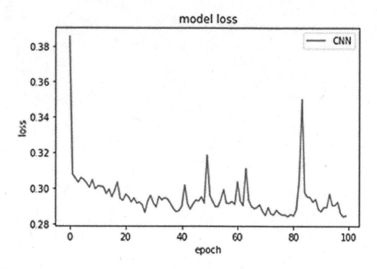

FIGURE 8.3 Model loss.

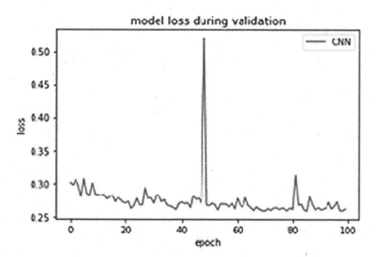

FIGURE 8.4 Model loss during validation.

the efficient generalization of the model. Figure 8.5 points out to the uniform decrease in training accuracy of the LSTM network indicating the ability of the network to learn patterns within the training dataset. Figure 8.6 provides the observation of the smoothening of the accuracy of LSTM validation following the 30th epoch indicating the saturation in generalization. Figure 8.7 shows the consistent decrease in the training loss pointing to the efficient training process. Figure 8.8 displays decrease in the validation loss decreases just like the training loss indicating the generalization in the network too. Figure 8.9 shows the consistent increase in training accuracy until

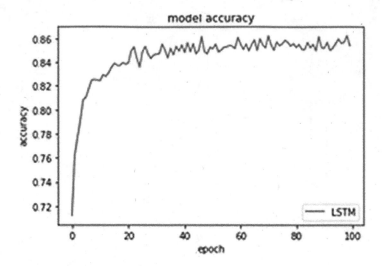

FIGURE 8.5 Model accuracy.

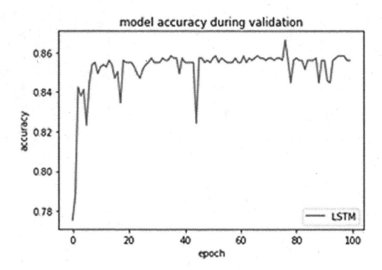

FIGURE 8.6 Model accuracy during validation.

reaching the 60th epoch followed by an overall saturated effect. Figure 8.10 shows the absence of any log change in the validation accuracy following the 30th epoch indicating the achievement of the maximum generalization of the model. Figure 8.11 displays the gradual decrease in the training loss showing that the process has reached local minima. Figure 8.12 exhibits a decrease in the validation loss also and a smoothing out after the 40th epoch indicating the model having reached its peak validation performance (with these hyper parameters).

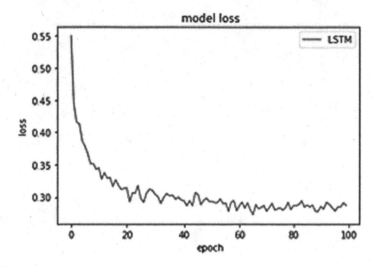

FIGURE 8.7   Model loss.

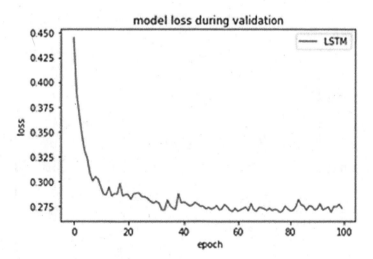

FIGURE 8.8   Model loss during validation.

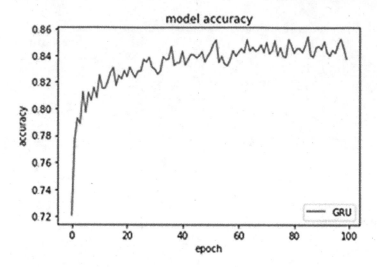

FIGURE 8.9   Model accuracy.

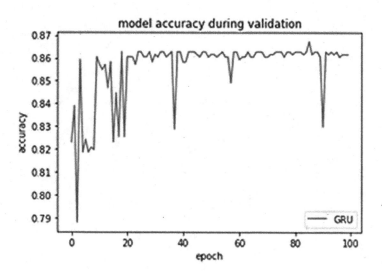

FIGURE 8.10   Model accuracy during validation.

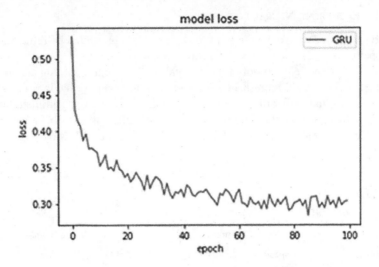

FIGURE 8.11 Model loss.

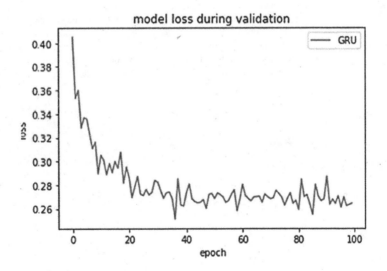

FIGURE 8.12 Model loss during validation.

8.16.2 RECURRENT NEURAL NETWORK

The parameters for recurrent neural network design are presented in Table 8.3.

The performance is presented in the following figures.

Figure 8.13 shows clear proof of the gradual increase in the training accuracy and instability in accuracy. Figure 8.14 shows validation accuracy having many peaks and depressions, indicating the model ending up at the same local minima after a few steps. Figure 8.15 shows training loss as the lowest at the 68th epoch, so the training process needs to be stopped at the 68th epoch following the early stopping protocol.

TABLE 8.3
Parameters of RNN

Hyper Parameters	Purpose	Value (Units)
Hidden Nodes	To specify the number of neurons in each layer	25, 128, 64, 32 (powers of 2)
Dropout	To specify how much information to forget and how much to remember	0.3 (optimal 0.1–0.6)
Activation	To define the output of each node	Softmax (works best for a multiclass problem)
Train_test_split	To separate the input data into train and test data	0.8, 0.2, i.e., 80%:20% (widely accepted optimal range)
Epochs	To specify the number of times to go through the training data	100 (after trial and error, found this to be suitable for chosen dataset)
Batch size	To specify the number of training samples in one pass	12 (for the dataset used, it seems to be a reasonable value)

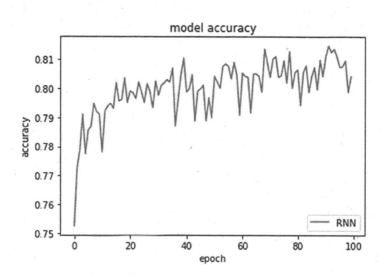

FIGURE 8.13 Model accuracy.

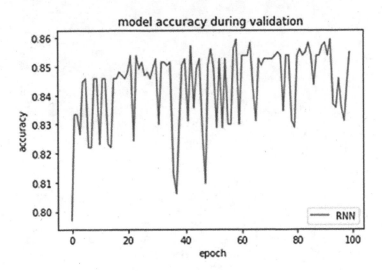

FIGURE 8.14   Model accuracy during validation.

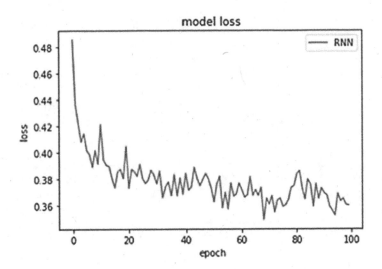

FIGURE 8.15   Model loss.

8.16.3   COMPARISON OF CNN, LSTM, GRU, RNN

Figure 8.16 shows the model loss during validation. Figure 8.17 displays the greater accuracy of LSTM compared to other architectures. The inference is that the performance of LSTM network is better on the training data. Figure 8.18 shows that, based on the accuracy during validation, LSTM outperforms other algorithms based on the accuracy seen during validation. (At many epochs, the LSTM accuracy is just a bit

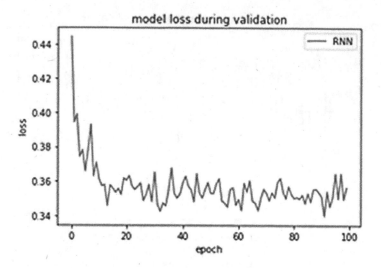

FIGURE 8.16   Model loss during validation.

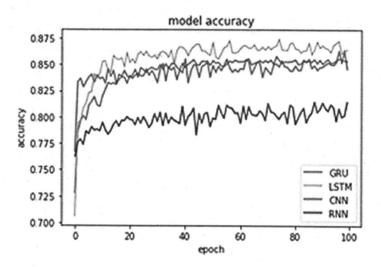

FIGURE 8.17   Comparison of model accuracy.

higher than other architectures.) Figure 8.19 indicates LSTM learning the training data very well. Figure 8.20 shows the model loss during validation. LSTM is seen having lower loss during training. The same is with the validation set. This shows the LSTM does not overfit the training data and performs well in terms of generalization.

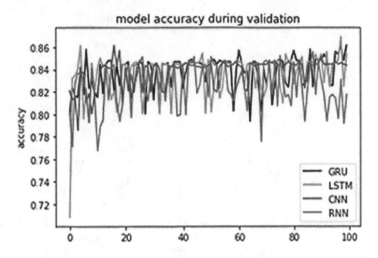

FIGURE 8.18   Comparison of model accuracy during validation.

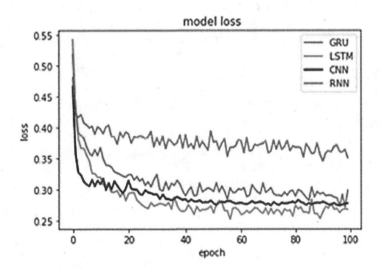

FIGURE 8.19   Comparison of model loss.

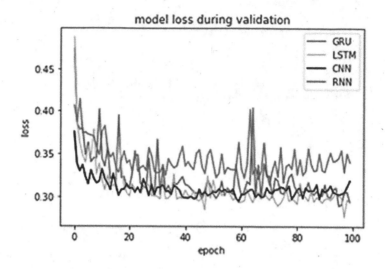

FIGURE 8.20 Comparison of model loss during validation.

8.17 SUMMARY

This chapter analyzed how CNN, GRU, LSTM, an RNN can be used for classifying the available dataset relevant to web services. The logs contain 180 requests and are classified. The deep learning architectures are evaluated with 70 percent for training and 30 percent for testing. The conclusion based on the graphs relating to training and validation is that the LSTM network outperforms the GRU and RNN in terms of accuracy in both the training data and validation data. The study concludes that these results can be providing insight for web user diagnostics with a higher level of accuracy. The limitations are:

(a) CNN, RNN, and GRU architectures have been explored for the first time with web user state logs.
(b) The research can be optimized for reducing the vanishing gradient problem.

REFERENCES

1. Goodfellow, I., Bengio, Y., and Courville, A. *Deep learning*, MIT Press, 2016.
2. LeCun, Y., Bengio, Y. and Hinton, G. "Deep learning", *Nature* 521, no. 7553, 2015: 436–444.
3. Bu, S.-J. and Cho, S.-B.. "A hybrid system of deep learning and learning classifier system for database intrusion detection", *International Conference on Hybrid Artificial Intelligence Systems*, Springer, (2017): 615–625
4. Sewak, M., Sahay, S. K., and Rathore, H. "Comparison of deep learning and the classical machine learning algorithm for the malware detection", *19th IEEE/ACIS International Conference on Software Engineering, Artificial Intelligence, Networking and Parallel/ Distributed Computing (SNPD)*, IEEE, (2018): 293–296

5. Xin, Y., Kong, L., Liu, Z., Chen, Y., Li, Y., Zhu, H., Gao, M., Hou, H., and Wang, C. "Machine learning and deep learning methods for cybersecurity", *IEEE Access* 6 (2018): 35365–35381

6. Paterakis, N. G., Mocanu, E., Gibescu, M., Stappers, B., and van Alst, W. "Deep learning versus traditional machine learning methods for aggregated energy demand prediction", *2017 IEEE PES Innovative Smart Grid Technologies Conference Europe (ISGT-Europe)*, (2017): 1–6.

7. Verma, D., White, G., and de Mel, G. "Federated ai for the enterprise: A web services based implementation", *IEEE International Conference on Web Services (ICWS)* (2019): 20–27.

8. Liu, H., Xu, Z., and Zou, Y. "Deep learning based feature envy detection", *Proceedings of the 33rd ACM/IEEE International Conference on Automated Software Engineering*, ACM, (2018): 385–396.

9. Ye, H., Cao, B., Peng, Z., Chen, T., Wen, Y., and Liu, J. "Web services classification based on wide and bi-lstm model", *IEEE Access* 7, (2019): 43697–43706.

10. Shi, M., Liu, J. et al. "Functional and contextual attention-based lstm for service recommendation in mashup creation", *IEEE Transactions on Parallel and Distributed Systems*, **30**, no. 5, (2018): 1077–1090.

11. Ouni, A., Daagi, M., Kessentini, M., Bouktif, S., and Gammoudi, M. M. "A machine learning-based approach to detect web service design defects", *IEEE International Conference on Web Services (ICWS)*, (2017): 532–539.

12. Bai, B., Fan, Y., Tan, W., and Zhang, J. "Dltsr: A deep learning framework for recommendation of long-tail web services," *IEEE Transactions on Services Computing* 13, no. 1, (2020): 73–85.

13. Xu, H., Zhang, C., Hao, X., and Hu, Y. "A machine learning approach classification of deep web sources", *Fourth International Conference on Fuzzy Systems and Knowledge Discovery (FSKD 2007)*, IEEE, vol. 4 (2007): 561–565.

14. Yang, Y., Ke, W., Wang, W., and Zhao, Y. "Deep learning for web services classification", *IEEE International Conference on Web Services (ICWS)*, IEEE, (2019): 440–442.

15. Miyagi, T., Rupasingha, R. A., and Paik, I. "Analysis of web service using word embedding by deep learning", *9th International Conference on Awareness Science and Technology (iCAST)*, IEEE, (2018): 336–341.

16. Blasch, E., Liu, S., Liu, Z., and Zheng, Y. "Deep learning measures of effectiveness, 'NAECON 2018-IEEE National Aerospace and Electronics Conference'", *IEEE National Aerospace and Electronics Conference* (2018): 254–261.

17. Liu, L., Wu, Y., Wei, W., Cao, W., Sahin, S., and Zhang, Q. "Benchmarking deep learning frameworks: Design considerations, metrics and beyond", In *2018 IEEE 38th International Conference on Distributed Computing Systems (ICDCS)*, IEEE, 2018: 1258–1269.

18. Loussaief, S. and Abdelkrim, A. "Deep learning vs. bag of features in machine learning for image classification", *International Conference on Advanced Systems and Electric Technologies (IC ASET)*, IEEE, (2018): 6–10.

19. Xie, F., Li, S., Chen, L., Xu, Y., and Zheng, Z. "Generative adversarial network based service recommendation in heterogeneous information networks", *IEEE International Conference on Web Services (ICWS)* (2019): 265–272.

9 D-SegNet
A Modified Encoder-Decoder Approach for Pixel-Wise Classification of Brain Tumor from MRI Images

K. Aswani and D. Menaka

Noorul Islam Center for Higher Education, Kumaracoil, India

CONTENTS

9.1 INTRODUCTION

Brain tumor segmentation from MRI images has started decades back. The need for image processing in tumor analysis came from the fact that human inspection of MRI images can be misjudged and information may be lost during the process. The study of the human brain has greatly improved in terms of details because of the development of advanced image processing tools. These tools' ability to zoom in, better region-of-interest selection, ability to select multiple slices in a window, better registration, segmentation, and MRI processing algorithms are expanding the capability of automatic tumor segmentation horizon [1]. Analysis of MRI images using image processing started from conventional methods, and later developed into a machine learning (ML) process. The latter features are extracted from the images using mathematical procedures, which are then used to train a model. Though the process seems simple, the difficulty in image feature extraction, determining how the feature size required, and the performance of the model trained made the ML methods incompatible with medical standards.

Deep learning (DL) is another sophisticated method and is widely popular at this time. The advantage of DL methods is that they combine the feature extraction and training process, thus reducing the human effort considerably. Like ML methods, DL methods are also divided into supervised and unsupervised learning methods. In unsupervised learning, image patterns are identified from the data and learn to classify the tumor from other pixels. This method has the advantage that previous data is not required for pattern identification. But supervised learning methods perform better than unsupervised methods in performance measures. Massive volumes of data required for training the model still pose a problem for using supervised DL models for image processing in medical fields. The reason is the availability of medical images. Medical images availability is limited due to a variety of legal and other related issues. This is overcome by a public database made available by BRATS in early 2012 by releasing its first public database named BRATS2012 [2] for tumor segmentation and analysis. The database has been improved over the years, with its different types of data including basic sequence like T1-weighted imaged, more enhanced T2-weighted images, and T2-FLAIR and excellent ground truth images for supervised learning.

Supervised DL methods mainly depend on convolutional neural networks (CNN) for feature extraction. Networks like U-Net and SegNet use convolutional layers in their architecture for feature extraction from MRI images. Since the scope of DL is large, we only focus on the instance pixel-wise classification of brain tumors from MRI images here. U-Net or SegNet perform the semantic segmentation using encoder-decoder architecture, and thus can be considered as a convolutional network with full connection between the layers. The major difference between U-Net and SegNet is that SegNet saves the pooling indices and will transfer it to an expansion path for its operation, which results in lower memory requirements, whereas in U-Net all feature maps are transferred, resulting in higher memory requirements. Thus in SegNet, the trainable parameters are reduce to 17.4MB of available memory, compared to the 134MB of U-Net. During decoding using the max pooling indices, SegNet can find the corresponding encoder layer and the weights can be applied, making the training process easier. At its core, a SegNet uses VGG16 as its encoder section. It is implemented using VGG16 [3] with all the convolutional layers in it. The encoder and decoder parts complement each other. The decoder section also uses a pixel classification layer for segmentation. The architecture of SegNet is shown in Figure 9.1.

Traditional SegNet uses square patches in its training procedure [4]. For agricultural images taken by satellites SegNet has used patch sizes 96×96, 160×160, 192×192, with the 92×92 patch size lately emerging as the most accurate one. The square patches are easy to apply for filtering operations, but in the case of brain tumors, the complexity in their spatial variation results in most of the information being lost if square patches are used. Here we employ a non-square patch for feature extraction MRI images. Two patches in horizontal and vertical directions are extracted

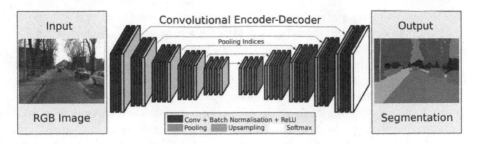

Input — Convolutional Encoder-Decoder — Output

Pooling Indices

Conv + Batch Normalisation + ReLU
Pooling   Upsampling   Softmax

RGB Image — Segmentation

FIGURE 9.1 SegNet architecture.

from images for detailed analysis. These patches were processed using dual encoder architecture. The features obtained from the dual encoders were then optimized and fused to apply for decoding. This modified SegNet is called dual SegNet (D-SegNet). The contribution of this work is termed below.

- We avoid traditional square patches and employ patches in horizontal and vertical direction to get more spatial information from MRI images.
- A dual encoder structure is proposed for processing patches in horizontal and vertical directions.
- Measured features were optimized using singular value decomposition (SVD) and fused and fed into the decoder for final processing.

9.2   LITERATURE REVIEW

Automatic segmentation of tumors from MRI images has started almost three decades ago. From simple PCA it is developed using DL methods. The advancement in the field is mainly due to the accuracy in segmentation needed for medical analysis. We present the development of brain tumor studies [5] in detail. That study analyzes various PCA methods, machine learning, and deep learning methods in detail and presents their advantages and disadvantages.

Since the development of CNN, tumor segmentation using deep learning methods has received considerable attention. Different CNN architectures are available for the classification and segmentation of tumors. One of these types is presented in [6]. Here the authors present a CNN network for segmentation of HGG and LGG types of tumors. Six convolutional layers were used for HGG and for convolutional layers for LGG. The kernel of 3 × 3 size is used, which, the authors claim, allows to avoid overfitting, reduces the number of weights, and facilitates the design of deep architecture. Both BRATS2013 and BRATs 2015 datasets were used and obtained a dice similarity value of .88 and .78, respectively. The authors of [7] implemented a CNN with multichannel input for feature extraction. The input image is segmented using super pixel segmentation by using saliency, and the obtained super pixels are applied to different CNN architecture. The obtained features from multichannel CNN are pooled to get the final features. Other multichannel architectures like exception model and the dense net are given in [8, 9]. They claim that a high feature recognition rate was achieved. A large database, similar to that used in machine learning, is required to train the network.

Generative adversarial network (GAN) is another DL-based model used for tumor analysis. The core part of the network consists of a generator–discriminator combination. The former produces the sample results from noisy input, and the latter classifies them as real or fake according to the real data. In [10] authors present a GAN for the tumor detection. The study presents the GAN method to generate various complex brain images like noise-to-image (pathological image from noise) and image-to-images (malignant image from benign images). This reduces the lack of data usually present in the deep learning methods for tumor analysis. Here the authors present a two-step GAN with domain adaptation (DA) [10]. As per the result, a sensitivity of 93 percent is obtained compared to the classic DA method. An unpaired residual network called RescueNet based on GAN is presented in [11] tumor clustering in brain. Preparing vast amounts of labeled data for deep network training is a time-consuming and difficult operation in automatic brain tumor analysis. The study presents an unpaired training strategy to train the suggested network to avoid the necessity for paired data. The results were tested on BRATS12015 and BRATS 2017 databases and the dice similarity scores were measured. The authors claim a dice score of 94.6 percent was obtained, which outperforms all the similar methods. A 3D GAN is presented in [12] for three-dimensional MRI images. The authors present a method called Vox2Vox, which segments the tumor from three-dimensional images in an accurate way. A whole tumor dice score of 87.2 percent was obtained.

One of the main drawbacks of supervised tumor detection methods is the huge database required for its training. The availability of medical data is restricted compared to other data used for classification or segmentation. The researchers are trying to solve the problem by treating the tumor as an anomaly found in the brain. Here only normal MRI images are required for training, which are easier to collect than tumor images. Autoencoder-based brain tumor segmentation is presented in [13]. The primary purpose of these efforts is to compress and restore healthy data to learn a model of normal anatomy. This method has the following advantages: it needs only normal data to train; can detect tumor parts that even supervised methods fail to detect; and can use different image resolutions and different model architectures. Latent regularized adversarial network [14] is another method for tumor detection. Only healthy and normal images are trained in this model. Furthermore, the method initially constrains the latent space with singular values before jointly optimizing the image space with multiple loss functions, which improves the feature-level separation of normal and abnormal samples. For tumor segmentation BRATS dataset is used, and the obtained results shows the merit of semi-supervised methods over supervised ones. In [15] the authors propose the unsupervised Medical Anomaly Detection Generative Adversarial Network (MADGAN), a unique dual technique for detecting problems in brain tissues using multi-sequence MRI with a GAN for MRI slice regeneration. They mainly used T1-weighted brain MRI images for diagnosing Alzheimer's disease and brain metastases/various illnesses. The AUC score shows the MDGAN is efficient in detecting AD. We have done some research in this area and published our contribution in [16]. We employ dual autoencoder-based architecture for a semi-supervised method where only normal MRI images are trained. Tumor pixels are detected as anomaly pixels and classified by a simple distance classifier. The model is trained on BRATS2015 dataset. The method is matched against supervised and unsupervised methods, with commendable results.

Pixel-wise segmentation is another area where the tumor pixels are classified as instance segmentation. In [4] an architecture named SegNet is presented, which employs pixel-wise segmentation of images via an encoder–decoder arrangement. The architecture is topologically similar to VGG16 [17] network. The decoder network's job is to convert the feature map from encoder to a full-feature map suitable for pixel-wise classification. SegNet employs a unique mechanism for up-sampling the encoder feature maps. The pooling indices saved from the encoder stage are later used in the decoder stage for up-sampling. The method performs well compared to methods in the same area in terms of memory usage and lower training time. A 3D semantic segmentation network based on ResNet50 [18] is presented in [19]. The method is tested using the BRATS2019 dataset. A Deep Supervised U-Attention Net for pixel-wise brain tumor segmentation is presented in [20]. The method combines U-Net, attention net, and a supervised stage. The method can generate feature maps for all the images with any resolution. A dice similarity of 83 percent is achieved for a whole tumor.

9.3 SYSTEM MODEL

The proposed D-SegNet architecture is shown in Figure 9.2. The main modules in the model are the patch extraction, encoder, feature fusion, and decoder.

9.3.1 DATABASE

Here we consider two types of patches: horizontal and vertical. In traditional SegNet only square patches are used. This can cause information loss because of the complex spatial variation of tumors in the brain. The length of the horizontal or vertical patch is determined based on the image size used for training. Here we use the BRATS2015 and BRATS2019 datasets for training and testing the model.

BRATS2015 and BRATS2019 are datasets containing images for brain tumor segmentation. Glioma is one of the common tumor found in the brain, so the analysis of gliomas is the most interesting tumor segmentation in brain tumor challenges. The BRATS2015 consists of 220 high-grade gliomas (HGG) and 54 low-grade gliomas

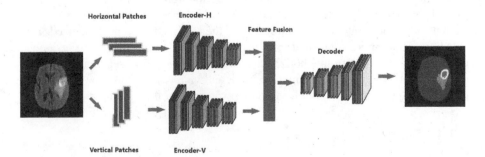

FIGURE 9.2 The proposed D-SegNet model.

(LGG) while BRATS2019 has 255 HGG and 76 LGG images [21]. Both datasets have 30 manually annotated images from the previous version BRATS2013. The remaining data in BRATS2015 contain pre- and post-operation images, which are labeled by experts, while BRATS2019 removed all post-operation images and all the images are relabeled again. Each MRI volume in both datasets has a size of $220 \times 220 \times 155$ and has for modalities based on contrast T1, T1c, T2, and FLAIR. Each ground truth tumor part is labeled for different sub-regions. They are Necrosis (NCR), Edema (ED), Non-Enhancing Tumor (NET), Enhancing/Active Tumor (AT), and Everything Else. This can be used for the acute analysis of tumor parts in a better way.

9.3.2 DATA PREPROCESSING

No further spatial processing is needed, since all the voxels in the image have an isotropic resolution of 1 mm^3. We mainly perform image normalization to bring the intensity of the images in the range of 0 to 1 as done in [22]. Image resizing is also needed to remove the black regions present. In this case, the size of each image is reduced to 128×128 from the original size. To remove outliers, each voxel is clipped from 2nd to 98th percentile. Even though the tumor has subregions, we are interested only in the tumor as a whole. So, we manually relabel all the subregion labels to 1 and non-tumor regions to 0 before fed to training in D-SegNet. The entire dataset is finally divided for training (80%) and testing (20%). The preprocessed images are then fed to patch extraction.

9.3.3 PATCH EXTRACTION

Here we perform patch extraction both horizontally and vertically. For horizontal patch extraction, we employed the following sizes 64×16 and 64×8, 32×16, and 32×8. For vertical patches, we use 16×64, 8×64, 16×32, and 8×32. These complementary patches are employed to identify local features as well as broad contextual data. Furthermore, without providing any new parameters to train, these patches are simple to sample. In general, it is known that, in a given region, a patch with non-squared dimension capture more information than the squared patches. This integrates contextual and symmetrical information simultaneously covers the entire tumor along one path from side to side. During the training process, these patches can help each other. After the feature extraction stage, the features obtained from horizontal and vertical patches are optimized and the best feature value is selected. This helps in gaining more contextual information about the tumor pixels. For example, if the feature obtained from a horizontal patch is not enough to segment as a tumor pixel, the vertical patch feature may be used, and vice versa. Thus the two different patches complement each other for faster convergence of the training process.

9.3.4 ENCODER

The proposed architecture has two encoders, a single decoder, and a pixel classification layer. The two encoders are named Encoder-H for horizontal patches and Encoder-V for vertical patches. There is an architecture difference in both encoders, as they are processing different types of patches. The convolutional layers of the network are derived from VGG16. It is designed for object classification so the initial weights in both encoders will be of classification. The final convolutional layer provides the high-resolution feature map of tumor MRI images. Using a set of filter banks the encoder performs convolution to produce feature maps. The obtained features are then fed to a batch normalization layer. After that, an activation using ReLU is performed. The dimension of the feature map is reduced by the resulting features from ReLU and pooled using a max-pooling layer of size 2 × 2 with a nonoverlapping stride. The output from max pooling is then subsampled by a factor of 2. Since we are using non-square patches, there is a chance of spatial shifts in different regions of the patches. Max pooling operation helps reduce these spatial shifts. A higher number of max pooling and subsampling layers can produce higher translation invariance for robust classification, which affects the spatial resolution of the feature maps. This is not helpful for image segmentation. As a result, boundary information must be captured and stored. It is not practical to store the entire feature map generated by the max-pooling process. Instead in SegNet, we store only the max-pooling indices having high values. This can be done using 2bits of memory for a max-pooling window of size 2 × 2. This reduces the accuracy slightly but is more efficient for practical applications. The process is illustrated in Figure 9.3. The figure depicts the process in horizontal patches, but it is also true for vertical patches in the opposite direction.

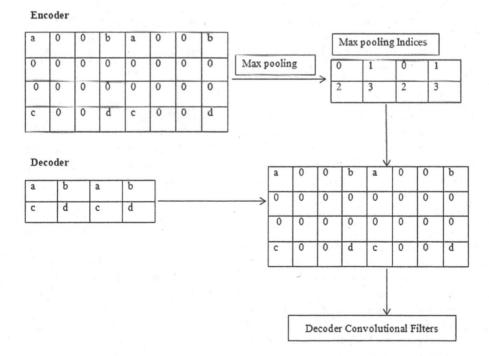

FIGURE 9.3 Encoder and decoder process in D-SegNet for horizontal (vertical) patches.

9.3.5 FEATURE FUSION

The two encoders perform feature extraction from dual patches, and these features are concatenated to generate higher-dimensional features. This also avoids the limitation of a single encoder feature extraction. But more features leads to higher connectivity correlation and redundancy of information. As a result, we use singular value decomposition (SVD) to pick features and reduce their dimensionality. The eigenvalue statistical rate is defined in this work, with eigenvalues maintained by SVD to the total number of components. The statistical rate of eigenvalue is set to 50 percent, which means 50 percent of the main components will be used.

9.3.6 DECODER

For each encoder layer, there is a corresponding decoder in D-SegNet architecture. Each layer in the decoder up-samples the features corresponding to the encoder layer from the max-pooling indices saved during encoding. The D-SegNet process is illustrated in Figure 9.3. A filter bank is used to convolve the feature maps to a dense feature map. Batch normalization is performed further on these feature maps. The decoder produces a multi-channel feature map. Each of these features are with same dimension as the encoder input. A softmax layer produces a probability map at the output of the final decoder. This probability map differentiates each pixel to tumor or non-tumor.

We compare the performance of D-SegNet with other semantic networks such as U-Net [23] and DeconvNet [24]. U-Net transfers the entire feature maps for decoding and thus suffers memory issues. With its fully connected layers, DeconvNet has a substantially bigger parameterization, requires more computing resources, and is more difficult to train end-to-end. The pixel classification layer categorize each pixel into tumor or non-tumor also it ignores any pixel not labeled during the training.

9.3.7 TRAINING

We use the BRATS 2015 and BRATS 2019 databases for training and evaluation. The images are preprocessed to a resolution of 128 × 128. The subregions in the labels are relabeled to a single tumor region so there are only two classes to classify the tumor and non-tumor pixels. Other than this local contrast normalization is also performed on the images.

Pretrained weights are applied to the encoder and decoder initially. The weights are obtained from a VGG16 network trained for object classification. The optimization is done using Stochastic Gradient Descent (SGD) with a fixed learning rate of 0.1 and momentum of 0.9. The basic SegNet architecture is obtained from the Caffe model and restructured for D-SegNet. The variants are trained until the training loss is converged. The training data is shuffled on during iterations with a mini batch of eight images, guaranteeing that each image is only used once every epoch. On a validation dataset, we choose the model that performs the best. We selected binary entropy as the objective function, and the loss for each mini-batch is summed up. The validation model with minimum loss is selected as the trained model.

9.3.8 EVALUATION

The performance of the proposed system is measured using tree assessment measures such as dice similarity coefficient (DSC), positive predictive value (PPV), and sensitivity. DSC is a measure of overlap between ground truth and segmented result. Sensitivity shows how much positive proportions are measured correctly.

$$DSC = 2TP / (FP + 2TP + FN) \qquad (9.1)$$

$$PPV = TP / (TP + FP) \qquad (9.2)$$

$$Sensitivity = TP / (TP + FN) \qquad (9.3)$$

where TP, FP, FN, FP are the true positive, false positive, false negative, and false positive detections, respectively.

9.4 RESULTS AND DISCUSSION

Here we present the results obtained using D-SegNet and its comparison with other similar methods. We give a section-wise analysis to provide a better understanding of the working of D-SegNet.

At first, the front-facing image slice is selected from the BRATS2015 and BRATS2019 databases. Some of these images are shown in Figure 9.4. The images are then preprocessed and patches were extracted. Different patch size 64 × 16, 64 × 8, 32 × 16, and 32 × 8 for horizontal patches and vertical patches were obtained by inverting the horizontal patches. The best result is obtained for 64 × 16 for horizontal and 16 × 64 for vertical patches respectively. These patches illustrated in Figure 9.5. The images show the spatial variations included in the non-squared patches.

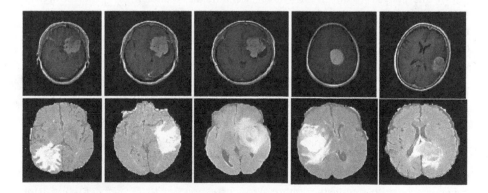

FIGURE 9.4 Top row shows samples images from the BRATS2015 dataset and the bottom row shows sample images from the BRATS2019.

FIGURE 9.5   Horizontal and vertical patches from the BRATS2015 and the BRATS2019.

The training procedure has to be repeated for all the patch sizes, while only vertical patch as its inverted form of horizontal is tested.

Both databases contain more than 500 images each with a size of 128. So the total number of horizontal patches comes around 8,000 and so as vertical patches for a patch size of 64 × 16. So the total number of patches comes around 16,000. These patches then fed to the dual encoders for feature extraction. The encoder takes a batch of patches for feature extraction. A mini batch size is 8 is found to be giving the best accuracy and speed in processing. Some of the feature maps obtained is shown in Figure 9.6. Each layer of the encoder produces a multiple of feature maps while its size is reduced. A total of 13 convolutional layers perform these operations.

Even though the feature maps does not contribute for any visual analysis the conv4 and conv13 (final layer) we can see that the spatial filtering performed on the patches. This reduce the edge information considerably so D-SegNet we keep the max-pooling indices for decoders to perform the edge analysis successfully. The obtained features are then optimized using SVD and fused to a single feature map for decoding. SVD generate a sparse representation of the features from the horizontal and vertical feature map set. The eigenvectors factorize a real or complex matrix to a Hermitian matrix. This is a stable and successful strategy for dividing a system into a set of linearly independent components, each of which has its own energy component. Image feature fusion is done by combining the sparse nonzero elements. This keeps most of the useful information in the original image. The final combined feature map shown in Figure 9.7. The fused feature maps then applied to the single decoder for up-sampling.

The decoder up-sample the feature maps corresponding to the encoder while using the max-pooling indices to keep the edge information. The final pixel classification

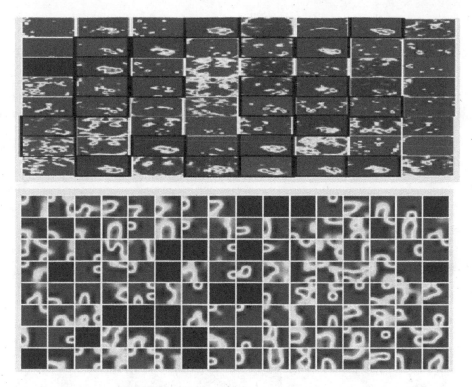

FIGURE 9.6 Top row shows the feature maps of conv4 layer while the bottom row shows the final convolutional layer for horizontal patches.

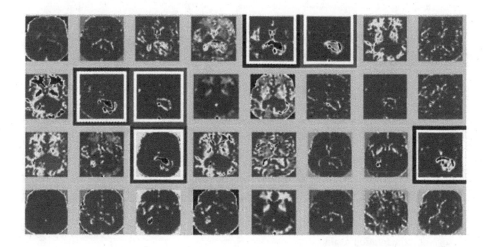

FIGURE 9.7 Combined feature map of both the horizontal and the vertical patches.

layer converts the features to a probability map for final classification. The obtained result for the BRATs2015 and the BRATS2019 dataset is shown in Figure 9.8.

In BRATS2015 it found that the tumor inside the skull region is segmented properly while at the edges the skull region also segmented as tumor parts. This can be avoided by some preprocessing methods like skull region removal in the initial processing steps. The BRATS2019 results were shown in Figure 9.9. The obtained results are promising similar to BRATS2015. The performance of both datasets was measured using DSC, PPV and sensitivity and presented in Table 9.1

The performance of D-SegNet is compared with traditional SegNet and SegNet and GAN combination known as SegAN.

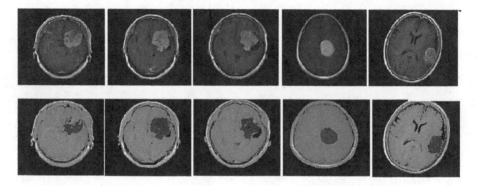

FIGURE 9.8 Segmentation result obtained for The BRATS2015 dataset. The top row shows the original tumor images and the bottom shows the D-SegNet segmentation result.

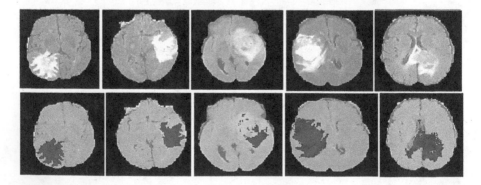

FIGURE 9.9 Top row shows the original BRATS2019 images and the bottom row shows the D-SegNet segmentation result.

TABLE 9.1
Comparison of D-SegNet

Model	BRATS2015			BRATS2019		
	DSC	PPV	Sensitivity	DSC	PPV	Sensitivity
SegAN	0.705	0.759	0.694	0.766	0.745	0.834
SegNet	0.825	0.901	0.785	0.814	0.850	0.840
D-SegNet	**0.855**	**0.924**	**0.832**	**0.842**	**0.880**	**0.861**

9.5   CONCLUSION

Here we propose a modified SegNet architecture knows as D-SegNet. The name comes from the fact that the model employs two encoders for different complementing patches. The patches were able to keep more spatial information compared to the traditional square patches. The obtained features are then optimized and fused using SVD. This keeps most of the useful information in the original image. The final decoder and pixel classification layers perform the up-sampling and segmentation, respectively. The method is compared with traditional SegNet and variation of SegNet known as SegAN and performs better in terms of DSC, PPV, and sensitivity. A DSC of 0.855 is obtained for BRATS2015 and 0.842 for BRATS2019 database while all other methods scores are significantly lower than this. This proves the efficiency of the proposed method. End-to-end learning of deep segmentation structures is a more difficult task, and in future we hope that this vital issue receives more attention.

REFERENCES

1. Vachan Vadmal, Grant Junno, Chaitra Badve, William Huang, Kristin A. Waite, and Jill S Barnholtz-Sloan, MRI image analysis methods and applications: an algorithmic perspective using brain tumors as an exemplar, *Neuro-Oncology Advances*, 2, no. 1, January–December 2020, vdaa049, https://doi.org/10.1093/noajnl/vdaa049
2. Bjoern H. Menze et al., The Multimodal Brain Tumor Image Segmentation Benchmark (BRATS), *IEEE Trans. Med. Imaging*, 34, no. 10, 1993–2004, 2015.
3. Vijay Badrinarayanan, Alex Kendall, and Roberto Cipolla, SegNet: A Deep Convolutional Encoder-Decoder Architecture for Image Segmentation, Computer Vision and Pattern Recognition (cs.CV); Machine Learning (cs.LG); Neural and Evolutionary Computing (cs.NE), 2016, https://arxiv.org/abs/1511.00561
4. V. Badrinarayanan, A. Kendall, and R. Cipolla, "SegNet: a deep convolutional encoder-decoder architecture for image segmentation," in *IEEE Transactions on Pattern Analysis and Machine Intelligence*, 39, no. 12, 2481–2495, 1 Dec. 2017, doi:10.1109/TPAMI.2016.2644615.
5. K. Aswani, D. Menaka, and M.K. Manoj, "On the methods for detecting brain tumor from MRI images," *International Journal of Innovative Technology and Exploring Engineering (IJITEE)*. 9, no. 9S, July 2020, ISSN: 2278-3075.

6. S. Pereira, A. Pinto, V. Alves, and C. A. Silva, "Brain tumor segmentation using convolutional neural networks in MRI images," *IEEE Transactions on Medical Imaging*, 35, no. 5, 1240–1251, May 2016, doi:10.1109/TMI.2016.2538465.

7. A. Yang, X. Yang, W. Wenrui, H. Liu, and Y. Zhuansun, "Research on feature extraction of tumor image based on convolutional neural network. Special section on new trends in brain signal processing and analysis," *IEEE Access*, 7, 24204–24213, 2019.

8. K. Hu, Q. Gan, Y. Zhang, S. Deng, F. Xiao, W. Huang, C. Cao, and X. Gao, "Brain tumor segmentation using multi-cascaded convolutional neural networks and conditional random feld," *IEEE Access*, 7, 92615–92629, 2019.

9. M. Havaei, A. Davy, and D. Warde-Farley, "Brain tumor segmentation with deep neural networks," *Med Image Anal.* 35, 18–31, 2017.

10. C. Han, L. Rundo, R. Araki, Y. Nagano, Y. Furukawa, G. Mauri, H. Nakayama, and H. Hayashi, "Combining noise-to-image and image-to-image GANs: brain MR image augmentation for tumor detection," *IEEE Access*, 2019. https://doi.org/10.1109/ACCESS.2019.2947606

11. A. Choudhary, L. Tong, Y. Zhu, and M. D. Wang, "Advancing medical imaging informatics by deep learning-based domain adaptation," *Yearbook of Medical Informatics*, 29(1), 129–138, 2020. https://doi.org/10.1055/s-0040-1702009

12. S. Nema, A.A. Dudhane, S. Murala, and S. Naidu, "RescueNet: An unpaired GAN for brain tumor segmentation," *Biomed. Signal Process. Control*, 55, 101641, 2020.

13. C. Baur, B. Wiestler, S. Albarqouni, and N. Navab, "Deep autoencoding models for unsupervised anomaly segmentation in brain MR images," In: Crimi A., Bakas S., Kuijf H., Keyvan F., Reyes M., and van Walsum T. (eds) *Brainlesion: Glioma, Multiple Sclerosis, Stroke and Traumatic Brain Injuries. BrainLes 2018*. Lecture Notes in Computer Science, vol. 11383. Springer, Cham, 2019. https://doi.org/10.1007/978-3-030-11723-8_16

14. N. Wanga, C. Chena, Y. Xiea, and L. Maa, "Brain tumor anomaly detection via latent regularized adversarial network," *Computer Vision and Image Understanding*, 2020, https://doi.org/10.48550/arXiv.2007.04734

15. C. Han, L. Rundo, K. Murao et al. "MADGAN: unsupervised medical anomaly detection GAN using multiple adjacent brain MRI slice reconstruction," *BMC Bioinformatics* **22**, 31, 2021. https://doi.org/10.1186/s12859-020-03936-1

16. K. Aswani and D. Menaka, "A dual autoencoder and singular value decomposition based feature optimization for the segmentation of brain tumor from MRI images," *BMC Med Imaging* **21**, 82, 2021. https://doi.org/10.1186/s12880-021-00614-3

17. T. Kaur and T. K. Gandhi, "Automated brain image classification based on VGG-16 and transfer learning," *2019 International Conference on Information Technology (ICIT)*, pp. 94–98, 2019, doi:10.1109/ICIT48102.2019.00023.

18. Kaiming He, Xiangyu Zhang, Shaoqing Ren, and Jian Sun, "Deep residual learning for image recognition," *Proceedings of the IEEE Conference on Computer Vision and Pattern Recognition (CVPR)*, 2016, pp. 770–778.

19. A. Myronenko and A. Hatamizadeh, "Robust semantic segmentation of brain tumor regions from 3D MRIs." In: Crimi A., Bakas S. (eds) *Brainlesion: Glioma, Multiple Sclerosis, Stroke and Traumatic Brain Injuries. BrainLes 2019*. Lecture Notes in Computer Science, vol 11993. Springer, Cham, 2020, https://doi.org/10.1007/978-3-030-46643-5_8

20. J.H. Xu, W.P.K. Teng, X.J. Wang, and A. Nürnberger, "A deep supervised U-attention net for pixel-wise brain tumor segmentation," In: Crimi A., Bakas S. (eds) *Brainlesion: Glioma, Multiple Sclerosis, Stroke and Traumatic Brain Injuries. BrainLes 2020*. Lecture Notes in Computer Science, vol 12659. Springer, Cham, 2021, https://doi.org/10.1007/978-3-030-72087-2_24

21. C. Persello, V.A. Tolpekin, J.R. Bergado, and R.A. de By, "Delineation of agricultural fields in smallholder farms from satellite images using fully convolutional networks and combinatorial grouping," *Remote Sensing of Environment*, 231, 111253, Sepember 2019, doi:10.1016/j.rse.2019.111253.

22. E. Giacomello, D. Loiacono, and L. Mainardi, "Brain MRI tumor segmentation with adversarial networks," *2020 International Joint Conference on Neural Networks (IJCNN)*, 1–8, 2020, doi:10.1109/IJCNN48605.2020.9207220.

23. O. Ronneberger, P. Fischer, and T. Brox, "U-net: convolutional networks for biomedical image segmentation," *MICCAI*, Springer, pp. 234–241, 2015.

24. H. Noh, S. Hong, and B. Han, "Learning deconvolution network for semantic segmentation," *CoRR*, vol. abs/1505.04366, 2015.

10 Data Analytics for Intrusion Detection System Based on Recurrent Neural Network and Supervised Machine Learning Methods

Yakub Kayode Saheed
American University of Nigeria, Nigeria

CONTENTS

DOI: 10.1201/9781003307822-12

10.1   INTRODUCTION

Safeguarding our private information from unauthorized users in this digital era is becoming a difficult task. As the prevalence of internet access and internet connectivity has generated an enormous amount of security risks to information technology worldwide, the need to secure our personal information on digital platforms has become a global concern [1]. Many public databases are becoming more accessible to highly classified information, and many social media platforms, such as Telegram, YouTube, Twitter, Facebook WhatsApp, and Instagram, contain a wealth of vital personal information. In addition, numerous e-commerce sites, like Ali express, eBay, Konga, Amazon, and Jumia, have seen an increase in their use for many online transactions [2]. Our identities, debit or credit card numbers, and other personal data are all over these digital media sites and social media websites. As a result, protecting our online applications from third parties such as eavesdroppers and phishers has now become a significant issue for many security investigators.

An intrusion detection system (IDS) is a methodology for tracking network activity in order to identify potential dangers by determining whether they violate confidentiality, integrity, and availability (CIA) fundamentals [3]. The main goal of an IDS [4] is to protect a network device by identifying antagonistic assaults on a computer network, monitoring ongoing activities in a network, and examining them for indications of intrusion. Machine learning (ML) [2] and data analytics [5] techniques have become critical in the development of IDS and algorithms. ML classifiers are employed to create models that study from their experiences and uncover new forms within a dataset. In general, they are classified as supervised [6], which includes SVM, ANN, and NB; and unsupervised [7], which includes clustering. Data analytics [8] is a relatively new field of study that unifies algorithms and methods from a variety of disciplines, including mathematics, data mining, high-performance computing, statistics, and machine learning, in order to effectively manage large amounts of data.

Traditional IDSs include flaws such as high false alarm, low detection accuracy, and poor performance in detecting novel types of threats [9, 10]. As a result, it is critical to create powerful IDS capable of increasing detection accuracy, reduce false alarm rates, and speed up the discovery of new forms of assaults. ML technologies have been extensively researched in order to develop IDS proficient in operating optimally in order to meet network security needs. ML is a growing area of computational procedures that mimic human intellect. ML approaches make use of arithmetical models to find forms in massive amounts of data [11]. The preceding ML approaches have been extensively employed in the area of IDS research and innovation: SVM [12, 13], L-SVM [14], ICA [15], KNN [16–18], ANN [19], DT [18], NB [20], genetic algorithm [21], extreme gradient boosting [22], and random forest [23].

Due to the increasing availability of computing cost, RNNs that have existed for years only recently are having their full potential realized; for example, CNN has recently gained considerable advancement in the realm of deep learning [24]. RNNs have made significant contributions to recent advances in NLP, computer vision, speech recognition, semantic understanding, language modeling, human action recognition, translation, object detection, and image description [25, 26].

DL-based algorithms, in contrast to typical ML algorithms, deal with big datasets with a variety of attributes (inputs). Some of the traits are necessary to solve a precise classification challenge, while others are unnecessary and redundant. Moreover, datasets with many feature vector dimensions are difficult to use to perform training and testing. As a result, doing feature engineering (FE) over a multidimensional dataset is critical for improved efficiency. In ML and DL research, FE has received a lot of attention [27, 28]. The idea of integrating or separating inputs to enhance performance of a classifier is known as FE. In this chapter, we used PSO for feature selection in which 19 features have been chosen, which is subsequently been trained by the RNN and supervised ML models: extra tree, cat boost, RF, and GB.

The remainder of this chapter is organized as follows. Section 10.2 discusses the corresponding work. Section 10.3 presents the proposed approach. In Section 10.4, we explain the experiment results and discussion. Finally, in Section 10.5, we conclude the discussion and explore future directions.

10.2 RELATED WORK

Previously, different techniques based on ML and DL were investigated and implemented to address the IDS issue. In this section, we carry out a review of current ML- and DL-based strategies utilize in IDS.

Recently, Saheed and Hamza-usman [29] proposes a novel method for feature selection that combines the Information Gain and Ranker (IG+R) method using the NB, SVM, and KNN classifiers. On the NSLKDD dataset, the performance of these IG+R-KNN, IG+R-NB, and IG+R-SVM was evaluated. The results obtained gave an accuracy of 99.4 percent.

Kasongo and Sun [30] developed a scheme for detecting network intrusions using deep learning and a filter technique for attribute reduction. The classifier utilized for their work is based on the IG philosophy. The FFDNN-IDS were compared to the next classifiers: NB, DT, KNN, RF, and SVM. The findings displayed that the IG-FFDNN-IDS outperforms the other classifiers implemented. The FFDNN-IDS attained a binary classification accuracy reaching 99.37 percent of the data training and 87.74 percent on the test data utilizing the abridged NSL-KDD set of attributes.

The authors in [31] presented a method for intelligent IDS using DNN. The researchers did not employ any feature extraction techniques in this instance. Numerous experiments were conducted, and the DNN design was evaluated by comparing to traditional ML approaches. The experiments used publicly accessible datasets like the NSL-KDD, the UNSW-NB15, the KDD Cup 99, and the WSN-DS. By using KDDCup 99, the DNN model with five layers gave a 92.7% accuracy. On the NSL-KDD, the DNN model with five folds achieved 78.9% detection accuracy. Also, on WSN-DS, a DNN with five layers achieved 98.2% accuracy. The DNN with five folds attained accuracy reaching 76.1% on the UNSW-NB15.

According to [32], the author developed a WIDS based on the AWID and use an ACO algorithm to extract classification model. They used a correlation-based method to implement a filter feature extraction method in their experiments. The AWID's entire feature space was decreased to an array of 35 attributes as a result of this procedure. The findings of their experimentations indicated that the RF model achieved

TABLE 10.1

Summary of Existing Approaches

References	Classifiers Employed	Feature Selection	Dataset	Accuracy (%)
[30]	Feed-Forward DNN	Filter	NSL-KDD	81.19
[31]	DNN	Nil	NSL-KDD	78.50
[36]	DFNN	Wrapper	NSL-KDD	98.60
[36]	DT-GA-LR	Wrapper	UNSW-NB15	81.42
[37]	ANN	Filter	UNSW-NB15	81.34
[38]	APCA I-ELM	Wrapper	UNSWW-NB15	70.51
[33]	SVM	Wrapper	KDDCup 99	93.00
[39]	SAE	Wrapper	AWID	98.57
[32]	ACO	Filter	AWID	98.87

an overall accuracy of 98.87% for multiclass classification and 99.10% for binary classification strategies, respectively.

Chang et al. [33] presented a NIDS using the RF and SVM. The features selection process was carried out using RFs premised on a feature importance score technique. The KDD Cup 99 dataset was employed to assess the approach. With the SVM as the classification model, the implementation results indicated that a lowered group of attributes consisting of 14 features accomplished a classification accuracy reaching 93% of the training data, compared to 90% for the complete set of forty-one attributes.

The authors of [34] suggested an evolutionary FFNN-LSO IDS based on the locust swarm optimization technique. To determine the FFNN-performance, LSO's both the UNSW-NB15 and NSL-KDD entities were used. FFNN-LSO seemed to have a DA of 95.24% and a FAR of 9.40% when tested on the UNSW-NB15. DA of 86.44% and FAR of 29.1% were achieved by the FFNN-GA. DA of 89.09% and FAR of 5.62% were obtained for the FFNN-PSO. According to the results presented above, the FFNN+LSO surpassed the FFNN+GA and the FFNN+PSO.

Vinayakumar et al. [35] proposed an LSTM-based IDS. The authors assessed the quality of their methodology by utilizing the CIDDS dataset. The DA was the primary metric used to assess the LSTM IDS's efficiency. Additionally, the model was compared to a diversity of other methods, including NN, SVM, and the MLP. The findings indicated that the LSTM-IDS outpaced its associates, achieving an 84.83 percent detection accuracy on validation data. We present the existing works summary in Table 10.1.

10.3 PROPOSED SYSTEM

The units in terms of inputs, output, and the hidden units form RNN, with the hidden unit performing most of the effort. The RNN is simply a one-way information flow between the input and the output units. We can think of hidden units as the network's storage, which retains endwise knowledge. When an RNN is unfolded, we discover that it embodies deep learning. For supervised categorization learning, an RNNs approach can be employed. The fundamental distinction between (RNN) and typical

FFNNs is the presence of a directed loop that may remember earlier knowledge and implement it to the current output (FNNs). The previous output of a series is also tied to the output current, as well as the nodes that connect them both the concealed folds are no more connection oriented; they now have connections. Not only do the input's output nodes influence the input of the concealed fold, but also the output of the final concealed fold influences on input of the hidden units.

10.3.1 Methodology

Figure 10.1 explains the proposed IDS utilizing RNN and supervised ML models: extra tree, Cat boost, RF, and GB that consists of the modules: the data attainment, the data preprocessing, wrapper feature selection, the classification, and model assessment.

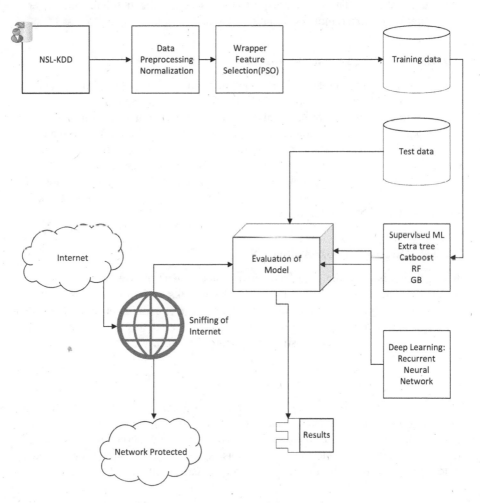

FIGURE 10.1 Architecture of proposed IDS model.

10.3.2 Description of the Dataset

The NSL-KDD data [40] is a more advanced form of KDD'99 and contains critical information for updating the KDD'99 data. The attack categories classified in the NSL-KDD is given as:

1. Denial of Service: Attacks affecting the victim's capability to react to valid needs are considered denial of service attacks.
2. Probing: The basic objective of a probing attack is to get crucial information about remote user.
3. User to root: By acquiring illegal access to the user's local superuser (root) rights, this form of assault enables the eavesdropper to access the user's account.
4. Root to local: This form of attack enables unauthorized access from a distant computer. The attacker acquires local access to the victim machine after breaking into a remote workstation.

10.3.3 Particle Swarm Optimization

Kennedy and Eberhart created particle swarm optimization (PSO), a concurrent evolutionary process computation approach. The included tuning parameters have a significant impact on the performance of the PSO algorithm, which is commonly known as the exploration–exploitation balancing act, where exploration refers to the capacity to evaluate numerous regions throughout the problem space in order to discover a good optimal, ideally the global one [41]. The PSO method has been used to tackle a variety of issues in a variety of areas. In this chapter, PSO was used for feature selection to select 19 attributes, and subsequently the reduced features were fed to the ML models and the DNN model for classification.

10.3.4 Recurrent Neural Network

RNN, which is a variant of a feed-forward neural network, tends to make use of sequential data. The term "recurrent neural networks" refers to the fact that they complete the same task for each element of a sequence, with the outcome dependent on the previous computation [42]. Because RNNs include cyclic connections, they are particularly well suited for simulating sequences [43].

10.3.5 Extra Tree

ET is a supervised ML strategy similar to RF. Additional tree classification [44] is nothing more than a completely random tree categorization. Additionally, because the entire sample is used in tree measurements, decision bounds should be viewed as random. This approach enables the use of bootstrap replicas of sample training and the determination of the optimum cutoff position for each randomized feature at a node.

10.3.6 CAT BOOST

Cat boost effectively handles category characteristics during training and avoids the requirement for them to be converted before to training [45]. It enhances decision trees using gradient boosting. It requires less training time than other gradient-boosting methods. Additionally, this approach is unique in that it instantly converts categorical attributes to numerical attributes.

10.3.7 RANDOM FOREST

The RF ensemble algorithm is used to improve the accuracy of classifications. The RF classifier is a meta-word estimation technique that employs numerous DTs on a single dataset to predict an instance's label [46, 47]. When compared to other traditional classification algorithms, RF has a low classification error [48].

10.3.8 GRADIENT BOOSTING

GB is a very powerful approach for uniting numerous base classifiers to yield a committee in which the performance is far better than any of the base classifier. The chief idea of the boosting algorithm is to complement new models to the ensemble model sequentially. GB allows optimization of loss function that are arbitrary differentiable [49]. It transforms a group of weak classifiers into a powerful one [50].

10.4 RESULTS AND DISCUSSION

In this section, we present the findings of the proposed method. We started with the experimental analysis of the deep learning recurrent neural model. Subsequently, we present the ML models and, finally, the comparison with existing methods.

10.4.1 EXPERIMENTAL FINDINGS OF PSO-RNN

As can be seen in Table 10.2, the PSO-RNN gave an accuracy of 96.08%, recall of 85.63%, sensitivity of 85.63%, and precision of 98.15.

TABLE 10.2
Classification Performance of PSO-RNN Model

Technique	Accuracy	Recall	Sensitivity	Precision
PSO-RNN	96.08	85.63	85.63	98.15

10.4.2   EXPERIMENTAL FINDINGS OF PSO-EXTRA TREE, PSO-CAT BOOST, PSO-RF, PSO-GB

As can be seen in Table 10.3, the extra tree gave an accuracy of 100, recall of 100, sensitivity of 100, and precision of 100. The PSO-Cat boost gave an accuracy of 100, recall of 100, sensitivity of 100, and precision of 100. The PSO-RF obtained an accuracy of 100, recall of 100, sensitivity of 100, and precision of 100. The PSO-GB obtained an accuracy of 99.9, recall of 99.9, sensitivity of 100, and precision of 100. (All figures in %.)

As noticed in Table 10.2, Table 10.3, and Figure 10.2, the proposed ML models— PSO-extra trees, PSO-Cat boost, PSO-RF, and PSO-GB—all outperformed the deep learning PSO-RNN model in terms of the accuracy, recall, sensitivity, and precision. This is as a result of the tree-based model requiring very little data preprocessing and preparation. Tree-based models also work on any form of data and are very intuitive.

10.4.3   COMPARISON WITH EXISTING STUDIES REPORTED IN THE LITERATURE

The comparison of our proposed ML models and RNN with the existing models is reported in Table 10.4. The comparison was made in terms of the classifiers used, the dataset for the experimental analysis, and the performance metric in terms of the accuracy.

TABLE 10.3

Classification Performance of PSO-Extra Tree, PSO-Cat Boost, PSO-RF, PSO-GB

Techniques	Accuracy	Recall	Sensitivity	Precision
PSO-Extra Trees	100	100	100	100
PSO-Cat Boost	100	100	100	100
PSO-RF	100	100	100	100
PSO-GB	99.99	99.99	100	100

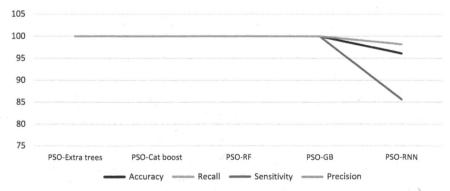

FIGURE 10.2   Classification performance of the proposed ML models and RNN model.

TABLE 10.4

Comparison with the Existing Studies

References	Classifiers Employed	Dataset	Accuracy (%)
[30]	Feed-Forward DNN	NSL-KDD	81.19
[31]	DNN	NSL-KDD	78.50
[36]	DFNN	NSL-KDD	98.60
[36]	DT-GA-LR	UNSW-NB15	81.42
[37]	ANN	UNSW-NB15	81.34
[38]	APCA I-ELM	UNSWW-NB15	70.51
[33]	SVM	KDDCup 99	93.00
[39]	SAE	AWID	98.57
[32]	ACO	AWID	98.87
Proposed	**PCO-RNN**	**NSL-KDD**	96.08
Proposed	**PCO-Extra tree**	**NSL-KDD**	100
Proposed	**PCO-Cat boost**	**NSL-KDD**	100
Proposed	**PCO-RF**	**NSL-KDD**	100
Proposed	**PCO-GB**	**NSL-KDD**	99.99

Comparison with existing studies

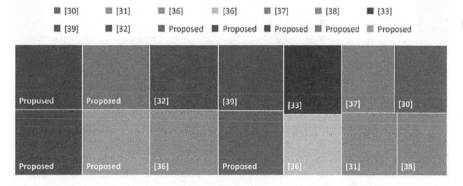

FIGURE 10.3 Comparison with state-of-the-art model.

Our proposed ML models and deep learning neural network models outperformed other existing studies in terms of the accuracy of detection as seen in Figure 10.3. The best-performing model of the existing system [32] gave an accuracy of 98.87%, while our proposed model's lowest performing accuracy was 99.9%. The findings revealed that our proposed models performed competitively versus the existing models.

10.5 CONCLUSION AND FUTURE WORK

In this chapter, data analytics for IDS based on ML models and RNN model was proposed. The ID was constructed using the PSO for feature selection from the pre-processed NSLKDD data. An efficient FS has been identified as one of the major bottlenecks in IDS. We employed a wrapper-based efficient FS for dimensionality reduction in which the relevant attributes were selected and fed into the ML models and RNN model. The experiment was performed on a popular dataset known as the NSLKDD for IDS. The findings of our proposed methods revealed that the ML models outperformed the RNN model. In comparison with the state-of-the-art methods, our proposed ML models and RNN model gave competitive results in terms of the accuracy. In future research, we will focus on employing GPU acceleration to shorten training time and investigate the classification performance of the LSTM deep neural network algorithm in the field of intrusion detection.

REFERENCES

[1] J. Jang-Jaccard and S. Nepal, "A survey of emerging threats in cybersecurity," *J. Comput. Syst. Sci.*, vol. 80, no. 5, pp. 973–993, 2014, doi:10.1016/j.jcss.2014.02.005.

[2] O. A. Sarumi, A. O. Adetunmbi, and F. A. Adetoye, "Discovering computer networks intrusion using data analytics and machine intelligence," *Sci. African*, vol. 9, p. e00500, 2020, doi:10.1016/j.sciaf.2020.e00500.

[3] N. Moustafa, G. Creech, and J. Slay, "Big data analytics for intrusion detection system: Statistical decision-making using finite dirichlet mixture models," In Palomares Carrascosa, I., Kalutarage, H., Huang, Y. (eds), *Data analytics and decision support for cybersecurity*. Cham: Springer, pp. 127–156, 2017, doi:10.1007/978-3-319-59439-2_5.

[4] A. K. Pathan and F. Group, "The State of the Art in Intrusion Preventio and Detection." In Khan Pathan Al-Sakhib (ed.), *Introduction to Wireless Intrusion Detection Systems*. Berlin: Spinger, pp. 336–352, 2013.

[5] O. A. Sarumi, C. K. Leung, and A. O. Adetunmbi, "Spark-based data analytics of sequence motifs in large omics data," *Procedia Comput. Sci.*, vol. 126, pp. 596–605, 2018, doi:10.1016/j.procS.2018.07.294.

[6] H. K. Gianey and R. Choudhary, "Comprehensive review on supervised machine learning algorithms," *Proc. - 2017 Int. Conf. Mach. Learn. Data Sci. MLDS 2017*, vol. 2018-Janua, pp. 38–43, 2018, doi:10.1109/MLDS.2017.11.

[7] C. Bauckhage, A. Drachen, and R. Sifa, "Clustering game behavior data," *IEEE Trans. Comput. Intell. AI Games*, vol. 7, no. 3, pp. 266–278, 2015, doi:10.1109/TCIAIG.2014.2376982.

[8] O. A. Sarumi and C. K. Leung, "Exploiting anti-monotonic constraints in mining palindromic motifs from big genomic data," *Proc. - 2019 IEEE Int. Conf. Big Data, Big Data 2019*, pp. 4864–4873, 2019, doi:10.1109/BigData47090.2019.9006397.

[9] R. Samrin and D. Vasumathi, "Review on anomaly based network intrusion detection system," *Int. Conf. Electr. Electron. Commun. Comput. Technol. Optim. Tech. ICEECCOT 2017*, vol. 2018-Janua, pp. 141–147, 2018, doi:10.1109/ICEECCOT.2017.8284655.

[10] T. Mehmood and H. B. M. Rais, "Machine learning allgorriitthms IIn conttextt off inttrusiion dettecttiion," *Comput. Inf. Sci. (ICCOINS), 2016 3rd Int. Conference*, pp. 369–373, 2016.

[11] A. B. R. Shatte, D. M. Hutchinson, and S. J. Teague, "Machine learning in mental health: A scoping review of methods and applications," *Psychol. Med.*, vol. 49, no. 9, pp. 1426–1448, 2019, doi:10.1017/S0033291719000151.

[12] J. Gu and S. Lu, "An effective intrusion detection approach using SVM with naïve Bayes feature embedding," *Comput. Secur.*, vol. 103, p. 102158, 2021, doi:10.1016/j.cose.2020.102158.

[13] Y. Tao, S. Sui, K. Xie, and Z. Liu, "Intrusion detection based on support vector machine using heuristic genetic algorithm," *Proc. - 2014 4th Int. Conf. Commun. Syst. Netw. Technol. CSNT 2014*, pp. 681–684, 2014, doi:10.1109/CSNT.2014.143.

[14] A. K. Oladejo, T. O. Oladele, and Y. K. Saheed, "Comparative evaluation of linear support vector machine and K-nearest neighbour algorithm using microarray data on Leukemia Cancer Dataset," *African Journal of Computing & ICT*, vol. 11, no. 2, pp. 1–10, 2018.

[15] S. Y. K. Rasheed, G. Jimoh, Ridwan M. Yusuf, and Yusuf O. Olatunde, "Application of dimensionality reduction on classification of colon cancer using ica and K-NN algorithm," *Anale. Ser. Informatică*, vol. 6, no. 10, pp. 55–59, 2018.

[16] R. Wazirali, "An improved intrusion detection system based on KNN hyperparameter tuning and cross-validation," *Arab. J. Sci. Eng.*, vol. 45, no. 12, pp. 10859–10873, 2020, doi:10.1007/s13369-020-04907-7.

[17] A. A. Aburomman, M. Bin, and I. Reaz, "A novel SVM-kNN-PSO ensemble method for intrusion detection system," vol. 38, pp. 360–372, 2016.

[18] P. Sukarno and M. A. N. IIham Ramadhan, "Comparative analysis of K-nearest neighbor and decision tree in detecting distributed denial of service," *2020 8th International Conference on Information and Communication Technology (ICoICT)*, 2020, pp. 16–19, doi:10.1109/ICoICT49345.2020.9166380.

[19] W. W. Lo, S. Layeghy, M. Sarhan, M. Gallagher, and M. Portmann, "E-GraphSAGE: A graph neural network based intrusion detection system," no. Ml, pp. 1–12, 2021.

[20] A. S. Talita, O. S. Nataza, and Z. Rustam, "Naïve bayes classifier and particle swarm optimization feature selection method for classifying intrusion detection system dataset," *J. Phys. Conf. Ser.*, vol. 1752, no. 1, 2021, doi:10.1088/1742-6596/1752/1/012021.

[21] Y. Saheed and A. Babatunde, "Genetic algorithm technique in program path coverage for improving software testing," vol. 7, no. 5, pp. 151–158, 2014.

[22] A. Bansal and S. Kaur, *Extreme gradient boosting based tuning for classification in intrusion detection systems*, vol. 905. Singapore: Springer, 2018.

[23] S. Waskle, L. Parashar, and U. Singh, "Intrusion detection system using PCA with random forest approach," *Proc. Int. Conf. Electron. Sustain. Commun. Syst. ICESC 2020*, no. Icesc, pp. 803–808, 2020, doi:10.1109/ICESC48915.2020.9155656.

[24] A. Turchin and D. Denkenberger, "Classification of global catastrophic risks connected with artificial intelligence," *AI Soc.*, vol. 35, no. 1, pp. 147–163, 2020, doi:10.1007/s00146-018-0845-5.

[25] X. Peng, L. Wang, X. Wang, and Y. Qiao, "Bag of visual words and fusion methods for action recognition: Comprehensive study and good practice," *Comput. Vis. Image Underst.*, vol. 150, pp. 109–125, 2016, doi:10.1016/j.cviu.2016.03.013.

[26] W. Nie, A. Liu, W. Li, and Y. Su, "Cross-view action recognition by cross-domain learning," *Image Vis. Comput.*, vol. 55, pp. 109–118, 2016, doi:10.1016/j.imavis.2016.04.011.

[27] F. Gottwalt, E. Chang, and T. Dillon, "CorrCorr: A feature selection method for multivariate correlation network anomaly detection techniques," *Comput. Secur.*, vol. 83, pp. 234–245, 2019, doi:10.1016/j.cose.2019.02.008.

[28] S. S. Saha, S. Rahman, M. J. Rasna, T. Bin Zahid, A. K. M. M. Islam, and M. A. R. Ahad, "Feature extraction, performance analysis and system design using the DU mobility dataset," *IEEE Access*, vol. 6, no. c, pp. 44776–44786, 2018, doi:10.1109/ACCESS.2018.2865093.

[29] Y. K. Saheed and F. E. Hamza-Usman, "Feature selection with IG-R for improving performance of intrusion detection system," *International Journal of Communication Networks and Information Security (IJCNIS)*, vol. 12, no. 3, pp. 338–344, 2020.

[30] S. M. Kasongo and Y. Sun, "A deep learning method with filter based feature engineering for wireless intrusion detection system," *IEEE Access*, vol. 7, no. DL, pp. 38597–38607, 2019, doi:10.1109/ACCESS.2019.2905633.

[31] R. Vinayakumar, M. Alazab, K. P. Soman, P. Poornachandran, A. Al-Nemrat, and S. Venkatraman, "Deep learning approach for intelligent intrusion detection system," *IEEE Access*, vol. 7, no. c, pp. 41525–41550, 2019, doi:10.1109/ACCESS.2019.2895334.

[32] F. D. Vaca and Q. Niyaz, "An ensemble learning based Wi-Fi network intrusion detection system (WNIDS)," *NCA 2018 - 2018 IEEE 17th Int. Symp. Netw. Comput. Appl*, pp. 1–5, 2018, doi:10.1109/NCA.2018.8548315.

[33] Y. Chang, W. Li, and Z. Yang, "Network intrusion detection based on random forest and support vector machine," *Proc. - 2017 IEEE Int. Conf. Comput. Sci. Eng. IEEE/ IFIP Int. Conf. Embed. Ubiquitous Comput. CSE EUC 2017*, vol. 1, pp. 635–638, 2017, doi:10.1109/CSE-EUC.2017.118.

[34] I. Benmessahel, K. Xie, M. Chellal, and T. Semong, "A new evolutionary neural networks based on intrusion detection systems using locust swarm optimization," *Evol. Intell.*, vol. 12, no. 2, pp. 131–146, 2019, doi:10.1007/s12065-019-00199-5.

[35] S. A. Althubiti, E. M. Jones, and K. Roy, "LSTM for anomaly-based network intrusion detection," *2018 28th Int. Telecommun. Networks Appl. Conf. ITNAC 2018*, pp. 1–3, 2019, doi:10.1109/ATNAC.2018.8615300.

[36] M. AL-Hawawreh, N. Moustafa, and E. Sitnikova, "Identification of malicious activities in industrial internet of things based on deep learning models," *J. Inf. Secur. Appl.*, vol. 41, pp. 1–11, 2018, doi:10.1016/j.jisa.2018.05.002.

[37] N. Moustafa and J. Slay, "The evaluation of network anomaly detection systems: Statistical analysis of the UNSW-NB15 data set and the comparison with the KDD99 data set," *Inf. Secur. J.*, vol. 25, no. 1–3, pp. 18–31, 2016, doi:10.1080/19393555.2015. 1125974.

[38] J. Gao, S. Chai, B. Zhang, and Y. Xia, "Research on network intrusion detection based on incremental extreme learning machine and adaptive principal component analysis," *Energies*, vol. 12, no. 7, 2019, doi:10.3390/en12071223.

[39] M. E. Aminanto and K. Kim, *Improving detection of Wi-Fi impersonation by fully unsupervised deep learning*, vol. 10763 LNCS. Springer International Publishing, 2018.

[40] L. M. Ibrahim, D. B. Taha, and M. S. Mahmod, "A comparison study for intrusion database (KDD99, NSL-KDD) based on self organization map (SOM) artificial neural network," *J. Eng. Sci. Technol.*, vol. 8, no. 1, pp. 107–119, 2013.

[41] M. H. Ali, B. A. D. Al Mohammed, A. Ismail, and M. F. Zolkipli, "A new intrusion detection system based on fast learning network and particle swarm optimization," *IEEE Access*, vol. 6, no. c, pp. 20255–20261, 2018, doi:10.1109/ACCESS.2018.2820092.

[42] T. A. Tang, L. Mhamdi, D. McLernon, S. A. R. Zaidi, and M. Ghogho, "Deep recurrent neural network for intrusion detection in SDN-based networks," *2018 4th IEEE Conf. Netw. Softwarization Work. NetSoft 2018*, no. NetSoft, pp. 462–469, 2018, doi:10.1109/ NETSOFT.2018.8460090.

[43] J. Kim, J. Kim, H. L. T. Thu, and H. Kim, "Long short term memory recurrent neural network classifier for intrusion detection," *2016 Int. Conf. Platf. Technol. Serv. PlatCon 2016 - Proc.*, 2016, doi:10.1109/PlatCon.2016.7456805.

[44] B. A. Ashwini and S. S. Manivannan, "Supervised machine learning classification algorithmic approach for finding anomaly type of intrusion detection in wireless sensor network," *Opt. Mem. Neural Networks (Information Opt)*, vol. 29, no. 3, pp. 244–256, 2020, doi:10.3103/S1060992X20030029.

[45] A. Lazar, A. Sim, and K. Wu, "GPU-based classification for wireless intrusion detection," pp. 27–31, 2020, doi:10.1145/3452411.3464445.

[46] N. B. Olaniyi, Abdulsalam Sulaiman, Saheed Yakub Kayode, Hambali Moshood Abiola, T.T. Salau-Ibrahim, "Student's performance analysis using decision tree algorithms," *Ann. Comput. Sci. Ser.*, vol. XV, pp. 55–62, 2017.

[47] Y. K. Saheed, T. O. Oladele, A. O. Akanni, and W. M. Ibrahim, "Student performance prediction based on data mining classification techniques," *Niger. J. Technol.*, vol. 37, no. 4, p. 1087, 2018, doi:10.4314/njt.v37i4.31.

[48] N. Farnaaz and M. A. Jabbar, "Random forest modeling for network intrusion detection system," *Procedia Comput. Sci.*, vol. 89, pp. 213–217, 2016, doi:10.1016/j.procs.2016.06.047.

[49] M. A. Hambali, Y. K. Saheed, T. O. Oladele, and M. D. Gbolagade, "Adaboost ensemble algorithms for breast cancer classification," *J. Adv. Comput. Res. Q.*, vol. 10, no. 2, pp. 1–10, 2019.

[50] P. Verma, S. Anwar, S. Khan, and S. B. Mane, "Network intrusion detection using clustering and gradient boosting," *2018 9th Int. Conf. Comput. Commun. Netw. Technol. ICCCNT 2018*, 2018, doi:10.1109/ICCCNT.2018.8494186.

Section III

Applications

11 Triple Steps for Verifying Chemical Reaction Based on Deep Whale Optimization Algorithm (VCR-WOA)

Samaher Al-Janabi, Ayad Alkaim and G. AL-Taleby
University of Babylon, Babylon, Iraq

CONTENTS

11.1 INTRODUCTION

Intelligent computation represents the ability of the device to learn from data or observations of experiments to perform a specific task. Although it is synonymous with soft computing, there is no agreed definition of computational intelligence. The feature "intelligence" is usually attributed to humans. Recently, many devices and

DOI: 10.1201/9781003307822-14

183

items are referred to as "smart", an inherent characteristic with interpretation and decision-making [1].

Optimization represents that under specific conditions the best results can be obtained. Engineers have several stages to make many technological and administrative decisions to design and engineering system. The objective of these decisions is to either increase interest or reduce the effort required. Since we have a specific decision function, optimization can be defined as the way to discover conditions that give a function maximum or minimum value [2–4]. There are two kinds of objective functions optimization: single-objective function and multiple-objective function. In single-objective optimization, solutions are accepted or rejected according to the value of the objective function, and there is just one search space. Multi-objective optimization may have many possible conflicting objectives. Therefore, there exists a trade-off among objectives, i.e., making concessions to the objective to improve another one. There is no optimum solution simultaneously for all objective functions. Therefore, multiple-objective functions will be under a specified set of constraints [5].

Many of the chemical reactions carried out in the laboratories are incorrect or inaccurate, and the ongoing revolution in the world of technology and computing can help those who work in chemical laboratories and make their work easier, reducing material costs, and freeing up more time for creativity and innovation. This chapter seeks to solve the issues in chemical research, particularly that of time, through the use of catalysts. We attempt to design an optimal model to find optimal materials by evaluating the candidate materials computationally before applying them to lab experiments, based on cooperation between deterministic selection techniques and Whale optimization.

11.2   MAIN CONCEPTS RELATED TO PROBLEM

The key concepts linked to this study and the role of each term in handling the problem are presented in this section.

11.2.1   TOKENIZATION PROCESS

The method of breaking text into a collection of small parts called tokens, such as words, symbols, and other text components, is tokenization. Punctuation marks, white spaces,-or line-breaks can be-distinguished by traditional tokenization, and can be removed from the list of words in another preprocessing step.

There are several [6–8] kinds of methods of tokenization, such as Treebank, which is a Penn Treebank word tokenizer implementation method. It operates based on the regular expressions-to fragment-the text into-words. The-English compressions-are broken. As a word separator, punctuation marks are considered. If the punctuation marks are accompanied by white space, the text is broken into words. The downside of this strategy is the inability to distinguish the underscore or the dot added to the phrase.

In this study the tokenization is used to split the sequence of interaction into sets of material based on a periodic table. The tokenizer splits the sequence in different lengths of token = 1, 2, 3, 4, and 5.

11.2.2 Coding

Coding converts the sequence of word strings into short terms or numbers; in other words, a character is coded by a number similar to cypher [2, 9] (such as, for example, each letter of the English alphabet receiving a corresponding number between 1 and 26). The main benefit of this process is to simplify the string/character relation and perform the mathematical processing on it. In general, in this work, we are coding for all the elements in the periodic table—in other word, coding each token related to interactions.

11.2.3 Selection Algorithms

Selection algorithm [10–12] is an algorithm used to locate the smallest (or biggest) kth number in a set or sequence. The number is called statistic of the kth size. It contains the different cases for having list or an array of the minimum, maximum, and median elements. To locate the minimum (or maximum) item by iterating over the array, we keep track of existing minimum (or maximum) elements that have happened so far, and it is linked to the sort of collection.

11.2.4 Optimization

Finding an alternative under the defined constraints with the most cost-effective or feasible efficiency is achieved by maximizing desirable conditions and minimizing undesirable ones [13, 14]. Maximization involves trying to obtain the best or optimum effect or consequence without reference to risk or benefit. The exercise of optimization is constrained by the scarcity of sufficient knowledge, and the scarcity of time to determine what data is available. Problems of optimization may be split into two groups, based on whether the factors are continuous or discrete: An issue of continuous variables is defined as continuous optimization [15, 16], in which an optimum value needs to be derived from a continuous function. These can contain limited problems and multimodal problems [7, 17]. A problem of optimization of discrete variables is defined as a discrete optimization, in which an entity such as a number, permutation, or graph may be extracted from a countable set. In the next part we will talk about some of the well-known optimization techniques: multilevel coordinate search (MCS) and Whale optimization algorithm (WOA) [18].

11.3 BUILDING VCR-WOA

A lot of time and money is wasted during preparing interactions in many laboratories in different fields (i.e., chemical, physical, medical, and biology) [12, 19]. Some interactions lead to legal interaction while others are illegal interaction; therefore, how to avoid this loss and avoid incorrect interactions is one of the important challenges. In general, the process of finding a correct interaction before entering laboratories of various scientific fields is one of the most important challenges in the scientific research [5] as a result of the progress achieved in the field of intelligent computing. Therefore, in this section, we will seek to solve the above challenge by building an integrated software model to test the interactions and ensure their accuracy before they are performed inside the laboratories.

This research introduces the VCR-WOA model for predicting optimal interactions. VCR-WOA consists of several stages: the first stage separates the group of interaction into their primary elements, then the model selects the roots to build the set of possible interactions, where the root is not chosen randomly but rather specifically through using (DSA), after that the best set of interactions is found (finding the set of optimal rules) through the use of our algorithm (LR-WO). This algorithm does not only give a set of interactions but also finds an optimal set of possible interactions, and the optimal interaction with VCR-WOA represents the least expensive and time-consuming interaction, and the last stage is the evaluation of results through the use of the five measures related to conflict matrix.

11.3.1 THE VCR-WOA DESIGN STAGES

Building an effective prediction model for a chemical interaction has three major stages. The first stage involves dataset collection and preprocessing. The second stage finds pivot (i.e., number of search agents) of interactions based on deterministic selection algorithm (DSA). In the third stage, the Whale optimization algorithm with process is used to create a new optimizer called LR-WO. The last stage is evaluation the results by measures of conflict matrix, as shown in Algorithm #1 and Figure 11.1.

ALGORITHM #1:   BUILDING VCR-WOA

Input: *Multi compounds related to interaction*
Output: Determine the validity of the interaction
// Pre-processing
  1: **For** each raw in dataset
  2:       **For** each column in dataset
  3:             **Call** split chemical compound into primary element
  4:       **End** For
  5: **End** For
  6: **For** each raw in compound
  7:       **For** each column in compound
  8:             **Call** coding procedure
  9:       **End** For
 10: **End** For
 11:       **For** i in range(1 : total number of compound)
 12:             **Call** split based on DSA
 13:       **End** For

// *Build VCR-WOA Predictor*
14: For each subgraph in training dataset
15: **Call** LR-WO
16: End For
// *Evaluation Stage*
17: Call *Evaluation*

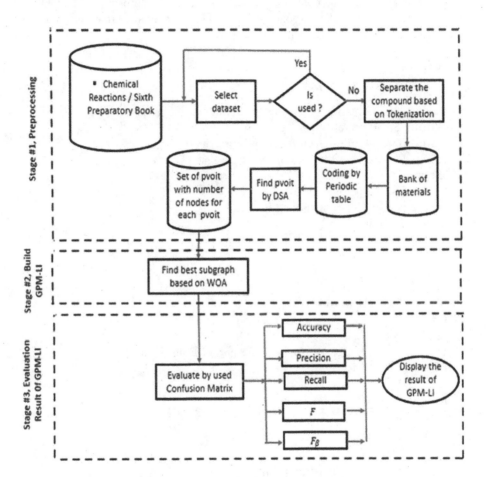

FIGURE 11.1 Block diagram of guide prediction model for the legal interactions.

11.3.1.1 Preprocessing Stage

After the dataset is collected, it is split into two files, namely the training dataset and testing dataset. As programmers can't work on that component directly, this step needs to be handled before entering into VCR-WOA.

A. Token Strategy

For chemical compositions data set [8, 20], the chemical formulas are complex, and thus we can't work on it without analyzing its primary elements. This stage is achieved through tokenization, where the token separates the elements according to the section number of elements (five syllables, four syllables, three syllables, two syllables, and one syllable) according to the periodic table.

B. Choose Pivot by DSA

After separating the complex chemical dataset into the primary elements, each element is coded through the index of buffer contained in it; the coding values are shown in Algorithm #2.

ALGORITHM #2:   DSA

Input: dataset of string of chemical material
Output: Set of search agent
// Split Dataset_id into multi groups and sort each group
  1: Split Dataset_id into 5 groups, and sort each group
  2: create empty matrix called C number of element n\5
  3: P = Dselect (C, N\5, N\10)
  4: Patriation Dataset_id around P
  5: For I in range 1 to N -J>
  6:   **For** j in range N> -I>to N
  7:   **IF I=J**
  8:   Return P
  9:   **End IF**
  10:   **IF J < I**
  11:   Return Dselect (1st part of Dataset_id, J-1, I)
  12:   **Else**
  13:   Return Dselect (2nd part of Dataset_id, N-J, I-J)
  14:   **End IF**
  15:   **End for**
  16: End for
End Dselect

11.3.1.2   Building VCR-WOA Predictor

WOA is a metaheuristic optimization approach inspired by nature. We develop that algorithm using the same strategy with fitness function as explain in Algorithm #3.

The best material for an ideal chemical interaction will be found using the Whale optimizer, along with tracking the path taken during the interaction by storing the location of each node through which it was crossed to reach the target. This algorithm called Legal Reaction by Whale Optimization (LR-WO), as shown in Algorithm #3.

ALGORITHM #3:   LR-WO

Input: *# set of search agents*
Output: *Optimal predicted interaction*
Initialization   *a: vector [2:0];, ub, lb*
//Build the Cognitive agent to search and determine the main perimeters
the whale algorithm
 1: *For each interaction in* data set
 2:        Compute *OBF*
 3:        *If OBF value better than Best_solution*
 4:                *Best_solution = result(OBF)*
 5:                *Xleader = X(t) of Best_solution*
 6:      *End*
 7: *End*
 8: *For i=1 to MaxIt*
 9:         *For each interaction in* data set
10:             Calculate main parameters A,C
11:             *If* abs(A) > 1
12:                    Calculate D and $X(t + 1)$
13:             *Else if abs(A)<=1*
14:                    Calculate D and $X(t + 1)$ through X_{leader}
15:          *End*
16:          *X(t) = max (X(t), lb)*   *// Bounded Whale*
17:          *X(t) = min (X(t), ub)*
18:          *For each reaction in updated* data set
19:                Compute *OBF*
20:                *If OBF value better than old Best_solution*
21:                     *Best_solution = OBF value   //Update leader*
                       position and fitness value
22:                     *Xleader − X(t) of Best_solution*
23:                 *End*
24:          *End*
25:        *End*
26:      *End*
27: *End*

11.3.1.3   Evaluation Stage

In this stage, we will use the five measures related to a confusion matrix to validation from the result obtaining by LTI-WO. Algorithm #4 displays evaluation performance of GPM-LI.

ALGORITHM #4:   PERFORMANCE THE EVALUATION OF VCR-WOA

Input: *predication values, real values*
Output: Efficiency Measures
  1: Initial value of True Negative, False Negative, True Positive, False Positive
     (True Negative = 0 , False Negative = 0, True Positive = 0,
     False Positive = 0)
     //Create confusion matrices
  2: **For** i=0 to length (values predication)
  3:     If values real [i] == values predication [i]: Then
  4:        TP += 1
  5:     If values predication [i] == 1 and values real[i]! = values predication
        [i]: Then
  6:        FP += 1
  7:     If values real [i] == values predication [i]: Then
  8:        TN += 1
  9:     Else If values predication [i] == 0 and values real[i] != values
        predication [i]
10:        FN += 1
11: **End** For
12: **Return** (True>Negative, False>Negative, True>Positive and
     False>Positive) values.
     //Compute Evaluation the Performance of VCR-WOA
13:     *Accuracy = TP + TN /(TP + FN + FP + TN)*
14:     *Precision = TP /(TP + FP)*
15:     *Racall = TP /(TP + FN)*
16:     $F_{-measure} = 2 * Precision * Racall/(Precision + Racall)$
17:     $F\beta = (1 + \beta^2). Precision * Racall/(\beta^2. Precision + Racall)$
18: *End*

11.4   IMPLEMENTATION AND RESULTS OF VCR-WOA

This section presents the results and details in each stage of VCR-WOA.

11.4.1   DESCRIPTION OF DATABASE

We take the real and true interactions from the sixth-grade textbook to prove the performance of the suggested model VCR-WOA. These interactions were characterized by being balanced and accurate. They were divided into two parts. The first part formed 60 percent of the data volume in the model building process, while the other interactions (40 percent) were used to test the accuracy of the proposed model (i.e., testing dataset).

11.4.2 CODING ELEMENTS OF PERIODIC TABLE

Because the periodic table consists of 118 elements, these elements have been coded so that we can deal with them later in the next steps that step represent step #1, explained in Table 11.1.

11.4.3 TOKENIZATION

Step #2, we split the dataset (chemical compounds) into primary elements, then apply the Dselect algorithm to it to obtain five groups of tokens, the first group that consists of elements that have five tokens as shown below:

A5

['NaNo3', 'ZnSO4', 'H3PO4',....]

While other elements have four tokens

A4

['NaCl', 'AgCl', 'KNO3,...']

Its tokens of other elements are three, so we saved in buffer 3

A3

['CH4', 'CO2', 'H2O', 'HCl', 'C', 'SO4', 'NO3', 'CL5',.....]

And the element that has length two put in the buffer 2

A2

['O2', 'H2', 'Na', 'Cl', 'Ag', 'No', 'C3', 'O2', 'Zn', 'Cu',....]

As well as some of them consisting of a single token put in buffer 1.

A1

['H', 'K', 'C', 'P',....]

11.4.4 APPLYING WHALE OPTIMIZATION STEPS

Step 3: Draw the graph showing the relationship among the materials of the real dataset of the chemical interaction.

Step 4: Apply the Dselect algorithm to find best pivots.
The graph obtained from the previous step is inserted as the input in the Dselect algorithm, allowing to find the most optimal number of pivots. This allows to divide the graph into a number of subgraphs (i.e., determined number of search agent to next step related to Whale)

Step 5: Find the optimal subgraphs generated based on training dataset.
In this step the WOA is implemented to the results obtained from step 4 (i.e., set of subgraphs). The best value of fitness is found to be 0.56769. This value is obtained after determining the main parameters related to WOA as shown below.

In this section, a detailed computational process is provided for the WOA using the objective function. In the objective function, the input parameters are all search agents (SA). The result of OF(.) function is an N-dimensional column vector with the objective function values for each search agent SA_j for the whole SA population.

TABLE 11.1
Coding of Periodic Table

Elements	Coding	Elements	Coding	Elements	Coding	Elements	Coding	Elements	Coding	Elements	Coding	Elements	Coding
H	1	K	19	Rb	37	Cs	55	Ta	73	Pa	91	Mt	109
He	2	Ca	20	Sr	38	Ba	56	W	74	U	92	Ds	110
Li	3	Sc	21	Y	39	La	57	Re	75	Np	93	Rg	111
Be	4	Ti	22	Zr	40	Ce	58	Os	76	Pu	94	Cn	112
B	5	V	23	Nb	41	Pr	59	Ir	77	Am	95	Nb	113
C	6	Cr	24	Mo	42	Nd	60	Pt	78	Cm	96	Fi	114
N	7	Mn	25	Tc	43	Pm	61	Au	79	Bk	97	Mc	115
O	8	Fe	26	Ru	44	Sm	62	Hg	80	Cf	98	Lv	116
F	9	Co	27	Rh	45	Eu	63	Tl	81	Es	99	Ts	117
Ne	10	Ni	28	Pd	46	Gd	64	Pb	82	Fm	100	Og	118
Na	11	Cu	29	Ag	47	Tb	65	Bi	83	Md	101		
Mg	12	Zn	30	Cd	48	Dy	66	Po	84	No	102		
Al	13	Ga	31	In	49	Ho	67	At	85	Lr	103		
Si	14	Ge	32	Sn	50	Er	68	Rn	86	Rf	104		
P	15	As	33	Sb	51	Tm	69	Fr	87	Db	105		
S	16	Se	34	Te	52	Yb	70	Ra	88	Sg	106		
Cl	17	Br	35	I	53	Lu	71	Ac	89	Bh	107		
Ar	18	Kr	36	Xe	54	Hf	72	Tb	90	Hs	108		

$$OF\left(SA_i\right) = \sum_{j=1}^{D} SA^2_{i,j} \tag{11.1}$$

In this optimization, there are four search agents and nine design variables.

In the first step, the position of the leader is set to zero and its objective value is set to an initial value (infinity for a **minimization problem**). The leader search agent is updated by the best solution found in the population.

In the second step, an initial population is developed by randomly generating values for the design variables within the permitted solution domain. The initial population is:

$SA_1 = \{15, 17, 1, 8, 1, 15, 8, 1, 17\}$
$SA_2 = \{6, 1, 8, 0, 6, 8, 0, 1, 8\}$
$SA_3 = \{19, 17, 47, 102, 47, 17, 0, 19, 102\}$
$SA_4 = \{30, 29, 16, 8, 30, 16, 8, 29, 0\}$

In the third step, the main loop of the algorithm starts and continues until termination criteria are satisfied. Within this loop, the objective values for the population of search agents are evaluated as:

OF $(SA_1) = 1159$
OF $(SA_2) = 266$
OF $(SA_3) = 26526$
OF $(SA_4) = 4122$

In the fourth step, the position and objective function value of the leader search agent is updated based on the best-found solution. In this example, the **new leader is SA₂**:

$$Leader\_position = \{6, 1, 8, 0, 6, 8, 0, 1, 8\}$$

$$Feader\_score = 266$$

In each iteration two different random numbers are produced between 0 and 1 to calculate A and C as follows:

$$r_1 = \{0.28574 \quad 0.58519 \quad 0.6489 \quad 0.39206 \quad 0.24139$$
$$0.7164 \quad 0.62251 \quad 0.61385 \quad 0.47705\}$$

By r_1, A is Calculate as Equation (2.3)

$$A = \{-0.85703 \quad 0.34074 \quad 0.59561 \quad -0.43176 \quad -1.0344$$
$$0.86561 \quad 0.49003 \quad 0.45542 - 0.091802\}$$

$$r_2 = \{0.53716 \quad 0.12088 \quad 0.16505 \quad 0.14303 \quad 0.33079$$
$$0.016261 \quad 0.50645 \quad 0.076257 \quad 0.33882\}$$

By r_2, C is Calculate as Equation (2.4)

$$C = \{1.0743 \quad 0.24177 \quad 0.33011 \quad 0.28606 \quad 0.66159$$
$$0.032522 \quad 1.0129 \quad 0.15251 \quad 0.67765\}$$

An important fact about humpback whale behaviors is the way their approach their prey by moving in a shrinking circle. The shrinking circle method based on the randomly selected leader is used to update its position. To this end, rand _leader _ index, the second search agent is a leader. In this case, the position of the search agent is updated using the following equation:

Calculate D and $X(t+1)$ through Xleader if abs$(A) <= 1$

In this case study, these values are:

$$D = |(1.0743 * 6) - 15| = 8.55405$$

$$SA(1,1) = 6 - (-0.85703 * 8.55405) = 13.3310$$

In the same method find the other value of vector D & SA(i, j) based on absolute value of coefficient vector A, until the fifth value in vector (−1.0344) found result as below:

Calculate D and $X(t+1)$ if abs$(A) > 1$

These values are:

$$\text{Rand}(k) = 2$$

$$D = |(0.66159 * 6) - 1| = 2.96953$$

$$SA(1,5) = 6 - (-1.0344 * 2.96953) = 9.0718$$

By same method other positions are found

$$D = \{8.55405 \quad 16.7582 \quad 1.64084 \quad 8 \quad 2.96953$$
$$14.7398 \quad 8 \quad 0.8474851 \quad 1.5788\}$$

$$SA1 = \{13.3310 \quad -4.7102 \quad 7.0227 \quad 3.4541 \quad 9.0718$$
$$-4.7589 \quad -3.9202 \quad 0.6140 \quad 9.0630\}$$

For the second search agent the new position is obtained using:
The updated position is computed as:

$$D = \{7.10641 \quad 2.13699 \quad 11.3722 \quad 0 \quad 4.18061$$
$$16.3597 \quad 0 \quad 0.232503 \quad 1.5064\}$$

$$SA_2 = \{19.3135 \quad -1.5567 \quad 35.2923 \quad 0 \quad 9.9334$$
$$-0.0573 \quad 0 \quad 1.1041 \quad 10.9192\}$$

For the third search agent the shrinking encircling mechanism is utilized for updating the position. As a result, the third search agent uses the following information for updating its position:

$$D = \{11.62099 \quad 21.56645 \quad 32.52633 \quad 102 \quad 43.78439$$
$$17.10636 \quad 0 \quad 31.49408 \quad 100.0792\}$$

$$SA_3 = \{23.1923 \quad 38.0225 \quad -5.89389 \quad 4.8870$$
$$-18.0766 \quad 18.6600 \quad 0 \quad -7.2449 \quad 2.3628\}$$

The fourth search agent is updated with the following result:

$$D = \{23.4742 \quad 16.7356 \quad 10.1565 \quad 8 \quad 24.775$$
$$0.945466 \quad 8 \quad 28.6338 \quad 6.26814\}$$

$$SA_4 = \{-18.0143 \quad 41.6321 \quad 2.8209 \quad -7.4259$$
$$29.9623 \quad 7.4951 \quad -2.9950 \quad 22.6104 \quad 20.0838\}$$

Next, the boundary conditions are checked and every violated individual is pushed back into the permitted solution domain.

$Valid\_SA_1 = \{13.3310 \quad -4.7102 \quad 7.0227 \quad 3.4541 \quad 9.0718 \quad -4.7589$
$-3.9202 \quad 0.6140 \quad 9.0630 \}$
$Valid\_SA_2 = \{19.3135 \quad -1.5567 \quad 35.2923 \quad 0 \quad 9.9334 \quad -0.0573 \quad 0$
$1.1041 \quad 10.9192\}$

Valid_SA$_3$ = {23.1923   38.0225   −5.8938   94.8870   −18.0766   18.6600
            0   −7.2449   2.3628}
Valid_SA$_4$ = {−18.0143   41.6321   2.8209   −7.4259   29.9623   7.4951
            −2.9950   22.6104   20.0838}

The OF values are computed for each SA as:

OF (Valid _SA$_1$) = 386.2627
OF (Valid_SA$_2$) = 402.3173
OF (Valid_SA$_3$) = 592.8084
OF (Valid_SA$_4$) = 628.2488

The final step, the leaders OF value and position are updated based on the best-found solution.

$$\text{Best solution position} = SA_2 = \{6, 1, 8, 0, 6, 8, 0, 1, 8\}$$

$$\text{Leader}\_\text{score} = SA_2 = 266$$

Comparison of the best solution score and the previous best solution score found the last score to be the best and the leader for the next iteration. Hence, in above Table 11.1 to Table 11.8, we can see the evaluation results of our proposed work in detail. The other best solution for each iteration is found as the same procedure of the first iteration, as shown in Table 11.9. This table display leader positions for 50 iterations to obtain the objective function (OF). Table 11.9 displays the best fitness for 50 iterations. Observed fitness value stability in some iteration, like in iteration 3: the fitness value (238.5518) is stable iteration 10. Stable state is also obtained in iterations 20 through 26 with best fitness value (55.1624), and the same state repeated in other iterations, until it reached the iteration 50, which is a 0.56769 fitness value.

11.4.5 Evaluation the Results

Here we present the evaluation of the results obtained based on the measures generated by the confusion matrix described in [10]

$$Accuracy = TP + TN / (TP + FN + FP + TN) = 0.94,$$
$$Precision = TP / (TP + FP) = 0.65,$$
$$Racall = TP / (TP + FN) = 0.86,$$
$$F_{-measure} = 2 * Precision * Racall / (Precision + Racall)$$
$$= 0.7404,$$
$$F\beta = (1 + \beta^2).Precision * Racall / (\beta^2.Precision + Racall)$$
$$= 1.040$$

TABLE 11.2
Population of Search Agents

	The Population of Search Agents								
SA$_1$	13.331	−4.7102	7.0227	3.4541	9.0718	−4.7589	−3.9202	0.6140	9.0630
SA$_2$	19.313	−1.5567	35.2923	0	9.9334	−0.0573	0	1.1041	10.9192
SA$_3$	23.192	38.0225	−5.8938	94.8870	−18.076	18.6600	0	−7.2449	2.3628
SA$_4$	−18.014	41.6321	2.8209	−7.4259	29.9623	7.4951	−2.9950	22.6104	20.0838

TABLE 11.3
First Whale in Population of Search Agents

	The Population of Search Agents								
SA$_1$	13.331	−4.7102	7.0227	3.4541	9.0718	−4.7589	−3.9202	0.6140	9.0630

TABLE 11.4
Cumulative Growth of Population of Search Agents

	The Population of Search Agents								
SA$_1$	13.331	−4.7102	7.0227	3.4541	9.0718	−4.7589	−3.9202	0.6140	9.0630
SA$_2$	19.313	−1.5567	35.2923	0	9.9334	−0.0573	0	1.1041	10.9192

TABLE 11.5
Cumulative Growth of Population of Search Agents

	The Population of Search Agents								
SA$_1$	13.331	−4.7102	7.0227	3.4541	9.0718	−4.7589	−3.920	0.6140	9.0630
SA$_2$	19.313	−1.5567	35.2923	0	9.9334	−0.0573	0	1.1041	10.9192
SA$_3$	23.192	38.0225	−5.8938	94.8870	−18.076	18.6600	0	−7.2449	2.3628

TABLE 11.6
Cumulative Growth of Population of Search Agents

	The Population of Search Agents								
SA$_1$	−1.461	−3.254	−3.1374	−4.2079	2.6279	0.92962	−0.9046	−20.884	16.8257
SA$_2$	−20.2074	14.8309	−9.0647	−4.9313	−9.3884	9.9343	−12.7284	3.538	−14.9092
SA$_3$	−4.372	22.8838	−14.2901	13.9465	2.1423	3.0014	−24.6069	−17.2609	11.7807
SA$_4$	−5.0778	1.7222	−25.1099	−4.3599	−6.2646	2.3318	2.0823	9.3937	15.8757

TABLE 11.7
Cumulative Growth of Population of Search Agents

The Population of Search Agents

SA$_1$	13.331	−4.7102	7.0227	3.4541	9.0718	−4.7589	−3.9202	0.6140	9.0630
SA$_2$	19.313	−1.5567	35.2923	0	9.9334	−0.0573	0	1.1041	10.9192
SA$_3$	23.192	38.0225	−5.8938	94.8870	−18.076	18.6600	0	−7.2449	2.3628
SA$_4$	−18.014	41.6321	2.8209	−7.4259	29.9623	7.4951	−2.9950	22.6104	20.0838

TABLE 11.8
Leader Position and Best Solution for Each Iteration

Itr.					Leader Position					OF
1	8	0	1	8	6	0	8	1	6	266
2	8	0	1	8	6	0	8	1	6	266
3	1.5617	2.4853	1.3653	−4.3479	7.6563	4.3776	−21.3106	−3.1727	4.6172	238.5518
4	1.5617	2.4853	1.3653	−4.3479	7.6563	4.3776	−21.3106	−3.1727	4.6172	238.5518
5	1.5617	2.4853	1.3653	−4.3479	7.6563	4.3776	−21.3106	−3.1727	4.6172	238.5518
6	1.5617	2.4853	1.3653	−4.3479	7.6563	4.3776	−21.3106	−3.1727	4.6172	238.5518
7	1.5617	2.4853	1.3653	−4.3479	7.6563	4.3776	−21.3106	−3.1727	4.6172	238.5518
8	1.5617	2.4853	1.3653	−4.3479	7.6563	4.3776	−21.3106	−3.1727	4.6172	238.5518
9	1.5617	2.4853	1.3653	−4.3479	7.6563	4.3776	−21.3106	−3.1727	4.6172	238.5518
10	1.5617	2.4853	1.3653	−4.3479	7.6563	4.3776	−21.3106	−3.1727	4.6172	238.5518
11	0.9900	−0.0081	−1.6567	−4.4365	6.7710	5.2744	−6.8026	−2.5459	1.7514	152.8969
12	0.9900	−0.0081	−1.6567	−4.4365	6.7710	5.2744	−6.8026	−2.5459	1.7514	152.8969
13	0.9900	−0.0081	−1.6567	−4.4365	6.7710	5.2744	−6.8026	−2.5459	1.7514	152.8969
14	0.9900	−0.0081	−1.6567	−4.4365	6.7710	5.2744	−6.8026	−2.5459	1.7514	152.8969
15	1.1301	0.2734	−2.3936	−2.8898	5.1452	1.0745	4.4406	−2.2203	4.9591	92.3015
16	1.1301	0.2734	−2.3936	−2.8898	5.1452	1.0745	4.4406	−2.2203	4.9591	92.3015
17	1.1301	0.2734	−2.3936	−2.8898	5.1452	1.0745	4.4406	−2.2203	4.9591	92.3015
18	1.9407	−0.1367	−1.6504	−1.4513	3.2402	3.8479	−2.5779	−2.3605	3.1992	56.3735
19	1.9407	−0.1367	−1.6504	−1.4513	3.2402	3.8479	−2.5779	−2.3605	3.1992	56.3735
20	−1.6040	0.0639	−3.0081	−1.3975	1.4064	4.6044	−2.3031	−1.3416	3.3618	55.1624
–	–	–	–							
30	1.7115	−0.0531	−1.8745	−1.6894	0.3087	−1.5641	2.6422	−2.6942	0.9428	26.97
31	2.4735	0.1532	−0.0760	−1.1346	0.8134	−2.2844	1.0108	−0.4823	−0.5389	14.8597
–	–	–	–							
40	2.2659	0.1409	−0.0940	−1.7441	0.686	0.9851	1.3203	−0.9915	−0.6892	12.8475
41	0.8233	−0.0227	−0.0844	−0.7519	1.0772	1.1013	−3.6941	−1.3695	−0.4333	10.4599
–	–	–								
45	1.6298	0.1046	−0.0454	−0.4013	0.0146	0.6543	1.2504	−0.2912	−1.1581	6.2481
46	1.7574	0.0579	−0.0725	−0.6326	0.0200	0.7084	0.4352	−0.1960	−1.1145	5.4696
47	1.1321	0.0710	−0.0930	−0.3921	−0.0888	0.3595	0.7864	−0.2409	−1.1113	3.4976
48	0.0587	0.0208	−0.1602	−0.3600	−0.0125	0.3353	0.6031	−0.7458	−1.3470	3.0061
49	0.0902	0.0095	−0.1938	−0.3189	−0.0041	0.2110	0.2278	−0.4603	−0.8146	1.1193
50	0.0816	0.0095	−0.0993	−0.2977	−0.0041	0.3152	0.1816	−0.0472	−0.5726	0.56769

TABLE 11.9
Best Solution for Each Iteration

Iteration	Best Fitness	Iteration	Best Fitness
1	266	2	266
3	238.5518	4	238.5518
5	238.5518	6	238.5518
7	238.5518	8	238.5518
9	238.5518	10	238.5518
11	152.8969	12	152.8969
13	152.8969	14	152.8969
15	92.3015	16	92.3015
17	92.3015	18	56.3735
19	56.3735	20	55.1624
21	55.1624	22	55.1624
23	55.1624	24	55.1624
25	55.1624	26	55.1624
27	26.97	28	26.97
29	26.97	30	26.97
31	14.8597	32	14.8597
33	14.8597	34	12.8475
35	12.8475	36	12.8475
37	12.8475	38	12.8475
39	12.8475	40	12.8475
41	10.4599	42	10.4599
43	8.04	44	7.2489
45	6.2481	46	5.4696
47	3.4976	48	3.0061
49	1.1193	50	0.56769

while the values generated based on testing dataset are

$$Accuracy = TP + TN / (TP + FN + FP + TN) = 0.62,$$
$$Precision = TP / (TP + FP) = 0.62,$$
$$Racall = TP / (TP + FN) = 0.55,$$
$$F_{-measure} = 2 * Precision * Racall / (Precision + Racall)$$
$$= 0.582,$$
$$F\beta = (1 + \beta^2).Precision * Racall / (\beta^2.Precision + Racall)$$
$$= 0.681$$

11.5 CONCLUSION AND FUTURE WORKS

Despite the accuracy and sensitivity of the data that we dealt with in this study, we were able to obtain a high performance for the training data and acceptable for the test data based on the five measures used to verify the accuracy of the proposed model.

The process of dividing the chains for chemical reactions or proteins is a question that needs infinite precision, and we have survived this by generating five intermediate buffers, each of which is transformed into tokens of a specific length, and then each token has been coded depending on the length of the token and the intermediate buffer that contains it for easy handling programmatically.

Dealing with interactions or predicting them by computer is a very important issue that makes researchers often move away from it and not discuss it and resort to using other data that are less complex and more readily available, so dealing with this type of data is in itself a challenge. In this study, a manually entered database was used to ensure its accuracy and reliability

The Dselect proved highly effective in determining pivots (i.e., number of search agents needed to discover the suitable material for each interaction). Therefore, we recommend its use in many other optimization algorithms based on the search agent in their work such as (Ant lion, partial swarm algorithms), because the Dselect dependence on the principles of division, arrangement, and selection continues to reach the best pivots.

A combination of computation techniques represented by Dselect and Whale reduces the time of searching related to whale and enhance their performance (i.e., reduce the computation). It may be possible to perform another objective function for that optimization algorithm, such as the polynomial functions or hyperbolic functions. It is possible to build a recommendations system based on one of the mining methods such as the FP-growth algorithm form optimal subgraph using other datasets, such as sequence of proteins or DNA.

REFERENCES

1. Ali, S. H., (2012), A novel tool (FP-KC) for handle the three main dimensions reduction and association rule mining, IEEE, *6th International Conference on Sciences of Electronics, Technologies of Information and Telecommunications (SETIT)*, pp. 951–961

2. Ray, A., Holder, L. B., and Bifet, A. (2019). Efficient frequent subgraph mining on large streaming graphs. *Intelligent Data Analysis*, 23(1), 103–132. https://doi.org/10.3233/IDA-173705

3. Dincer, I., Rosen, M. A., and Ahmadi, P. (2017). Modeling and optimization. *Optimization of Energy Systems*. https://doi.org/10.1002/9781118894484.ch2

4. Wang, Z. (2019). Research on subgraph distribution algorithm based on label null model. *Cluster Computing*, 22, 5521–5533. https://doi.org/10.1007/s10586-017-1359-5

5. Ali, S. H., (2012). "Miner for OACCR: Case of medical data analysis in knowledge discovery," *IEEE, 2012 6th International Conference on Sciences of Electronics, Technologies of Information and Telecommunications (SETIT)*, Sousse, pp. 962–975. https://doi.org/10.1109/SETIT.2012.6482043

6. Dönmez, A. (2020). Synthesis, structure and photoluminescence analysis of a Ho3+-cluster-based 3D coordination polymer: {Ho2(H2O)2(DMF)2(ATPA)3}n. *Journal of Cluster Science*, 4. https://doi.org/10.1007/s10876-020-01760-4

7. Churiwala, S. (2016). Designing with Xilinx® FPGAs: Using Vivado. Designing with Xilinx® FPGAs: Using Vivado, 1–260. https://doi.org/10.1007/978-3-319-42438-5

8. Zhao, Y., Tarus, S. K., Yang, L. T., Sun, J., Ge, Y., and Wang, J. (2020). Privacy-preserving clustering for big data in cyber-physical-social systems: survey and perspectives. *Information Sciences*, 515, 132–155. https://doi.org/10.1016/j.ins.2019.10.019

9. Zhang, C., Huang, Y., Wang, Z., Jiang, H., and Yan, D. (2018). Cross-camera multi-person tracking by leveraging fast graph mining algorithm. *Journal of Visual Communication and Image Representation*, 55, 711–719. https://doi.org/10.1016/j.jvcir.2018.08.006

10. Al-Janabi, Samaher and Alkaim, Ayad, (2022), A novel optimization algorithm (Lion-AYAD) to find optimal DNA protein synthesis, *Egyptian Informatics Journal*. https://doi.org/10.1016/j.eij.2022.01.004

11. Mirjalili, S. and Lewis, A. (2016). The Whale optimization algorithm. *Advances in Engineering Software*, 95, 51–67. https://doi.org/10.1016/j.advengsoft.2016.01.008

12. Guha, A. and Samanta, D. (2020). *Real-time application of document classification based on machine learning*. https://doi.org/10.1007/978-3-030-38501-9_37

13. Liu, J., Abbass, H. A., and Tan, K. C. (n.d.). *Complex Networks*. https://doi.org/10.1007/978-3-319-60000-0

14. Alkaim, A.F. and Al_Janabi, S. (2020). Multi objectives optimization to gas flaring reduction from oil production. In: Farhaoui, Y. (eds) *Big Data and Networks Technologies. BDNT 2019*. Lecture Notes in Networks and Systems (Vol. 81). Springer, Cham. https://doi.org/10.1007/978-3-030-23672-4_10

15. Preti, G., Lissandrini, M., Mottin, D., and Velegrakis, Y. (2019). Mining patterns in graphs with multiple weights. *Distributed and Parallel Databases*. https://doi.org/10.1007/s10619-019-07259-w

16. Balas, V. E. (2016). *Advances in intelligent systems and computing 634 soft computing applications* (Vol. 2).

17. Aridhi, S. and Mephu Nguifo, E. (2016). Big graph mining: frameworks and techniques. *Big Data Research*, 6, 1–10. https://doi.org/10.1016/j.bdr.2016.07.002

18. Qiu, C. and Dai, J. S. (n.d.). *Springer Tracts in Advanced Robotics 139 Analysis and Synthesis of Compliant Parallel Mechanisms — Screw Theory Approach*.

19. Tao, G. (2021). *The computer-aided design of miao costume patterns based on big data* (Vol. 2). https://doi.org/10.1007/978-3-030-51556-0_132

20. Chand Bansal, J., Kusum, Nagar, A. K., Johri, P., Kumar, J., Sudip, V., and Editors, P. (n.d.). Algorithms for Intelligent Systems Series Editors: Applications of Machine Learning. http://www.springer.com/series/16171

12 Structural Health Monitoring of Existing Building Structures for Creating Green Smart Cities Using Deep Learning

Nishant Raj Kapoor, Aman Kumar,
Harish Chandra Arora and Ashok Kumar
CSIR-Central Building Research Institute, Roorkee, India

CONTENTS

DOI: 10.1201/9781003307822-15

12.1 INTRODUCTION

Economic and social development of the country is based on the pillar of the construction industry [1, 2]. In 2018, the contribution of the global construction industry to the GDP was about 6 percent [3], but it is forecasted that by the end of 2023 this percentage can be increasing at the rate of 4.2 percent annually [4]. The CO_2 emission, GDP, and population growth of India are presented in Figures 12.1 and 12.2, with the CO_2 emission shown in accordance with the building sector from the last five decades [5]. Aging of building structures creates many structural (spalling [6, 7], elemental failure, and reinforcement corrosion) as well as non-structural (hair-line cracks, dampness, and sign of seepage, etc.) [8–10] defects that are responsible for the degradation of structures and sometimes cause catastrophic failure [11]. Maintenance plays a crucial role in the lifecycle of any structure (building, bridges, aircraft, roads, and mechanical infrastructures), and it becomes a concern to all countries as the number of older structures is increasing rapidly [12]. The maintenance costs of these structures increase with respect to time if suitable periodic maintenance was not done properly. The aging of the structure with maintenance and preventive measures is illustrated in Figure 12.3 concerning minor and major rehabilitation. The period of periodic maintenance depends on the type and age of the structure and includes present compressive strength of concrete [13, 14], density [15], humidity [16–18], carbonation level [19–21], corrosion level [22–24], non-structural cracks, etc.

The periodic maintenance needs specialized/trained staff to categorize the structural damages and destructions, and the process is also time-consuming. To address such kinds of issues, structural health monitoring (SHM) methods were presented in the 1960s. Firstly, the SHM technique was used in the railway to check the flaws and defects in the iron by normally hitting the hammer on the surface; this is a

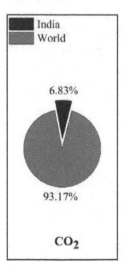 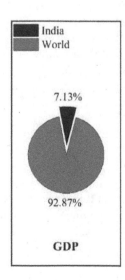 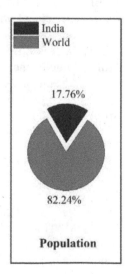

FIGURE 12.1 Plot of comparison of CO_2 emission, GDP and population of India with respect to world [5].

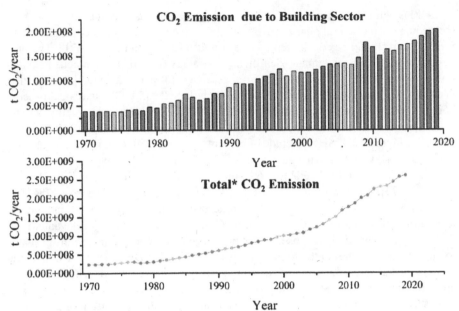

FIGURE 12.2 CO_2 emission due to buildings and the total amount of CO_2 emission from 1970 to 2019 [5].

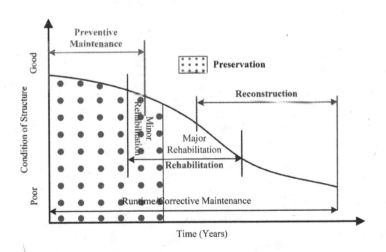

FIGURE 12.3 Plot between the condition of structures versus time.

sound-based phenomenon. Later, these types of techniques were adopted by the aerospace, mechanical, and civil engineering sectors. In civil engineering SHM is used in structures like bridges [25–31], roads [32, 33], buildings (concrete and masonry) [34–39], tunnels [40–43], dams [44–49], railways [50–54], and other steel structures [55].

SHM is defined by the various authors in the literature, as "SHM contains sensing techniques and structural characteristics analysis to detect structural damage or degradation and should be considered for the condition assessment" [56, 57]. "The process of implementing a damage identification strategy for aerospace, mechanical and civil engineering infrastructure is referred as SHM" [58]. The damage identification is carried out with six major fragments that include SHM [59–80], statistical process control (SPC) [81], non-destructive evaluation (NDE) [82], semi-destructive testing (SDE) [83], condition monitoring (CM) [84], and damage prognosis (DP) [85, 86] as shown in Figure 12.4. SHM includes fiber-optic sensors [59–61], accelerometer for SHM [62–64], vibrating wire transducers [65, 66], linear variable differential transformer (LVDT) [67], load cells [68, 69], inclinometer (slope indicator) [70, 71], tiltmeter [72, 73], acoustic emission sensor [74–77], and temperature sensors [78–80].

SHM is associated with the industry of aerospace, mechanical, and construction to identify the damages in the structures. Condition monitoring is relevant to the SHM, but predominately it is used in the power generation and manufacturing sector to identify the damages in the rotating parts of machines. NDE is used to evaluate the damage and characterize the type of damage based on strength, density, corrosion, and similar parameters. SPC is the process-based type of identification technique and used sensors to monitor structural damages. Damage prognosis is used for predicting the remaining life of a structure.

After its use in the aerospace and mechanical industry, SHM was firstly used in the civil engineering sector to monitor the dams [58]. This step was initially taken by the UK government after the failure of the 29 m long Dale Dyke dam near Sheffield, which resulted in the form of 254 casualties in 1864 [87]. In 1975, the legislation

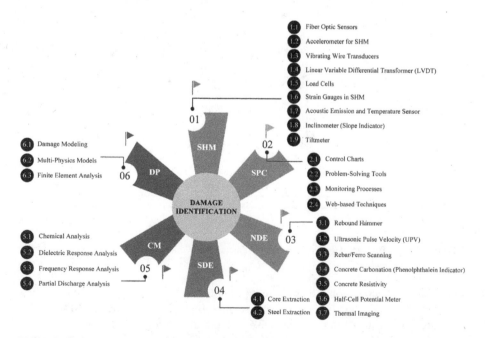

FIGURE 12.4 Damage identification techniques.

committee of the UK passed the Reservoir Act. In this act, it is necessary to appoint a supervising engineer for the surveillance dam and reservoir. The main responsibilities of the supervising engineer were to prepare the record of water level, meteorological conditions, structure temperature, etc.

12.2 FUNDAMENTAL OBJECTIVES OF MONITORING OF CIVIL STRUCTURES

Monitoring and maintenance of structures will surely prevent financial losses along with enhanced safety and health (public and structure). In the present era, the advancement in technological support is utilized to examine the health of structure effectively and efficiently [88]. The government of different countries implements strict rules and stringent laws concerning the procedure adopted and the time duration for periodic maintenance for masonry, steel, and concretes structures. The fundamental objective of SHM is reducing capital investment and accidental risks with maintaining structural health. In detail it is described as: (i) cost-effectiveness [89], (ii) detecting early risk [90], (iii) improved public safety, and (iv) the increased life span of the structure. The fundamental objectives of monitoring civil structures are shown in Figure 12.5.

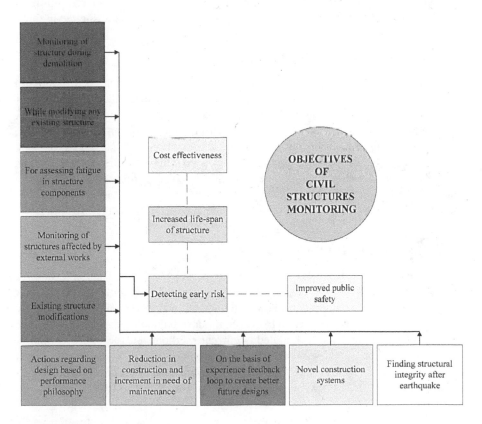

FIGURE 12.5   The fundamental objective of monitoring civil structures.

12.2.1 Cost-Effectiveness

Proper SHM implementation is responsible to reduce both the short- and long-term expenditures of structures. For increasing overall profit, the market and industry are quite interested in SHM. The researchers are putting continuous efforts to reduce maintenance costs based on the condition-based monitoring (CBM) technique. In CBM, sensors are used to keep an eye on structures as well as monitoring them continuously and when safety is threatened, providing the necessary maintenance to structures [91–93]. The detection of defects in structures helps in eliminating failures to elude major financial loss embedded in the process of demolition and reconstruction of structures entirely or partially [94–96].

12.2.2 Detecting Early Risk

Regular SHM enables engineers to identify defects in structures, the status of structure's health, sudden impacts (due to seismic activities and other natural calamities), as well as associated risks in the initial stages. The early assessment of structure prevents or reduces the risks associated with happenings like earthquakes, floods, etc. The sensors are installed in the dams, bridges, and other civil infrastructures at strategic locations to monitor the faults and movements. Based on collected information the failures can be prevented to a great extent if movements are spotted in time.

12.2.3 Improved Public Safety

The major benefit of SHM is increased public safety. Sensors deployed in modern SHM techniques provide appropriate results from the collected data. Critical structures are monitored as per government policies to ensure the safety of the public. Many weak points and cracks are developed with the increasing age of the structure. SHM enables engineers to identify faults and cracks at an early stage in structures, resulting in early rectification of problems associated with structures. If the problems are severe and cannot be rectified, the structure is isolated from the general public due to safety concerns. SHM increases public safety management as well as environmental concerns. SHM guarantees structure health with public safety [97, 98].

12.2.4 Increased Life Span of Structure

Continuous SHM enables engineers to identify cracks as well as possible failures in their early stages to enhance the structure's life span along with improving their efficiency. Conventional methods like visual inspection and NDT are not particularly effective due to accuracy concerns. However, modern technologies and methods like transient thermography, optical and eddy current methods, etc. equipped engineers to identify even the minutest failures. The identified minute cracks can be rectified at their initial stage so their further propagation is minimized or prevented. This results in postponing the failure of structure at their initial stages [99, 100].

12.3 ARTIFICIAL INTELLIGENCE

Artificial Intelligence (AI) is the field that can ingress a huge amount of heterogeneous technological solutions with great potential to enhance efficiency and solve issues related to merged interdisciplinary systems (medical, sciences, engineering and agricultural, etc.) [3, 4, 6–9]. AI is defined as "the capability of a machine to imitate intelligent human behaviour" [101].

In 1956, John McCarthy coined the term 'Artificial Intelligence' during a workshop at Dartmouth college [101, 102]. After the academic introduction of AI in the workshop, during the 1960s, AI research was funded primarily by the US Department of Defense. Afterward, AI projects see various ups and downs in research funding due to criticism and low success rate aligned in the path during the 1970s and 1980s known as 'AI winter' [103, 104]. During the late 1990s, AI gets its pace back again and began to use in real-time scenarios in sectors like medical, data mining, logistics, engineering, etc. [101, 105, 106]. Increased computational capabilities enable AI to show fascinating results when merged with the fields like mathematics, economics, and statistics [107–109]. Further, AI expands its area and enters more sectors. The entry of AI in civil engineering is reported back in the late 1990s and early years of the 21st century [102]. AI can benefit various applications extensively in the field of civil engineering including SHM [110], construction management, building materials, geotechnical engineering, transportation engineering, and hydraulic engineering as well as optimization, etc.

The upcoming decade will witness many advancements in AI and SHM due to the increasing popularity of the smart city concept at both global and local levels [101, 111–113]. Introducing AI in the SHM will give thrust to the infrastructure and construction sector with added safety and ease in maintenance. Maintenance personal and end-users can diagnose the real-time state as well as behavior of a structure more precisely and easily at any moment during the lifecycle of a structure. Issues concerning decision-making like abnormality detection, corrosion detection, damage detection, etc. can be easily diagnosed and solved by AI models with the highest level of accuracy, which is intellectually difficult to address by human beings. By gathering past information and experience, computers can learn to predict patterns and understand the structure of the information according to the concept hierarchy [114]. IoT, data mining, smart structures, ML, and DL are the companions of AI to perform SHM on various structures.

AI has a subdivision known as machine learning (ML). Further, ML has a subcategory known as deep learning (DL). ML is classified into two categories based on methods used: soft- computing methods (SCM) and hard-computing methods (HCM). Soft computing provides approximate results and includes neural sets, fuzzy logic, and probabilistic reasoning, whereas hard computing provides accurate results and contain crisp systems, numerical analysis, and binary logic. Soft computing is similar to computational intelligence (CI) and is capable to process data obtained from samples or experimental observations.

The share of AI in civil engineering increased profusely in the last decade. SHM is based on deep learning (DL), image processing (IP), pattern recognition (PR), and machine learning (ML). ML contains deep and shallow architecture based on model depth. Model depth can be understood as the difference between input and output layers. If the model is "deep," it represents that input layers are much more than output layers, whereas "shallow" denotes that there are fewer input layers in the process and the difference between the input and output layers is low. State-of-the-art DL technologies contain thousands of layers to process data. DL techniques are developed in the 1980s, but due to inadequate computer systems and software, they remain unpopular for many years in the starting.

12.3.1 Machine Learning

Machine learning enables computers to make predictions based on the data provided as an input by developing an algorithm after analyzing the input data [110]. ML enables computers to learn without creating particular programming [98]. ML creates both descriptive and predictive models according to the collected and analyzed data. In civil engineering, the scope of ML is spreading in all the sub-branches rapidly than other methods of AI. Apart from civil engineering, ML (subpart of AI) is extensively contributing to R&D activities of computer science engineering, finance, information technology, statistics, philosophy, and many other disciplines [115]. In ML the prime focus areas are IP, DL, and PR, where IP and object recognition are part of DL and in PR system trying to recognize the patterns in data and then classify them accordingly. The subcategories of machine learning such as supervised and unsupervised learning with their branch categories are shown in Figure 12.6.

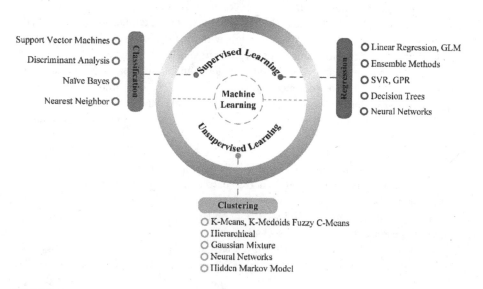

FIGURE 12.6   Machine learning technique.

12.3.2 DEEP LEARNING

DL is the emerging area of AI, and it has acquired consideration during the most recent years. DL comprises an architectural structure, created on the basis of numerous hidden layers. DL predicts the results as an output based on learnings from these hidden layers. In DL and PR, the system necessitates significant area expertise to extract the element (feature) information from the crude information (e.g., a picture) into a reasonable element (feature) vector from where it could categorize the input information pattern [116]. However, DL permits the input information to the learning algorithm without mining the element information. Compared to hand-coding, DL is the appropriate way to learn from the set of element data. Manual coding is used to mine information in hand-coding, whereas DL automatically processes the information [117].

12.4 ARTIFICIAL INTELLIGENCE IN CIVIL ENGINEERING

AI is enormous and retains infinite scope in civil engineering. No single subdisciplines of civil engineering are unimpaired from AI. Broadly subdomains of civil engineering like concrete technology, structural analysis, construction management, transportation engineering, green structures, and water management using AI extensively nowadays as shown in Figure 12.7 [118–122].

Presently, concrete is the most widely used building material among all the building materials if we did not consider water. Approximately three tons per person per year of concrete is utilized globally [123]. Concrete is a hard-strong composite building material; heterogeneous in nature and basically, it is the mixture of fine aggregate, coarse aggregate, cement, and water. In other words, concrete is a mass formed by coalescence of sand, grit/gravel/crushed stone, cement, and water. Durability and strength of concrete are significantly influenced by properties of ingredients, mix proportions, the technique of placing, compaction, and curing. Concrete inhibits properties like durability, impermeability, resistance to abrasion and fire, and high strength. AI is used to optimize and predict workability and compressive strength of mix proportions in concrete. AI is also used to classify concrete aggregates.

Strength and ease in placing the concrete on formwork depend on the workability of concrete. The concrete trials require time, material, manpower, and are significantly laborious, resulting in wastage of materials, manpower, and time. Additionally, it escalates the concrete production cost. To diminish wastage as well as reducing design cost, and time; the artificial neural network (ANN) assists in generating required concrete workability models. These models predict the concrete slump value precisely. The compressive strength of concrete depends on its constituents. The durability of concrete is dependent on the compressive strength.

12.4.1 ARTIFICIAL INTELLIGENCE IN SHM

In structural health monitoring, artificial intelligence tools such as image processing and data extraction tools are predominantly used. Mainly in civil infrastructures image processing tool is quite useful to detect and analyze the defects such as cracks,

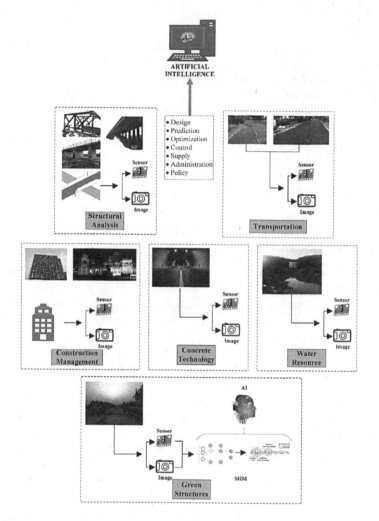

FIGURE 12.7   AI application in civil engineering.

dampness, seepage, thermal changes, etc. Recent studies show that the image-processing techniques for detecting the cracks in structures are boosting productivity. The crack information is enough alone to decide the rehabilitation/repair techniques [124]. Image binarization (IB) is commonly used in medical image processing and text pattern recognition, but in the process of crack identification, it is also showing excellent results [125–127]. Binarization is completely dependent on pixels of image, image quality, background noise, and other image-related parameters. Crack detection is also affected by the low contrast of an image, noise pollution, spalling of concrete, and uneven illumination.

Digital image correlation (DIC) is also used in the crack detection and measurement by equating the original images of the structure in healthy condition with the deteriorated images (images having cracks) at the present condition [128]. IB process

converts the grayscale image into black-and-white information. IB process transforms the bright and dark pixels in a grayscale image into a binary image with only
black-and-white information.

The general image-processing process and the structure of crack–model image
processing is shown in Figure 12.8(a) and (b), respectively.

12.4.1.1   Image Binarization (IB)

The binarization function is used to create binary images from the 2D or 3D grayscale images by replacing all the determined thresholds with 1s and setting other
values to 0s. In MATLAB most commonly used method of binarization is the "Otsu's
method," which simply minimizes the intraclass variance of the threshold white and
black pixels [129]. Color images should be initially converted into grayscale images
having threshold values from 0 to 255 for black-and-white information. In the process of binarization, "each pixel of the grayscale image is examined by equating its
pixel value with the threshold. Higher the pixel value then threshold function leads
to the one (white) in the binary image and lower values lead to zero (black)" shown
in Figure 12.9. Binarization parameters include the "window in which threshold calculation is conducted" and "sensitivity that controls the contribution of the statistical

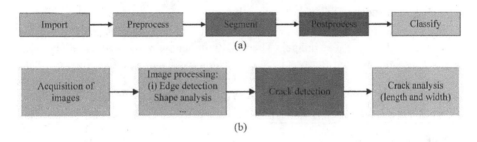

(a)

(b)

FIGURE 12.8   (a) General image-processing process (b) structure of crack-model image
processing.

Grayscale Image

121	200	117	119	128	110
117	118	115	124	78	80
115	130	128	75	81	112
121	200	140	80	117	119
80	75	77	64	113	115
130	120	140	160	110	124

Binary Image

1	1	1	1	1	1
1	1	1	1	0	0
1	1	1	0	0	1
1	1	1	0	1	1
0	0	0	0	1	1
1	1	1	1	1	1

FIGURE 12.9   Schematic demonstration of the conversion of grayscale image to binary image.

parameters of the pixels values to the threshold calculations" [130, 131]. The binarized image with pixel values 0 and 1 are shown in Figure 12.9.

12.4.1.2 Threshold Values

For a text and medical identification purposes, numerous IB techniques have been carried out to obtain binary images more efficiently and precisely. The threshold numbers by considering minimum and maximum "intensities of a selected window" are summarized by the various researchers [132–136] are tabulated in Table 12.1. The results of IB may differ with respect to the image binarization method/technique. The results of IB may be vary with the properties of images along with method of image binarization.

Otsu's method of thresholding. It is a clustering-based most commonly used method of thresholding and compatible with all types of images [137]. The principle of this method is to separate the pixels within the image into two groups. ω_0 and μ_0 are the ratios of the number of pixels and average gray level that are obtained from the separated image. Similarly, the background image is separated into ω_1 and μ_1. The total mean of the gray image is defined in the below expression:

$$\mu = \omega_0(t)\mu_0(t) + \omega_1(t)\mu_1(t) \qquad (12.1)$$

12.4.1.3 Concerns in Crack-Sensing Images

The prime objective of binarization is to identify the defects such as crack length and width within the processed image. "The sensitivity and window size should be properly selected to pinpoint the precise crack pixels from the grayscale image" [138]. The background pixel value of a grayscale image is higher than the pixel value of the crack element; it increases the window size and thus increases the threshold value of

---

TABLE 12.1
Methods to Determine the Threshold Values

Author	Equation	Application
Bernsen (1986) [132]	$\dfrac{Z_{max} - Z_{min}}{2}$	It is applicable for high-contrast images.
Niblack (1990) [133]	$T = m + k \times s$	It is adaptive for a less noisy background.
Sauvola & Pietikäinen (2000) [134]	$T = m \times \left\{ 1 - k \times \left(1 - \dfrac{s}{R} \right) \right\}$	It can work with a noisy background.
Wolf et al. (2004) [135]	$T = (1-k) \times m + k \times M + k \times \dfrac{s}{R} \times (m - M)$	This method is good to work with dark colors.
Khurshid et al. (2009) [136]	$T = m + k\sqrt{B + m^2}$	By adding square root to the variance remove the noisy background from the image.

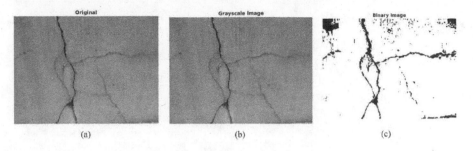

FIGURE 12.10 Conversion of an original image to binary image.

background pixels. This information leads to an overestimation of the crack in the binary image.

The binarization optimization criteria include (i) accuracy of crack length, (ii) identification of width crack, and (iii) processing (computational) time. All the color images are first converted into grayscale images and then binarization techniques are implemented to convert them into binary images as shown in Figure 12.10. Crack width is measured by calculating the crack pixels values at the exact places at which crack measurement is to be desired.

The final width of the crack in millimeters is calculated using the "camera pinhole model" [139].

$$W_r = D_p W_p = \frac{10 D_w}{P_c L_f} W_p \tag{12.2}$$

$$E_{\text{width}} = \frac{1}{n} \sqrt{\sum_{i=1}^{n} \left(\frac{d_c - d_m}{d_m} \right)^2_i} \tag{12.3}$$

The crack length is calculated using the given formula mentioned in the equation:

$$R_{\text{Length}} = \frac{L_{\text{Est}}}{L_{\text{Total}}} \tag{12.4}$$

The next setup is to generate the final image for crack detection by subtracting correcting image from the input/original image as shown in Figure 12.11. The output image is obtained by [140].

$$I_s(x_i) = \max \begin{cases} \text{median}_{x_j \in R_i} I(x_j) - I(x_i) \\ 0 \end{cases} \tag{12.5}$$

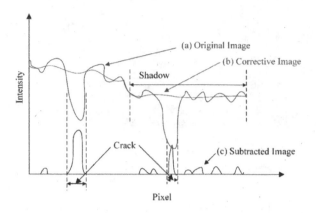

FIGURE 12.11   Removal of serious variations like shading [140].

12.5   CASE STUDY OF AN UNOCCUPIED BUILDING AT CSIR-CBRI CAMPUS

This is a 40-year-old masonry building situated in the northern part of India having coordinates 29°51'42" N and 77°54'20" E. The total plinth area of this building is approximately 50 m². Figure 12.13 illustrated the different types of damages in the building such as the sign of seepage of water, cracks near window openings, spalling, damage due to cracks, the sign of corrosion, as well as loss of plaster and exposure to weathering and material degradation. When the structure starts to degrade, the first indication is cracks in the walls or reinforced concrete members. In addition, an inspection of concrete and masonry structures on the basis of crack measurement and its patterns is helpful in the life prediction of structures. A total of 32 digital images of different locations were captured from this building including information on crack sizes, width, length, direction, and patterns using Canon 1500D camera. Some of the crack patterns and other information are quite similar, so authors categorized them into five categories on that basis, as shown in Figure 12.14. The plan of the inspected building and photographs taken of locations are shown in Figures 12.12 and 12.15, respectively.

The sample images of Figure 12.14 are considered for processing. The processed images for Location 1 to Location 5 are shown in Figure 12.17–12.21 respectively. The histogram is applied to get better RGB information about original images and grayscale images.

Digital images of the buildings were captured and prepare a huge amount of data. Then these images were further processed in MATLAB code to check the defects like quantification of the width of the crack, crack length and crack pattern, etc. Figure 12.13 presents the real images of outside the building. RGB images of these locations were load in MATLAB to detect defects and cracks. Figure 12.14 (3) shows the cracks in the building, and the corresponding distress condition is identified using developed algorithms. This algorithm helps in the quick assessment of the structures on the basis of photographs that further provide assistance in structural health monitoring. The manual measurement of crack width is shown in Figure 12.16.

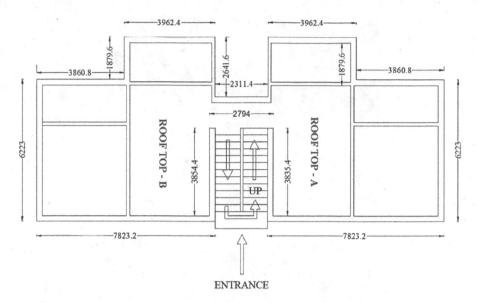

FIGURE 12.12   Plan of 50-year-old building (all dimensions are in mm).

12.5.1   RESULTS OF CRACKS IDENTIFICATION FROM THE PROPOSED IMAGES IN MATLAB

Location 1 has one horizontal directional crack, the maximum width of the crack and its length having the only error of 1.48 percent and 0.11 percent, respectively, when compared with the manual measurements. The original image of location 1 contains the wood signs at the top side, which creates noise in the processed image as shown in Figure 12.17. By neglecting that portion, overall accuracy of the processed image is good. Location 2 contains both the horizontal and vertical directional cracks as shown in Figure 12.18, in the horizontal direction the error in the length of the crack and maximum width are 0.36 percent and 4.41 percent, respectively, on comparing with manual measurements. In the vertical direction, the error in the length and maximum width size are 1.35 percent and 2.07 percent, respectively. Location 3 also contains the same horizontal and vertical directional cracks with different patterns as shown in Figure 12.19, in the horizontal direction the error in the length of the crack and maximum width size of the crack is 0.33 percent and 1.20 percent. But in the vertical direction, the values of error in length and maximum width of the crack are 0.57 percent and 2.64 percent, respectively.

Location 4 shows the diagonal crack pattern as illustrated in Figure 12.20, the total error in the length of the diagonal crack is 0.19 percent and the maximum width error is 4.11 percent. Location 5 shows both the vertical and diagonal directional cracks, in the vertical direction the error in the length of the crack and maximum width is 0.64 percent and 4.62 percent respectively by comparing with manual

1. Sign of seepage of water
2. Cracks near window openings
3. Spalling
4. Damage due to cracks
5. Sign of corrosion
6. Loss of plaster and exposed to weathering and material degradation

FIGURE 12.13   Various topologies of damages in the building structure.

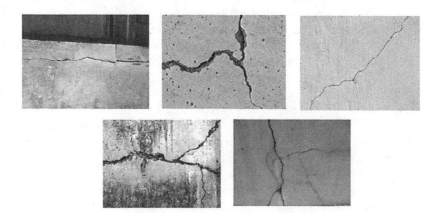

FIGURE 12.14   Different types of cracks in building structures.

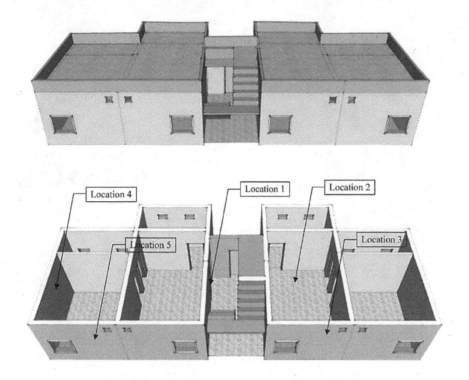

FIGURE 12.15 The image capturing locations for image processing.

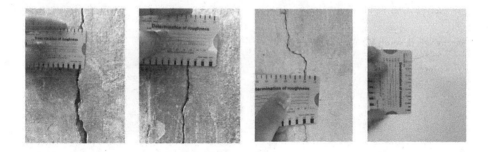

FIGURE 12.16 Manual measurement of cracks.

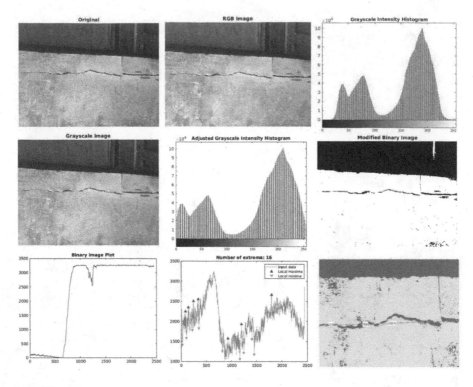

FIGURE 12.17   Analyzed image of location 1.

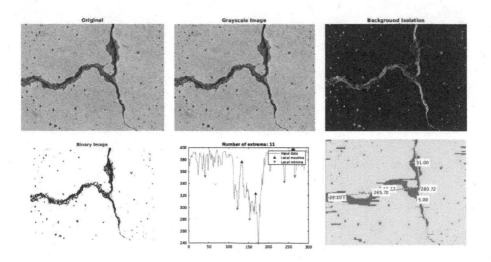

FIGURE 12.18   Analyzed image of location 2.

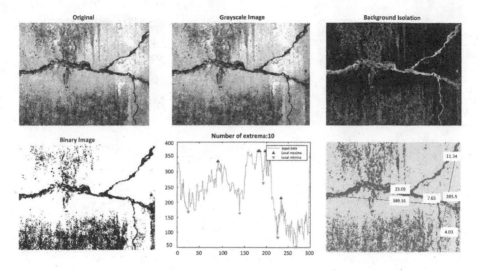

FIGURE 12.19 Analyzed image of location 3.

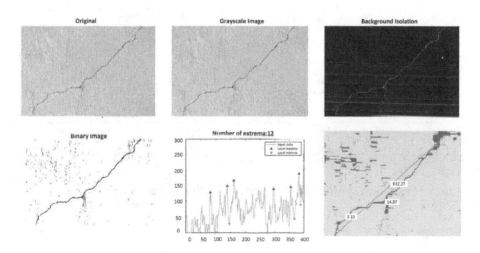

FIGURE 12.20 Analyzed image of location 4.

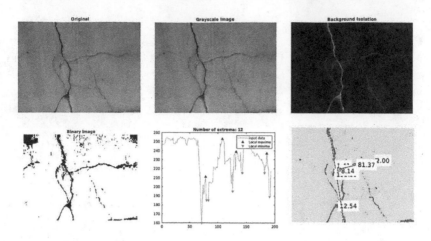

FIGURE 12.21   Analyzed image of location 5.

TABLE 12.2
Crack Length and Width Measurement from Processed Images

Location	H_{Lc} (mm)	V_{Lc}/D_{Lc} (mm)	Max W_{Hc} (mm)	Min W_{Hc} (mm)	Max $W_{Vc}/$ Max W_{Dc} (mm)	Min $W_{Vc}/$ Min W_{Dc} (mm)
1.	2886.97	—	66.20	13.53	—	—
2.	239.13	252.00	17.46	9.96	27.90	4.50
3.	350.24	256.95	20.78	6.88	10.20	3.18
4.	—	569.04	—	—	13.38	1.94
5.	—	174.15/ 73.23	—	—	12.54 / 7.25	1.27 / 1.80

TABLE 12.3
Crack Length and Width Measurement from the Manual Process

Location	HLc (mm)	V_{Lc}/D_{Lc} (mm)	Max W_{Hc} (mm)	Min W_{Hc} (mm)	Max $W_{Vc}/$Max W_{Dc} (mm)	Min $W_{Vc}/$ Min W_{Dc} (mm)
1.	2890.20	—	67.18	14.27	—	—
2.	240.84	255.40	18.23	10.62	28.48	4.91
3.	351.40	258.41	21.03	6.94	10.47	3.69
4.	—	570.12	—	—	13.93	2.05
5.	—	175.26 /73.62	—	—	13.12 /7.50	1.62 /2.01

measurements. In the diagonal direction, the error in the length and maximum width size is 0.53 percent and 3.45 percent, respectively. The test result values of processed images and manual measurements are tabulated in Tables 12.2 and 12.3. Table 12.4 shows the error in results of processed image and manual measurements.

TABLE 12.4
Error in Results of Processed Image and Manual Measurements

Location	Error in H_{Lc} (mm)	Error in V_{Lc}/D_{Lc} (mm)	Error in Max W_{Hc} (mm)	Error in Min W_{Hc} (mm)	Error in Max $W_{vc}/$ Max W_{Dc} (mm)	Error in Min $W_{vc}/$ Min W_{Dc} (mm)
1.	3.23	—	0.98	0.74	—	—
2.	1.71	3.4	0.77	0.66	0.58	0.41
3.	1.16	1.46	0.25	0.06	0.27	0.54
4.	—	*1.08*	—	—	*0.55*	*0.11*
5.	—	*1.11 / 0.39*	—	—	*0.58 / 0.25*	*0.35 / 0.21*

12.6 CONCLUSION

This chapter provides the crack-based information for structural health monitoring of building structures. This study created an IP-based tool to detect the surface cracks of both the concrete and masonry buildings. The digital images were taken for the image processing contain issues like noise, high-low divergence, and uneven brightness. So, with the help of the Otsu method, we can correct them for further analysis. The accuracy of this fabricated MATLAB code is quite good: in the horizontal direction the maximum error in the crack length is found as 0.36 percent, and for maximum crack width its value is 4.41 percent. For the case of the vertical direction, the maximum error in the crack length is 1.35 percent and the maximum error in crack width is 4.62 percent. When cracks are in the diagonal direction, the maximum error in crack length is 0.53 percent and the maximum error in crack width is 4.11 percent. The maximum range of error in all the horizontal, vertical, and diagonal directional cracks is less than 5 percent. This code can quickly analyze the length and width of cracks with additional information of minimum and maximum crack width. In the future, to increase the feasibility of this model by adding the repair techniques or solutions to these (grouting, epoxy filling, and rich mortar repair) for both the large and small cracks. Further, to enhance the structural assessment accuracy by adding infrared thermal imaging (ITI) and stereo mapping.

ABBREVIATION USED

Z_{max}	Histogram maximum pixel in each window
Z_{min}	Histogram minimum pixel in each window
k	Sensitivity of image
m	Mean value
s	Standard deviation
R	Regularising value of standard deviation factor
M	Minimum grayscale image pixel value
B	Variance.
t	Gray level of image
W_r	Original width of crack (mm)
D_p	Camera pixels (resolution)
W_p	Measured crack width in pixels (mm)

D_w Image capturing distance/working distance (mm)
P_c Camera used devices pixels per cm
L_f Camera focal length (mm)
d_c Crack width of binarization image
d_m Measured width using an optical microscope
L_{Est} Crack length estimation using IB method
L_{Total} Crack length from the reference image
$I(x)$ Intensity of pixel x
Ri   Region around pixel xi × Is (xi) (intensity of smoothened image)
H_{Lc} Horizontal length of crack (mm)
V_{Lc}/D_{Lc} Vertical/ *Diagonal* length of crack (mm)
Max W_{Hc} Maximum width of the horizontal crack (mm)
Min W_{Hc} Minimum width of the horizontal crack (mm)
Max W_{Vc} / *Max* W_{Dc} Maximum width of vertical/ *diagonal* crack (mm)
MIN W_{VC} / *MIN* W_{DC} Minimum width of vertical/ *diagonal* crack (mm)

REFERENCES

[1] Aravind, N., Amiya K. Samanta, Joseph V. Thanikal, and Dilip Kr Singha Roy. "An experimental study on the effectiveness of externally bonded corrugated GFRP laminates for flexural cracks of RC beams." *Construction and Building Materials* 136 (2017): 348–360. 10.1016/j.conbuildmat.2017.01.047

[2] Fares, Ali Issa, K. M. A. Sohel, K. Al-Jabri, and Abdullah Al-Mamun. "Characteristics of ferrochrome slag aggregate and its uses as a green material in concrete – a review." *Construction and Building Materials* 294 (2021): 123552. 10.1016/j. conbuildmat.2021.123552

[3] Rahman, M.M. and N.A.O. Ali. "An overview of construction related pollution." *IET Conference Proceedings* 54, no. 4–10 (2018).

[4] Global Construction Industry Report 2021. [available online: https://www.businesswire. com/news/home/20210111005587/en/Global-Construction-Industry-Report-2021-10.5-Trillion-Growth-Opportunities-by-2023---ResearchAndMarkets.com] Retrieved: 15 April 2021.

[5] EDGAR - Emissions Database for Global Atmospheric Research. Accessed 17 April 2021. [available online: https://edgar.jrc.ec.europa.eu/country_profile/IND]

[6] Kodur, Venkatesh and Srishti Banerji. "Modeling the fire-induced spalling in concrete structures incorporating hydro-thermo-mechanical stresses." *Cement and Concrete Composites* 117 (2021): 103902. 10.1016/j.cemconcomp.2020.103902

[7] Moccia, Francesco, Miguel Fernández Ruiz, and Aurelio Muttoni. "Spalling of concrete cover induced by reinforcement." *Engineering Structures* 237 (2021): 112188. 10.1016/j.engstruct.2021.112188

[8] Bojórquez, Juan, Sandra Ponce, Sonia E. Ruiz, et al. "Structural reliability of reinforced concrete buildings under earthquakes and corrosion effects." *Engineering Structures* 237 (2021): 112161. 10.1016/j.engstruct.2021.112161

[9] Gautam, Dipendra, Rabindra Adhikari, and Rajesh Rupakhety. "Seismic fragility of structural and non-structural elements of nepali RC buildings." *Engineering Structures* 232 (2021): 111879. 10.1016/j.engstruct.2021.111879

[10] Faqih, Faisal and Tarek Zayed. "Defect-based building condition assessment." *Building and Environment* 191 (2021): 107575. 10.1016/j.buildenv.2020.107575

[11] Guo, Hongyuan, You Dong, Emilio Bastidas-Arteaga, and Xiang-Lin Gu. "Probabilistic failure analysis, performance assessment, and sensitivity analysis of corroded reinforced concrete structures." *Engineering Failure Analysis* 124 (2021): 105328. 10.1016/j. engfailanal.2021.105328

[12] Islam, Rashidul, Tasnia Hassan Nazifa, Sarajul Fikri Mohammed, et al. "Impacts of design deficiencies on maintenance cost of high-rise residential buildings and mitigation measures." *Journal of Building Engineering* 39 (2021): 102215. doi:10.1016/j. jobe.2021.102215

[13] Yu, Baoying, Jianwei Zhou, Baojun Cheng, et al. "Compressive strength development and microstructure of magnesium phosphate cement concrete." *Construction and Building Materials* 283 (2021): 122585. 10.1016/j.conbuildmat.2021.122585

[14] Aïtcin, Pierre-Claude and Jean-Martin Lessard. "8 - the Composition and design of high-strength concrete and ultrahigh-strength concrete." In *Developments in the Formulation and Reinforcement of Concrete (Second Edition)*, edited by Sidney Mindess, pp. 171–192: Woodhead Publishing, 2019.

[15] Akkaya, Ahmet and İsmail Hakkı Çağatay. "Investigation of the density, porosity, and permeability properties of pervious concrete with different methods." *Construction and Building Materials* 294 (2021): 123539. 10.1016/j.conbuildmat.2021.123539

[16] Shi, Jinyan, Baoju Liu, Feng Zhou, et al. "Effect of steam curing regimes on temperature and humidity gradient, permeability and microstructure of concrete." *Construction and Building Materials* 281 (2021): 122562. 10.1016/j.conbuildmat.2021.122562

[17] Yu, P., Y. H. Duan, Q. X. Fan, et al. "Improved MPS model for concrete creep under variable humidity and temperature." *Construction and Building Materials* 243 (2020): 118183. 10.1016/j.conbuildmat.2020.118183

[18] Le, Huy Viet, Min Kyoung Kim, et al. "Electrical properties of smart ultra-high performance concrete under various temperatures, humidities, and age of concrete." *Cement and Concrete Composites* 118 (2021): 103979. 10.1016/j.cemconcomp.2021.103979

[19] Bonnet, Stéphanie and Jean-Paul Balayssac. "Combination of the Wenner resistivimeter and Torrent permeameter methods for assessing carbonation depth and saturation level of concrete." *Construction and Building Materials* 188 (2018): 1149–1165. 10.1016/j. conbuildmat.2018.07.151

[20] Gruyaert, Elke, Philip Van den Heede, and Nele De Belie. "Carbonation of slag concrete: effect of the cement replacement level and curing on the carbonation coefficient – effect of carbonation on the pore structure." *Cement and Concrete Composites* 35, no. 1 (01/01/2013): 39–48. 10.1016/j.cemconcomp.2012.08.024

[21] Al-Ameeri, Abbas S., M. Imran Rafiq, et al. "Impact of climate change on the carbonation in concrete due to carbon dioxide ingress: experimental investigation and modelling." *Journal of Building Engineering* 44 (2021): 102594. 10.1016/j.jobe.2021.102594

[22] Ngo, Tri Thuong, Ngoc Thanh Tran, Dong Joo Kim, et al. "Effects of corrosion level and inhibitor on pullout behavior of deformed steel fiber embedded in high performance concrete." *Construction and Building Materials* 280 (2021): 122449. 10.1016/j. conbuildmat.2021.122449

[23] Rodrigues, Romain, Stéphane Gaboreau, Julien Gance, Ioannis Ignatiadis, and Stéphanie Betelu. "Reinforced concrete structures: a review of corrosion mechanisms and advances in electrical methods for corrosion monitoring." *Construction and Building Materials* 269 (2021): 121240. 10.1016/j.conbuildmat.2020.121240

[24] Aggarwal, Paratibha and Yogesh Aggarwal. "7 - Carbonation and corrosion of SCC." In *Self-Compacting Concrete: Materials, Properties and Applications*, edited by Rafat Siddique, pp. 147–193: Woodhead Publishing, 2020. 10.1016/B978-0-12-817369-5.00007-6

[25] Sun, Limin, Zhiqiang Shang, Ye Xia, et al. "Review of bridge structural health monitoring aided by big data and artificial intelligence: from condition assessment to damage detection." 146, no. 5 (2020): 04020073. 10.1061/(ASCE)ST.1943-541X.0002535

[26] Qin, Xiaoqiong, Mingsheng Liao, Mengshi Yang, et al. "Monitoring structure health of urban bridges with advanced multi-temporal INSAR analysis." *Annals of GIS* 23, no. 4 (2017): 293–302. 10.1080/19475683.2017.1382572

[27] Arjomandi, Kaveh, Yumi Araki, and Tracy MacDonald. "Application of a hybrid structural health monitoring approach for condition assessment of cable-stayed bridges." *Journal of Civil Structural Health Monitoring* 9, no. 2 (2019): 217–231. 10.1007/s13349-019-00332-z

[28] Gatti, Marco. "Structural health monitoring of an operational bridge: a case study." *Engineering Structures* 195 (2019): 200–209. 10.1016/j.engstruct.2019.05.102

[29] Caicedo, Juan M. and Shirley J. Dyke. "Experimental validation of structural health monitoring for flexible bridge structures." 12, no. 3–4 (2005): 425–443. 10.1002/stc.78

[30] Li, Jun, Hong Hao, Keqing Fan, and James Brownjohn. "Development and application of a relative displacement sensor for structural health monitoring of composite bridges." *Structural Control and Health Monitoring* 22, no. 4 (2015): 726–742. 10.1002/stc.1714

[31] Li, Hui and Jinping Ou. "The state of the art in structural health monitoring of cable-stayed bridges." *Journal of Civil Structural Health Monitoring* 6, no. 1 (2016): 43–67. 10.1007/s13349-015-0115-x

[32] Ceravolo, Rosario, Gaetano Miraglia, and Cecilia Surace. "Strategy for the maintenance and monitoring of electric road infrastructures based on recursive lifetime prediction." *Journal of Civil Structural Health Monitoring* 7, no. 3 (2017): 303–314. 10.1007/s13349-017-0227-6

[33] Di Graziano, Alessandro, Vincenzo Marchetta, et al. "Structural health monitoring of asphalt pavements using smart sensor networks: a comprehensive review." *Journal of Traffic and Transportation Engineering (English Edition)* 7, no. 5 (2020): 639–651. 10.1016/j.jtte.2020.08.001

[34] Henke, Klaudius, Robert Pawlowski, Peter Schregle, and Stefan Winter. "Use of digital image processing in the monitoring of deformations in building structures." *Journal of Civil Structural Health Monitoring* 5, no. 2 (2015): 141–152. 10.1007/s13349-014-0091-6

[35] De Stefano, Alessandro, Emiliano Matta, and Paolo Clemente. "Structural health monitoring of historical heritage in Italy: some relevant experiences." *Journal of Civil Structural Health Monitoring* 6, no. 1 (2016): 83–106. 10.1007/s13349-016-0154-y

[36] Sun, Hao and Oral Büyüköztürk. "The MIT green building benchmark problem for structural health monitoring of tall buildings." *Structural Control Health Monitoring* 25, no. 3 (2018): e2115. 10.1002/stc.2115

[37] Mishra, Mayank. "Machine learning techniques for structural health monitoring of heritage buildings: a state-of-the-art review and case studies." *Journal of Cultural Heritage* 47 (2021): 227–245. 10.1016/j.culher.2020.09.005

[38] Yan, Kai, Yao Zhang, Yan Yan, et al. "Fault diagnosis method of sensors in building structural health monitoring system based on communication load optimization." *Computer Communications* 159 (2020): 310–316. 10.1016/j.comcom.2020.05.026

[39] Hattab, Oussama, Majdi Chaari, Matthew A. Franchek, et al. "An adaptive modeling approach to structural health monitoring of multistory buildings." *Journal of Sound and Vibration* 440 (2019): 239–255. 10.1016/j.jsv.2018.10.019

[40] Gómez, Judit, Joan R. Casas, and Sergi Villalba. "Structural health monitoring with distributed optical fiber sensors of tunnel lining affected by nearby construction activity." *Automation in Construction* 117 (2020): 103261. 10.1016/j.autcon.2020.103261

[41] Yang, Jian-Ping, Wei-Zhong Chen, Ming Li, Xian-Jun Tan, et al. "Structural health monitoring and analysis of an underwater TBM tunnel." *Tunnelling and Underground Space Technology* 82 (2018): 235–247. 10.1016/j.tust.2018.08.053

[42] Lin, Chao, Cheng-lin Zhang, and Jie-hua Chen. "Optimal arrangement of structural sensors in soft rock tunnels based industrial Iot applications." *Computer Communications* 156 (2020): 159–167. 10.1016/j.comcom.2020.03.037

[43] Hu, Min, Yunru Liu, Vijayan Sugumaran, et al. "Automated structural defects diagnosis in underground transportation tunnels using semantic technologies." *Automation in Construction* 107 (2019): 102929. 10.1016/j.autcon.2019.102929

[44] Kang, Fei, Junjie Li, Sizeng Zhao, et al. "Structural health monitoring of concrete dams using long-term air temperature for thermal effect simulation." *Engineering Structures* 180 (2019): 642–653. 10.1016/j.engstruct.2018.11.065

[45] Kang, Fei, Junjie Li, and Jianghong Dai. "Prediction of long-term temperature effect in structural health monitoring of concrete dams using support vector machines with Jaya optimizer and salp swarm algorithms." *Advances in Engineering Software* 131 (2019): 60–76. 10.1016/j.advengsoft.2019.03.003

[46] Milillo, Pietro, Daniele Perissin, Jacqueline T. Salzer, et al. "Monitoring dam structural health from space: insights from novel INSAR techniques and multi-parametric modeling applied to the Pertusillo Dam Basilicata, Italy." *International Journal of Applied Earth Observation and Geoinformation* 52 (2016): 221–229. 10.1016/j.jag.2016.06.013

[47] Pereira, Sérgio, Filipe Magalhães, Jorge P. Gomes, et al. "Vibration-based damage detection of a concrete arch dam." *Engineering Structures* 235 (2021): 112032. 10.1016/j.engstruct.2021.112032

[48] Zhao, Zhiyong, Bo Chen, Zhongru Wu, et al. "Multi-sensing investigation of crack problems for concrete dams based on detection and monitoring data: a case study." *Measurement* 175 (2021): 109137. 10.1016/j.measurement.2021.109137

[49] Dou, Si-qi, Jun-jie Li, and Fei Kang. "Health diagnosis of concrete dams using hybrid FWA with RBF-based surrogate model." *Water Science and Engineering* 12, no. 3 (2019): 188–195. 10.1016/j.wse.2019.09.002

[50] Du, Cong, Susom Dutta, Pradeep Kurup, et al. "A review of railway infrastructure monitoring using fiber optic sensors." *Sensors and Actuators A: Physical* 303 (2020): 111728. 10.1016/j.sna.2019.111728

[51] Narazaki, Yasutaka, Vedhus Hoskere, Koji Yoshida, et al. "Synthetic environments for vision-based structural condition assessment of Japanese high-speed railway viaducts." *Mechanical Systems and Signal Processing* 160 (2021): 107850. 10.1016/j.ymssp.2021.107850

[52] Hada, Akio, Kenichi Soga, Ruoshui Liu, et al. "Lagrangian Heuristic method for the wireless sensor network design problem in railway structural health monitoring." *Mechanical Systems and Signal Processing* 28 (2012): 20–35. 10.1016/j.ymssp.2011.05.020

[53] Carboni, Michele and Davide Crivelli. "An acoustic emission based structural health monitoring approach to damage development in solid railway axles." *International Journal of Fatigue* 139 (2020): 105753. 10.1016/j.ijfatigue.2020.105753

[54] Wang, Kai, Wuxiong Cao, Lei Xu, et al. "Diffuse ultrasonic wave-based structural health monitoring for railway turnouts." *Ultrasonics* 101 (2020): 106031. 10.1016/j.ultras.2019.106031

[55] Anastasopoulos, Dimitrios, Guido De Roeck, and Edwin P. B. Reynders. "One-year operational modal analysis of a steel bridge from high-resolution macrostrain monitoring: influence of temperature vs. retrofitting." *Mechanical Systems and Signal Processing* 161 (2021): 107951. 10.1016/j.ymssp.2021.107951

[56] Housner, G. W., L. A. Bergman, T. K. Caughey, et al. "Structural control: past, present, and future." 123, no. 9 (1997): 897–971. doi:10.1061/(ASCE)0733–9399(1997)123:9(897)

[57] Aktan, A. Emin, N. Farhey Daniel, L. Brown David, et al. "Condition assessment for bridge management." *Journal of Infrastructure Systems* 2, no. 3 (1996): 108–117. 10.1061/(ASCE)1076-0342(1996)2:3(108)

[58] Farrar, Charles R. and Keith Worden. "An introduction to structural health monitoring." *Philosophical Transactions of the Royal Society A: Mathematical, Physical and Engineering Sciences* 365, no. 1851 (2007): 303–315. 10.1098/rsta.2006.1928

[59] Han, Tianran, Gang Wu, and Yong Lu. "Crack monitoring using short-gauged brillouin fiber optic sensor." *Measurement* 179 (2021): 109461. 10.1016/j.measurement.2021.109461

[60] Tan, Xiao, Adi Abu-Obeidah, Yi Bao, et al. "Measurement and visualization of strains and cracks in CFRP post-tensioned fiber reinforced concrete beams using distributed fiber optic sensors." *Automation in Construction* 124 (2021): 103604. 10.1016/j.autcon.2021.103604

[61] Floris, Ignazio, Jose M. Adam, Pedro A. Calderón, et al. "Fiber optic shape sensors: a comprehensive review." *Optics and Lasers in Engineering* 139 (2021): 106508. 10.1016/j.optlaseng.2020.106508

[62] Kavitha, S., R. Joseph Daniel, and K. Sumangala. "Design and analysis of MEMS comb drive capacitive accelerometer for SHM and seismic applications." *Measurement* 93 (2016): 327–339. 10.1016/j.measurement.2016.07.029

[63] Kavitha, S., R. Joseph Daniel, and K. Sumangala. "High performance MEMS accelerometers for concrete SHM applications and comparison with COTS accelerometers." *Mechanical Systems and Signal Processing* 66–67 (2016): 410–424. 10.1016/j.ymssp.2015.06.005

[64] Kavitha, S., R. Joseph Daniel, and K. Sumangala. "A Simple analytical design approach based on computer aided analysis of bulk micromachined piezoresistive MEMS accelerometer for concrete SHM applications." *Measurement* 46, no. 9 (2013): 3372–3388. 10.1016/j.measurement.2013.05.013

[65] Grillanda, Nicola, Gabriele Milani, Siddhartha Ghosh, et al. "SHM of a severely cracked masonry arch bridge in india: experimental campaign and adaptive NURBS limit analysis numerical investigation." *Construction and Building Materials* 280 (2021): 122490. 10.1016/j.conbuildmat.2021.122490

[66] Miao, Hongchen and Faxin Li. "Shear horizontal wave transducers for structural health monitoring and nondestructive testing: a review." *Ultrasonics* 114 (2021): 106355. 10.1016/j.ultras.2021.106355

[67] Ribeiro, D., R. Santos, R. Cabral, G. Saramago, et al. "Non-contact structural displacement measurement using unmanned aerial vehicles and video-based systems." *Mechanical Systems and Signal Processing* 160 (2021): 107869. 10.1016/j.ymssp.2021.107869

[68] Alamandala, Sravanthi, R. L. N. Sai Prasad, et al. "Cost-effective load measurement system for health monitoring using long-period grating as an edge filter." *Optical Fiber Technology* 59 (2020): 102328. 10.1016/j.yofte.2020.102328

[69] Shahsavari, Vahid, Maryam Mashayekhi, Milad Mehrkash, et al. "Diagnostic testing of a vertical lift truss bridge for model verification and decision-making support." 5, no. 92 (2019). 10.3389/fbuil.2019.00092

[70] Hou, Shuang, Chuangshuo Zeng, Haibin Zhang, et al. "Monitoring interstory drift in buildings under seismic loading using MEMS inclinometers." *Construction and Building Materials* 185 (2018): 453–467. 10.1016/j.conbuildmat.2018.07.087

[71] Zhou, Yan, Zheng Dongjian, Chen Zhuoyan, et al. "Research on a novel inclinometer based on distributed optical fiber strain and conjugate beam method." *Measurement* 153 (2020): 107404. 10.1016/j.measurement.2019.107404

[72] Helmi, Karim, Todd Taylor, Ali Zarafshan, and Farhad Ansari. "Reference free method for real time monitoring of bridge deflections." *Engineering Structures* 103 (2015): 116–124. 10.1016/j.engstruct.2015.09.002

[73] Marković, Marko Z., Jovan S. Bajić, Milan Vrtunski, et al. "Application of fiber-optic curvature sensor in deformation measurement process." *Measurement* 92 (2016): 50–57. 10.1016/j.measurement.2016.06.001

[74] Ma, Guofeng and Qingjuan Du. "Optimization on the intellectual monitoring system for structures based on acoustic emission and data mining." *Measurement* 163 (2020): 107937. 10.1016/j.measurement.2020.107937

[75] Hesser, Daniel Frank, Shimaalsadat Mostafavi, Georg Karl Kocur, and Bernd Markert. "Identification of acoustic emission sources for structural health monitoring applications based on convolutional neural networks and deep transfer learning." *Neurocomputing* 453 (2021): 1–12. 10.1016/j.neucom.2021.04.108

[76] Mirgal, Paresh, Joy Pal, and Sauvik Banerjee. "Online acoustic emission source localization in concrete structures using iterative and evolutionary algorithms." *Ultrasonics* 108 (2020): 106211. 10.1016/j.ultras.2020.106211

[77] Fu, Tao, Yanju Liu, Quanlong Li, and Jinsong Leng. "Fiber optic acoustic emission sensor and its applications in the structural health monitoring of CFRP materials." *Optics and Lasers in Engineering* 47, no. 10 (2009): 1056–1062. 10.1016/j.optlaseng.2009.03.011

[78] Xu, Dongyu, Sourav Banerjee, Yanbing Wang, Shifeng Huang, and Xin Cheng. "Temperature and loading effects of embedded smart piezoelectric sensor for health monitoring of concrete structures." *Construction and Building Materials* 76 (2015): 187–193. 10.1016/j.conbuildmat.2014.11.067

[79] Rocha, Helena, Christopher Semprimoschnig, and João P. Nunes. "Sensors for process and structural health monitoring of aerospace composites: A review." *Engineering Structures* 237 (2021): 112231. 10.1016/j.engstruct.2021.112231

[80] Mieloszyk, Magdalena, Katarzyna Majewska, and Wieslaw Ostachowicz. "Application of embedded fibre Bragg grating sensors for structural health monitoring of complex composite structures for marine applications." *Marine Structures* 76 (2021): 102903. 10.1016/j.marstruc.2020.102903

[81] Leu, Sou-Sen and You-Che Lin. "Project performance evaluation based on statistical process control techniques." *Journal of Construction Engineering and Management* 134, no. 10 (2008): 813–819. 10.1061/(ASCE)0733-9364(2008)134:10(813)

[82] Concu, Giovanna and Nicoletta Trulli. "Direct and semi-direct ultrasonic testing for quality control of FRC-concrete adhesion." *Structures*, vol. 32, pp. 54–64. Elsevier, 2021. 10.1016/j.istruc.2021.02.061

[83] DETR 2001. List of Panel Engineers: Reservoirs Act 1975. Department of the Environment, Transportation and the Regions. [available online: www.dtatabases.detr. gov.uk/reservoir].

[84] Balamurugan, Saravanan and Rathinam Ananthanarayanan. "Condition monitoring techniques of dielectrics in liquid immersed power transformers-a review." In *2018 IEEE Industry Applications Society Annual Meeting (IAS)*, pp. 1–7. IEEE, 2018. 10.1109/IAS.2018.8544650

[85] Mahadevan, Sankaran, Kyle Neal, Paromita Nath, et al. "Quantitative diagnosis and prognosis framework for concrete degradation due to alkali-silica reaction." In *AIP Conference Proceedings*, vol. 1806, no. 1, p. 080006. AIP Publishing LLC, 2017. 10.1063/1.4974631

[86] Halabe, U. B. "Non-destructive evaluation (NDE) of composites: techniques for civil structures." In *Non-Destructive Evaluation (NDE) of Polymer Matrix Composites*, Edited by Vistasp M. Karbhari, pp. 483–517. Woodhead Publishing, 2013. 10.1533/9780857093554.4.483

[87] Lessons from historical dam incidents. GOV. UK. [available online: https://assets. publishing.service.gov.uk/government/uploads/system/uploads/attachment_data/ file/290812/scho0811buba-e-e.pdf]. Retrieved: 15 May 2021.

[88] Das, Swagato and Purnachandra Saha. "Structural health monitoring techniques implemented on IASC–ASCE benchmark problem: a review." *Journal of Civil Structural Health Monitoring* 8, no. 4 (2018): 689–718. 10.1007/s13349-018-0292-5

[89] Dong, Ting and Nam H. Kim. "Cost-effectiveness of structural health monitoring in fuselage maintenance of the civil aviation industry." *Aerospace* 5, no. 3 (2018): 87. 10.3390/aerospace5030087

[90] Alokita, Shukla, Verma Rahul, Kandasamy Jayakrishna, et al. "Recent advances and trends in structural health monitoring." In *Structural Health Monitoring of Biocomposites, Fibre-reinforced Composites and Hybrid Composites*, Edited by Mohammad Jawaid, Mohamed Thariq, and Naheed Saba, pp. 53–73. Woodhead Publishing, 2019. 10.1016/ B978-0-08-102291-7.00004-6

[91] Jardine, Andrew KS, Daming Lin, and Dragan Banjevic. "A review on machinery diagnostics and prognostics implementing condition-based maintenance." *Mechanical Systems and Signal Processing* 20, no. 7 (2006): 1483–1510. 10.1016/j.ymssp.2005.09.012

[92] Boller, Christian, Fu-Kuo Chang, and Yozo Fujino, eds. *Encyclopedia of Structural Health Monitoring*. Wiley, 2009.

[93] Peil, Udo. "Civil infrastructure load models for structural health monitoring." *Encyclopedia of Structural Health Monitoring* (2009). 10.1002/9780470061626.shm007

[94] Pines, Darryll and A. Emin Aktan. "Status of structural health monitoring of long-span bridges in the United States." *Progress in Structural Engineering and Materials* 4, no. 4 (2002): 372–380. 10.1002/pse.129

[95] Giurgiutiu, Victor. "Tuned Lamb wave excitation and detection with piezoelectric wafer active sensors for structural health monitoring." *Journal of Intelligent Material Systems and Structures* 16, no. 4.(2005): 291–305. 10.1177/1045389X05050106

[96] Giurgiutiu, Victor. *Structural Health Monitoring: With Piezoelectric Wafer Active Sensors*. Elsevier, 2007. 10.1016/C2013-0-00155-7

[97] Balageas, Daniel, Claus-Peter Fritzen, and Alfredo Güemes, eds. *Structural Health Monitoring*. Vol. 90. John Wiley & Sons, 2010. 10.1002/9780470612071.ch1

[98] Liu, Han, Zipeng Fu, Kai Yang, Xinyi Xu, and Mathieu Bauchy. "Machine learning for glass science and engineering: a review." *Journal of Non-Crystalline Solids* 557 (2021): 119419. 10.1016/j.jnoncrysol.2019.04.039

[99] Ko, J. M., and Yi Qing Ni. "Technology developments in structural health monitoring of large-scale bridges." *Engineering Structures* 27, no. 12 (2005): 1715–1725. 10.1016/j. engstruct.2005.02.021

[100] Glisic, B. "Fiber optic sensors for subsea structural health monitoring." In *Subsea Optics and Imaging*, pp. 434–470. Woodhead Publishing, 2013. 10.1533/9780857093523.3.434

[101] Kumar, Aman, and Navdeep Mor. "An approach-driven: use of artificial intelligence and its applications in civil engineering." *Artificial Intelligence and IoT: Smart Convergence for Eco-friendly Topography* 85 (2021): 201. 10.1007/978-981-33-6400-4_10

[102] Intelligence, Artificial. "Expert Systems for Engineers, CS Krishnamoorthy, S." (1996).

[103] Boobier, Tony. *Advanced Analytics and AI: Impact, Implementation, and the Future of Work*. John Wiley & Sons, 2018. 10.1002/9781119390961.ch2

[104] Thompson, Simon. "Artificial intelligence comes of age." *ICT Futures: Delivering Pervasive Real-Time and Secure Services* (2008): 153–164. 10.1002/9780470758656.ch12

[105] Fisher, Doug, Ling Xu, James R. Carnes, et al. "Applying AI clustering to engineering tasks." *IEEE Expert* 8, no. 6 (1993): 51–60.

[106] Faught, William S. "Applications of AI in engineering." *Computer* 19, no. 07 (1986): 17–27.

[107] Marzban, Caren. "Basic statistics and basic AI: neural networks." In *Artificial Intelligence Methods in the Environmental Sciences*, pp. 15–47. Springer, 2009. 10.1007/978-1-4020-9119-3_2

[108] Lenat, Douglas Bruce. *AM: An Artificial Intelligence Approach to Discovery in Mathematics as Heuristic Search.* Stanford University, 1976.

[109] Hoyles, Celia and Richard Noss. "What can digital technologies take from and bring to research in mathematics education?." In *Second International Handbook of Mathematics Education*, Edited by Alan J. Bishop, M. A. Clements, Christine Keitel, Jeremy Kilpatrick, and Frederick K. S. Leung, pp. 323–349. Springer Nature, 2003. 10.1007/978-94-010-0273-8_11

[110] Brownjohn, James MW. "Structural health monitoring of civil infrastructure." *Philosophical Transactions of the Royal Society A: Mathematical, Physical and Engineering Sciences* 365, no. 1851 (2007): 589–622.

[111] Allam, Zaheer and Zaynah A. Dhunny. "On big data, artificial intelligence and smart cities." *Cities* 89 (2019): 80–91. 10.1016/j.cities.2019.01.032

[112] Chatterjee, Sheshadri, Arpan Kumar Kar, and M. P. Gupta. "Success of IoT in smart cities of India: an empirical analysis." *Government Information Quarterly* 35, no. 3 (2018): 349–361. 10.1016/j.giq.2018.05.002

[113] D'Alessandro, Antonella, Filippo Ubertini, Simon Laflamme, and Annibale L. Materazzi. "Towards smart concrete for smart cities: recent results and future application of strain-sensing nanocomposites." *Journal of Smart Cities* 1, no. 1 (2015): 3. 10.18063/JSC.2015.01.002

[114] Chatterjee, Sankhadeep, Sarbartha Sarkar, Sirshendu Hore, et al. "Particle swarm optimization trained neural network for structural failure prediction of multistoried RC buildings." *Neural Computing and Applications* 28, no. 8 (2017): 2005–2016. 10.1007/s00521-016-2190-2

[115] Kiani, Jalal, Charles Camp, and Shahram Pezeshk. "On the application of machine learning techniques to derive seismic fragility curves." *Computers & Structures* 218 (2019): 108–122. 10.1016/j.compstruc.2019.03.004

[116] Machine Learning, [available online: https://in.mathworks.com/solutions/machine-learning.html]. Retrieved: 15 May 2021.

[117] Deep Learning, [available online: https://in.mathworks.com/solutions/deep-learning.html] Retrieved: 15 May 2021.

[118] Flood, Ian. "Towards the next generation of artificial neural networks for civil engineering." *Advanced Engineering Informatics* 22, no. 1 (2008): 4–14. 10.1016/j.aei.2007.07.001

[119] Abiodun, Oludare Isaac, Aman Jantan, Abiodun Esther Omolara, Kemi Victoria Dada, Nachaat AbdElatif Mohamed, and Humaira Arshad. "State-of-the-art in artificial neural network applications: a survey." *Heliyon* 4, no. 11 (2018): e00938. 10.1016/j.heliyon.2018.e00938

[120] Lu, Pengzhen, Shengyong Chen, and Yujun Zheng. "Artificial intelligence in civil engineering." *Mathematical Problems in Engineering* 2012 (2012). 10.1155/2012/145974

[121] Kaul, Vivek, Sarah Enslin, and Seth A. Gross. "History of artificial intelligence in medicine." *Gastrointestinal Endoscopy* 92, no. 4 (2020): 807–812. 10.1016/j.gie.2020.06.040

[122] Buch, Varun H., Irfan Ahmed, and Mahiben Maruthappu. "Artificial intelligence in medicine: current trends and future possibilities." *British Journal of General Practice* 68, no. 668 (2018): 143–144. 10.3399%2Fbjgp18X695213

[123] Gagg, Colin R. "Cement and concrete as an engineering material: an historic appraisal and case study analysis." *Engineering Failure Analysis* 40 (2014): 114–140. 10.1016/j.engfailanal.2014.02.004

[124] Rabah, Mostafa, Ahmed Elhattab, and Atef Fayad. "Automatic concrete cracks detection and mapping of terrestrial laser scan data." *NRIAG Journal of Astronomy and Geophysics* 2, no. 2 (2013): 250–255. 10.1016/j.nrjag.2013.12.002

[125] Chaki, Nabendu, Soharab Hossain Shaikh, and Khalid Saeed. "A comprehensive survey on image binarization techniques." *Exploring Image Binarization Techniques* (2014): 5–15. 10.1007/978-81-322-1907-1

[126] Woods, Richard E., Steven L. Eddins, and Rafael C. Gonzalez. *Digital Image Processing using MATLAB*, McGraw-Hill. 2009.

[127] Kim, Hyunjun, Eunjong Ahn, Soojin Cho, Myoungsu Shin, and Sung-Han Sim. "Comparative analysis of image binarization methods for crack identification in concrete structures." *Cement and Concrete Research* 99 (2017): 53–61. 10.1016/j.cemconres.2017.04.018

[128] Gehri, Nicola, Jaime Mata-Falcón, and Walter Kaufmann. "Automated crack detection and measurement based on digital image correlation." *Construction and Building Materials* 256 (2020): 119383. 10.1016/j.conbuildmat.2020.119383

[129] Otsu, Nobuyuki. "A threshold selection method from gray-level histograms." *IEEE Transactions on Systems, Man, and Cybernetics* 9, no. 1 (1979): 62–66.

[130] He, Jingyu, Q. D. M. Do, Andy C. Downton, and JinHyung Kim. "A comparison of binarization methods for historical archive documents." In *Eighth International Conference on Document Analysis and Recognition (ICDAR'05)*, pp. 538–542. IEEE, 2005. 10.1109/ICDAR.2005.3

[131] Bukhari, Syed Saqib, Faisal Shafait, and Thomas M. Breuel. "Adaptive binarization of unconstrained hand-held camera-captured document images." *J. Univers. Comput. Sci.* 15, no. 18 (2009): 3343–3363. 10.3217/jucs-015-18-3343

[132] Bernsen, John. "Dynamic thresholding of gray-level images." In *Proc. Eighth Int'l conf. Pattern Recognition*, Paris, 1986. 1986.

[133] Niblack, Wayne. *An Introduction to Digital Image Processing*. Strandberg Publishing Company, 1985.

[134] Sauvola, Jaakko and Matti Pietikäinen. "Adaptive document image binarization." *Pattern Recognition* 33, no. 2 (2000): 225–236. 10.1016/S0031-3203(99)00055-2

[135] Wolf, Christian and J-M. Jolion. "Extraction and recognition of artificial text in multimedia documents." *Formal Pattern Analysis & Applications* 6, no. 4 (2004): 309–326. 10.1007/s10044-003-0197-7

[136] Khurshid, Khurram, Imran Siddiqi, Claudie Faure, and Nicole Vincent. "Comparison of Niblack inspired binarization methods for ancient documents." In *Document Recognition and Retrieval XVI*, vol. 7247, p. 72470U. International Society for Optics and Photonics, 2009. 10.1117/12.805827

[137] AliArshad Kothawala (2021). Image segmentation using Otsu method. [available online: https://www.mathworks.com/matlabcentral/fileexchange/51297-image-segmentation-using-otsu-method, MATLAB Central File Exchange]. Retrieved: 4 May 2021.

[138] Li, Shengyuan, and Xuefeng Zhao. "Automatic crack detection and measurement of concrete structure using convolutional encoder-decoder network." *IEEE Access* 8 (2020): 134602–134618. 10.1109/ACCESS.2020.3011106

[139] Liu, Yufei, Soojin Cho, Billie F. Spencer Jr, and Jiansheng Fan. "Automated assessment of cracks on concrete surfaces using adaptive digital image processing." *Smart Structures and Systems* 14, no. 4 (2014): 719–741. 10.12989/sss.2014.14.4.719

[140] Fujita, Yusuke, and Yoshihiko Hamamoto. "A robust automatic crack detection method from noisy concrete surfaces." *Machine Vision and Applications* 22, no. 2 (2011): 245–254. 10.1007/s00138-009-0244-5

13 Artificial Intelligence– Based Mobile Bill Payment System Using Biometric Fingerprint

A. Kathirvel, Debashreet Das and Stewart Kirubakaran
Karunya Institute of Technology and Sciences, Coimbatore, India

M. Subramaniam
Sree Vidyanikethan Engineering College, Tirupati, India

S. Naveneethan
SRM Institute of Science and Technology, Chengalpattu, India

CONTENTS

DOI: 10.1201/9781003307822-16

233

13.1   OVERVIEW OF PAYMENT TRANSACTIONS

Monetary transactions have been an integral part of human lives for millenia. The system of monetary exchange has evolved from the barter system, which was practiced until trade has become diverse enough that it was no longer possible to accurately estimate the value of goods and services being exchanged against each other. A more standardized transaction system came into existence using coins made of valuable materials such as gold and silver. This method was convenient, as it had a standardized value for every good or service. With the formation of modern-era nation-states and the growth of economies to the degree where the existing supply of precious metals in circulation would no longer suffice, currency bills and smaller-denomination coins became more common. Paper bills, or cash, are still popular and in common use today, although with the growth of technologies and advancements in digitization, alternative payment vehicles such as credit cards, e-wallets, and bank-linked direct exchanges (e.g., PayPal, Venmo, Zelle) are growing in popularity.

The similarity in all these transactions is that they depend on a material to complete the payment. Users need to carry cash, credit/debit cards, or their smart phones to identify their payment method. Then the transaction needs to be validated using OTP, PIN, or password to prove its authenticity. After verification is completed from the server side, the transaction is complete, and the amount gets deducted from the payer. This process needs to repeat involving the bank and the payment gateway to credit amount the back to the payee. Also, people carrying valuables such as a wallet worry about safeguarding them and be conscious not to misplace them. With the advancement in technology, this process could be simplified and yet be more secured.

This chapter introduces a novel method of material-less payment that makes the process of payment hassle-free. The customers need not carry any form of cash, debit/credit cards, or smart phone to make the payment. It allows the users to stop worrying about possessing and protecting their valuables while going out shopping.

A secure system involving a fingerprint developed in this project identifies every individual user uniquely. A fingerprint is unique for every single human being [1] and acts as a security gateway for the system. It involves minutiae extraction and minutiae comparison algorithms at the back end for analyzing the fingerprints as discussed in the algorithm section of this chapter.

The user needs to complete a one-time registration after which the application lets the user enroll their fingerprint to initiate the transaction and pay to any vendor. A brief description of a few other payment methods in comparison to the proposed system can be found in the literature review segment of this chapter.

13.2 LITERATURE REVIEW

The need for goods has been a part of human lives since the dawn of time. In a civilization, people demanded something valuable in exchange for goods. Before the invention of money, a barter system supported the economy by allowing people to exchange goods for other goods, goods for services, or services for goods. Eventually, it was no longer possible to accurately evaluate the value of each good and service in the marketplace, and a standardization of some kind was required. This led to the emergence of currency, specifically coins or tokens made of precious metals – or cash.

As recently as a few decades ago, cash transactions—now using paper bills of exchange—were the most widely used method of financial transaction. Bank checks were used for particularly large transactions, and credit cards were slowly gaining in popularity. In terms of government revenue, however, cash transactions are undesirable because they are not easily traceable [2]. Checks, money orders, traveler's checks and other forms of "bank drafts," while better traceable, represented a much slower transaction process, requires days for the funds to transfer from the payer to the payee.

13.2.1 CURRENT SCENARIO

Improvements in technology have led to the development of various new, more efficient methods of payment. Credit cards have become more secure and easier to use [3]. Debit cards have replaced paper checks for those instances where a payer wishes to have the funds for a transaction picked up directly from their bank account. Both methods have become even more secure with the introduction of geolocation; the issuing bank can immediately see where the transaction is taking place and raise a red flag if the location is in an unusual location given the account owner's place of residence or usual travel habits. New payment vehicles such as e-wallets and bank-linked user-to-user services also have emerged, in many cases eliminating the need to carry a wallet filled with cash and credit cards [4].

13.2.1.1 Disadvantages of Current Payment Methods

On the user side, no matter how convenient it is to use credit cards or smart phone–based payment vehicles, either one of these can be lost or stolen, creating the risk of unauthorized use. On the merchat side, the disadvantages of payment cards is that the payee is required to have a card reader machine to process the transaction. This results in additional costs, both in terms of acquiring the card reader and paying a percentage of the transaction as a fee to the bank.

13.2.2 MOBILE BANKING

Mobile banking has become handy for users with the use of smart phones. Payment through smart phones is convenient for people [5]. There are many applications provided by banks to transfer funds, but the payer needs the account details of the payee to be added as a beneficiary to complete the transaction. Although the transaction is completed online, adding the payee details takes more time in many circumstances

[6]. It is not a preferred option to fill in payee account details while making a payment at the location. Also, uninterrupted internet connection is required to make these transactions.

13.2.3 e-Wallets

Many private companies have successfully established e-wallets in which users can load money and pay using QR codes. It is a time-efficient method to complete a transaction, as the user has to scan the QR code [7] with their smart phone. The users always need to have money preloaded in these applications or have them connected to their bank account, and these also require an uninterrupted internet connection. It also means that the user must agree to the conditions and trust these third-party applications with their money [8].

13.2.3.1 NFC Chips

An advanced method broadly used for payments in developed countries is near field communication (NFC). Most smart phones sold in developed countries have built-in NFC chips. It makes payment transaction simple, as the users need to tap their device against another device to complete the transactions. It is highly time efficient and has no intermediate steps for the user to perform [9]. A management authentication server communicates with the device and the application server using an adaptive protocol to complete the transaction. It may not be successful in developing countries, as the smart phones available there are not equipped with NFC chips. Also, this technique does not include any level of authentication, so it may not be the safest method to use.

13.2.3.2 Face Recognition

This technique, when implemented as a payment method, allows users to pay by scanning their face by the camera installed at the billing counter [10]. The problem is the registration, as it requires a minimum of thousand images of input for a single person to be identified accurately. The database and server for processing and storing these data would be so expensive as to be impractical. Also, the system fails to differentiate between identical twins. Iris recognition provides more accurate results, but the hardware required to recognize irises is expensive [11], and installing it in every shop would not be financially a good idea for most shops.

13.2.4 Biometrics Method

Biometrics is efficient and generates accurate results, but the cost of implementation is a drawback.

13.2.4.1 QR Code Method

An innovative method of payment is the one involving both QR code and face recognition. It uses QR to identify the user and the account details and uses face recognition as an authentication mechanism [12]. It is highly secure, as it combines the advantages of both methods; of course, the drawbacks are also combined. It also increases the overall process time.

13.2.4.2   IoT Method

A separate device has been built using Internet-of-Things (IoT) components. It is a combination of the fingerprint sensor, a Wi-Fi module, a keypad, and an LCD connected to a raspberry pi that acts as a processor [13]. It is a stand-alone device that is portable and can be at any billing counter. The main drawback is that the IoT devices have not delivered notable result in fingerprint matching. Proper training must be provided to employees to use the device. Failure of even a single component would lead to hindrance of the whole system. This device requires to be paired up via Wi-Fi with a computer or smart phone to send the collected data depending on the host, and transfer of data through Wi-Fi is prone to network and safety issues.

13.2.4.3   Fingerprint Method

The use of fingerprint inspired many inventors to improvise the idea. A paper discussed the implementation of the fingerprint sensor on an existing contactless debit/credit card. It aids the user to register a fingerprint in their card itself. Use it to make payments without entering the PIN. It ensures only the account owner can make the payment, and the process self-authenticates as the user holds the card with the right finger on the sensor [14]. The challenge faced in this method is that the sensor needs to have a power supply to function properly. The card requires power to function as expected. It ultimately leads to opting for an adaptor for it, at extra expenses. It also has the usual disadvantages of using a card, which was discussed earlier in the chapter.

13.2.4.4   E-Cash Transaction

An intriguing and unusual proposal for payments using offline e-cash transfer has been put forth. Emphasis is on using virtual cash instead of real hard cash with the help of blockchain technology. The idea involves payment tasks such as withdrawal, transfer, and so on but with e-cash [15]. It requires the user to register with their preferred bank and get a card and a mobile application for e-cash processes. It mentions that the transaction is authenticated using the payer's signature on the smart phone itself. However, it only was conceptually discussed, and a working model currently does not exist.

13.2.4.5   Merits and Demerits of Biometric

Considering both advantages and disadvantages of all the above-discussed techniques, a biometric payment application using fingerprint is developed. The following section discusses potential upsides and drawbacks.

13.3   BILL PAYMENT SYSTEM USING BIOMETRIC FINGERPRINT

The concept of material-less payment with the use of fingerprint developed as an application for smart phones. The practice of carrying wallets and securing them is no longer needed, as the users are encouraged to complete the transaction by just using their fingertip. This process requires a one-time registration where the users fill in their details with their fingerprint and a PIN for security. For data privacy reasons, sensitive data such as the fingerprint gets converted into numerical values inserted in a byte array. All the information gets securely stored in the real-time cloud database, functioning seamlessly without a server. After this process, the user can enter any shop using this application and pay the bill using their fingerprint and PIN.

13.3.1 Architecture Description

The architecture involves two roles, the payer and the payee. In this system, the payer is not required to carry any materials, wallet or otherwise, to make the payment. The payee has the application connected to a USB fingerprint scanner as depicted in Figure 13.1. The payee logs into the application, after which the amount payable gets entered. The customer gives their details to complete the payment.

The application directly opens into the make payment activity for convenience where an option to register is present. The application also has a registration activity where the application prompts the user for their details and linking of their preferred payment account. Figure 13.2 depicts the actions performed by the user on the application. This registration is a one-time process where the details are securely stored in the real-time database, after which the user can directly make the payment using their fingerprint and PIN. The application authenticates the data by contacting the database. After proper validation, the amount is debited from the payer and credited to the payee's account. The application directly communicates with the database without any middlemen such as payment gateway, which makes it an efficient architecture.

13.3.2 Minutiae Extraction and Comparison Algorithm

The working of the algorithm comprises five steps, namely fingerprint acquisition, fingerprint preprocessing, fingerprint enhancement, feature extraction, and minutiae matching [16].

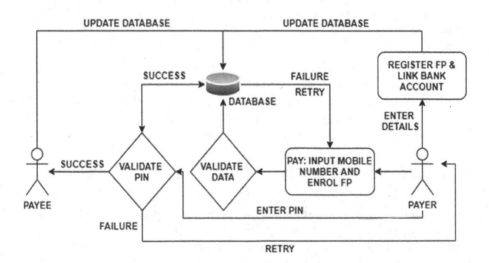

FIGURE 13.1   AI-based biometric architecture model.

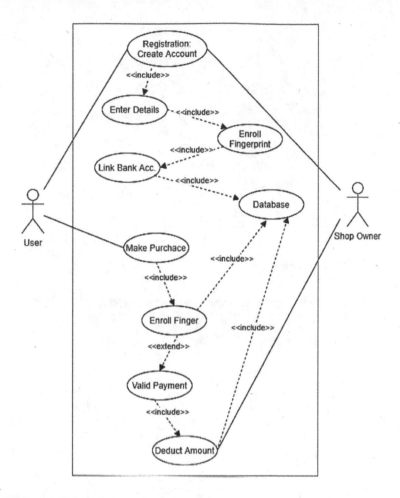

FIGURE 13.2 AI-based biometric payment method.

13.3.2.1 Fingerprint Acquisition

It is the process where the application retrieves the fingerprint input from the user through the fingerprint scanner. The scanner captures an image of the fingerprint placed on its surface. The application communicates with the scanner using device drivers and retrieves the fingerprint image into the application for further processing.

13.3.2.2 Fingerprint Preprocessing

In preprocessing, the acquired image gets converted to pure grayscale, i.e., black and white. It makes sure that the ridges, ridge endings, bifurcations, valleys and whorls are made distinct as shown in Figure 13.3.

13.3.2.3 Fingerprint Enhancement

At this stage, the image quality is enhanced to the maximum to better differentiate between minutiae and white space. The image undergoes a quality check to ensure

FIGURE 13.3   Representation of minutiae.

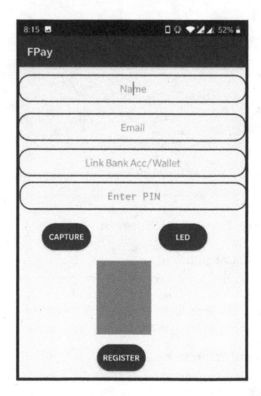

FIGURE 13.4   Payment registration.

that it is adequate for the extraction process. Binarization makes every black ridge in an image considered as 0 and the white space considered as 1. It helps identify the features of the fingerprint in the Figure 13.4 extraction process.

13.3.2.4 Feature Extraction

The image gets fully rooted for the binary bits with the value 0 as features. Every feature gets determined by the value it holds in each pixel.

These binary values and the pixel values are computed using (13.1) and stored in a byte array [17].

This byte array represents the entire fingerprint.

$$CN = 1/2 \sum_{i=1}^{8} \left| P_i - P_{i+1} \right| \tag{13.1}$$

where CN is Cross Number, P_i is the binary pixel value in the neighbourhood of P with $P_i = (0 \text{ or } 1)$.

13.3.2.5 Minutiae Matching

Since the byte array represents the entire fingerprint, the byte arrays of the desired two fingerprints get compared. As fingerprint input is not constant and tends to change orientation every time even for the same finger, a matching score gets generated as shown in Figures 13.5 and 13.6. This matching score gives information regarding

FIGURE 13.5 Payment activity.

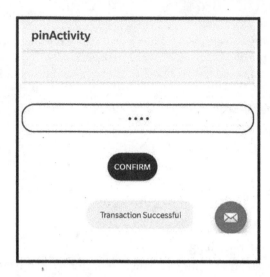

FIGURE 13.6   Payment success message.

the similarity of the fingerprints taken into consideration. It finds whether the fingerprints match or not. If the generated result is above 100, then the fingerprints are similar upon an agreed standard. It gets considered as a match. Any outcome below that value gets considered as not a match.

13.4   IMPLEMENTATION

The application consists of two main activities, namely biometric payment and user registration. When the user clicks the Register button, the registration activity opens. This module prompts the user to give input details for the registration process. The details such as name, mobile number, and e-mail are collected.

The users are required to enter their bank account number and link their preferred payment account with the application. Finally, for identification and security purposes, the user's fingerprint is collected. The user must press the capture fingerprint button and place their preferred fingertip on the external fingerprint scanner. It captures an image of the fingerprint for further processing. The user also must enter a secure PIN for authentication of upcoming payments.

The fingerprint gets encoded to a byte array using the minutiae extraction algorithm. The PIN is also securely hashed. So, there is no storage of sensitive information. All these data are stored securely in a real-time cloud database. It is a one-time registration after which the user can use this application at any location that accepts this form of payment. The user is notified with a success message instantly after signup. After registration, the users of this application are free to use this payment method wherever available.

The user need not carry any payment material to the shop, as they can complete the shopping and scan their fingerprint, authenticate the payment, and complete the transaction. The bill amount gets entered by the shopkeeper in the application.

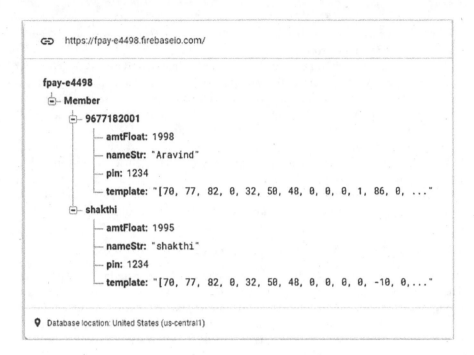

FIGURE 13.7 Could database of AI-based biometric system.

The user must enter their mobile number, scan their fingerprint, and enter the PIN to complete the transaction.

The process comprises three subprocesses: identification, validation, and authentication. In the identification process, the user's mobile number is used as a primary key to select the details in the database. In the validation process, the byte array containing the fingerprint is matched with the existing byte array in the database using the minutiae-matching algorithm. When a successful match gets found, the application checks for sufficiency in the account balance. Once enough credit is available, the user receives a prompt with the PIN for authentication to inform the user that they do not have sufficient balance to continue with the payment.

Once the PIN matches, the application contacts the database (Figure 13.7) and debits the specified amount. At the same time, the debited amount gets credited to the payee's account. Finally, a transaction success message gets displayed to the user. Fingerprints are unique for every person. They cannot get manipulated or forged by anyone, which adds security to this method.

13.5 EXPERIMENTAL RESULTS AND DISCUSSION

Thus, biometric payment application got designed, developed, and implemented successfully. Also, a new technique of material-less payment got introduced to society. It reduces the pressure on people to safeguard their wallets everywhere. The application uses fingerprint and PIN for security, which is simple and causes less confusion for the customers, unlike OTP and two-step authentications. The transaction gets completed with a smaller number of inputs. It saves users from entering long account digits and speeds up the process.

The use of fingerprints makes it easy to prevent unauthorized use, as fingerprint is unique for every user. In terms of the minutiae-matching algorithm accuracy, regression testing got 100 percent accurate results. In terms of the database, real-time database implementation makes data retrieval instant and does not require a server. It ensures zero server downtime.

The sensitive data such as fingerprints are converted into bytes and stored as a byte array. In terms of data security, the application is safe to use. No sensitive data get lost. Finally, the payment transaction is done seamlessly and quickly without involving any middlemen such as payment gateways. Also, it is a good alternative instead of a card swiping machine, which requires an annual subscription.

13.6   CONCLUSION AND FUTURE SCOPE

The biometric payment application paves a way to overcome material-based payment. The application combines all crucial upsides and eliminates most drawbacks discussed in the literature review. The application uses automation to solve the problem of the material dependency. It also provides various other advantages, discussed in the result section of the paper. The application makes the users less worried about safeguarding their wallet or carrying the exact change to places. The overall user experience is added comfort for both the payee and the payer. People adapt to this method without hassle, as there are not many materials to be carried or processes to be done from the user's side.

In the future, a few new features will get released as updates. The application will get modified to register more than one fingerprint for every user. It ensures the user can use this system even if they have any problem with the previously registered fingerprint. A backup payment method will get added to cope with any unexpected failure in the fingerprint sensor. Aadhar-enabled payment system (AEPS) lets users make payment using their Aadhar card, as it is already linked with their bank account. The proposed biometric payment application could collaborate with India Stack, the developers of Aadhar, to make payment simple. It also makes the user skip the registration process, as Aadhar card already has registered the user's fingerprint. It also enables an option to link a bank account or change an existing bank account associated with the biometric payment application entirely online. A few more basic features such as forgot PIN, report bug, and a feedback mechanism could get added as an update based on the requirements of the investor and convenience of the users.

REFERENCES

1. Yankov, M. P., Olsen, M. A., Stegmann, M. B., Christensen, S. S., and Forchhammer, S., 2020. Fingerprint entropy and identification capacity estimation based on pixel-level generative modelling, *IEEE Transactions on Information Forensics and Security*, vol. 15, pp. 56–65, doi:10.1109/TIFS.2019.2916406.

2. Hanzal, P. and Homan, J., 2019. Electronic exchange SAF-T standard of data from organizations to tax authorities or auditors - situation in the Czech Republic, *2019 9th International Conference on Advanced Computer Information Technologies (ACIT)*, pp. 405–408, doi:10.1109/ACITT.2019.8780001.

3. Sajić, M., Bundalo, D., Bundalo, Z., Stojanović, R., and Sajić, L, 10–14 June 2018. Design of digital modular bank safety deposit box using modern information and communication technologies. *7th Mediterranean Conference on Embedded Computing MECO 2018*, pp. 107–112.

4. Zolotukhin, O. and Kudryavtseva, M., 2018. Authentication method in contactless payment systems. *2018 International Scientific-Practical Conference Problems of Infocommunications. Science and Technology (PIC S&T)*.

5. Sun, Y. and Havidz, S., 2019. Factors impacting the intention to use M-payment. *2019 International Conference on Information Management and Technology (ICIMTech)*.

6. Tounekti, O., Ruiz-Martinez, A., and Skarmeta Gomez, A., 2020. Users supporting multiple (mobile) electronic payment systems in online purchases: an empirical study of their payment transaction preferences. *IEEE Access*, 8, pp. 735–766.

7. Liu, W., Wang, X., and Peng, W., 2020. State of the art: secure mobile payment. *IEEE Access*, 8, pp. 13898–13914.

8. Islamiati, D., Agata, D., and Anom Besari, A., 2019. Design and implementation of various payment system for product transaction in mobile application. *2019 International Electronics Symposium (IES)*.

9. Al-Haj, A. and Al-Tameemi, M., 2018. Providing security for NFC-based payment systems using a management authentication server. *2018 4th International Conference on Information Management (ICIM)*.

10. Zhang, W. and Kang, M., 2019. Factors affecting the use of facial-recognition payment: an example of Chinese consumers. *IEEE Access*, 7, pp. 154360–154374.

11. Caron, F., 2018. The evolving payments landscape: technological innovation in payment systems. *IT Professional*, 20(2), pp. 53–61.

12. Ximenes, A., Sukaridhoto, S., Sudarsono, A., Ulil Albaab, M., Basri, H., Hidayat Yani, M., Chang Choon, C., and Islam, E., 2019. Implementation QR code biometric authentication for online payment. *2019 International Electronics Symposium (IES)*.

13. Hualin, Z., Qiqi, W., and Yujing, H., 2018. Design fingerprint attendance machine based on C51 Single-chip microcomputer. *2018 IEEE International Conference of Safety Produce Informatization (IICSPI)*.

14. Suwald, T. and Rottschafer, T., 2019. Capacitive fingerprint sensor for contactless payment cards. *2019 26th IEEE International Conference on Electronics, Circuits and Systems (ICECS)*.

15. Luo, J. and Yang, M., 2018. Offline transferable e-cash mechanism. *2018 IEEE Conference on Dependable and Secure Computing (DSC)*.

16. Liban, A. and Hilles, S., 2018. Latent fingerprint enhancement based on directional total variation model with lost minutiae reconstruction. *2018 International Conference on Smart Computing and Electronic Enterprise (ICSCEE)*.

17. Gudkov, V. and Lepikhova, D., 2018. Fingerprint model based on fingerprint image topology and ridge count values. *2018 Global Smart Industry Conference (GloSI)*.

14 An Efficient Transfer Learning–Based CNN Multi-Label Classification and ResUNET Based Segmentation of Brain Tumor in MRI

V. Abinash, S. Meghanth, P. Rakesh, S. A. Sajidha, V. M. Nisha and A. Muralidhar
Vellore Institute of Technology, Chennai

CONTENTS

DOI: 10.1201/9781003307822-17

14.1   INTRODUCTION

Brain tumors are collections of abnormal cells in the brain. Brain tumors are classified into various types based on the complexity and position of the tumor. Brain tumors can be noncancerous (benign) and cancerous (malignant). As malignant or benign tumors grow, the pressure on the patient's skull increases. It can cause brain damage, which is often life-threatening. Therefore, identification and treatment of the brain tumor at the early phase are essential.

Brain tumors are divided into primary and secondary. Primary brain tumors originate in the patient's brain. A secondary brain tumor is classified as a condition in which cancer cells spread from other organs (such as the breast or kidney) to the brain. Generally, tumors are diagnosed by neurological examinations such as magnetic resonance imaging (MRI) scans, computer tomography scan (CT scan), and other examinations like lumbar puncture, angiography, etc. However, in most cases, doctors prefer to use MRI scans over CT scans, because the latter expose patients to ionizing radiation. The amount of radiation used during the test is more than that used in X-rays. Therefore, computed tomography scans slightly increase the risk of side effects, such as developing cancer. Many researchers and health professionals have proposed various approaches to classify brain tumors and identify the tumor position in MR images. However, due to low accuracy and high false-positive rate, manual classification is still used to classify tumors. This chapter proposed a multi-label classification model using CNN and a pretrained VGG16 model for extracting features from MR images. It also includes a segmentation model developed using ResUNET. Cheng [1] is used to test the efficacy of the proposed models.

The rest of the chapter is organized as follows: Section 14.2 provides an overview of related previous work; Section 14.3 presents details about the dataset and preprocessing; Section 14.4 presents the methodology used to develop the proposed classification and the segmentation models; the implementation of the proposed classification and segmentation models are discussed in Section 14.5; the results of the segmentation model are provided in Section 14.6; and conclusions are presented in Section 14.7.

14.2   REVIEW OF RELATED WORK

Zhang et al. [2] explored the effectiveness of the Attention Gate Residual U-Net model for segmenting brain tumors. Data from BraTS 2017, BraTS 2018, and BraTS 2019 are used to evaluate the effectiveness of the proposed approaches. Observe that the approaches with attention gate units, i.e., AGResU-NET and AGU-Net, outperformed their baseline models ResU-Net and U-Net, respectively. The average DSC score recorded by the AGResUNet method was 0.83. Dong et al. [3] presented a fully automatic method for segmenting brain tumors using deep convolutional networks based on U-Net. BRATS 2015 dataset is used to test the robustness of the proposed method. The DSC achieved by the segmentation model was 0.81. Similarly, Naser and Deen [4] developed a deep learning model for segmenting brain tumors and a classifier to grade brain tumors. A pretrained VGG16 model is used for tumor grading and UNET is used for segmenting brain tumors. The segmentation model achieved the mean DSC of 0.84.

Vani et al. [5] introduce a classification system to classify cancerous and noncancerous brain tumors using support vector machine (SVM). This classification method provides an accuracy of 82 percent. Deepak and Ameer [6] presented a classification model to distinguish brain tumors among pituitary, meningioma, and glioma tumors. Transfer learning is adopted to develop the classification model. Pretrained GoogLeNet is used for extracting features from MR images of the brain. Cheng [1] analyzed the effectiveness of the classification model. Similarly, Swati et al. [7] worked on multiclass brain tumor classification using pretrained CNN and adopted transfer learning. Finally, a fivefold cross-validation test is carried out to ensure the effectiveness of the proposed multiclass classification model. Through fivefold cross-validation, the average accuracy reaches 94.82 percent. Ismael and Abdel-Qader [8] introduced a framework that combines statistics features and neural network algorithms to classify multi-label brain tumors. 2D Gabor filter and 2D Discrete Wavelet Transform (DWT) techniques are used for the feature selection. To test the impact of selected features, a back-propagation neural network classifier is used for multi-label brain tumor classification. Cheng [1] is used to test the effectiveness of the classifier. The accuracy yield by the classifier is 91.9 percent. Furthermore, CNN architecture was developed in the research of Pashaei et al. [9] to extract features from brain MR images. The CNN model shows an accuracy of 81 percent. To improve the model performance, CNN features are combined with the extreme learning machine (ELM) classifier model. The KELM-CNN method shows 93.68 percent accuracy. Díaz-Pernas et al. [10] introduced fully automated brain tumor classification and segmentation methods using DeepCNN with a multiscale method. The classification model yields an accuracy of 97.3 percent. Kang et al. [11] presented a method to classify brain tumors using ensemble ML classifiers and features extracted by DL models. Various pretrained CNN models are used for extracting features from MR images. These extracted features are then used by various ML classifiers for the prediction of brain tumors. Among all tested ML classifiers, SVM with RBF kernel achieved better results. Nisha and Jeganathan [12] developed a cellular automata-based model to detect abnormalities in the human brain. Rammurthy and Mahesh [13] presented an optimization-based approach, called Whale Harris Hawks (WHH) optimization, for detecting brain tumors in MR images. Cellular automata and Rough set theory are used to segment brain tumors. The Local Optical Oriented Pattern (LOOP), Kurtosis, Variance, Tumor Size, and Mean are used to extract features. The proposed WHHO based DeepCNN reaches 81.6 percent accuracy.

14.3   DATASET AND PREPROCESSING

The data used for evaluating the proposed multi-label classification model and segmentation model performance were taken from the Brain tumor dataset ([1] from the public website figshare by Jun Cheng. It contains 3,064 CE-MRI brain slices from 233 patients. This dataset is a collection of three unique brain tumors: meningiomas (708 slices), pituitary (930 slices), and gliomas (1,426 slices) in the standard views (sagittal, axial, and coronal). Eighty percent (2,452 images) of the dataset are used for the purposes of training, and the remaining 20 percent (612 images) are used to test the effectiveness of the proposed models. The splitting of the data ensures that specific patient data do not appear in both test data and training data simultaneously. The brain tumor dataset ([1] in figshare by Jun Cheng is organized in a MATLAB data format [.mat file]. Each file contains a structure with the patient's identification number, the tumor label, and the tumor mask: a binary image where the position of the tumor contains the value 1, and the non-tumor position contains the value 0.

During training, image augmentation is adopted to avoid overfitting the network. Image augmentation follows a set of processes by taking in existing images from training data and applying different geometric transformations to them, such as shearing, zooming, translation, and rotation, to obtain new versions of the images. For the classification model, we preprocessed the data such that each image in the dataset is resized to 224 × 244. For the segmentation model, images are resized to 256 × 256. Finally, each image is scaled with pixel values of (0, 255) to a value between (0, 1) because the deep learning model performs well with smaller inputs.

14.4 METHODS USED

The multi-label classification model proposed in our study is developed using CNN and uses a pretrained VGG16 model for extracting features from the input MR images. The proposed segmentation model is developed using ResUNET architecture.

Figure 14.1 illustrates the architecture of the proposed system. Initially, the dataset is preprocessed before it is used for the model training purpose as described in Section 14.4. After the data is preprocessed, the pretrained VGG16 model is used for extracting features from MR images. These extracted features are used to classify brain tumors. The newly trained model is utilized to predict the test data classes. In addition, the proposed multi-label CNN classification model utilizes a new activation function called Swish rather than the commonly used ReLU activation function. Compared with ReLU and LeakyReLU, Swish is smoother.

The mathematical notation of the Swish function is defined in Equation (14.1)

$$f(x) = \frac{x}{1 + e^{-\beta x}} \tag{14.1}$$

Here $\beta \geq 0$ is a parameter that can be learned during the training of model. When $\beta \to \infty$, $f(x)$ looks more like the ReLU activation function, only smoother. When $\beta = 0$, $f(x)$ becomes a linear activation function.

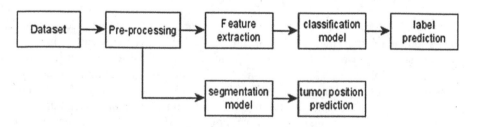

FIGURE 14.1   Architecture of the proposed system.

The same dataset is utilized for training the proposed segmentation model developed using ResUNET. The proposed segmentation model is utilized to identify the position of tumor in the test data.

14.4.1 VGG16 Model

VGG16 is a CNN model introduced by Simonyan and Zisserman [14]. The VGG16 model is a 16-layer convolutional and fully connected network trained on the ImageNet dataset for solving image classification and recognition problems. The VGG16 model is constructed using 13 convolutional layers with 3×3 convolutional filters followed by max-pooling layers for down-sampling. It is connected by two fully connected hidden layers. Each hidden layer has 4,096 units, followed by 1,000 dense neurons. Each neuron refers to an image class present in the ImageNet dataset. We fine-tuned the VGG 16 model by introducing our fully connected dense layers to classify the brain tumor MR images. VGG16 model is used because it has a simple homogeneous structure of sequentially arranged convolutional and pooling layers. It contains 16 learning layers and works very well, which means the filters and the generated feature maps, can capture important features.

14.4.2 Convolutional Neural Network

Convolutional Neural Network (CNN) is a DL algorithm, proposed in 1980 by Yann LeCun et al. [15]. The CNN algorithm can take an image as input and assign weight to several aspects in the image and differentiate one from the other. CNN requires less prepossessing, compared with other classification algorithms. The structure of CNN is similar to the structure of neural connections in the human brain. The basic architecture of CNN consists of two main parts, as presented in Figure 14.2.

- Feature Extraction: The convolution process of identifying and separating various features of an image for analysis.

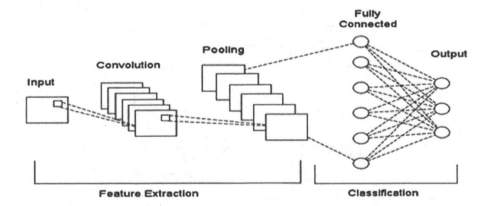

FIGURE 14.2 Basic CNN architecture.

- The fully connected layer accepts the results of the convolution process and predicts the image category based on the features extracted in the previous stage.

14.5   TRANSFER LEARNING (TL)

Transfer learning is a ML approach in which a model trained for a problem (i.e., pretrained model) is reused as a starting point for a new problem, as shown in Figure 14.3. Transfer learning is especially useful when the training data set is small. The advantage of pretrained models is that they are versatile enough to be used in other real-world applications. For instance, the VGG16 model that we have used is trained on ImageNet.

14.5.1   ResUNET Model

ResUNET is an encoder-decoder architecture developed by Zhang et al. [16] for semantic segmentation inspired by deep residual learning and UNET architecture. ResUNET was chosen for creating the segmentation model because it improves the existing UNET architecture. In addition, ResUNET uses advantage of both the Deep Residual Learning and UNET architecture. ResUNET comprises a decoding network, encoding network, and a bridge connection between the networks. Figure 14.4 represents the architecture of the ResUNET model.

Advantages of ResUNET:

- The residual units make it effortless to train the network.
- The skip connections in the network can facilitate information propagation without degradation and allow the use of a few parameters to design the neural network.

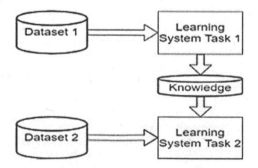

FIGURE 14.3   Concept of transfer learning.

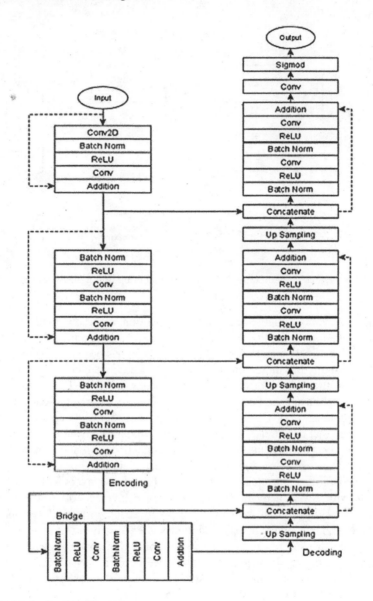

FIGURE 14.4 ResUNET architecture.

14.6 IMPLEMENTATION

14.6.1 CLASSIFICATION MODEL

Transfer learning is a concept of overcoming the isolated learning paradigms and exploitation of the acquired knowledge from a completed task to resolve the target drawback, introduced by Shao et al. [17]. We utilized the VGG16 pretrained model considered the basic model. The VGG16 model is specifically used to build dense

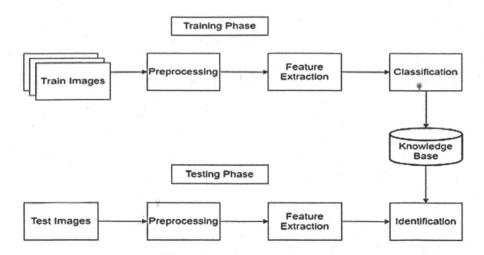

FIGURE 14.5   Block diagram of proposed multi-label brain tumor classification system.

convolution networks for large-scale visual recognition, making it an ideal choice for tumor classification. Using the Keras deep learning library, we loaded VGG16 as the basic model. The final output layer of the basic model has been removed because the basic model usually has more units than required. Later, we can add the final output layer based on the number of classes present in our problem. The 13 layers of the pretrained model have been frozen to ensure that the weights in these levels will not be updated after each epoch. If the weights are updated after every epoch, we will lose all the learning that has already occurred. Hence, the last activation layer in VGG16 (block5 pool) gives us the features map. We have flattened the features map of the base model so that they can be used in our fully connected classifier (refer Figure 14.5).

We created a fully connected classifier using three dense layers with 128, 512, and 1024 units with Swish activation. The third dense layer is followed by dropout. Dropout is a regularization method for the neural network model proposed by Srivastava et al. [18]. It also helps avoid the issue of overfitting of neural networks. We have set the dropout rate to 0.2. The final output layer has three neurons that correspond to the number of categories in which we need to classify the input image. The network hyperparameters are adjusted to promote the concurrence of the loss function in the process of training.

14.6.2 CLASSIFIER METRICS AND EVALUATION

Our multi-label classification model uses "Adam" as the optimizer because it has a reasonable learning rate and adaptability to specific learning rate parameters. The initial learning rate is set to 0.001. Choosing a higher learning rate can avoid the loss function from causing overshoot and converging. A very low learning rate will increase learning time. The minimum batch size is set to 32. Categorical cross-entropy is utilized as the loss function because it compares how close the predicted distribution is to the actual distribution. The maximum epochs are limited to 50 (see Table 14.1).

As illustrated in Figure 14.6, classification accuracy of the proposed multi-label classification model is 100 percent on training data and 98.22 percent on the test data (Figure 14.7).

Table 14.2 describes the class-specific performance of the proposed multi-label classification model. Precision, Recall, and F1-Score are calculated using Equations (14.2), (14.3), and (14.4) respectively.

$$\text{Precision} = \frac{TP}{TP + FP} \tag{14.2}$$

$$\text{Recall} = \frac{TP}{TP + FN} \tag{14.3}$$

$$\text{F1 Score} = 2 \times \frac{\left(\text{Precision} \times \text{Recall}\right)}{\left(\text{Precision} + \text{Recall}\right)} \tag{14.4}$$

TABLE 14.1

Experimental Parameters of the Proposed Classification Model

Parameter	Setting (Values)
Initial learning rate	0.001
Batch size	32
Optimizer	Adam
Loss function	Cross-entropy
Maximum epochs	50

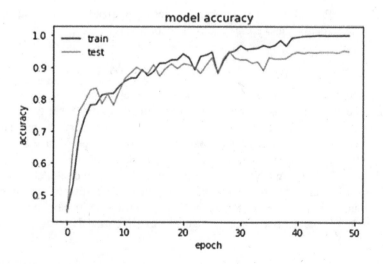

FIGURE 14.6   Accuracy of the classifier model during training.

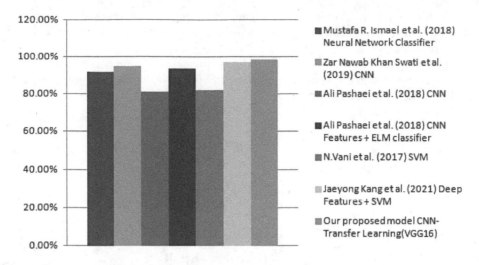

FIGURE 14.7   Comparison of the proposed model with some existing approaches.

TABLE 14.2

Class-Specific Observation of Proposed Multi-Label Brain Tumor Classifier

Tumor Type	Precision	Recall	F1-Score
Meningioma	0.96	0.97	0.96
Glioma	0.90	0.98	0.94
Pituitary	0.97	0.99	0.98

where TP, TN, FP, and FN are the number of cases categorized as True Positive, True Negative, False Positive, and False Negative, respectively.

14.6.3 COMPARISON WITH RELATED CLASSIFICATION MODELS

We compared the effectiveness of the proposed multi-label classification model with some of the existing models on specific problems of classifying three types of brain tumors (Figure 14.7). Table 14.3 presents a comprehensive performance analysis based on classification accuracy. Our proposed model has outperformed Ismael and Abdel-Qader [8] by 6.32 percent, Zar Nawab Khan Swati et al. [7] by 3.4 percent, Ali Pashaei et al. [9] using CNN by 17.22 percent, Ali Pashaei et al. [9] using CNN features and ELM classifier by 4.54 percent, N. Vani et al. [5] by 16.22 percent, and Jaeyong Kang et al. [11] by 1.05 percent. Our proposed multi-label classification model provides better accuracy than some of the existing models.

TABLE 14.3
Performance Analysis with Some Existing Methods

Authors	Classification Method	Accuracy (%)	Improvement of the Proposed Model
Ismael and Abdel-Qader [8]	Neural Network Classifier	91.9	6.32
Zar Nawab Khan Swati et al. [7]	CNN	94.82	3.4
Ali Pashaei et al. [9]	CNN	81	17.22
Ali Pashaei et al. [9]	CNN Features + ELM classifier	93.68	4.54
N.Vani et al. [5]	SVM	82	16.22
Jaeyong Kang et al. [11]	Deep Features + SVM	97.17	1.05
Our proposed model	CNN-Transfer Learning(VGG16)	98.22	-

14.6.4 SEGMENTATION MODEL

The segmentation model is developed using ResUNET (refers to Deep Residual UNET) as shown in Figure 14.8. ResUNET uses residual units as an essential building block instead of a plain convolutional block. We created a residual unit (Figure 14.8) for constructing our model that includes two 3 × 3 convolutional blocks followed by batch norm and identity mapping. Identity mapping is used to connect the results and input of the residual unit.

We create a convolution block consisting of one batch normalization layer, one ReLU activation function layer, and one convolution layer as shown in Figure 14.9.

Figure 14.10 discusses about proposed segmentation model architecture. The encoder takes the input image and passes it through different encoder blocks. The encoder in our model consists of four encoder blocks, which are constructed using the residual units.

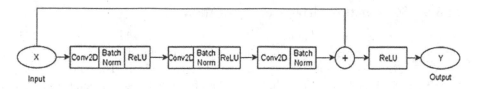

FIGURE 14.8   The architecture of residual block (R).

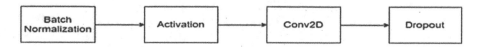

FIGURE 14.9   The architecture of convolution block (C).

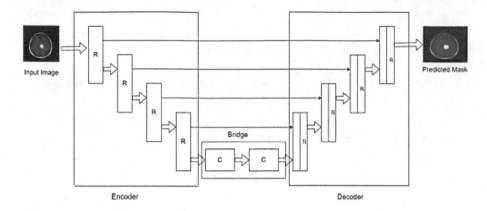

FIGURE 14.10 Proposed segmentation model architecture (R represents residual block, C represents convolution block).

Every encoder block output performed as a skip connection for the corresponding decoder block. To reduce the spatial dimensions (width and height) of the feature maps, the first 3 × 3 convolution layer uses a stride of 2 in the second and the third encoder block. The stride value of 2 decreases to half of the spatial dimensions, i.e., 256 to 128. The bridge is created using two convolution blocks. The decoder takes the feature map from the bridge and the skip connections from different encoder blocks and learns a higher semantic representation used to generate a segmentation mask. The decoder of our model consists of four decoder blocks. Each decoder block starts with a 2 × 2 up-sampling, which doubles the spatial size of the feature maps. These feature maps are then combined with the appropriate skip connection from the encoder block. These skip connections assist the decoder block to get the feature learned by the encoder network. Finally, a 1 × 1 convolution is applied with sigmoid activation to obtain the brain tumor segmentation. Data argumentation was adopted on the train and test dataset.

14.6.5 SEGMENTATION METRICS AND EVALUATION

The optimizer used during training is 'Adam' and the initial learning rate is 0.05. Early stopping is used during the model training, which helps stop the model's training if validation loss did not improve in 10 epochs consecutively. The batch size was set to 32. Focal Tversky Nabila is chosen as a loss function because it helps deal with class imbalance discussed in Abraham and Khan [19]. Focal Tversky Loss (FTL) is a generalization of the Tversky loss as shown in Equation (14.5).

$$FTL = (1 - TI)\gamma \tag{14.5}$$

γ is the parameter that controls the nonlinearity of the loss. TI represents the Tversky Index. Mathematically notation of TI is given in Equation (14.6)

$$TI = TP / (TP + \alpha \times FN + \beta \times FP) \tag{14.6}$$

TI provides parameters α and β, where $\alpha + \beta = 1$. In the case of $\alpha = \beta = 0.5$, it is simplified to the coefficient of the dice. When $\alpha = \beta = 1$, it is simplified to the Jaccard index. In our proposed segmentation model, we set the α value to 0.7, β to value to 0.3, and the γ value to 0.75. The number of epochs is limited to 100.

The segmentation model was able to achieve a Focal Tversky of 95.5 percent and Dice Similarity Coefficient of 0.861 on the test data (Figure 14.11).

14.6.6 COMPARISON WITH SOME EXITING SEGMENTATION MODELS

Table 14.4 provides a comprehensive comparison of the improvement percentage of the Dice Similarity Coefficient (DSC). Figure 14.12 represents improvement percentage of DSC compared with some existing methods. We see that our proposed ResUNET based segmentation model has an improvement percent of DSC over Jianxin Zhang et al. [2] by 3.7 percent, Hao Dong et al. [3] by 6.2 percent, and Mohamed et al. (2020) by 2.5 percent.

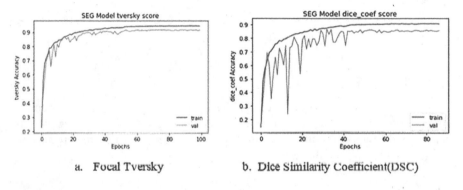

a. Focal Tversky   b. Dice Similarity Coefficient(DSC)

FIGURE 14.11 Focal Tversky (a) and Dice coefficient (b) of segmentation during training.

TABLE 14.4

Performance Analysis of the Proposed Segmentation Model with Some Existing Methods

Authors	Segmentation Method	DSC	Improvement % of DSC with Exiting Methods
Jianxin Zhang et al. [2]	AGResU-Net	0.83	3.7%
Hao Dong et al. [3]	U-net	0.81	6.2%
Mohamed A. et al. (2020)	U-net	0.84	2.5%
Our Model	ResUNET	0.861	—

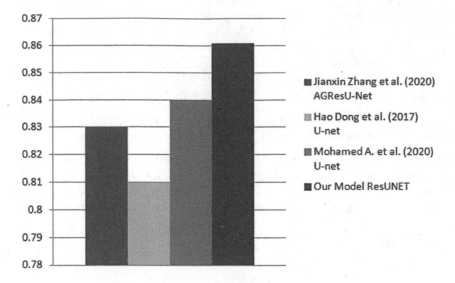

FIGURE 14.12 Comparison of the proposed segmentation model with some existing approaches.

14.7 RESULTS

Figure 14.13 illustrates the results of the proposed segmentation model. The images on the left are the growth truth of the tumor position: the red-colored region is the location of the tumor. The images on the right are predicted images: the green area is the predicted location of the tumor.

1. Meningioma Tumor

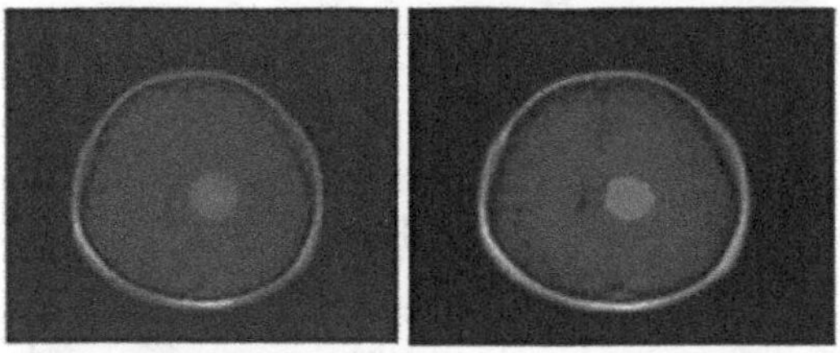

a. Ground Truth   b. Generated Mask

FIGURE 14.13 Sample result of proposed segmentation model.

2. Glioma Tumor

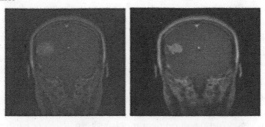

a. Ground Truth   b. Generated Mask

3. Pituitary Tumor

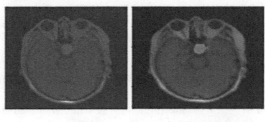

a. Ground Truth   b. Generated Mask

FIGURE 14.13 (*Continued*)

14.8 CONCLUSION

This chapter presented a multi-label brain tumor classification model using CNN architecture and a brain tumor segmentation model that uses ResUNET architecture. We used openly available T1-weighted MRI data to test the effectiveness of the proposed models. Image augmentation was adopted to avoid overfitting. The proposed multi-label classification model achieved 98.22 percent accuracy on test data, and the segmentation model achieved a Tversky of 95.5 percent and a Dice Coefficient of 86.1 percent. Our proposed segmentation model and classification model can assist health care professionals in diagnosing brain tumors. Further research in this area can focus on improving tumor estimation time using various ensemble functions. The proposed model can also be tested with the remaining tumor types.

REFERENCES

1. Cheng, J., 2017. *Brain tumor dataset*. 10.6084/M9.FIGSHARE.1512427.V5
2. Zhang, J., Jiang, Z., Dong, J., Hou, Y., and Liu, B., 2020. Attention gate ResU-net for automatic MRI brain tumor segmentation. *IEEE Access* 8, 58533–58545.
3. Dong, H., Yang, G., Liu, F., Mo, Y., and Guo, Y., 2017. Automatic brain tumor detection and segmentation using u-net based fully convolutional networks, in: *Communications in Computer and Information Science*, Springer International Publishing, pp. 506–517.
4. Naser, M.A. and Deen, M.J., 2020. Brain tumor segmentation and grading of lower-grade glioma using deep learning in MRI images. *Computers in Biology and Medicine* 121, 103758.

5. Vani, N., Sowmya, A., and Jayamma, N., 2017. Brain tumor classification using support vector machine. *International Research Journal of Engineering and Technology (IRJET) 4*, 1724–1729.
6. Deepak, S. and Ameer, P.M., 2019. Brain tumor classification using deep CNN features via transfer learning. *Computers in Biology and Medicine* 111, 103345.
7. Swati, Z.N.K., Zhao, Q., Kabir, M., Ali, F., Ali, Z., Ahmed, S., and Lu, J., 2019. Brain tumor classification for MR images using transfer learning and fine-tuning. *Computerized Medical Imaging and Graphics* 75, 34–46.
8. Ismael, M.R. and Abdel-Qader, I., 2018. Brain Tumor Classification via statistical features and back-propagation neural network, in: *2018 IEEE International Conference on Electro/Information Technology (EIT)*.
9. Pashaei, A., Sajedi, H., and Jazayeri, N., 2018. Brain tumor classification via convolutional neural network and extreme learning machines, in: *2018 8th International Conference on Computer and Knowledge Engineering (ICCKE)*.
10. Díaz-Pernas, F.J., Martínez-Zarzuela, M., Antón-Rodríguez, M., and González-Ortega, D., 2021. A deep learning approach for brain tumor classification and segmentation using a multiscale convolutional neural network. *Healthcare* 9, 153.
11. Kang, J., Ullah, Z., and Gwak, J., 2021. MRI-based brain tumor classification using ensemble of deep features and machine learning classifiers. *Sensors* 21, 2222.
12. Nisha, V.M. and Jeganathan, L., 2019. A symmetry based anomaly detection in brain using cellular automata for computer aided diagnosis. *Indonesian Journal of Electrical Engineering and Computer Science 14*(1), pp. 471–477.
13. Rammurthy, D. and Mahesh, P.K., 2020. Whale Harris hawks optimization based deep learning classifier for brain tumor detection using MRI images. *Journal of King Saud University - Computer and Information Sciences*.
14. Simonyan, K. and Zisserman, A., 2014. Very deep convolutional networks for large-scale image recognition. *arXiv preprint arXiv:1409.1556*.
15. LeCun, Y., Bengio, Y., and Hinton, G., 2015. Deep learning. *Nature* 521, 436–444.
16. Zhang, Z., Liu, Q., and Wang, Y., 2018. Road extraction by deep residual U-Net. *IEEE Geosci. Remote Sensing Lett.* 15, 749–753.
17. Ling Shao, Fan Zhu, and Xuelong Li, 2015. Transfer learning for visual categorization: a survey. *IEEE Trans. Neural Netw. Learning Syst.* 26, 1019–1034.
18. Srivastava, N., Hinton, G., Krizhevsky, A., Sutskever, I., and Salakhutdinov, R., 2014. Dropout: a simple way to prevent neural networks from overfitting. *The Journal of Machine Learning Research 15*(1), pp. 1929–1958.
19. Abraham, N. and Khan, N.M., 2019. A novel focal Tversky loss function with improved attention U-net for lesion segmentation, in: *2019 IEEE 16th International Symposium on Biomedical Imaging (ISBI 2019)*.
20. Mohamed Hibat-Allah, Martin Ganahl, Lauren E. Hayward, Roger G. Melko, and Juan Carrasquilla *Phys. Rev. Research* 2, 023358 – Published 17 June 2020.

15 Deep Learning–Based Financial Forecasting of NSE Using Sentiment Analysis

Aditya Agarwal, Romit Ganjoo, Harsh Panchal and Suchitra Khojewe
MIT-World Peace University Pune, Maharashtra, India

CONTENTS

DOI: 10.1201/9781003307822-18

15.1   INTRODUCTION

Stock market is a place where continued trade of capital and shares takes place between investors and companies, where investors invest in any company with the goal of gaining as much profit as possible and companies try to accumulate huge amounts of capital. Therefore, the market is a reflection of a country's growth, investment, jobs, economy, and business. There are generally two methods used to attempt to predict stock price: technical analysis, which uses data such as opening price, volume traded, low price, and high price; and fundamental analysis, which is related to economic policies, current situation in the country, trade relations of the country with global partners, public opinion (nowadays obtained from social media as much as, if not more than, from conventional news media). Inaccurate prediction by an analyst can lead to substantial economic losses among investors. Therefore, the ability to analyze all data that can influence economic performance—and, consequently, the stock price—of whole industries as well as individual companies is crucial for anyone looking to generate profits in stock market trading.

For a long time, one of the most common tools for stock performance prediction has been analysis of past stock performance [1–3]. In reality, however, a variety of factors affect stock prices. In this chapter we take those factors into account to showcase how news and public sentiment can influence the stock markets.

First we have implemented some of the basic ML algorithms, keeping in mind different ways of preprocessing of textual data in sentiment analysis. We have incorporated two different techniques of word embedding, namely TF-IDF and Countvectorizer, before training with any of ML algorithms, to find out which one among these gives the best results for market sentiment between "bearish" and "bullish." The dataset used in these cases consisted of both news headlines taken from different websites and people's opinions taken from microblogging site Twitter, as further explained in the coming sections.

Second, for stock prediction using historical data, with help of algorithms like mutual info regression and correlation heat mapping, feature selection is performed to get the most relevant data for our target closing price. Raw data are imported from websites like Kaggle and Yahoo! Finance [4–8]. Third, relevant data are then used for the training process of future stock prices. Algorithms such random forest regressor, decision tree regressor, gradient boost, and different types of LSTM are used for the learning process. The purpose of choosing multiple algorithms was to get the most accurate prediction.

15.2   RELATED WORK

A vast amount of research to date is done on finding various approaches to stock prediction. Most of them involve considering the technical analysis of stocks. There has been proven a strong correlation between stock prices and the news reported relating to that particular stock.

Saloni Mohan et al. [9] have used three different algorithms, ARIMA, Fb-Prophet, and RNN-LSTM, for stock price prediction. The RNN-LSTM model using textual news information shows the best results among all others. For sentiment analysis, they have used NLTK sentiment analyzer to classify the polarity of which only negative and positive ones are taken into account. For finding out polarity of each text, maximum absolute positive or negative sentiment is calculated and an average of the results is taken, i.e.,

$$\text{Polarity}_i^c = \left(+/-\right)\max\left(\text{abs}\left(N_i^c, P_i^c\right)\right)$$

$$\text{Polarity}_i^c = \frac{1}{k}\sum_{i=1}^{k}\text{Polarity}_i^c$$

where N_i^c and P_j^i are negative and positive values corresponding to words in the ith of k documents about company.

H. Alostad et al. [1] have worked on hourly stock prices. In their study they have observed 30 different stocks for a duration of six months and corresponding news articles from the NASDAQ website. In addition to news articles, they have collected tweets of those companies for sentiment analysis. Li et al. [2] collected stock market's four different factors for each company listed in HKEX. Also, they collected financial articles to showcase a relation between the articles and the stock prices. Ashraf S. Hussein et al. [15] has used multi-layer perceptron for technical indicators. Above-mentioned algorithms were used in Egyptian companies EL Nasr clothing, Egyptian Electrical Cables, and EFG Hermes Holding, as well as Microsoft. The maximum accuracy gained in prediction of each company using the above-mentioned algorithm was 83 percent. Mehar Vijh et al. [14] have performed stock closing price prediction using machine learning using two different algorithms, ANNs and Random Forest techniques, and the prediction was evaluated using RMSE and MAPE indicators. Historical data of seven different companies was taken for 10 years and was converted into different variables to train the model [14]. Overall, ANN outperformed RF given RMSE of 0.42 and MAPE of 0.77. Nonita Sharma et al. [18] have performed predictions of future stock for 1–10, 15, 30, and 40 days in advance based on historical data. Prediction is performed with Random Forest using LSboost and is then compared with support vector machine (SVM). Tejas Mankar et al. [20] have performed sentiment along with prediction of stock price using historical prices, using two classifiers for sentiment analysis. Aparna Nayak et al. [22] have performed multiple experiments of one model of daily prediction with sentiment analysis, producing an accuracy of 70 percent; their second experiment included monthly prediction using historical data to find correlation between any two-month trends [22]. A careful evaluation proved a correlation between them. Sneh Kalra et al. [21] have evaluated the effect of news on stock price prediction, using Naive Bayes classifier for sentiment analysis.

15.3 SYSTEM DESIGN

The system model comprises the different algorithms used for stock price prediction from historical dataset and sentiment classification of the tweets and news headlines. Figure 15.1 represents the system model for forecasting using historical dataset. It comprises three different prediction models:

1. Prediction Model A: In this model high price, open price, low price, and volume are used as training data. This data is then fed to different regressor models for prediction.
2. Prediction Model B: In this model, closing price of a particular stock is used as training data. For predicting the prices for the coming days, two different algorithms, i.e, Vanilla LSTM and Stacked LSTM, are used.
3. Prediction Model C: In this model, EMA14, EMA50, MA14, and MA50 data are fed to different regression algorithms for price prediction.

Figure 15.1 represents the model for sentiment analysis using news headlines and tweets.

It consists of two different methods of sentiment analysis:

1. Method A: In this method, word embedding is done using tf-idf vectorization and then the SVM and logistic regression algorithms are applied for classification.
2. Method B: In this method, word embedding is done using CountVectorization and then the classification is done using SVM and logistic regression.

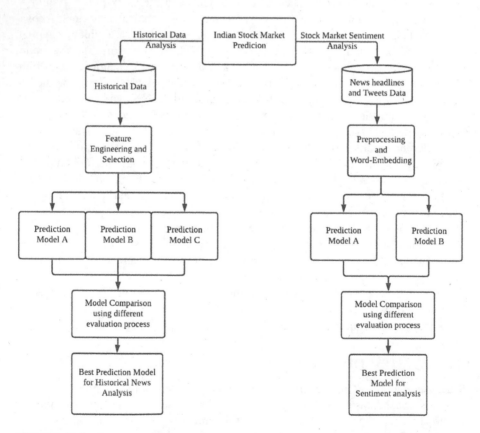

FIGURE 15.1   System model.

15.4   DATA COLLECTION AND PROCESSING

In this section data collection and preprocessing of both sentiment analysis and stock prediction using historical data are discussed. Data preprocessing after data collection is an important step for better performance and accuracy for machine learning algorithms.

15.4.1   STOCK PRICE PREDICTION USING HISTORICAL DATA

There are many methods for obtaining and forming the dataset. Various websites like Kaggle and Yahoo! Finance provide historical stock market dataset for the past 10–15 years. Application programming interface (API) is also available, which allows transfer of data without actually opening the application [10–13, 16–19]. These APIs help access data in real time. For stock market prediction using historical data we have retrieved a total of 1,227 pieces of data from March 3, 2016 to March 1, 2021 of NIFTY-50 along with that to see the impact of crude oil price and dollar price on the prediction accuracy. We have imported same amount of data from Kaggle and Yahoo! Finance. Raw data after importing were converted into different statistical variables, with the goal of removing unnecessary noise from the data. The statistical variables were created using the ta-lib library in Python. The statistical variables generated were:

(a) EMA14: Stock closing price fourteen days Exponential Moving Average
(b) EMA100: Stock closing price hundred days Exponential Moving Average
(c) EMA200: Stock closing price two hundred days Exponential Moving Average
(d) EMA50: Stock closing price fifty days Exponential Moving Average (e) MA14: Stock closing price fourteen days Moving Average
(e) MA50: Stock closing price fifty days Moving Average (g)MA100: Stock closing price hundred days Moving Average
(f) MA200: Stock closing price two hundred days Moving Average
(g) RSI14: Stock closing price fourteen days Relative Strength Index
(h) RSI100: Stock closing price hundred days Relative Strength Index
(i) RSI200: Stock closing price two hundred days Relative Strength Index

Including High Price, Low Price, Open Price, Volume, Dollar Close Price and Crude oil Close Price, a total of 17 different variables were generated, as shown in Table 15.1. Considering such a large number of variables for prediction is a difficult task, so in order to remove variables that are completely irrelevant, feature selection is performed. Tara Rawat et al. [26] have worked on different feature engineering tools and methodology and determined their use according to different purposes. The overall purpose of using feature engineering was to fix the problem of missing data, remove noise from the variables, and, through feature selection, get the input variable that is highly correlated with the target set (Closing Price), as well as to get the best accuracy from our models. In feature selection we have used three different algorithms for proper evaluation, Mutual Info Regressor, ExtraTree Regressor,

TABLE 15.1
Different Variables

High	Low	Open	Volume	MA 14	MA 50	MA 100	MA 200	EMA 14	EMA 50	EMA 100	EMA 200	RSI 200	RSI 100	OP	DP
8111	8020	8030	1785	8082	8258	8480	8246	8070	8228	8295	8242	53.0	50.0	56	68.2
8197	8114	8119	1276	8083	8248	8476	8250	8085	8227	8293	8241	53.45	51.0	56	67.9
8219	8148	8196	1273	8081	8228	8469	8256	8110	8224	8289	8240	53.47	51.0	55	68.1
8218	8180	8202	1324	8084	8217	8464	8260	8121	8222	8287	8239	53.47	51.0	56	68.2
14854	146511	4782	7441	15057	14358	13336	11999	14914	14324	13544	12626	56.47	59.1	65	72.4
15008	145041	4729	4038	15063	14388	13373	12028	14923	14350	13573	12649	57.24	60.1	67	72.3

and Correlation Matrix with HeatMap, to get the set of most correlated variables. There are two types of correlation, namely Pearson correlation and Spearman correlation. In this case, feature selection is done using Pearson correlation, as our data are normally distributed. Value of correlation lies between −1 and 1; if value is zero, it means there is no linear association between variables. Formula used for calculating correlation is

$$r_{xy} = \frac{n\sum x_i y_i - \sum x_i \sum y_i}{\sqrt{n\sum x_i^2 - (\sum x_i)^2}\sqrt{n\sum y_i^2 - (\sum y_i)^2}}$$

where r_{xy} is Pearson correlation, n is the sample space, x is input variable, and y is output variable.

Pierre Geurts et al. [27] have compared ExtraTree Regressor and classifier with other algorithms such as single CART Tree, Tree Bagging, Random Subspace, and Random Forest on accuracy and computational efficiency. ExtraTree Regressor is an ensemble algorithm that takes the arithmetic average of multiple decision trees collected in a forest to produce regression output.

Mutual Info Regressor is a widely used powerful technique for feature selection process that measures not only linear dependencies between dataset but also nonlinear dependencies between two discrete and continuous datasets. According to M. A. Sulaiman et al. [28], mutual information estimator suffers from three limitations: it depends on smoothing parameters; greedy methods lack stopping criteria; and similar estimators are used for both classification and regression problems. This study works on improving the three limitations of mutual info estimators. The formula that follows is for mutual information (MI),

$$I(X:Y) - \iint_{XY} p(x,y) \log \frac{p(x,y)}{p(x)p(y)} dxdy$$

where $I(X:Y)$ is the MI between two variables X and Y, where X can be one of our input variable and Y our target variable (closing price), $p(x, y)$ is the combined probability density function of X and Y, and $p(x)$, $p(y)$ can be represented as marginal density function. In case X and Y are completely independent of each other, the value of $p(x, y)$ will be equal to $p(x) p(y)$; in that case the value of $I(X:Y)$ or mutual information will be zero. Higher value of MI implies that there is a lot of common information between variable X and Y or vice versa; lower values indicate the variables are either independent or share very little information.

15.4.2 Textual Data Collection for Sentiment Analysis

News headlines and tweets are considered in the current situation of NSE companies. Data collection is done manually using web scraping. Tweets have been collected from various accounts of analysts and financial firms and by using appropriate hashtags to retrieve maximum tweets related to the NIFTY50. News headlines are scraped from the website MoneyControl using Python library BeautifulSoup, which is used for retrieving appropriate data from HTML tags. Few headlines are also picked manually from different websites such as Finviz Inc. Once all data are retrieved, they are combined and passed for preprocessing. The textual data collected is converted into a suitable and clean format in the following manner:

(A) The string is converted to lowercase format.
(B) Various special characters such as '@', '$', '#', '&', ' []' are removed from the data including the HTML tags and white spaces.
(C) Duplicated data is removed
(D) Different stop words such as "the," "are," "is," and "etc." are eliminated because they do not carry any valuable information.
(E) Strings are tokenized to apply word lemmatization. Tokenization is a process of splitting a sentence into individual words.
(F) After tokenization, word lemmatization is applied on the tokenized string. Lemmatization is a process of combining all similar-meaning words into a single word hence, reducing redundancy and size of the sentence.

This paper compares *tfidf* and CountVectorizer approaches for sentiment analysis. The *tfidf* is a way to convert textual data into numerical form. *tfidf* yields a vector value that is the product of *tf* and *idf*. *tf* (*termfrequency*) denotes the contribution of a particular word in the document and is calculated using

TABLE 15.2
Number of Tweets and News according to Their Topics

No.	Category	News Count	Tweet Count	Total Count
1	Announcements	113	0	113
2	Auto	10	19	29
3	Business	205	146	351
4	Companies	43	25	68
5	Finance	19	35	54
6	Crypto Currency	11	6	17
7	Current Affairs	22	16	38
8	Earnings	144	21	165
9	Economy	87	32	119
10	Entertainment	43	14	57
11	India	337	106	443
12	Markets	94	57	151
13	Mutual Funds	18	8	26
14	Sports	10	29	39
15	Start-ups	37	15	52
16	Stocks	78	51	129
17	World	133	55	188
18	Technology	43	24	67
19	Politics	27	16	43
	Total	1474	675	2149

$$tf = \frac{number\ of\ term\ t\ appears\ in\ a\ headline\ /\ tweet}{total\ number\ of\ terms\ in\ a\ document}$$

To measure the frequency of words in any article, *idf* (inverse document frequency) is used. *idf* gives the relevance of a particular word in any document and is calculated using

$$idf = \log \frac{total\ number\ of\ heading\ /\ tweets}{number\ of\ documents\ with\ term\ t\ in\ it}$$

Once we have *tf* and *idf*, *tfidf* can be calculated using

$$tfidf = tf * idf$$

The *tfidf* compares the words based on their rarity, such that words that are less occurring are considered of high relevance. The parameters of *tfidf* are shown in Table 15.3.

min_df: It ignores those terms that have a document frequency strictly lower than the given threshold.

max_df: It ignores those terms that have a document frequency strictly higher than the given threshold.

ngram_range: It is a tuple of lower and upper boundary of the range of n-values for different n-grams to be extracted.

CountVectorizer is a widely used method for text feature extraction [25]. It converts each word into a word frequency matrix, and fit_transform is used to calculate the number of times each word occurred. This is performed only when the stop words are removed. For a count vectorizer, two different parameters, i.e., Stop words and max_feature, have to be defined, as shown in Table 15.4.

TABLE 15.3
Tf-Idf Parameters

Parameter	min_df	max_df	n_gram
Value	113	0	(1,10)

TABLE 15.4
CountVectorizer Parameters

Parameter	Stop words	max_feature
Value	and, the, is, of, to	4

15.5   EVALUATION METHODOLOGY

For evaluating the model performance on different algorithms, four different evaluation factors are taken into consideration, based on which an optimal algorithm is identified.

15.5.1   ACCURACY

Accuracy is the ratio of number of correct predictions to the total number of predictions. In a simpler language, accuracy is the number of values that the model has predicted correctly. Accuracy immediately tells whether a model is being trained correctly and how well it may perform. The formula to calculate accuracy is:

$$\text{Accuracy} = \frac{\text{Number of Correct Predictions}}{\text{Total Number of Predictions}}$$

15.5.2   *F1* SCORE

$F1$ score is a measure of precision and recall. Precision is a measure to determine how precise the prediction of our model is, i.e., how many predicted values are actually true. Recall is defined as the number of true positives per the total number of values, i.e., positive + negative. The output of recall ranges from 0 to 1. $F1$ score is calculated using the formula:

$$F1 = 2 \times \left(\frac{\text{Precision} \times \text{Recall}}{\text{Precision} \times \text{Recall}} \right)$$

15.5.3   MEAN ABSOLUTE ERROR

Absolute error in machine learning models refers to the magnitude difference between the predicted value and the true value. In this study we evaluate our regression models by computing mean absolute error (MAE). MAE evaluates the average of absolute errors for a set of predictions as an estimation of the generalized value of error for an entire set. MAE is calculated using:

$$\text{MAE} = \frac{\sum_{i=1}^{n} (y_i - x_i)}{n}$$

where

y_i = Predicted values
x_i = Actual values
n = Total number of predictions

15.5.4 ROOT MEAN SQUARE ERROR

Root mean square error calculates error between the predicted values and the observed values. RMSE is always positive, and the lower the value of RMSE, the smaller the error.

$$\sqrt{\frac{\sum_{i=1}^{n}(y_i - y_i)^2}{n}}$$

where

n = Total number of values
$y\Gamma_i$ = Predicted value
y_i = Observed value

15.6 EXPERIMENTAL SETUP

This section discusses the flow of experiment along with the explanation of the different models used.

15.6.1 STOCK PRICE PREDICTION

Once the preprocessing part, which included the feature selection process as well, is completed, a total of nine variables highly correlated with our target variable (closing price) are chosen. The chosen variables are split into two different sets: Set 1 contains Low Price, High Price, Open Price, and Volume as input variables; and Set 2 contains ma100, ma14, rsi200, ema14, and ema100 as an input variables. For each set, closing price is the target variable. Both sets are trained with random forest regressor, gradient boosting, and decision tree regressor algorithms separately, and each algorithm hyperparameters were tuned using GridSearchCV and RandomizedSearchCV. Along with those, times series analysis is also performed with the help of the LSTM algorithm, and within the LSTM algorithm a proper comparison is done between two types of LSTM, Vanilla LSTM and Stacked LSTM, as well as by choosing different sets of batch sizes and epochs. All the machine learning algorithms were performed using the Scikit-Learn package in Python, and deep learning algorithms like types of LSTM were implemented using Tensorflow library and Keras interface in Python.

15.6.1.1 Decision Tree Regressor

Decision tree regressor is the advanced regression technique that not only can give the prediction for linear variables but also is capable of prediction of nonlinear variables and can also consider large numbers of different input variables at a time. It is important to understand how the basic splitting process takes place in regression, which depends on two main points: (1) divide the space of prediction into different spaces $(X_1, X_2,...X_i$ into different regions $R_1, R_2,...R_j)$. For every observation that falls into the region R_j, all predictions are made by taking the mean of the observation which lies in a particular Region (R_j). To elaborate step 1, usually the prediction space is divided into higher dimensions so that interpretation of the prediction model can be done easily. The main aim is to find the value of $R_1, R_2,....R_j$ capable of giving the minimum value of residual sum of squares (RSS).

$$\sum_{i=1}^{J}\sum_{i \in R_j}\left(y_i - \hat{y}R_j\right)^2$$

where Y_i is the actual value and Y_{Rj} is the mean of all the observations of that region. But the following methodology is computationally infeasible. Looking into this problem, an approach called top-down, recursive binary splitting, or greedy, is considered. It is top-down because it begins at the top of the tree with a single unit and then keeps on splitting into predictive space, and each split creates two branches. It is computationally feasible because at a time only the best split is considered rather than taking care of the split that will give a better tree in future. Now, to perform, recursive binary splitting predictor X_j and cutoff point s are selected such that it divides the predictor space into two different regions $\{X_j < s\}$ and $\{X_j > s\}$, those value of $X_1, X_2,...X_i$ and cutoff point s are considered that give the lowest RSS value for both regions.

$$R_1\left(j,s\right) = \{Xj < s\} \text{ and } R_2\left(j,s\right) = \{Xj > s\}$$

and formula used for RSS value is

$$\sum_{i:x_i \in R_1(j,s)}\left(y_i - \hat{y}R_1\right)^2 + \sum_{i:x_i \in R_2(j,s)}\left(y_i - \hat{y}R_2\right)^2$$

where yR_1 is the mean response of training observations in region R_1 and yR_2 is the mean response of training observations in region R_2. Now, within the region, the same process of obtaining a split by keeping RSS value lowest is repeated, and the process is continued until a required criterion is reached.

Above is an example of splitting that takes place in a decision tree regressor with the process we have discussed before.

15.6.1.2   Random Forest Regressor

Random forest regressor (RFR) is an ensembling technique that takes the aggregate of different predictions rather than depending on any individual model.

It works by constructing a large number of different decision trees, for distribution of data to different trees. The row sample replacement process is followed, and some data (D1) are distributed to Tree1 where (D1, D2...D$(N + 1) < $D); while distributing further data, they are randomly resampled into smaller subsets. It is also called

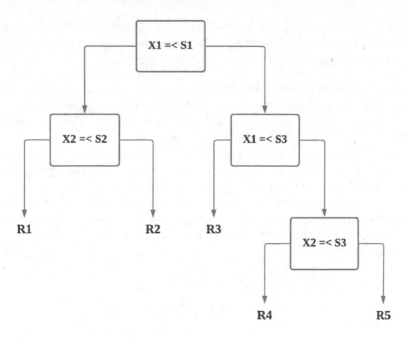

FIGURE 15.2   Diagram for decision tree prediction.

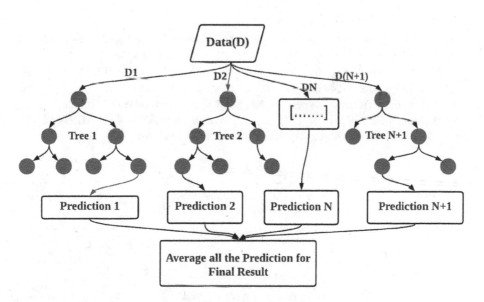

FIGURE 15.3   Diagram for random forest regressor prediction.

bagging or bootstrap aggregation, as final prediction is a mean of all the independent predictions obtained from different trees, which is an aggregation process; distribution of subsets of data to different trees is a bootstrap process.

15.6.1.3 Gradient Boosting Regressor

Gradient boosting regressor (GBS) is a widely used ensembling and boosting technique where prediction is made sequentially rather than independently. In this process the new predictor learns from the mistake of the previous one.

Figure 15.4 presents a complete explanation of the working of a gradient-boosting algorithm, where initially residual data (R) are obtained by subtracting mean of actual data by actual data, and that is given as an input to the next tree. Similar process is continued until the last tree (N), but while performing this continuous additive process, there is a significant risk of overfitting. To protect our prediction process from overfitting, we use alpha or learning rate whose value ranges from 0 to 1. Final prediction can be given as

$$y(pred) = y_1 + (\alpha \times R) + (\alpha \times R_1) + \ldots + (\alpha \times R_n)$$

where

α = Learning rate,
R1,2,...n = Residual value.

15.6.1.4 Long Short-Term Memory

Sima et al. [29] have conducted an experiment where advanced RNN model LSTM is compared with general regression-based models like ARIMA, and LSTM has been proven to be a superior model. They have also compared it with BiLSTM, a variant of the LSTM model. BiLSTM has much better prediction than ARIMA or general LSTM, but the performance speed of BILSTM was found to be slower than that of LSTM. Steven Elsworth et al. [31] have compared raw LSTM with ABBA-LSTM and found that ABBA reduces the sensitivity of the model toward hyperparameters,

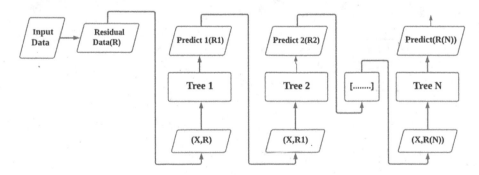

FIGURE 15.4 Block diagram for gradient-boosting regressor prediction.

leading to better results for historical prediction. Akbar Siami Namin et al. [32] have performed forecasting of economic and financial time series using ARIMA and LSTM algorithms on multiple sets of data, including N225, IXIC, HSI, GSPC, and Dow Jones and compared the overall prediction of all models.

Long short-term memory is an advanced or improved version of RNN, developed to overcome vanishing gradients and other shortcoming problems of RNN. An architecture of LSTM can be divided into three portions: forget gate, input gate, and output gate.

(6.1.E.1.) *Forget Gate.* As new values keep pouring in, past value becomes irrelevant, so the forget gate plays an important role of removing irrelevant values from the cell. Due to presence of sigmoid activation function σ, forget gate output ranges from 0 to 1.

(6.1.E.2.) *Input Gate.* Input gate is responsible for deciding which new information is needed to be added. The first layer of sigmoid activation function acts as filter of values in the Input gate. If the output of the sigmoid function is 0, then the value is rejected, and if it is 1, then the value is kept, and the second layer tanh function creates a vector of new value from −1 to 1. At last, output obtained from both layers is multiplied.

(6.1.E.3.) *Output Gate.* An output layer is responsible for selecting relevant information from the memory cell and showing it in an output. The tanh function converts the values from the memory cell into a vector from −1 to 1, and at last the result is multiplied with an output of the sigmoid function. Value of the final output ranges from −1 to 1.

(6.1.E.4.) *Stacked and Vanilla LSTM.* These are types of LSTM in which the hidden layer of LSTM is changed. If the model has one hidden LSTM layer, it is called Vanilla LSTM, and if the model has more than one layer of hidden LSTM, it is called Stacked LSTM. Both types of LSTM have a single output prediction layer.

15.6.2 Sentiment Analysis

For sentiment analysis the dataset is divided into two portions: 80% for training and 20% for testing. Three different machine learning algorithms are applied on the collected textual dataset. The sections that follow give a detailed explanation of the algorithms and how they have been applied on the dataset.

15.6.2.1 Logistic Regression

Logistic regression model is used for the classification of binary class problems. It helps in modeling the probability of the default model class. It can predict the probability of those instances that can be classified into 0 or 1. Modeling of an input (A) belonging to a default class ($B = 1$) can be represented formally as:

$$P(X) = P(Y = 1|X)$$

Logistic regression model can be mathematically represented by [23]:

$$P = \frac{\exp\left(c_0 + c_1 x_1 + c_2 x_2 + \ldots + c_n x_n\right)}{1 + \exp\left(c_0 + c_1 x_1 + c_2 x_2 + \ldots + c_n x_n\right)}$$

The above equation is used for classifying the sentiment of the stock. To predict the stock price trend, the value of P at any instance 'i' is calculated. For any instance i, the value of P is either '0' or '1'. '0' represents the negative sentiment of the news headline and will lead to a drop in the stock price value. On the other hand, '1' represents the positive sentiment of the news headline and that the stock prices will go up.

15.6.2.2 Support Vector Machine

Support vector machines (SVM) is one of the frequently used binary classifiers. SVM creates a separation boundary to differentiate certain values from others such that the values lie to either side of the separation [24, 30]. For an n dimensional feature vector x = $(X_1, X_2, X_3, \ldots, X_n)$, the linear separation boundary is defined as:

$$\beta_0 + \beta_1 X_1 + \beta_2 X_2 + \ldots + \beta_n X_n = \beta_0 + \sum_{i=1}^{n} \beta_i X_i = 0$$

The element category comprises binary value, i.e., in one category the sum can either be less than 0 or it can be greater than 0. The equation to represent the label 'y' is:

$$y = \beta_0 + \sum_{i=1}^{n} \beta_i X_i$$

The range of values of y is $\{-1,1\}$

Sahil Madge [24] has used SVM classifier for predicting stock price and has obtained a mean prediction accuracy of around 60 percent and maximum accuracy of more than 80 percent.

15.6.3 Hyperparameter Optimization

Hyperparameter optimization is a machine learning technique that intends to find a hyperparameter of any particular machine learning algorithm that protects a model from overfitting, underfitting while training, and also to give best prediction accuracy from a model. In this paper two different types of hyperparameter are discussed, GridSearchCV and randomized SearchCV, both of which are applied using the Scikit-learn library of Python. GridSearchCV checks each parameter among parameters passed to it to find the best combination, whereas randomized SearchCV randomly checks the combination of parameters.

TABLE 15.5

Parameters for Prediction through Historical Data

No	Algorithm	Hyper Parameter	OPV (Open)	OPV (EMA)
1	Decision Tree Regressor	Randomized SearchCV	criterion = 'mse', max_depth = 340, max_features = 'auto', min_samples_leaf = 1, min_samples_split = 5, splitter = 'random'	criterion = 'friedman_mse', max_depth = 780, max_features = 'auto', min_samples_leaf = 8, min_samples_split = 2, splitter = 'random'
		Grid SearchCV	criterion = 'friedman_mse', max_depth = 560, max_features = 'log2', min_samples_leaf = 1, min_samples_split = 5, splitter = 'best'	criterion = 'friedman_mse', max_depth = 1000, max_features = 'auto', min_samples_leaf = 12, min_samples_split = 20, splitter = 'random'
2	Random Forest Regressor	Randomized SearchCV	n_estimators = 50, criterion = 'mse', max_depth = 450, min_samples_split = 6, min_samples_leaf = 20, max_features = 'log2'	n_estimators = 50, criterion = 'mae', max_depth = 670, min_samples_split = 2, min_samples_leaf = 20, max_features = 'log2', max_leaf_nodes = None
		Grid SearchCV	criterion = 'mse', max_depth = 406, max_features = 'log2', min_samples_leaf = 6, min_samples_split = 10, n_estimators = 50	criterion = 'mse', max_depth = 858, max_features = 'log2', min_samples_leaf = 10, min_samples_split = 14, n_estimators = 50
3	Gradient Boost Regressor	Randomized SearchCV	criterion = 'mae', learning_rate = 0.1, loss = 'ls', max_depth = 780, max_features = 'auto', min_samples_leaf = 1, min_samples_split = 2, n_estimators =750, subsample=1.0, tol = 0.0001	criterion = 'mae', learning_rate = 1, loss = 'ls', max_depth = 1000, max_features = 'sqrt', min_samples_leaf = 8, min_samples_split = 10, n_estimators = 550 subsample = 1.0, tol = 0.0001
		Grid SearchCV	criterion = 'mae', learning_rate = 1, loss = 'ls', max_depth = 10, max_features = 'sqrt', min_samples_leaf = 4, min_samples_split = 14, n_estimators = 50, random_state = None, subsample = 1.0, tol = 0.0001	criterion = 'mae', learning_rate = 1, loss = 'ls', max_depth = 10, max_features = 'sqrt', min_samples_leaf = 4, min_samples_split = 5, n_estimators = 525, subsample = 1.0, tol = 0.0001

TABLE 15.6

Hyperparameters for Prediction of Sentiment Analysis

No.	Algorithm	Hyper Parameter	OPV (tf-idf)	OPV (CountVectorizer)
1	Support Vector Machines	Randomized SearchCV	C = 10, cache_size = 200, decision_function_shape = 'ovr', degree = 3, gamma = 0.1, kernel = 'rbf', max_iter = −1, tol = 0.001, verbose = False	C = 10, cache_size = 200, decision_function_shape = 'ovr', degree = 3, gamma = 0.01, kernel = 'rbf', max_iter = −1, tol = 0.001, verbose = False
		Grid SearchCV	C = 1, cache_size = 200, decision_function_shape = 'ovr', degree = 3, gamma = 1, kernel= 'rbf', max_iter = −1, tol = 0.001, verbose = False	C = 1000, cache_size = 200, decision_function_shape = 'ovr', degree = 3, gamma = 0.0001, kernel = 'rbf',max_iter = -1, tol = 0.001, verbose = False
2	Logistic Regression	Randomized SearchCV	C=10, fit_intercept = True, intercept_scaling = 1, max_iter = 100, multi_class = 'auto'; penalty= 'l1'; solver = 'liblinear', tol = 0.0001	C = 1.0, intercept_scaling = 1, max_iter = 100, multi_class = 'auto', penalty = 'l1', solver = 'liblinea', tol = 0.0001
		Grid SearchCV	C = 10, fit_intercept = True, intercept_scaling = 1, l1_ratio = None, max_iter = 100, multi_class = 'auto'; penalty = 'l1'; solver = 'liblinear', tol = 0.0001	C = 100, max_iter = 100, multi_class = 'ovr', penalty = 'l1', solver = 'liblinear', tol = 0.0001

15.7   RESULT AND ANALYSIS

15.7.1   FEATURE SELECTION

In our simulation results, Figures 15.1–15.12 shows that performance comparison of feature selection process ExtraTree ReGressor, Mutual info Regressor, and Pearson Correlation, i.e., use heatmap to choose top nine features for prediction of Adj closing price. With ExtraTree Regressor High that obtained values more than 0.20, Low, Open, EMA14, MA14 variables having values more than 0.15, EMA50, MA50, EMA100, MA100 were identified as top nine features when compared with Adj Close.

With Pearson (Figure 15.10) Correlation, HeatMap High, Low, Open, MA14, EMA14, EMA50, MA50, EMA100, and MA50 were most correlated variables with our target variable Adj Close.

With Mutual Info Regressor, Low, High, Open, EMA14, MA14, EMA200, MA200, EMA50 and EMA100 were identified as top variables that shared almost the same information as Adj Close (Table 15.7).

Among three algorithms, ExtraTree Regressor and Pearson Correlation HeatMap were found to have High, Low, Open, MA14, EMA14, MA50, and EMA50 to be most correlated features with our target variable, due to which we have used those variables as input features for our prediction algorithms.

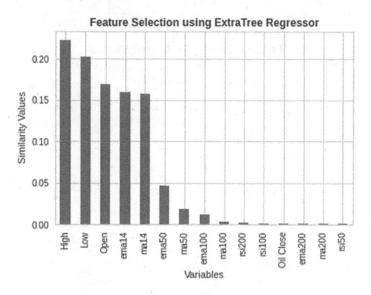

FIGURE 15.5 Feature selection bar graph for ExtraTree regressor.

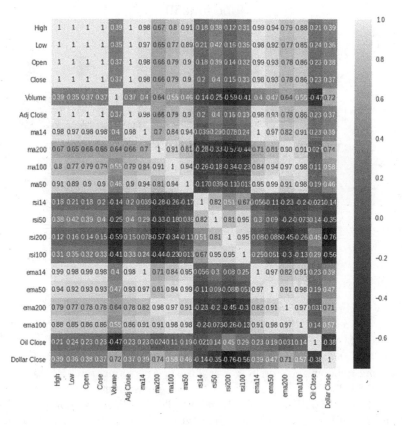

FIGURE 15.6 Feature selection heat for ExtraTree regressor.

TABLE 15.7

Feature Selection Using Mutual Infor Regressor Feature Selection Using Mutual Info Regressor

Low	3.465
High	3.29
Open	2.744
EMA14	2.09
MA14	1.94
EMA200	1.84
MA200	1.8095
EMA50	1.8090
EMA100	1.609
MA50	1.68
MA100	1.64
RSI200	1.63
RSI100	1.35

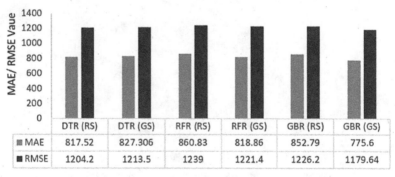

Result Table for Feature Set: ma50, ma14, ema14 and ema50

	DTR (RS)	DTR (GS)	RFR (RS)	RFR (GS)	GBR (RS)	GBR (GS)
■ MAE	817.52	827.306	860.83	818.86	852.79	775.6
■ RMSE	1204.2	1213.5	1239	1221.4	1226.2	1179.64

■ MAE ■ RMSE

FIGURE 15.7 Comparative analysis of RMSE and MAE achieved using feature set MA14, MA50, EMA14, and EMA50.

15.7.2 HISTORICAL DATA ANALYSIS

Boosting algorithm Gradient Boosting Regressor tuned using GridSearchCV achieves the lowest RMSE and MAE values among all the different algorithms, and while using MA14, EMA14, EMA50 and MA50 as a feature set, values achieved were 1179.8 and 775.306 and was the best performer. Random Forest Regressor tuned using RandomizedSearchCV was the worst performer with RMSE 1239 and MAE 860.83. Evaluating overall performance GridSearchCV achieved lower and better RMSE and MAE value than RandomizedSearchCV in most of the results.

Here as well Boosting algorithm Gradient Boosting Regressor achieved the lowest RMSE and MAE values. Gradient Boosting Regressor tuned using Randomized

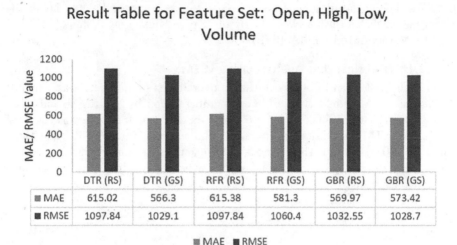

FIGURE 15.8 Comparative analysis of RMSE and MAE achieved using feature set open, high, low, and volume.

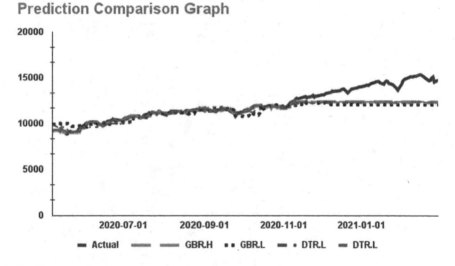

FIGURE 15.9 Prediction comparative analysis of various ML model.

SearchCV achieved lowest MAE value of 569.97 and tuned using GridSearchCv achieved lowest RMSE value of 1028.7 were the two best performance values among all. Decision Tree Regressor and Random Forest Regressor both achieved similar highest and worst RMSE and MAE values 1097.84 and 615.38. Evaluating overall performance GridSearchCV achieved lower and better RMSE and MAE value than RandomizedSearchCV in most of the results.

Figure 15.9 shows the prediction comparison graph between the actual data and predicted data of using Decision Tree Regressor (DTR), RandomForest Regressor

(RFR), and Gradient Boosting Regressor (GBR), and each algorithm tuned with different parameter and using two datasets of [Open, High, Low, Volume] (H) and [MA14, MA50, EMA14, EMA50] (L)

15.7.2.1   Historical Data Analysis Using LSTM

From Table 15.8 it can be observed that the overall best performance was achieved by Stalked LSTM with batch size 128 and number of epochs 200, RMSE and MAE values obtained were 143.06 and 104.67. And the worst performance was achieved by Vanilla LSTM while using batch size 128 and epochs 300 with RMSE and MAE values 1024.0 and 494.01. There were no significant and substantial improved results achieved by increasing batch size and epochs, whereas in some cases increasing it also led to overfitting.

TABLE 15.8
Parameter Tuning for LSTM

Batch Size	Epochs	Metrics		Algorithm			
				Vanilla	LSTM	Stacked	LSTM
	100	MAE	RMSE	197.9	250.6	119.82	153.39
32	200	MAE	RMSE	110.48	149.44	139.84	190.09
	300	MAE	RMSE	124.9	165.0`	230.0	335.20
	100	MAE	RMSE	234.57`	321.78	219.31	273.37
64	200	MAE	RMSE	201.94	275.09	122.96	155.04
	300	MAE	RMSE	124.36	169.18	137.51	181.08
	100	MAE	RMSE	197.15	270.56	269.33	347.50
128	200	MAE	RMSE	193.51	255.49	104.67	143.06
	300	MAE	RMSE	494.01	1024.0	125.35	158.68

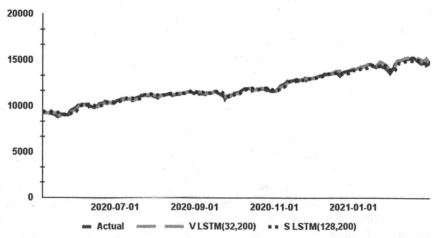

Prediction Comparison Graph

FIGURE 15.10   Prediction comparison graph of LSTM with choosing best hyperparameter.

For sentiment analysis of news headlines and tweets, three different algorithms, i.e., support vector machines and logistic regression is implemented using two different vectorizers, i.e., count vectorizer and tf-idf vectorizer. For F_1 score (Figure 15.11) and accuracy (Figure 15.12), logistic regression shows maximum score using GridSearchCV.

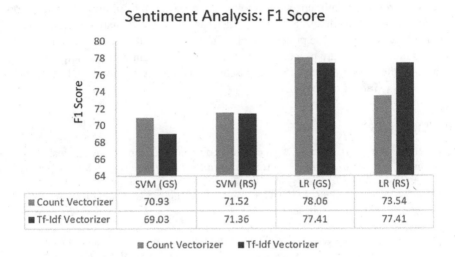

FIGURE 15.11 F_1 score comparison for sentiment analysis.

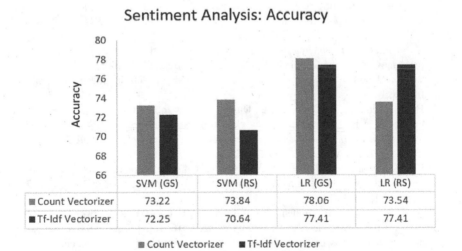

FIGURE 15.12 Accuracy comparison for sentiment analysis.

15.8 CONCLUSION AND FUTURE SCOPE

The current share market boom in India also adds more risk in investment for any particular stock. The model proposed in this paper for stock price prediction and sentiment analysis using public opinion and news headlines gives better insights about a particular stock, which considers previous performance and current situation of the stock. Feature engineering was proposed to handle missing data and for the feature selection process. Sentiment analysis was done on public opinion extracted from Twitter and news headlines categorizing them as positive or negative helping predict sudden hikes or dips in the price of stock. There are few other things that need to be worked on, which we are proposing as future work. To begin with, an automated system for gathering news headlines can be implemented. Automatic headline retrieval will make the model more dynamic.

REFERENCES

[1] H. Alostad and H. Davulcu, "Directional prediction of stock prices using breaking news on twitter," in *2015 IEEE/WIC/ACM International Conference on Web Intelligence and Intelligent Agent Technology (WIIAT)*, December 2015, vol. 1, pp. 523–530.

[2] X. Li, H. Xie, Y. Song, S. Zhu, Q. Li, and F. L. Wang, "Does summarization help stock prediction? A news impact analysis," *IEEE Intelligent Systems*, May 2015, vol. 30, no. 3, pp. 26–34.

[3] D. Duong, T. Nguyen, and M. Dang, "Stock market prediction using financial news articles on ho chi minh stock exchange," in *Proceedings of the 10th International Conference on Ubiquitous Information Management and Communication, ser. IMCOM '16*. New York, NY, USA: ACM, 2016, pp. 71:1–71:6.

[4] Y. Wang, D. Seyler, S. K. K. Santu, and C. Zhai, "A study of feature construction for text-based forecasting of time series variables," in *Proceedings of the 2017 ACM on Conference on Information and Knowledge Management, ser. CIKM '17*. New York, NY, USA: ACM, 2017, pp. 2347–2350.

[5] Y. Shynkevich, T. McGinnity, S. A. Coleman, A. Belatreche, and Y. Li, "Forecasting price movements using technical indicators: Investigating the impact of varying input window length," *Neurocomputing*, 2017, vol. 264, pp. 71–88, machine learning in finance.

[6] H. D. Huynh, L. M. Dang, and D. Duong, "A new model for stock price movements prediction using deep neural network," in *Proceedings of theEighth International Symposium on Information and Communication Technology, ser. SoICT 2017*. New York, NY, USA: ACM, 2017, pp. 57–62.

[7] R. P. Schumaker and H. Chen, "Textual analysis of stock market prediction using breaking financial news: The azfin text system," *ACM Trans. Inf. Syst.*, Mar. 2009, vol. 27, no. 2, pp. 12:1–12:19.

[8] A. de Myttenaere, B. Golden, B. L. Grand, and F. Rossi, "Mean absolute percentage error for regression models," *Neurocomputing*, 2016, vol. 192, pp. 38–48, advances in artificial neural networks, machine learning and computational intelligence.

[9] Saloni Mohan, Sahitya Mullapudi, Sudheer Sammeta, Parag Vijayvergia, and David C. Anastasiu, "Stock price prediction using news sentiment analysis," in *2019 IEEE Fifth International Conference on Big Data Computing Service and Applications (BigDataService)*.

[10] Shangkun Deng, Takashi Mitsubuchi, Kei Shioda, Tatsuro Shimada, Akito Sakurai. "Combining technical analysis with sentiment analysis for stock price prediction," in *2011 Ninth IEEE International Conference on Dependable, Autonomic and Secure Computing*.

[11] Zhigang Jin, Yang Yang, Yuhong Liu, "Stock closing price prediction based on sentiment analysis and LSTM," in *Neural Computing and Applications*, September 19 2019.

[12] Mehak Usmani, Syed Hasan Adil, Kamran Raza, and Syed Saad Azhar Ali, "Stock market prediction using machine learning techniques," in *2016 3rd International Conference on Computer And Information Sciences (ICCOINS)*.

[13] Lingling Zhang, Saiji Fu, and Bochen Li, "Research on stock price forecast based on news sentiment analysis—a case study of Alibaba", Springer International Publishing AG, part of Springer Nature, 2018.

[14] Mehar Vijha, Deeksha Chandolab, Vinay Anand Tikkiwalb, and Arun Kumar, "Stock closing price prediction using machine learning techniques," in *International Conference on Computational Intelligence and Data Science (ICCIDS2019)*, 2019

[15] Ashraf S. Hussein, Ibrahim M. Hamed, and Mohamed F. Tolba, "An efficient system for stock market prediction," in *Springer International Publishing Switzerland 2015*, D. Filev et al. (eds.), Intelligent Systems' 2014, Advances in Intelligent Systems and Computing, p. 23.

[16] A.J. Smola, and B. Scholkopf, "A tutorial on support vector regression," *Stat Comput*, 2004, vol. 14(3), pp. 199–222.

[17] T. Fischer and C. Krauss, "Deep learning with long short-term memory networks for financial market predictions," *Eur J Oper Res.*, 2017, S0377221717310652.

[18] N. Sharma and A. Juneja, "Combining of random forest estimates using LSboost for stock market index prediction," in *2017 2nd International Conference for Convergence in Technology (I2CT)*, 2017, pp. 1199–1202, doi:10.1109/I2CT.2017.8226316.

[19] K. Ryota and N. Tomoharu, "Stock market prediction based on interrelated time series data," in *2012 IEEE Symposium on Computers & Informatics (ISCI)*, 2012, pp. 17–21, doi:10.1109/ISCI.2012.6222660.

[20] T. Mankar, T. Hotchandani, M. Madhwani, A. Chidrawar, and C. S. Lifna, "Stock Market prediction based on social sentiments using machine learning," in *2018 International Conference on Smart City and Emerging Technology (ICSCET)*, 2018, pp. 1–3, doi:10.1109/ICSCET.2018.8537242.

[21] S. Kalra and J. S. Prasad, "Efficacy of news sentiment for stock market prediction," in *2019 International Conference on Machine Learning, Big Data, Cloud and Parallel Computing (COMITCon)*, 2019, pp. 491–496, doi:10.1109/COMIT-Con.2019.8862265.

[22] Aparna Nayak, M. M. Manohara Pai, Radhika M. Pai, "Prediction models for Indian stock market," *Procedia Computer Science*, ISSN 1877-0509.

[23] Jibing Gong and Shengtao Sun, "A new approach of stock price trend prediction based on logistic regression model," in *2009 International Conference on New Trends in Information and Service Science*.

[24] Saahil Madge, "Predicting stock price direction using support vector machines," Independent work report spring 2015, Princeton University.

[25] JinShan Yang, ChenYue Zhao, Hao TongYu, and HeYang Chena, "Use GBDT to predict the stock market", *Procedia Computer Science*, 2020, vol. 174, pp. 161–171.

[26] Tara Rawat and Vineeta Khemchandani. Feature Engineering (FE) tools and techniques for better classification performance, 2019, doi:10.21172/ijiet.82.024.

[27] P. Geurts, D. Ernst, and L. Wehenkel, Extremely randomized trees. *Mach Learn*, 2006, vol. 63, pp. 3–42.

[28] M. A. Sulaiman and J. Labadin, "Feature selection with mutual information for regression problems," in *2015 9th International Conference on IT in Asia (CITA)*, 2015, pp. 1–6, doi:10.1109/CITA.2015.7349826.

[29] S. Siami-Namini, N. Tavakoli, and A. S. Namin, "The performance of LSTM and BiLSTM in forecasting time series," in *2019 IEEE International Conference on Big Data (Big Data)*, 2019, pp. 3285–3292, doi:10.1109/BigData47090.2019.9005997.

[30] R. Ganjoo and A. Purohit, "Anti-spoofing door lock using face recognition and blink detection," in *2021 6th International Conference on Inventive Computation Technologies (ICICT)*, 2021, pp. 1090–1096, doi:10.1109/ICICT50816.2021.9358795.

[31] Steven Elsworth, Stefan Güttel, Time Series Forecasting Using LSTM Networks: A Symbolic Approach, 2020, arXiv:2003.05672. Available at: https://arxiv.org/abs/2003.05672

[32] Sima Siami-Namini and Akbar Siami Namin, Forecasting Economics and Financial Time Series: ARIMA vs. LSTM, 2018, arXiv:1803.06386. Available at: https://arxiv.org/abs/1803.06386

16 An Efficient Convolutional Neural Network with Image Augmentation for Cassava Leaf Disease Detection

Ratnavel Rajalakshmi, Abhinav Basil Shinow, Aswin Murali and Kashinadh S Nair
Vellore Institute of Technology, Chennai, India

J. Bhuvana
Sri Sivasubramaniya Nadar College of Engineering, Chennai, India

CONTENTS

DOI: 10.1201/9781003307822-19

16.1 INTRODUCTION

Cassava is a perennial shrub, and people consume its roots as vegetables. Cassava leaves also are very useful and are rich in vitamins and protein. Cassava hay is widely used for animal feed and in textile industries. Cassava also serves as a substitute for rice and has several applications as a raw material for producing starch, other bio-based products, and animal feed. It also provides more energy than the other staple foods like rice, maize, etc. Cassava is a staple food specifically for the people of Africa, Indonesia, and several countries in Asia. Parts of the Cassava plant including its leaves, hay, and roots offer several medicinal benefits namely weight loss, treating migraines, healing wounds, fever, diarrhea, and increasing energy and appetite.

Most of the population around the world is relying on agriculture mostly for food and employment. Around 40 percent of productivity is lost every year, which leads to loss of income and rise in the demand of that produce along the demand-supply chain. Factors that usually affect the yield of food crops include the environmental causes like soil fertility, soil erosion, water quality, pests, diseases, weather, natural disasters, etc. These factors are categorized into abiotic and biotic ones, where the soil and climatic-related factors are referred to as abiotic and the pests-related factors are biotic [1]. The abiotic climatic changes affect the agricultural yield in three ways, namely directly via morphological changes, indirectly through soil fertility and socioeconomic changes like change in trade, policy, etc.

Among all these environmental factors, it has been observed that the yield is reduced only due to diseases or pests by 50–80 percent. Plant diseases can be due to parasitic or nonparasitic causes. Parasitic causes include pests, weeds, and pathogens, whereas the nonparasitic causes include nutrition loss, water quality, and temperature. The losses due to these, namely economic and ecological, may lead to starvation. Cassava is grown by farmers across the world in large and medium scales across Nigeria, Thailand, Indonesia, Brazil, Ghana, and Congo . There is always a decline in productivity due to several environmental factors, among which the primary factor is due to the diseases affecting the Cassava leaves. Viruses, bacteria, fungi, and pests detrimentally affect the growth of cassava. The cassava farmers are losing their crops and their livelihood is affected. All these challenges demand the need for assessing the growth of the plant along with its quality that predicts the presence of diseases that cause harm to the plant yield and leading to losses in all dimensions.

In this work, we aim to address this problem by identifying the diseases in an early stage by applying suitable image-processing techniques. Appropriate features are necessarily extracted from the leaf images to discriminate them into the categories of diseases. Choosing such discriminative hand-crafted features using machine learning approaches is tedious. In order to handle the difficulty of manual feature engineering, deep learning approaches come in handy, where the features are automatically extracted from the images and help in classifying them.

In this work, we have employed convolutional neural networks [2] and applied augmentation techniques for improving the performance of the classifier. We also applied a transfer learning technique to learn the significant features from the image that helps in efficiently identifying the type of disease. We have applied the Cut-Mix algorithm for data augmentation and used the EfficientNet architecture for obtaining better performance, independent of scale variations. By extensive experiments on the cassava leaves dataset, we have shown that an accuracy of 88.41 percent can be achieved by the proposed method, which outperforms other state-of-art techniques.

The chapter is organized as follows: related works are presented in Section 16.2, materials and methods are detailed in Section 16.3, followed by results and discussion in Section 16.4. The concluding remarks are presented in Section 16.5.

16.2   RELATED WORKS

Detecting the state of the leaves is the utmost requirement to maintain the crop yield. Usually, the farmers carry out a manual inspection of leaves to detect the same, using the symptoms exhibited by the inspected plant leaves. Symptoms like blight, blotch, wilt, mold, mildew, spots, and holes are the ones the farmers look for.

Manual inspection of leaves is tedious, time-consuming, and prone to errors. Hence, automatic approaches that make use of computer vision–based techniques have been widely used to assess the quality of the leaves [3]. The computer vision–based image-processing techniques use automatic or manual methods for input image acquisition. Digital cameras and unmanned aerial vehicles (drones) are used for acquiring images. The acquired images are preprocessed for further processing stages, and the region of interest is segmented. From the segmented parts of the leaves the features are extracted and given to a plethora of classifiers available to distinguish the features appropriately into their classes of diseases. The features include LBP, HOG, SURF, GLCM, MSER, Histogram, and Wavelets, which are extracted from the segmented regions of the leafy images. Some metaheuristic optimization techniques have also been employed to choose the optimal features for classification.

Many types of research have been carried out for detecting various leaf diseases, but cassava leaf disease detection has not been explored much. Cassava green mite (CGM), cassava brown streak virus disease (CBSD), cassava mosaic disease (CMD), and cassava bacterial blight (CBB) are the most common diseases identified in cassava leaves. Each of these diseases has unique symptoms to identify them. White spots on the leaves that tend to enlarge and affect the process of photosynthesis due to a drop in chlorophyll content is CGM. CBSD can be identified with the presence of yellow veins. CMD reduces the size of the leaves due to mosaic and twisted leaf edges. CBB is caused by bacteria that lead to wilting of leaves prematurely.

Several image-processing methods have been used to evaluate the quality of plants, such as remote sensing, hyperspectral sensing technique, unmanned aerial vehicle (UAV) multispectral imagery, etc. Custom-generated dataset of 18,000 images of cassava leaves [4] has been used to classify them as healthy or unhealthy at the first level and the category of the disease at the second level using a machine learning approach. Preprocessing is done to remove poor and irregular instances, and the rest are normalized. Bag of features is used for feature extraction, and principal component analysis (PCA) is used to reduce the dimension of the features extracted. Among the several classifiers trained with fivefold cross-validation, cubic support vector machine has achieved the highest accuracy of 83.9 percent.

Due to the development of high-speed computing systems, deep learning has emerged as a potential approach in problem solving in several application domains, especially in image processing, natural language processing, and speech processing. The deep learning approach follows representational learning in the image processing domain, with many convolutional layers stacked to learn the composite features from the low-level image features across the layers. The features are extracted automatically, where human interference in choosing the best possible features is not necessary in deep learning networks.

Kaggle dataset with five classes and 10,000 labeled images was given to a CNN architecture for leaf disease prediction [5]. The dataset is inherently imbalanced and has employed four different schemes to handle this problem. The training set size is increased through class-weight, focal loss, and SMOTE along with h data augmentation techniques such as flipping, shearing, scaling cropping, shifting height and width, etc. CNN has three convolutional layers with four fully connected layers to classify the diseases of cassava leaves. The results are observed with and without a mechanism to handle data imbalance and have shown a 5 percent increase in accuracy in the prediction of diseases. The mobile-based deep learning model for disease identification is used by authors of [2]. They have used conventional neural networks, particularly MobileNet, the efficient net that provides the most accurate result.

Transfer learning approaches have been popularly used for image classification. This learning approach makes use of the pretrained models that have been constructed and trained already with massive datasets like ImageNet. These networks are trained on one problem and can be reused in similar problems to avoid training from scratch. These models can be used in several ways: as a pretrained network for feature extraction, or by fine-tuning or freezing the pretrained network by training a few layers with the custom dataset. In computer vision, VGG-16, VGG-19, Inception V3, XCeption, ResNet-5, and EfficientNet are few of the potential transfer learning models.

Authors of [6] have used INC-VGGN, a combination of VGGNet and Inception network, two pretrained deep convolutional architectures, to classify the four classes of Maize dataset of Plantvillage database with 3,852 images. Accuracy of 80.38 percent has been observed by using their proposed architecture. INC-VGGN has used a swish activation function in place of ReLU. An additional convolution layer at the end of VGG followed by the two inception modules made up the INC-VGGN architecture for leaf disease classification.

Transfer learning network MobileNetV2 [7] is used to classify cassava leaves, whose size is scaled to 224×224 pixels and has achieved an accuracy of 65.6 percent. A custom dataset fed to a hybrid network combining CNN and MobileNetV2 was implemented [8] to detect the diseases on cassava leaves. This hybrid combination is used for feature extraction and is fed to three fully connected layers. The system has obtained a testing accuracy of 85.38 percent on its custom dataset. The Inceptionv3 model is used as a feature extractor and fed to three different classifiers such as Inceptionv3 softmax, SVM, and KNN for leaf disease detection in cassava plants. A custom-created dataset with 11,650 images [9] was used to test the performance of the proposed network. SVM is found to be the best classifier that has obtained an accuracy greater than the other two classifiers. Similarly, ResNet is used for the same purpose [10], and Single Shot Multibox (SSD) model with the MobileNet detector and classifier is used for cassava disease prediction [11] with 83.9 percent accuracy.

All these surveyed works gave a motivation to use a pretrained model to detect the diseases of the cassava plant leaves. The best suitable model has been identified through our proposed system for disease classification.

16.3 MATERIALS AND METHODS

16.3.1 DATA SET DESCRIPTION

In this work, we have used the cassava leaf dataset obtained from Kaggle. The sample images are shown in Figure 16.1. It consists of five classes, namely Cassava Bacterial Blight (CBB - labeled as 0), Cassava Brown Streak Disease (CBSD labeled as 1), Cassava Green Mottle (CGM), Cassava Mosaic Disease (CMD), and Healthy Cassava (labeled as 4). The class distribution is plotted in Figure 16.2. From the plot, we can observe that CMD is the predominantly seen disease.

FIGURE 16.1   Sample cassava images from the dataset.

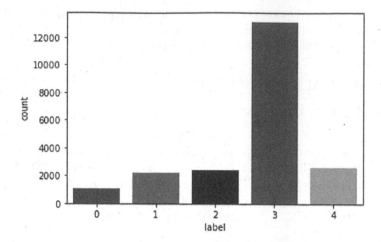

FIGURE 16.2   Class-wise distribution of cassava leaf instances.

16.3.2   Methodology

The proposed method consists of different stages that include preprocessing, data augmentation, and transfer learning. The details are presented below.

16.3.2.1   Preprocessing and Augmentation

The image is resized into 512 × 512, and the proposed system has used the image data generator class in Keras for data augmentation. Image data generator is applied to augment the images in real time while training rather than augmenting the images beforehand. This helps save a lot of space taken by the model to train. The initial parameters used for augmentation are tabulated in Table 16.1. But upon further analysis, we were able to find that the image data generator gave a very poor performance. Initially, we replaced the image data generator by adding augmentation to the images by making use of the augmentation layers provided by Keras. We implemented this by adding these augmentation layers in between the input layer and the CNN feature extractor layers in our model's architecture. This workaround was not

TABLE 16.1

Parameters Used for Data Augmentation

Parameter	Value
Rotation_range	40
Width_shift_range	0.2
Height_shift_range	0.2
Shear_range	0.2
Zoom_range	0.2
Horizontal_flip	True
Vertical_flip	True
Fill_mode	Nearest

viable due to the compatibility issues of TPU with Keras augmentation layers. For our final best-performing model that was trained on a TPU, augmentation was done by creating a function that we then passed into the image decode function.

In addition to the image data generator, we also tried using CutMix augmentation in the EfficientNet B4 model. In CutMix augmentation we cut and pasted random patches between the training images, and the original labels were mixed based on the proportion of the patches in each image. Upon training, we observed a decrease in accuracy when CutMix was implemented.

16.3.2.2   CNN Feature Extractors

To classify leaf diseases based on their images, we have implemented various available CNN architectures. We trained and tested on the following architectures: VGG, ResNet, MobileNet, Inception, Xception, and EfficientNet.

Traditionally an artificial neural network learns by first assigning a random set of weights, which then gets changed to minimize the loss function with each epoch. Artificial neural networks can be used for image classification by flattening the image vector into a one-dimensional vector. But the issue with this is that flattening the image vector results in the loss of the spatial features that determine the position of each pixel in the image. Since the loss function in artificial neural networks is done through back-propagation by gradient descent, the loss of spatial features of the image could result in a vanishing gradient when trained using an artificial neural network and could provide unusable results. Thus, to avoid this diminishing effect, we have used convolutional neural networks as the feature extractors.

To train our image classification model, we have implemented transfer learning by using the pretrained weights and then adding additional pooling and flattening layers and finally a fully connected, dense layer with softmax activation function, which will give the probability of each class as output. We trained and tested several CNN architectures on our dataset. Among the various architectures, EfficientNetB4 [12] provided the best results.

16.3.2.3   EfficientB4 Transfer Learning Architecture

Generally, in CNN architectures, scaling is done in any one of the dimensions, namely depth, width, or resolution. By applying a highly effective method, the accuracy of the model can be improved. In the proposed method, EfficientNet is employed, which scales in all three dimensions using an effective compound coefficient [12].

Initially, all the CNN architectures were trained using Nvidia Tesla P100 GPU, but this resulted in several hardware limitations, as our dataset consisted of almost 21,000 images, and the GPUs did not provide enough computational power to train enough parameters, so because of this, our proposed system had to rely largely on the pretrained parameters, which severely affected our model's performance. Upon training with the GPU, EfficientNetB4 performed the best by providing an accuracy of 81 percent on the test set consisting of roughly 1,000 images.

These limitations were solved by switching to a TPU (Tensor processing unit), which provided much more computational power. The EfficientNet model that provided the best results when trained using GPU/CPU provided much better performance and efficiency in terms of training time by switching the training pipeline to

TPU, which allowed the training of much more parameters. The final weights that provided the best results are saved into a .h5 file format, which can then be used to classify the disease in cassava leaves for various applications like deploying to the web or using as weights for another classification model.

To train and test the proposed transfer learning–based image classification model, the cloud computing environment provided by Kaggle was used.

16.3.2.4   GPU Training

The cassava dataset was directly loaded from the cloud into the notebook's virtual environment. Initially, for training, the Nvidia Tesla P100 GPU provided by Kaggle was utilized with a weekly quota of 40 hours. The initial training of the various CNN architectures using transfer learning took an average of 3–4 hours for each of the CNN architectures.

16.3.2.5   TPU Training

GPUs were taking too long to train the image classification models, so it was decided to optimize the proposed pipeline to work with TPUs. Traditionally loading of data as we did in the case of GPU to the virtual environment is not possible in the case of TPU, as this would cause bottlenecks due to the inability of the data stream to keep up with the speed of the TPU. So, to run on TPU, we loaded the data from Google's Cloud Storage Bucket in the form of TF record files. On training using the TPU and further streamlining our pipeline by optimizing the code, we were able to reduce the training time to just a few minutes.

16.3.2.6   Parameters on GPU and TPU

Initially, while training using GPU due to hardware limitations, only 8,965 parameters were trained and the rest of the parameter values were the pretrained ones. The model had a total of 17,682,788 parameters, of which 8,965 were trainable ones. By switching to TPU we were able to train much more parameters, and this helped improve the model's performance by a considerable margin. Now with TPU, the model had a total of 17,682,788 parameters, among which 17,557,581 were trainable ones.

16.3.2.7   Loss Functions Used

Loss function plays an important role in statistical models, particularly for determining whether a prediction is a good one or not. They define an objective function, using which the performance of the model is evaluated against the parameters learned by the model and are determined by minimizing a chosen loss function. Our proposed system has used three types of loss functions: (i) categorical cross-entropy, (ii) sigmoid focal cross-entropy, and (iii) sparse categorical cross entropy.

(i)   Categorical cross-entropy is a loss function that is used in multiclass classification tasks. This task shows that the item belongs to one out of many possible categories, and the model must decide which one. It is designed to quantify the difference between two probability distributions. This loss is a very good measure of how distinguishable two discrete probability distributions are from each other.

(ii) When highly unbalanced classes are involved, sigmoid focal cross-entropy is extremely useful. It focuses on hard examples and many irregularities and weighs well-classified examples. It is mainly used in object detection techniques when scenarios like the imbalance between background class and other classes are extremely high. It can be referred to as extended cross-entropy.

(iii) Since the image data generator took too long to train, it was decided to replace it and to further optimize our code so that training could be done faster. The image data generator used One Hot encoded labels, which is why our proposed model used categorical cross-entropy as the loss function, since we no longer used One Hot encoded labels and had to replace the loss function with sparse categorical cross-entropy, which is the same loss function but for normal image labels.

16.3.2.8 Optimizer

During training, the neural network adjusts the weights in such a way that the loss can be minimized, to provide better predictions. The fine-tuning of weights based on the loss is done by an optimizer. In our model, we used Adam optimizer. The adaptive moment estimation is the optimizer function that we have used across all our models with a learning rate of 0.000001(1e-3). The Adam optimizer combines both the functions of Rms-prop and momentum-based gradient descent.

16.3.2.9 Learning Rate Function

The function used for fixing the learning rate during training is ReduceLrOnPlateau. The monitored value that was used to change the learning rate is the validation loss, as we are trying to increase the validation accuracy of the model. Since the lower the loss function, the better the outcome, we set the mode to min and patience to 2, so that when the validation loss shows no further decrease after two consecutive epochs, the learning rate is reduced by a factor of 0.2 (Figures 16.3 and 16.4).

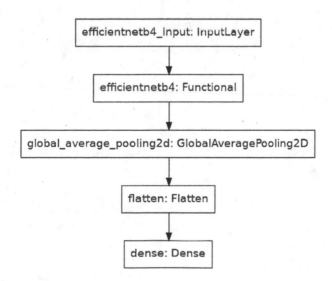

FIGURE 16.3 Efficient net architecture.

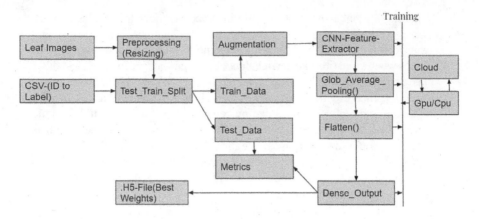

FIGURE 16.4 GPU training pipeline (schematic representation).

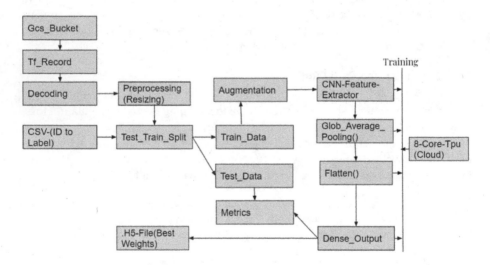

FIGURE 16.5 TPU training pipeline (schematic representation).

The pipeline used for GPU training and TPU training is shown in Figures 16.5 and 16.6, respectively.

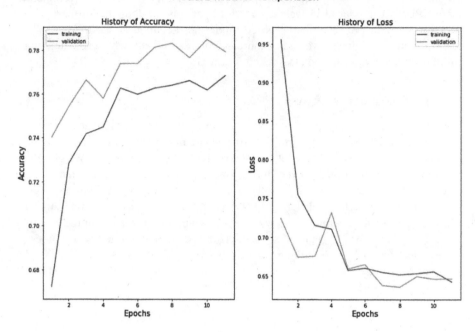

FIGURE 16.6   Performance of VGG16.

TABLE 16.2

Comparative Study of Different Architecture with the Proposed Model

Model	Reported Accuracy (test data from test_train split at 0.05 ratio), seed = 21
Inceptionnet	75.55%
Xception	75.79%
Vgg16	78.13%
Resnet	78.50%
Efficient Net(B5)	78.69%
Mobilenet_v2	79.43%
Efficient Net(B4) with CutMix Augmentation	80.84%
Efficient Net(B4) (Updated Weights)	81.12% **(Best Model)**

16.4   EXPERIMENT RESULTS AND DISCUSSION

Several experiments were carried out on different transfer learning architectures, testing accuracy across the models trained as shown in Table 16.2. The shift in the training pipeline from GPU/CPU to TPU enabled the training of many more parameters, which helped in improving the model performance. Efficient Net (B4) architecture using GPU/CPU produced an accuracy of 81.12 percent. By doing the formerly mentioned change/shift to TPU, the proposed model has acquired an accuracy of 88.41 percent. Thus, by doing so we had an increase of 7.29 percent, which is a huge margin of difference in the image classification domain.

16.4.1 PERFORMANCE ANALYSIS

The training accuracy and loss across seven different transfer learning models experimented with are shown in Figures 16.7–16.14. The fluctuation of accuracy and loss across the classification models show that Efficient Net(B4) (Updated Weights) has performed better than others even during training, showing a gradual increase in accuracy and decrease in the loss both in terms of training and validation. Figure 16.15 depicts the accuracy difference between the best-performing model and the other models during the training. Hence, we can see that Performance of the Efficient Net(B4) (Updated Weights) model has outperformed all other models tested in terms of classification accuracy (see Figures 16.6–16.15). Finally, it can be inferred that the EfficientNet-based model has performed better than the other models.

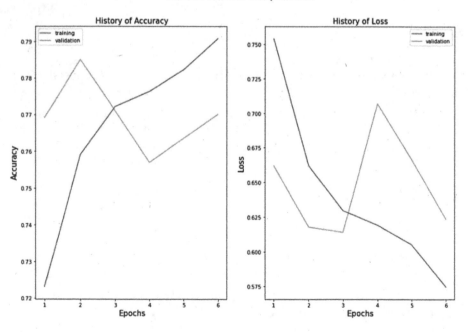

FIGURE 16.7   Performance of ResNet.

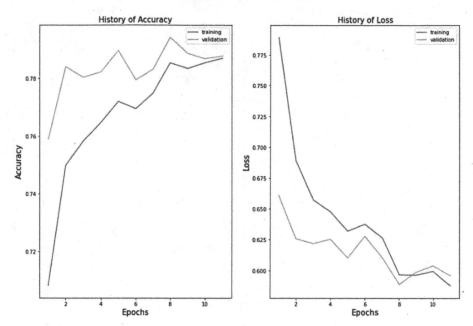

FIGURE 16.8   Performance of MobileNet.

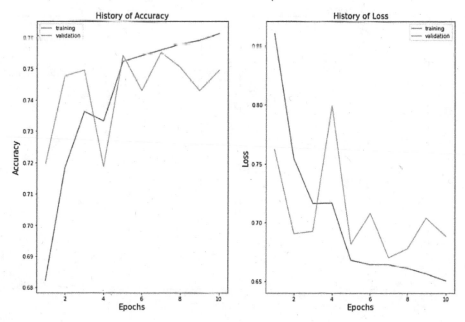

FIGURE 16.9   Performance of InceptionNet.

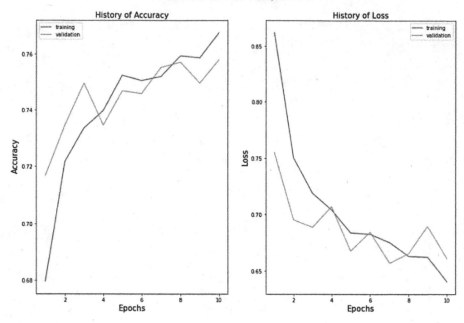

FIGURE 16.10   Performance of XceptionNet.

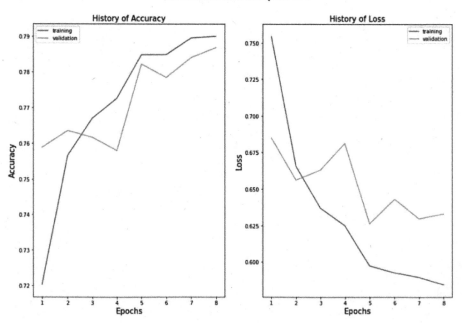

FIGURE 16.11   Performance of Efficient-Net-B5.

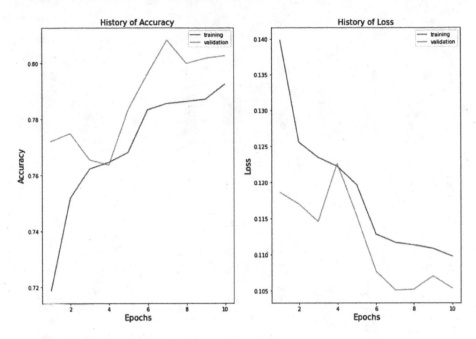

FIGURE 16.12   Performance of Efficient-Net-B4.

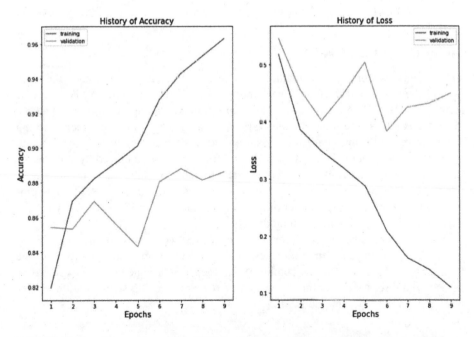

FIGURE 16.13   Best performance of Efficient Net(B4) with the higher number of parameters.

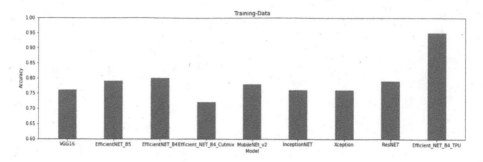

FIGURE 16.14   Performance comparison in terms of accuracy on training data.

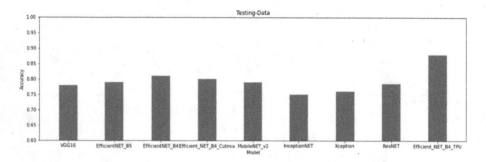

FIGURE 16.15   Performance comparison in terms of accuracy on testing data.

16.5   CONCLUSION

In this work, we proposed a methodology to detect diseases in cassava plants all around the world and fix the farmers' biggest problem by identifying issues. This should be of significant help to farmers and minimize damage to food production. We have analyzed the images using various transfer learning–based deep learning architectures and found that EfficientNet provides better accuracy of 88.41 percent, compared to all other existing works. This performance was achieved by shifting the implementation platform from GPU-based computation to TPU-based computation, which has allowed the proposed system to train more parameters. GPU-based computation has restricted the number of trainable parameters, which has constricted the performance of the classification model.

This work could be extended for other diseases as well, in the future considering more plants. To improve the efficiency of the classification model, more than one transfer learning model can be combined and their performance can be explored. A generalized diseases detection system can be developed using segmentation, detection, and classification methods.

REFERENCES

1. Liliane, Tandzi Ngoune and Mutengwa Shelton Charles. "Factors affecting yield of crops." *Agronomy-Climate Change & Food Security* (2020): 9. 10.5772/intechopen.90672
2. Simonyan, Karen, and Andrew Zisserman. "Very deep convolutional networks for large-scale image recognition." arXiv preprint arXiv:1409.1556, 2014.
3. Dhingra, Gittaly, Vinay Kumar, and Hem Dutt Joshi. "Study of digital image processing techniques for leaf disease detection and classification." *Multimedia Tools and Applications* 77, no. 15 (2018): 19951–20000.
4. Emuoyibofarhe, Ozichi, Justice O. Emuoyibofarhe, Segun Adebayo, Adebamiji Ayandiji, Oloyede Demeji, and Oreoluwa James. "Detection and classification of cassava diseases using machine learning." *International Journal of Computer Science and Software Engineering (IJCSSE)*, 8, no. 7 (2021): 166–176.
5. Sambasivam, G. and Geoffrey Duncan Opiyo. "A predictive machine learning application in agriculture: Cassava disease detection and classification with imbalanced dataset using convolutional neural networks." *Egyptian Informatics Journal* 22, no. 1 (2021): 27–34.
6. Chen, Junde, Jinxiu Chen, Defu Zhang, Yuandong Sun, and Yaser Ahangari Nanehkaran. "Using deep transfer learning for image-based plant disease identification," *Computers and Electronics in Agriculture* 173 (2020): 105393.
7. Ayu, H. R., A. Surtono, and D. K. Apriyanto. "Deep learning for detection cassava leaf disease." In *Journal of Physics: Conference Series*, vol. 1751, no. 1, p. 012072. IOP Publishing, 2021.
8. Surya, Rafi and Elliana Gautama. "Cassava leaf disease detection using convolutional neural networks." In *2020 6th International Conference on Science in Information Technology (ICSITech)*, pp. 97–102. IEEE, 2020.
9. Ramcharan, Amanda, Kelsee Baranowski, Peter McCloskey, Babuali Ahmed, James Legg, and David P. Hughes. "Deep learning for image-based cassava disease detection." *Frontiers in Plant Science* 8 (2017): 1852.
10. Choi, Hong Chong and Tsung-Chih Hsiao. "Image Classification of Cassava Leaf Disease Based on Residual Network." In *2021 IEEE 3rd Eurasia Conference on Biomedical Engineering, Healthcare and Sustainability (ECBIOS)*, pp. 185–186. IEEE, 2021.
11. Ramcharan, Amanda, Peter McCloskey, Kelsee Baranowski, Neema Mbilinyi, Latifa Mrisho, Mathias Ndalahwa, James Legg, and David P. Hughes. "A mobile-based deep learning model for cassava disease diagnosis." *Frontiers in Plant Science* 10 (2019): 272.
12. Tan, Mingxing and Quoc Le. "Efficientnet: rethinking model scaling for convolutional neural networks." In *International Conference on Machine Learning*, pp. 6105–6114, PMLR, 2019.

Section IV

Post–COVID-19 Futuristic
Scenarios–Based Applications:
Issues and Challenges

17 AI-Based Classification and Detection of COVID-19 on Medical Images Using Deep Learning

V. Pattabiraman and R. Maheswari
Vellore Institute of Technology, Chennai, India

CONTENTS

17.1 INTRODUCTION

The novel coronavirus (SARS-CoV-2) causes an extreme respiratory syndrome leading to the disease called COVID-19, which is a respiratory infection that mainly affects the nasal tract and the lungs. Taking into consideration the alarmingly high levels of spread of the disease throughout the world, the World Health Organization (WHO) is looking into ways and measures to protect mankind. Another team is also working on finding a solution to identify the disease and find out its severity in our neighborhood. The WHO has announced COVID-19 to be a global pandemic with many lives lost.

The visible signs of the coronavirus include fever, sore throat, dry coughing, breathlessness, stomach upset, and loss of the senses such as taste and smell. This in turn leads to extreme respiratory disease that often requires the afflicted person to be admitted to an intensive care unit. Initially the intensity and severity of COVID-19 were directly proportional to the age of the individual, and the death rate was high among the elderly population. As a consequence, COVID-19 is considered a high-risk emergency, and early diagnosis of the disease by following the symptoms carefully is a target, according to WHO, in order to break the chain of transmission and thereby monitor the virus's spread. Medical imaging of the chest has been a commonly used diagnostic tool in clinical research during the past several years to examine abnormalities in the cardiac region of the human in order to detect and monitor the development of many pulmonary diseases including lung cancer, chronic bronchitis, lung inflammation, lung disease, and asthma, to name a few. In this scenario of COVID-19 disease, chest medical images such as X-ray scans showed many symptoms and patterns of lung malformation including bilateral anomalies, interstitial irregularities, lung aggregation, and surface opacities. Mostly as an outcome, the study of suspicious chest X-ray images provides an opportunity to aid in the diagnostic processes and early identification of the severity of COVID-19 disease in the affected individual, which may help save the individual's life.

AI and deep learning can be implemented to carry forward the testing process in a more efficient and accurate manner. Given the significance of the subject in the sense of the ongoing universal epidemic triggered due to the COVID-19 blast, several scholars suggested analytical frameworks for the coronavirus identification on chest X-ray images by applying the deep learning methodologies in the recent months.

In the recent times, artificial intelligence and deep learning techniques have made clinical experts' job easier to identify and detect errors in many cases. These techniques have portrayed great potential in classifying the X-ray images to give the desired outcome. The descriptive knowledge of the dataset characteristics aids in identifying the three categories of images found in our collected dataset with greater precision. The dataset is divided by three attributes, namely COVID-19, pneumonia (viral), and normal. There are many deep learning algorithms that can be used to produce the desired outcome, such as logistic regression (LR), random forest, support vector machine, etc.

Several chest X-ray image processing and classification methods have been proposed in the last 20 years by researchers and scholars. This is done to be more precise by considering many applied deep learning models for X-ray image detection and processing to derive at important conclusion. The classifiers are mainly divided into two processes. The first process being considered here is feature extraction; the second one is classification. Classification takes place with the help of an activation function and a convolution layer over chest X-ray image as depicted in Figure 17.1. With regard to deep neural networks methods for image detection and classification, famous classification algorithms such as support vector machine (SVM) and regression analysis are employed to find insights from the datasets. These algorithms are usually single layered. These layers in the deep learning framework depict the layers present in the retinal cortex of the human eye. Human brain performs object detection and recognition tasks using several layers present in the retinal cortex. Similarly, artificial intelligence algorithms extract the essential information by preprocessing and processing in a dynamic manner, preserving knowledge features, and are therefore assumed to be capable of higher recognition and classification accuracy than normal, steeper classifiers. These deep learning algorithms are mostly utilized to achieve promising outcomes in a variety of areas, including recognition of abnormalities and image detection tasks. Therefore, in this work the system will exploit the various models used by other researchers and propose a model to aid in detecting COVID-19.

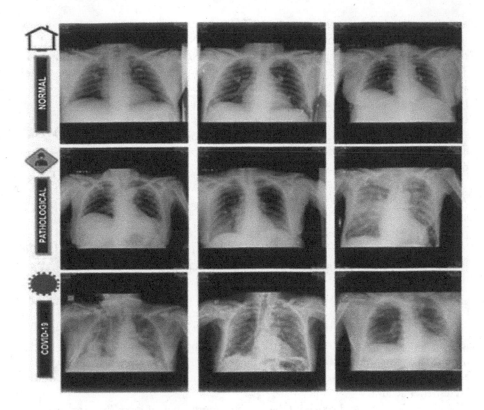

FIGURE 17.1   Representation of chest X-ray images.

17.2   LITERATURE SURVEY

Shin et al. [1] have taken the dataset of chest X-ray medical images from openly accessible sources. The dataset consisted of more than 3,500 images from the Indiana Network for Patient Care. This study enables us to learn the utilization of deep CNN model as a classification algorithm, as it is easy to train large datasets. The most commonly used AlexNet and a state-of-the-art CNN model also known as GooLeNet model were also implemented to detect and to assure a more sustainable accuracy and performance in identification and classification in comparison to the several other native frameworks used for the purpose of image classification. The native and traditional methodologies are inclusive of SVM-based models. The image weights are loaded into the classification model to begin the training and testing procedure. However, this approach did not satisfy the high-performance chart; hence, other algorithms were considered for implementation.

De Moura et al. [2] have used different deep learning–built models by varying the number of learning layers in each model employed for identification and classification, such as deep belief networks (DBN) and convolutional neural networks (CNN) such as DenseNet-161. A feed-forward network is practiced inside each of the dense blocks to obtain maximum transmission of data between the layers. These architecture networks are classified into various networks, and features extractor is used to extract data categorically. In this work, CNN models have been used and the number of layers has been increased and reduced to see which produces better results. They have used stochastic gradient descent (SGD) for optimizing the training model with a standard learning rate of 0.01. In this work it is observed that the accuracy percentage obtained from the analysis is reasonably better when compared with the other traditional methods to detect the abnormalities in the X-ray images.

Sadman et al. [3] implemented data augmentation of radiograph images (DARI) algorithm with state-of-the-art CNN model to intertwine AI with deep learning. The result was a customized convolutional neural network (CNN) model, a generic adversarial network (GAN) in DL-CRC, which gave them an accuracy of 93.94 percent, which, when compared to accuracies from other models, was the highest.

Xu et al. [4] created a novel approach to detect the abnormalities in chest X-ray images by using Inception V3 CNN architecture. The modified version of CNN changes the kernel size to discover variations in the convolution layer. In this work it is under that deeper the layer in the architecture, and the results obtained were of higher accuracy.

Rajaraman et al. [5] have implemented deep learning ensembles by using multiple CNN models with pruning the layers to get a predicted outcome. Once the predicted outcomes were acquired, they have combined the outcomes into an individual deep learning model, which proved to provide a superior prediction when compared to training the entire dataset in one model only. Many approaches are available to build an ensemble model. Therefore, this modified version of CCN model is proven to yield better accuracy.

Anis et al. [6] have discovered the various approaches of deep learning to study the chest radiographs using COVID-Net, a deep learning CNN model that helps in detecting the coronavirus in the chest X-ray images. The researchers have made use of SqueezNet architecture for training along with Adam optimizer for optimization. However, Bayesian optimization process showed a greater performance by giving 98.4 percent accuracy when compared to Adam optimizer.

Shuaijing et al. [7] have come up with a new deep learning–based architecture to detect any suspiciousness in the medical images, i.e., the chest X-ray images using CVXNet-m1mode, which can be achieved by fine-tuning the images characteristics and pruning the layers of the original CNN architecture, as presented in Figure 17.2. As CXNet-m1 had some complications while computing the irregularities in the X-ray images, they are trained by another set of binary classifier. Although this process is extremely tough considering the lack in COVID-19 X-ray images and people to carry out the process, data scientists and AI engineers have found solutions to identify the disease with minimal human intervention.

Jamshidi et al. [8] have used AI and deep neural network learning techniques to diagnose the coronavirus from chest X-ray medical imagery. The COVID-19 epidemic put the entire planet in extremely challenging circumstances, resulting in millions of lives lost and disrupted, and therefore it is of prime importance to find a feasible solution to detect and treat the patient affected with COVID-19 as soon as possible. Table 17.1 represents the comparative analysis on the algorithms and the results pertaining to the literature survey references.

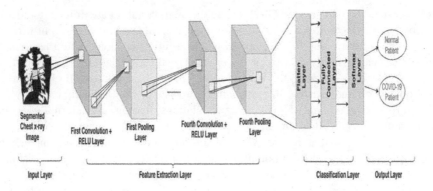

FIGURE 17.2 CNN architecture for chest X-ray image classification.

TABLE 17.1

Comparative Analysis on the Algorithms and Results-Literature Survey References

Research Work	Methodology	Results
Learning to Read Chest X-Rays: Recurrent Neural Cascade Model for Automated Image Annotation	Alex Net, RNN Framework	Accuracy obtained for the Chest-X-rays using RNN – 82%
Deep convolutional approaches for the analysis of Covid-19 using chest X-ray images from portable devices	Convolution Neural Network – DenseNet-161	Accuracy for the COVID-19 dataset implemented using portable devices – 89.76%
DL-CRC: Deep Learning Based Chest Radiograph Classification for COVID-19 Detection: A Novel Approach	DL-CRC: Inception-ResNet v2 Deep Learning-Based Chest Radiograph Classification	Accuracy obtained on the test data using DL-CRC model – 93.4%
Deep Chest Xray: Automatic Diagnoses of Diseases on Chest X-Rays Using DNN	Inception V3 (CNN architecture), Random Forest model	Accuracy for Random forest model on test data – 88%
Iterative Pruning Employing Deep Learning Ensembles for COVID-19 Detection in Chest X-Rays	Customized CNN models	Accuracy for modified CNN model – 85%
CXNet-m1: Anomaly Detection on Chest X-Rays With Image-Based Deep Learning	DenseNet model and ResNet model	Accuracy for the testing dataset. – 88.52%

17.2.1 Methodology

In the field of image classification and feature detection, deep learning and artificial intelligence play and major role. COVID-19 and other related respiratory illnesses require a strong learning model to detect and predict the diseases accurately [9]. There are several AI-based deep learning and machine learning techniques that can be used to train and test the dataset. One of them is the deep recurrent neural network

(RNN), which is in likeness to CNN, where the input variables are trained iteratively. The output obtained after the first iteration set is carried forward as an input variable for the second iteration [10]. This process was a little strenuous with a large data-set set and yielded only 82 percent accuracy. The famous classification algorithm, K-Nearest Neighbors (KNN), is known to be one of the fundamental classification methods in computer vision. It corresponds to the supervised learning category and is widely used in recognizing patterns and relations, finding any external user, and aggregating data [11]. It is commonly applicable in day-to-day circumstances because in most cases it is nonparametric, which means it does not connect to any underlying conclusions regarding distribution of data. CNN is a prominent image classification model because the architecture of CNN classifiers requires subject knowledge or the fixing of constraints [12, 13]. The CNN model can be modified based on the size and depth of the image dataset, which makes it easy for the algorithm to train large datasets, thus making it suitable for performing an in-depth exploration of the data provided. The application of deep learning CNN model with AI-based techniques aids in diagnosis of COVID-19 in a faster manner and in turn helps in monitoring the treatment improvement of the individual. In this work, the methodology proposed is VGGNet-16, which is a modified CNN model. This model was presented to Large Scale Visual Recognition Challenge 2014 [14].

17.3 PROPOSED MODEL

The model proposed in the work is an AI-based deep learning technique, which is used primarily for image classification. Furthermore, this classification technique will evaluate the real-time efficiency in order to arrive at the correct predictions. VGGNet-16 Neural Network is a modified version of CNN architecture with 16 lay-ers that possess some weights of the parameters. VGGNet-16 is known for its unique characteristic of including a large number of parameters and hyperparameters [15]. Similar to that of CNN architecture, the VGGNet-16 model primarily consists of three phases. Python scripts on Google Colab notebook were implemented using Keras to include this AI-based technique. The dataset was split into three folders, namely normal chest X-ray, pneumonia chest X-ray, and COVID-19 chest X-ray. The evaluation is performed by data preprocessing by setting the learning rate as 1e-3, i.e., 0.001 for the image with size ($224 \times 224 \times 3$) as mentioned in Table 17.2. The number of epochs is taken as 10 and the batch size is 8. The VGGNet-16 architecture can broadly be classified into convolution layer with an activation function (ReLU), followed by the max-pooling layer, which is then followed by the fully connected layer with the same ReLU activation function. The model finally ends with a softmax layer that gives out the end prediction. The input data is passed through the first set of convolution layers, which includes a small-size filter to capture the notable features of the images.

The VGGNet-16 is then followed by the max-pooling layer as implemented over a filter size of 2×2 and stride 2. In this step the input data is flattened and further filtered for the activation function. The third part of this model is the fully connected layer that works steadily alongside the base model layer. The optimization of the model is done by using Adam optimizer. The Adam optimization algorithm is a

TABLE 17.2

Hyperparameter of the AI-Based Deep Learning Model of Chest X-Ray Images

S. No.	Hyperparameter	Count
1	Learning rate	0.001
2	Epoch	10
3	Batch size	8
4	Image size	224
5	First convolution layer – number of filters	28
6	Second convolution layer – number of filters	56
7	Third convolution layer – number of filters	112
8	Fully connected layer	224

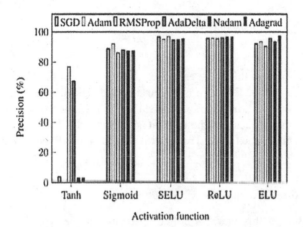

FIGURE 17.3   Comparison of precision offered by activation functions.

modified version of the gradient descent algorithm. Adam optimizer is preferred when compared to stochastic gradient descent (SGD) optimizer, as it allows to update the weights of the parameters iteratively. This enables us to understand the model and predict more accurately based on the training and testing dataset. Figure 17.3 shows the precision percentage of the different activation function.

Deep residual neural network (ResNet-50) is used for image recognition and classification. This ResNet-50 is a variant of the original ResNet architecture. The ResNet-50 consists of 48 deep convolution layers that are followed by one max-pooling layer and another average pooling layer. This AI-based deep learning model is proved to be the most efficient to study visual images.

The evaluation is performed by building the pretrained ResNet-50 model on Keras. The activation function used at the dense layers is a sigmoid activation function with a train size of 38 and validation size of 12. The learning rate of the model was taken as (1e-4) × 1, i.e., 0.0001, and the number of epochs was taken as 400. Adam optimizer is used as an optimization function for this model as well. As mentioned above, Adam optimizer is the novel work implemented in this study, as it yields the highest accuracy when compared to other activation functions such as ReLU, SELU, ELU, and tanh. This algorithm enables to update the parameter weights iteratively.

To aim is to evaluate the outcome of the classification model; the weighted precision and F1 score measurement have been taken from Equations (17.1) and (17.2). The main purpose of the weighted precision is to evaluate how accurate the classification of the model is. The indicator measures the precision of classification performed by the model by taking into consideration the number of input sample images in each class denoted as 'I'. $|Y|$ denotes the complete number of sample data in all classes.

$$\text{Weighted Precision} = \sum_{i=1}^{C} \frac{|y_i|}{|Y|} \times \frac{TP_i}{TP_i + FP_i} \tag{17.1}$$

$$\text{Weighted F1 score} = \sum_{i=1}^{C} \frac{|y_i|}{|Y|} \times 2\left(\frac{P_i \times R_i}{P_i + R_i}\right) \tag{17.2}$$

The F1-score used in this work estimates the accuracy of the classification model on the given dataset. The F1-score is a metric of the classifier that utilizes the precision and recall of the test. In Equations (17.1) and (17.2), the expressions P and R are taken as precision and recall of the test data, respectively. The expressions given in Equation (17.1) guarantees TP as True Positive, FP as False Positive, and FN as False Negative.

17.3.1 DATASET DESCRIPTION

The dataset used in this work is collected from Kaggle, which originated from 'Optical Coherence Tomography and Chest X-ray – Raw Images for Classification,' an open-source page in the Internet. The chest X-ray dataset folder is bifurcated into three subfolders: pneumonia, normal, and COVID-19 chest X-ray. The total number of images in all three categories is 5,863. The typical normal chest X-ray medical images show healthy lungs with no regions of irregular opacities. The pneumonia chest X-ray is distinguished by the centralized lobar aggregation, and more severe cases of bacterial pneumonia show a more diffused pattern in the chest X-ray radiographs. COVID-19 chest X-rays were selected and collected from observational samples of children aged 1–5 years at women and children's medical centers in different parts of the world. The chest X-ray radiograph screening was performed as a part of their patients' regular health care service. The number of samples of COVID-19 radiographs is relatively smaller when compared to pneumonia and normal chest X-ray, as COVID-19 is the first of its kind and people in the medical field are finding it quite hard to collect this disease chest X-rays at the moment.

17.4 RESULT AND DISCUSSION

COVID-19 diagnosis is mostly based on patients' conditions, immunological record, bacterial DNA detection, immunity-building technologies, and other such factors. Therefore, in this work the system has used a structured approach to understand which of the AI-based deep learning algorithms yield a better classification outcome. The model was implemented using Python language's Keras and Tensor flow framework on Google Colab Notebook. The system configurations were suitable to load the large dataset and implement the model.

The dataset was trained with different CNN algorithms, and the layers were modified by varying the number of layers in the model. The framework was applied first to the train dataset, which was then followed by the test dataset of COVID-19 chest X-ray, pneumonia, and normal images. These patterns can be observed and classified according to their respective images. In this work, a modified CNN model was implemented, which yielded an accuracy of 94.74 percent. All the results obtained in this work using the modified CNN model (VGGNet-16) and AI-based ResNet model are given in Table 17.3. As mentioned, two models have been implemented in this project, namely VGGNet-16 and ResNet. Both models were implemented using Tensorflow and Keras as the base platform on Google Colab Notebook. It is observed from Table 17.3 that when compared to DL-CRC and AlexNet model, VGGNet-16 and ResNet yielded a better accuracy for the COVID-19 dataset. The accuracy of VGGNet-16 of 16 layers network resulted was 94.74 percent accuracy, and the ResNet model yielded 91.43 percent accuracy. Therefore, after comparing the results of the models implemented, VGGNet-16 can classify the COVID-19 chest X-ray dataset to get the better accuracy, whereas the pneumonia dataset is classified by chest radiograph classification (DL-CRC) deep learning algorithm to yield an accuracy of 88.94 percent. The DL-CRC model is a modified version of a convolution neural network varying in the number of layers.

In Figure 17.4 the training loss and accuracy on COVID-19 dataset is depicted in the line graph using the gg plot library in Python language. The loss in the model is calculated using the binary cross-entropy loss algorithm. This loss function is similar to that of the sigmoid function. Binary cross-entropy evaluates the correctness of the classification model. Since it is binary, the outcome is either 0 or 1.

The analysis in Table 17.4 shows the comparison of the accuracy obtained by using the various CNN architectures along with the area under the curve score. It is observed that the proposed ResNet architecture is much advanced at estimating the

TABLE 17.3

Model Implementation Results

Model	Normal (%)	Pneumonia (%)	COVID-19 (%)
VGG-Net	97.23	86.54	94.74
CRC	95.82	88.94	89.85
ResNet	97.63	73.66	91.43
AlexNet	92.01	75.64	67.62

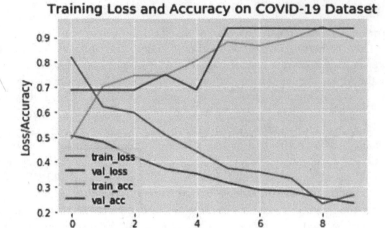

FIGURE 17.4   Training loss and accuracy using VGGNet-16.

TABLE 17.4
CNN Architectures Analysis

Model	Normal (%)	Pneumonia (%)	COVID-19 (%)	AUC Score (%)
DL-CRC	95.23	87.54	94.74	0.9453
Inception – ResNet V2	96.82	79.94	89.85	0.9326
ResNet	98.63	75.66	91.43	0.9213
DenseNet	99.01	73.64	67.62	0.8659

highest accuracy percentage for the COVID-19 dataset. The AI-based deep learning algorithms proposed in this work outperformed the remaining models.

VGGNet-16 achieves an accuracy of 97.23 percent and ResNet achieves an accuracy of 98.63 percent. The AUC score more firmly testifies that the proposed models are better in terms of accuracy when compared to other models. In Figure 17.4, the loss and accuracy on the classification of the COVID-19 dataset are presented in a graphic format. The loss of the model decreases as the number of epochs increases; the accuracy of the model is gradually increasing as the epoch count increases.

17.5   CONCLUSION

The discussed topic is related to the evolving problems of detecting COVID-19. Many people affected with this severe illness are unreported due to lack of efficient treatment equipment and staff. There is a shortage in the staff and the equipment needed in the rural as well as developing regions. Since there are not many to help in detecting COVID-19, it is of paramount importance to build a model that is able to detect the disease without any human intervention. This study showed how the use of chest X-ray images of COVID-19 patients and normal chest X-rays enabled the implementation to display the desired outcomes. The images possessed all the potential characteristics needed to perform this method of detection of the disease. The ResNet and VGG-Net algorithm implementation on the radiograph works out cheaper and more efficient when compared to the long procedural test that are conducted in the hospitals using the CT scan machines. Moreover, these machines are expensive and often not affordable to small hospitals located in rural regions. Hence this methodology of detecting the disease using artificial intelligence and deep learning is found to serve the purpose and also be cost effective when compared to the traditional method of scanning chest X-rays. The proposed algorithm is concentrated with the VGG-Net 16 framework, which is a modified version of a convolution neural network of 16 layers. The second framework implemented is the ResNet framework, which has proven to be highly accurate by giving an accuracy of 91.43 percent. In the further study, one can improvise on other AI-based models and can implement them on the new set of COVID-19 radiographs available in the Image Hub. Therefore, for the future work of this system, the existing models can be improvised by varying the number of layers to get a better result.

REFERENCES

[1] Shin, H. C., Roberts, K., Lu, L., Demner-Fushman, D., Yao, J., & Summers, R. M. (2016). Learning to read chest X-rays: recurrent neural cascade model for automated image annotation. In *Proceedings of the IEEE conference on computer vision and pattern recognition*, pp. 2497–2506.

[2] De Moura, J., García, L. R., Vidal, P. F. L., Cruz, M., López, L. A., Lopez, E. C., & Ortega, M. (2020). Deep convolutional approaches for the analysis of covid-19 using chest X-ray images from portable devices. *IEEE Access*, 8, 195594–195607.

[3] Sakib, S., Tazrin, T., Fouda, M. M., Fadlullah, Z. M., & Guizani, M. (2020). DL-CRC: deep learning-based chest radiograph classification for covid-19 detection: a novel approach. *IEEE Access*, 8, 171575–171589.

[4] Xu, X., Guo, Q., Guo, J., & Yi, Z. (2018). DeepCX-ray: automatically diagnosing diseases on chest X-rays using deep neural networks. *IEEE Access*, 6, 66972–66983.

[5] Sivaramakrishnan, R., Jen, S., & Philip, O. A. Iteratively modified deep learning model for COVID-19 detection in chest X-rays. arXiv preprint arXiv:2004.08379.

[6] Anis, S., Lai, K. W., Chuah, J. H., Ali, S. M., Mohafez, H., Hadizadeh, M., & Ong, Z. C. (2020). An overview of deep learning approaches in chest radiograph. *IEEE Access*, 8, 182347–182354.

[7] Xu, S., Wu, H., & Bie, R. (2018). CXNet-m1: anomaly detection on chest X-rays with image-based deep learning. *IEEE Access*, 7, 4466–4477.

[8] Sharma, A., Rani, S., & Gupta, D. (2020). Artificial intelligence-based classification of chest X-ray images into COVID-19 and other infectious diseases. *International Journal of Biomedical Imaging*, 2020, Article ID 8889023.

[9] Karanam, S., Li, R., Yang, F., Hu, W., Chen, T., & Wu, Z. (2020). Towards contactless patient positioning. *IEEE Transactions on Medical Imaging*, 39(8), 2701–2710.

[10] World Health Organization. (2020). *Coronavirus disease (COVID-19)*.

[11] Wang, W., Xu, Y., Gao, R., Lu, R., Han, K., Wu, G., & Tan, W. (2020). Detection of SARS-CoV-2 in different types of clinical specimens. *Jama*, 323(18), 1843–1844.

[12] Rubin, G. D., Ryerson, C. J., Haramati, L. B., Sverzellati, N., Kanne, J. P., Raoof, S., & Leung, A. N. (2020). The role of chest imaging in patient management in the COVID-19 phase: a worldwide consensus statement from the Fleischner Society. *Chest*, 158(1), 106–116.

[13] Hosseiny, M., Kooraki, S., Gholamrezanezhad, A., Reddy, S., & Myers, L. (May 2020). Radiology perspective of coronavirus disease 2019 (COVID-19), *Amer. J. Roentgenol.*, 214, no. 5, 1078–1082, doi:10.2214/AJR.20.22969.

[14] Udugama, B., Kadhiresan, P., Kozlowski, H. N., Malekjahani, A., Osborne, M., Li, V. Y. & Chan, W. C. (2020). Diagnosing COVID-19: the disease and tools for detection. *ACS Nano*, 14(4), 3822–3835.

[15] Jain, R., Gupta, M., Taneja, S., & Hemanth, D. J. (2021). Deep learning based detection and analysis of COVID-19 on chest X-ray images. *Applied Intelligence*, 51(3), 1690–1700.

18 An Innovative Electronic Sterilization System (S-Vehicle, $NaOCl.5H_2O$ and CeO_2NP)

Samaher Al-Janabi and Ayad Alkaim
University of Babylon, Babylon, Iraq

CONTENTS

18.1 INTRODUCTION

Today, the world suffers from a very large number of people infected with the COVID-19 virus, and their numbers are constantly increasing due to the lack of an effective treatment for this virus until this day, which made prevention and sterilization the currently accepted ideal solution to preserve the lives of people and reduce the number of cases of this epidemic [1–3]. In addition, many people were exposed to infection as a result of performing their work in sterilizing the affected areas or contacting injured people while performing their medical work. This led to an increase in infected people and the failure of hospitals to absorb the disease in their increasing numbers, in addition to increasing the total costs of dealing with the epidemic.

DOI: 10.1201/9781003307822-22

Therefore, the process of finding an effective and efficient sterilization method that is managed remotely without approaching people from the affected areas is the best solution currently to preserve the lives of people and the possibility of infection. Therefore, it was necessary to think about creating a method that adopts modern technologies to reduce the incidence of the epidemic and the effort exerted by the teams to sterilize areas and make their work safe and easy, as well as reduce the material costs spent on such emergency situations by the state. The idea of this work was developed and implemented in a practical way in order to address a set of realistic problems that society suffers from as a result of the epidemic of COVID-19, specifically assisting teams to sterilize and disinfect areas and make their work done through an electronic sterilization system completely remotely managed by small vehicles (Robots) run by smart phones, which is called Vehicles, which represents it in the form of a triangular problem. How to find an effective, lightweight, and highly effective oil sterilizer with sterilization in which the droplets of it are sufficient to sterilize the area was the first challenge. How the design of the drones can be developed and made to be controlled by smartphones in terms of their movement and pumping of sterile liquid spray into the areas or the delivery of drugs from one affected area to another was the second challenge. As for the third challenge, how can artificial intelligence techniques be employed to complete the work quickly in addition to making the system less expensive so that it can be used widely, as shown below in Figure 18.1

Self-driving car, autonomous car (AV), connected and autonomous vehicle (CAV), robotic car, driverless or self-driving vehicle are different names for a vehicle capable of feeling its surroundings and moving safely without human intervention is widespread, as it has been applied in many fields, as it is used by courier service companies in the field of mail services delivery as well as used to transport goods [4–6]. These vehicles are also used as part of smart cities, which are considered a modern trend for most countries because they preserve the environment from pollution through their reliance on charging batteries or electric or solar energy instead of gasoline as their fuel. This work will focus on the development of this type of vehicle by producing a new vehicle, called S-Vehicle, for the purpose of sterilizing large areas, hospitals, operating wards, and the purpose that contains people infected with viruses

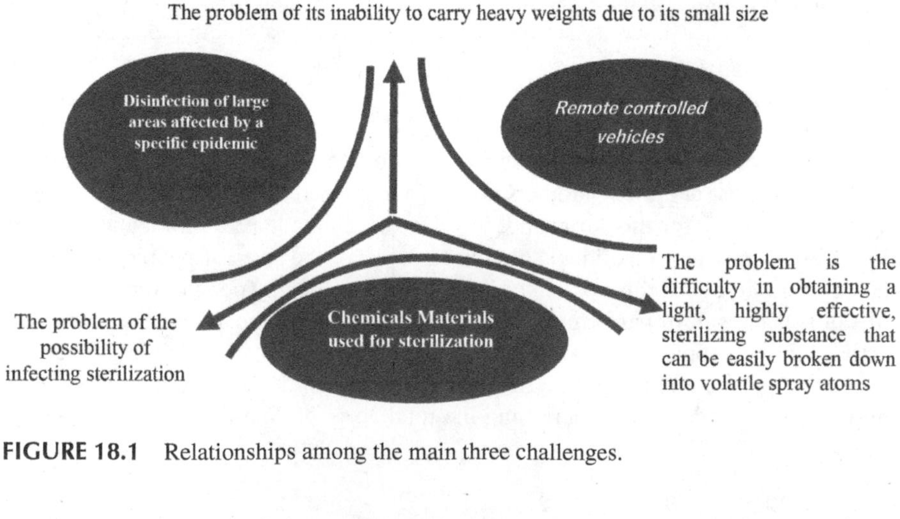

FIGURE 18.1   Relationships among the main three challenges.

or specific epidemics, as well as it can be used to deliver medicines between hospital wards. It was primarily designed to reduce the number of infections generated by the most difficult virus that humanity has suffered in this century—COVID-19.

On the other hand, researchers discovered that the emerging coronavirus is characterized by remaining active and contagious on contaminated metal, glass, or plastic surfaces for an average of 9 days at room temperature, which ranges between 15 and 20°C on average. But if the temperature of contaminated surfaces drops to 4°C, the virus can remain active for up to 28 days, while the degree of infection decreases if the surfaces temperature ranges between 30 and 40°C.

As for sterile chemicals that have proven effective to eliminate the virus, tests conducted on various sterilization solutions showed that disinfectants with high effectiveness to eliminate the virus are those containing ethanol compounds at a concentration between 6 and 71 percent, hydrogen peroxide at a concentration of 0.5 percent, or sodium hypochlorite at a concentration of 0.1 percent. It has been proven that if surfaces and areas contaminated with infection are disinfected with the appropriate concentrations of these disinfectants, they reduce the numbers of infectious coronaviruses from one million pathogenic particles to only 100 within one minute. On the other hand, tests showed that there are other disinfection solutions that proved less effective in combating coronavirus infection, which are benzalkonium chloride compounds with a concentration between 0.05 and 0.2 percent) and chlorhexidine digluconate compounds with a concentration of 0.02 percent. Our work here will focus on benefiting from the principle of driving automation for relatively small vehicles. In general, the level of driving automation for vehicles is divided into five basic levels, from level 0 that are fully manually managed to level 5 autonomous as shown in Table 18.1.

This work attempts to take advantage of the idea of small-sized vehicles that can be operated and controlled remotely by smart phones so that they are sent to specific areas infected with the virus to perform a sterilization process for those areas and then return to the starting area. It can also be used to deliver medicines from one place to another, and that by downloading the map of those areas. Note that the work assumes that there is internet coverage for those areas to benefit from the Wi-Fi feature, so this work will attempt to address those emergency situations by developing an integrated structure for the system whose basis is the vehicles that are driven by smart phones (S-Vehicles), equipped with a location tracking system and a tank containing sterilization solutions and sprays that perform sterilization, which are opened or closed by a mobile device.

18.2 RELATED WORKS

There are many researchers who sought to solve this problem by using multiple techniques to deal with it, most of which focused on testing and exploring antibiotics to reduce the spread of the virus. Health care personnel are among the most vulnerable to infection, due to their extensive contact with some infected people while providing treatment. Some medical personnel also risk becoming infected as a result of contact with surfaces or tools where people carrying the virus are present. Thus sterilizing surfaces and places that are frequently touched and things that are frequently handled with effective types of disinfectants/sterilizers is an optimal solution to protect

TABLE 18.1

Driving Automation Levels

			Driving Automation Levels			
SAE. level	Name	The Definition	Car Steering and Acceleration/ Deceleration Implementation	Driving Environment Monitoring	Backup Performance for Dynamic Driving Mission	System Capacity (Drive Modes)
The human driver monitors the driving environment						
0	Not automatic	Full human driver performance of all aspects of a dynamic driving task, even when "enhanced by warning or intervention systems"	Human driver			n/a
1	Driver assistance	Implementation of driving mode by driver assistance system "either steering or acceleration/ deceleration"	The driver and the human system	Human driver	Human driver	
2	Partial automatic	Drive mode specific implementation by one or more driver assistance systems of "steering and acceleration/ deceleration"	System			Some driving modes

Automated driving system monitors the driving environment

				System	System	Human driver	Some driving modes
3	Conditional automatic	Drive mode specific performance with Autopilot for all aspects of a dynamic driving mission	With the expectation that "the human driver will respond appropriately to the request for intervention"	System	System	Human driver	Some driving modes
4	High automatic			*Even if the human driver does not respond appropriately to the request for intervention*		System	Several driving modes
5	Fully automatic			*Under all roads and environmental conditions, a human driver can operate*	System		All driving modes

people from infection. The issue is in how the sterilization process can be carried out without human intervention, and managing it remotely is the biggest challenge. Here we will review the most important research that sought to solve this problem.

Kovac et al. [7] manufacture a sterilizer that uses xenon UV rays to clean surfaces, reduce microbes more efficiently and faster than manual cleaning, and achieve lower infection rates in homes and hospitals, operating on UV disinfection protocols so that UV energy can destroy bacteria by going through their cell walls and breaking up their DNA. This work is similar to our work in which we seek to design a robot that can be operated automatically to disinfect areas without human intervention.

Jung Yun et al. [8] focused on demonstrating the importance of robots in all disinfection and food and drug delivery operations without human assistance in monitoring patients' condition to help with disease management and prevention, which is evolving and extending into many areas such as mobile software. This work is related to robots tracing contact with infected people and alerting others, thus reducing the cost and risk to people working to disinfect and clean most touch surfaces. This work only highlights key points without including any actual design or construction aspect of any system. In contrast, our proposed work to design of an integrated system includes a robot managed remotely by smart phones to sterilize potentially contaminated areas.

Ki Ho, Honk et al. [9] explore several general methods used for the purpose of diagnosis and interpretation of diagnostic results obtained for HIV testing. The purpose of the study was to identify all the key determinants for the purpose of building an integrated robot that can diagnose infected persons by building a complete record for each patient and to determine the therapeutic procedures that are taken with him automatically. This work was satisfied with identifying all the determinants of symptoms, diagnosis, and prevention as an integrated database that can be updated for people under diagnosis/examination and stressed that to make the robot and software capable of dealing with events, they must be aware of all the determinants, factors, and addresses and leave the stage of building the robotic system as a future work for it.

Trunk Thiem et al. [10] set up a sterilization room controlled by a system with three levels of protection against coronavirus, where a main system was divided into three substages. The first stage included automatic hand sterilization, while the second stage was intended to check body temperature. In that stage, the patient's entire body was sprayed with silver nano-solvent, and if the infrared sensor read the body temperature above 37°C, it would send it to the processor to be displayed on the screen. It is specific and difficult to transfer. While our proposed work includes the design of an integrated system, Robert, managed remotely by smart phones, and is actually applied to sterilize areas/surfaces for infested individuals that can move according to the specified area. Table 18.2 shows a comparison between all previous works.

18.3   MAIN TOOLS AND MATERIALS

The idea of the work is to develop a simplified robot structure that is managed remotely by smart phones to perform a sterilization process for different areas and surfaces contaminated with different types of viruses. As for the most important tools used in building this system in an integrated manner, we will explain them below.

TABLE 18.2
Comparison of Previous Works

The Names of the Researchers and the Year	Suggested Robot Type	Methodology	Methods for Evaluating Results	Advantages	Disadvantages
Christine R. Kovac et al., 2020	Xenon Pulsed Ultraviolet Disinfection Device	Use the principle of learning. In building a robot for sterilization based on ultraviolet rays	• Collect baseline ATP measurements from the clean surface for disinfection • Check elapsed time	The device is proven to perform xenon UV disinfection much better than manual cleaning	It is poor in terms of design. Its true efficacy cannot be proven without clinical trials
Jung Yun et al., (2020)	Highlight all kinds of robots that can be used in sterilization and disease diagnosis	Highlight the most common methods of sterilization and help mankind	Compare the results between traditional methods and various robots and devices that are used for the same purpose	• Emphasize the need to use robots for tiring and risky work instead of human cadres • He stressed the need for a real trend by researchers to develop robots to deal with epidemics and viruses that threaten human life	The lack of actual robots to confront the current and ancient epidemics facing humanity

(Continued)

TABLE 18.2 (Continued)
Comparison of Previous Works

The Names of the Researchers and the Year	Suggested Robot Type	Methodology	Methods for Evaluating Results	Advantages	Disadvantages
Ki Ho, Honk et al., (2020) [9]	• The Robot was not designed, but all tests specified by the US Food and Drug Administration have been performed. (EUA)	A set of instructions and special tests	–	• Conducting COVID-19 tests and distinguishing its symptoms from respiratory diseases	• Some systems may take longer time to make decisions if they are not equipped with all the required information and due to the lack of confirmed knowledge about COVID-19, so there are many obstacles and challenges in designing feed bots databases
Trunk Theme et al., (2020)	sterilization system	CDC	• Type Sensor (BRQPS 10M-TDTA-C type NPN) • JMNano silver solution	• Hand washing • Temperature measurement • Sterilization with silver nanoparticles • Greatly help to inhibit and kill the virus	• Inability to manage the system remotely • It is characterized as a fixed system that cannot be moved easily

18.3.1 PLATFORM WASPMOTE [11]

It is a platform available to everyone to process the information obtained from the sensors and send it wirelessly, designed by the Spanish company Libelium. It runs on battery and is mainly characterized by being low energy consumption and relatively cheap. This type of platform contains four types of methods to reduce energy consumption, namely.

On, Sleep, Deep Sleep, and Hibernate, which helps extend the life of the node (Life time). The basic rule to reduce the price of the node designed using Waspmote is to build units assembled according to the specific application and according to the actual need only. For these reasons Waspmote has become one of the appropriate platforms for developing applications for wireless sensor networks as well as Internet of Things (IoT) applications.

18.3.2 LORA MODEM

It is a special modulation method developed by Semtech company based on Spread-Spectrum Modulation technology to obtain long-range transmission and relatively low data transfer speed. This unit contains an electronic chip SX1272, which operates within the 868 and 900 MHz ISM frequency bands and depends on the principle of point-to-point communication, so it is a star-shaped network that can carry each transmitted data packet with a maximum of 250 bytes.

The unit uses the SPI protocol to communicate with the platform, which is characterized by the speed of information transfer, and it will also free up URALs ports to be used for other purposes. Also, one of the advantages of this unit is that it can reach a transmission range of 1.4 km using it, according to a specific setting.

18.3.3 AUTONOMOUS VEHICLES (AVs) [12, 13]

Autonomous vehicles (AVs) are driverless vehicles that can communicate with other systems and make driving decisions for themselves [7]. Decisions made by AVs may range from following the vehicle, cruise control, and choosing a lane to making decisions by processing data from sensors or other vehicles. With the current development in vehicle automation and artificial intelligence (AI), it is believed that a large role will be played by connected and automated vehicles (CAVs), with the possibility of future in health care as on-demand robotic shuttles to hospitals (for use by patients and staff), to deliver medical supplies, or even as a mobile workplace for health-on-demand services such as biometrics, laboratory work management, or counseling units with nurses. These options are very promising, especially for increasing access to health care in stricken communities or in the event of infection with rapidly spreading or unexpected viruses, such as COVID-19.

18.3.4 GPS MODULE [14]

It is an updated GPS Module [NEO-6M] that can be used with the Ardupilot Mega (APM). This GPS module uses the latest technology to provide the best possible location information, allowing for improved performance using Ardupilot or any other multi-engine control system. Also included is Honeywell's latest High Accuracy Digital Magnetometer (HMC5883L), which provides a convenient way to mount a compass away from sources of interference that may be located near a multistage vehicle control device.

GPS features are:

- A fully independent GPS receiver
- U-blox NEO-6M GPS module
- HMC5883L magnetometer
- Anti-jamming technology
- Supports SBAS, WAAS, EGNOS, MSAS, GAGAN
- The u-blox 6 50-channel GPS engine with over 2 million active links
- Operating temperature range: from 40 to 85°C
- NetLogo Simulation [15, 16]

It is a free modeling environment capable of simulating complex situations such as natural and social phenomena. Suitable for research and teaching, it can be defined as an environment simple enough to enable students and researchers to create their own models using Java programming language. They are particularly suited for the formation of complex systems that evolve over time. Designers can give instructions to hundreds or thousands of independent "agents" that all work concurrently. This makes it possible to run more than one sterilizing vehicle at the same time. It allows users to simulate different environments with agents and to explore their behavior under different conditions. Agents move through a network of "patches" using multiple rules to modify their path toward the goal, and they have the ability to overcome any obstacles on their way in programmable ways. All agents can interact with each other and perform multiple tasks simultaneously.

18.3.5 CONTROL SYSTEM [17]

A control system is a device or group of devices that manage, direct, or regulate the behavior of other devices or systems. Industrial control systems are used to control equipment or machines. There are two common categories of control systems: open-loop control system and closed-loop control system. In open-loop control systems, the output is generated based on the input, as happens in an electronic washing machine system when we specify the spin period according to the degree of soiling of the clothes. This means that the user does not need to check whether the clothes are clean or not because the results are known according to the specified time.

In closed-loop control systems, the current output is taken into account and corrections are made based on the feedback. For example, the human interaction with the computer, where it is a reciprocal process between the human development of the computer.

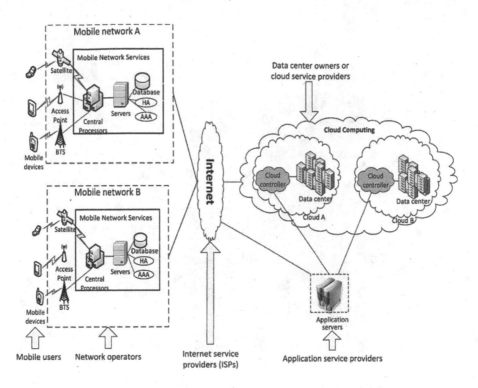

FIGURE 18.2 Mobile cloud computing.

18.3.6 Arduino UNO [13]

It is an electronic development board consisting of an electronic circuit with a computer-programmed microcontroller, designed to facilitate the use of interactive electronics in multidisciplinary projects. Arduino is mainly used in the design of interactive electronic projects or projects that aim to build different environmental sensors such as temperature, wind, light, pressure, air pollution, etc. The Arduino can be connected to various programs on the personal computer, and the programming codes for the Arduino language are similar to the Arduino language. C is one of the easiest programming languages used to write microcontroller programs. The Uno is based on the Microchip ATmega328P microcontroller, and the board is equipped with combinations of digital and analog input/output (I/O) pins that may be interlaced with various expansion boards (shields) and other circuits containing. The board has 14 digital pins and 6 analog pins and is programmable using the Arduino IDE (Integrated Development Environment). It can be powered by a USB cable or by an external 9V battery, although it accepts voltages between 7 V and 20 V.

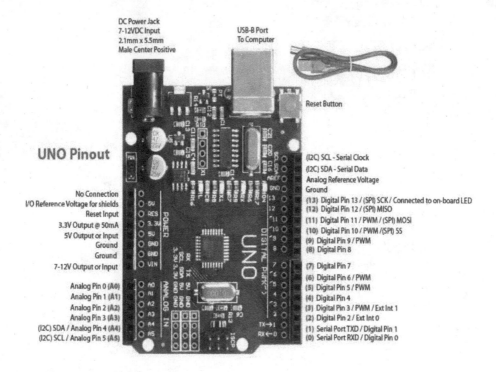

FIGURE 18.3   Arduino Uno.

18.3.7   ARDUINO UNO COMPONENTS

A. **POWER INPUTS/OUTPUTS**

- VIN or DC power jack: It is a port through which you can operate the Arduino through an external power source such as a battery or an adapter.
- 5V: It is a port that provides a voltage of 5 V that can be used for sensors or other circuits
- 3.3V: A voltage source with a value of 3.3 V and 50 mA is the maximum value of the current that can be used through this port
- Two ground ports: the land line.

B. **Control inputs and outputs (INPUT & OUTPUT PINS) (I/O)**
The number of digital ports can be used, which is 14 (Digital Pins 14), numbered from 0 to 13, which are ports used to input and output fixed digital signals 0 or 5, and each port can provide a current draw of up to 40 mA. Within these ports, the Arduino board contains six digital pins that support PWM digital modulation. There is also 6Pins Analog, starting from A0 to A5, which are ports used to input analog signals coming from the sensors and by default these inputs can measure voltages from zero to 5 volts.

C. **Powering the Arduino POWER UP**

The piece can be equipped via the computer from the USB port as well as from the charger port, where the charger port receives a voltage of 7 to 12 volts to be adjusted internally to 5 volts, but it is noted that the Vin port located within the power outlets is not connected to the voltage rating, so a regular voltage must be entered and its value is 5 volts.

D. **ICSP header**

There are six ports in the center of the board. These ports are used to program the Arduino from an external programmer, called ICSP header. There is a button on the board that restarts the program loaded on the Arduino.

18.4   DESIGNED SYSTEM

The designed system consists of three basic stages. The first stage is focused on developing the structure and electronic system of the remotely piloted vehicle by adding new physical parts to it and connecting them. The second stage focuses on preparing chemicals with high efficacy by sterilization and relatively low cost, and the last stage includes linking the developed electronic system for the vehicle. With a new application for remote control by smart phones, this stage is divided into the control of downloading the map of the area to be sterilized, the application of remote control quickly, the direction of the vehicle, and opening the nozzles of the sprinklers by phone. The following is an accurate description of each of these stages.

- **The first stage: developing the chassis for remotely piloted vehicles**

    In this work, the structure of the self-driving vehicle was developed so that its structure was carefully selected so that it has a suitable structure that allows carrying 12 liters of sterile solution in addition to a basket capable of carrying 2 kilograms of medicines. Types of engines: two of them are used for the purpose of moving the vehicle forward and backward and have a voltage of 12 volts, in addition to the third engine of the same voltage that is used for the purpose of rotating the vehicle. The most important parts of the electronic circuit of the S-Vehicle can be illustrated in Figure 18.4.

    The motors operate in DC power in three phases. Any three signals to control the voltage and thus control the speed, and this control depends on an electronic control piece called Electronic speed control (ESC) and here a controller type ESC w/BEC 5V/3A 2~4S Simon K Firmware was used as shown in Figure 18.5. It is an electronic circuit designed to limit the current that enters the motors by cutting the signal instead of giving the motor a constant voltage; that is, it controls the current directed to the motors, and from it you can control the speed by converting the DC into an analog signal.

    This type of ESC contains a scaling circuit called battery elimination circuit (BEC).

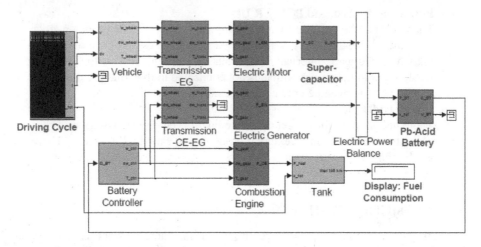

FIGURE 18.4 Circle of automatic vehicle.

FIGURE 18.5 Electronic speed control (ESC).

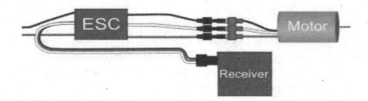

FIGURE 18.6 Connecting the motor and receiver with ESCs.

In this system, a Lipo Battery 3000 mAh 11.1 V 30C 3S with XT60 connector was used, which is a three-cell lithium battery with a capacity of 3000 mAh and discharge capacity.

C30, high energy with an excellent combination of weight, strength, and performance This type has several advantages:

- It is capable of achieving maximum continuous discharge rates of up to 30°C, this battery is among the most powerful Li-Po battery packs in its class.
- It is equipped with various connectors that are compatible with most balancers and other chargers.

- It is equipped with an EC3 connector on the mains power connections.
- Use Plug and Play with ESCs.

The battery contains two wires for connection, one of which is connected with the PCB board connected to the ESC to supply all parts of the vehicle with power, and the other wire is used to charge the battery using a charger.

Pumps are an essential part of our work to transfer sterilization solutions from the tank through the nozzle to disinfect the area, and at the same time we need them to save energy and work at a low power level to know that DC pumps use 40–150 watts which is much less than 220 volts pumps on the one hand. We used pumps of very small size in order to suit the size of the developed vehicle and do not take up much space, and it is also characterized by not making loud sounds or even random vibrations during its work, as we used in our work this pump shown in Figure 18.7, working on 24VDC 75GPD, a purification pump RO water.

In addition to the pumps, polyethylene tubes and elbows have been used, which are characterized by not being chemically altered by sterilizing fluid, good resistance to low temperatures, resistance to stress cracking, and good strength that will not break or leak liquids, even dealing with high-pressure BSP 4/1, which are really easy to connect to each other because they have little blue lock clips, as shown in Figure 18.8.

A 12-liter polyethene chemical storage tank was used because it is a real practical solution for transporting and storing many liquids, no toxic elements or sharp edges, thickness of only 5 cm, designed to ensure minimal impact on the environment, and long-life cycle, which reduces the need for replacement as shown in Figure 18.9.

The important point in our work was how to obtain very fine atomization of particles that allow sterilization/disinfection of all surfaces without leaving any negative impact on the lives of the people present in the sterilization areas. Thus, we had to

FIGURE 18.7 Pump.

FIGURE 18.8 Polyethylene tubes and elbows.

FIGURE 18.9   Chemical sanitizer tank.

FIGURE 18.10   Nozzles.

work to obtain nozzles that provide us with particles of a good and effective atomizer in terms of volume The drop depends on the strength of the chemical sterilizer chosen and the capacity of the nozzle. The nozzle we use creates a mist with a droplet size of less than 35 microns. Such a small size was used for a number of reasons. First is to make it comply with the conditions of health safety and chemical security and to protect the lungs where there are large chemical droplets of sterile liquid. We used two pieces of 0.3-mm high-pressure plastic spray mist nozzle, as shown in Figure 18.10.

Smart phones, which are one of the most popular means of communication in our time, and all phones come loaded with CPU, radios, screen, battery, ports, buttons, camera, sensors, and storage, while the CPU works like the human brain and has RAM to store the temporary application and programming the running devices; radios such as 3G, 4G, Wi-Fi, or Bluetooth; and a screen to interact with the user. In addition, each phone has an operating system such as Android or IOS. We focused in our work on creating an easy-to-use application for the purpose of operating and controlling the vehicle in terms of its movement directions, speed, and locations of sprinklers opening and closing, and here the vehicle that has been developed will be connected wirelessly via Wi-Fi. To ensure long-distance control, we use the Lora by connecting it with the Arduino, while the mobile phone is connected to the FPV receiver, as shown in Figure 18.11A and B.

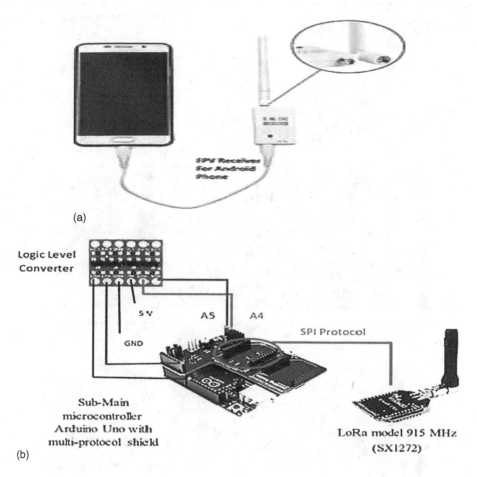

(a)

(b)

FIGURE 18.11 (A) Connect smartphone with FVP receiver. (B) Connect LoRa with sub-main microcontrollers Arduino.

Figure 18.12 shows the basic steps for connecting the support tools in order to develop the structure of the marching vehicle and make the process of controlling its movement and opening and closing the sprinklers nozzles by means of a mobile phone as well as connecting a special GPS device to it that determines the coordinates of the area at which we start the sterilization process, as well as the coordinates of the point where the sterilization process stops.

- The second stage: Preparation of sterilization materials, which are two substances, sodium hypochlorite, and cerium oxide atomizer [18–21].
  - A. **Sodium hypochlorite** is a yellowish-green solid with the chemical formula NaOCl or NaClO in its hydrated state (pentahydrate), and its chemical formula is NaOCl or NaClO, its partial weight is 74.44 g/mol, and its melting point is 18°C (in the case of the pentahydrate form). It decomposes at a temperature of 101°C and its density is 1.11 g/cm³. The

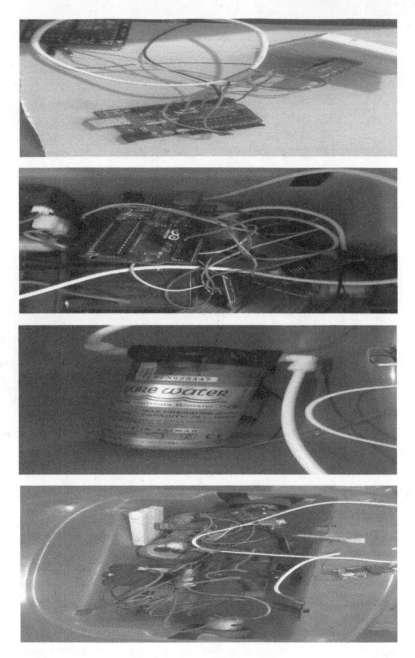

FIGURE 18.12   Connection the main components of S-Vehicle.

pure or anhydrous form of this substance is unstable and may degrade explosively. This substance is usually found in the aqueous form (pentahydrate) and its chemical formula is $NaOCl.5H_2O$, which is nonexplosive and stable if kept in the refrigerator. Hypochlorite is usually prepared through a process known as the Hooker Method reaction, In

FIGURE 18.12   (*Continued*)

which a solution of sodium hydroxide (NaOH) is treated with chlorine gas, to produce, in addition to hypochlorite, sodium chloride and water. Sodium hypochlorite is known as Javel water and is used for disinfection and bactericidal, which depends in its principle of action on the ability of hypochlorite to eliminate bacteria. Sodium hypochlorite is generally used in water in different concentrations for sterilization. Sodium hypochlorite in 0.5% w/v solution is called Dakine's solution and is used as an antiseptic to clean infected local wounds. Hypochlorite can be prepared by passing chlorine gas into a sodium hydroxide solution:

$$Cl_{2(g)} + 2NaOH_{(aq)} \rightarrow NaCl_{(aq)} + NaClO_{(aq)} + H_2O_{(aq)}$$

B. **Cerium oxide nanoparticles (nanoceria)**

Cerium is the first element in the lanthanide group with four electrons and has attracted a lot of interest from researchers in physics, chemistry, biology, and materials science. When combined with oxygen in a nanoparticle composition, cerium oxide adopts a fluorite crystal structure that stands out as a fascinating material. Cerium oxide nanoparticles (CeONP) have been extensively used in many engineering and biological applications, such as solid oxide fuel cells, high antioxidant protection materials, and potential pharmacological agents. Although the main application of CeONPs is beneficial due to its various properties and applications, it is in the field of catalysis, and stems from its unique structure and atomic properties compared to other materials. In recent years, materials containing CeONP and CeONP have come under intense scrutiny as catalysts and as structural and electronic catalysts for heterogeneous catalytic reactions. In industry, it has been widely used as an active ingredient in processes such as three-way catalysts for automobile exhaust gas treatments and oxidative coupling for methane and water gas conversion reaction. Recently, CeONP has been reported to have multiple enzymes, including superoxide dismutase, oxidase and oxidase, and mimetic properties, and it has emerged as a fascinating and profitable material in fields such as bioanalysis. This type of spray has the advantage that it is not sticky and will not be obvious when applied to a surface due to the nanoscale size of the disinfection particles it contains, but it is planned to sterilize continuously due to the regenerative nature of the nanoparticles.

- **The third stage: the interconnection between the electronic system and the control application**
  This stage is very important because it is where the vehicle's developed electronic system is combined with a new mobile application that allows controlling its speed and direction of movement, as well as controlling when the sprinkler nozzles are opened for the purpose of sterilizing the affected areas and when they are closed. On the other hand, the map of the area to be sterilized is downloaded to the application, and the vehicle is driven according to it, taking advantage of the GPS feature that was linked to the vehicle. The importance of this stage can be summarized, as it includes linking the electronic system of the vehicle S-Vehicles with an application developed using the Android environment for smart phones as shown in Figure 18.13 and the following code.

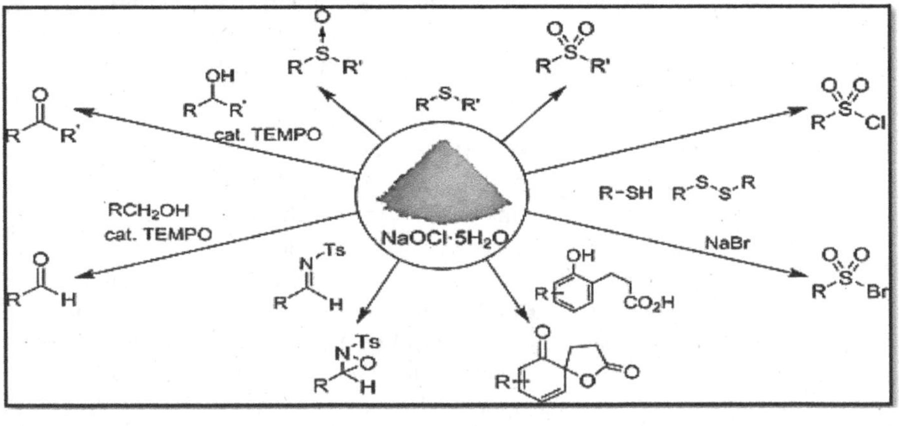

FIGURE 18.13   Main application of $NaOCl \cdot 5H_2O$.

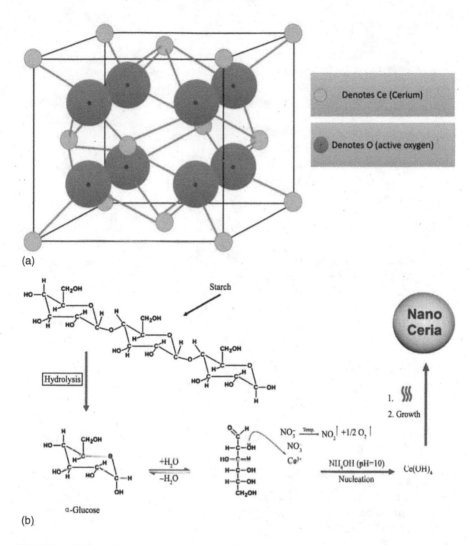

FIGURE 18.14 (A) A centered cubic face of cerium oxide (CeO_2) nanoparticles. (B) Preparation of cerium oxide (CeO_2) nanoparticles.

```
// Starting of control Program
//int led = 8;
char val;
void setup()
{
//pinMode(led, OUTPUT);   // Digital pin 13 set as output
   Pin
Serial.begin(9600);
}
void loop()
{
```

```
while (Serial.available() > 0)
{
val = Serial.read();
Serial.println(val);
}
if( val == '1') // Forward
  {
    analogWrite(6,0);
    analogWrite(9,255);
     analogWrite(10,255);
     analogWrite(11,255);
    delay(500);
  }
 if( val == '2') // Forward
  {
    analogWrite(9,0);
    analogWrite(6,255);
     analogWrite(10,255);
     analogWrite(11,255);
    delay(500);
  } if( val == '3') // Forward
  {
    analogWrite(10,0);
    analogWrite(9,255);
    analogWrite(6,255);
    analogWrite(11,255);
    delay(500);
  } if( val == '4') // Forward
  {
    analogWrite(11,0);
    analogWrite(9,255);
     analogWrite(10,255);
     analogWrite(6,255);
     delay(500);
  }
  if( val == '6') // Forward
  {
    analogWrite(3,100);
   analogWrite(5,0);
    delay(500);
  }
  if( val == '7') // Forward
  {
   analogWrite(5,100);
   analogWrite(3,0);
    delay(500);
  }}
// End of program
```

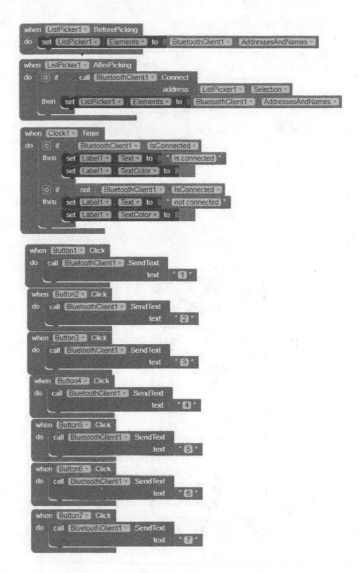

FIGURE 18.15 Steps to build the S-Vehicle mobile app.

It represents the designed and integrated structure in all its parts, which consists of four subsystems that work together in order for each device to perform the task required of it. The GPS (subsystem) and the Power subsystem.

The work of each of them is illustrated in the designed electronic circuit diagram. Here, an integrated network of the type (WAN) was designed in a star shape, based on a special type of data transmission and receiving devices called (LoRa modem). These devices are distinguished by the fact that they operate within the frequency 800/900 MHZ with 21 wireless communication channels (Wireless Channel), each channel accommodating 254 knots. As the communication between the main node /

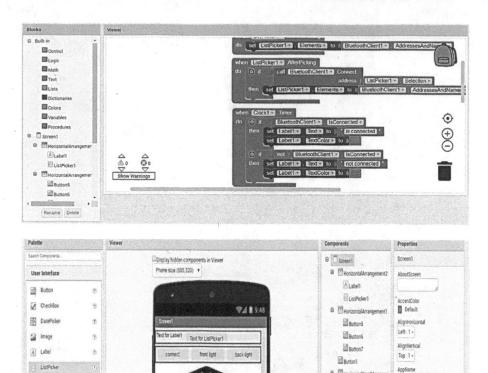

FIGURE 18.15   (*Continued*)

the starting point of the vehicle (Start Point of S-Vehicle) and the rest of the network is through the address of its own node/sites, whether rooms, hospital lobbies, corridors or halls to be sterilized. Here, an integrated electronic circuit (Interfacing circuit) has been designed and implemented to connect LORA with Waspam, as the Waspam platform was not merely used, but four supporting parts were added to it: Real Time Clock, Battery 3000m A/L, GPS Model, Remote Control Transmitter.

FIGURE 18.16   Structure of the S-Vehicles.

FIGURE 18.17   Steps of S-Vehicles.

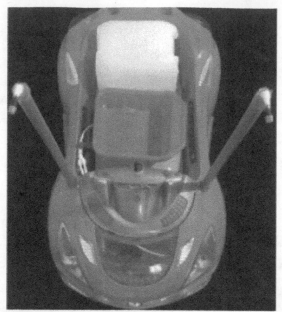

FIGURE 18.17   (*Continued*)

FIGURE 18.17 (*Continued*)

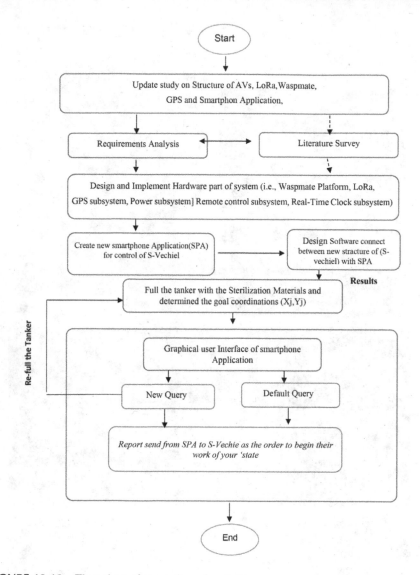

FIGURE 18.18 Flow chart of research work activities

The most important features of the achievements that have been reached can be summarized as follows:

A. Building an integrated advanced structure for a remote-managed vehicle that adopts the principle of control by smart phones and GPS) used to sterilize large areas that contain areas infected with a specific virus and be an aid to medical authorities in the country and sterile teams, and thus this structure saves effort and cost. It reduces the need for sterilization teams by finding a new, highly effective sterilization material and activating its role to raise the level of system performance, in addition to reducing effort, time, and cost.

B. Using smart phones to control the vehicle (S-Vehicle) and control the speed of spraying, when the sprinkler valves open or close and how long they remain open. GPS is also used to determine the coordinates of the area, and this increases the efficiency of the sterilization process and reduces effort and time wasted by using modern technologies in Iraq instead of the traditional methods.

C. The introduction of the technology of driverless vehicles (AV), which is controlled by smart phones, and this increases the efficiency of protection from the virus, as well as reduces the possibility of its spread, in addition to it reduces the effort and time wasted by using traditional and ordinary techniques used for this purpose for the first time in Iraq.

D. The system designed to control plants and plants from pests can be applied as well as can be used to achieve the goals of chemical security and safety by protecting people's lives through the use of sterilization materials with very little toxicity and preserving people's lives.

Pseudo code S-Vehicle
Input: *(Xi, Yi) coordinations for the Epidemic Areas.*
Output: *Optimal Strategy for Sterilization Areas by S-Vehicle*
Step 1: Building the hardware (S-Vehicle) part based on multi subsystems (i.e. Remote control, Real-Time Clock, Remote monitoring subsystem, GPS sensor)
Step 2: *Determined to coordinations of start points and goal points. In addition, satisfy the tanker is full by the Sterilization materials.*
Step 3: *Building smartphone application to control of S-Vehicle that software has five procedure, call these procedures sequentially (i.e., move forward, move backward, move left side, move right side, on-off valve)*
Step 4: *Forward the process*
         IF *start point=goal point & tanker <>0 Then*
                   Call *procedure of on-off valve*
         Else
                   Call *procedure of Move (Forward, backward, left and right)*
                            IF *current point=goal point & tanker <>0* **Then**
                            Call procedure of open valve
                            Else
                            Rechange the direction
                            End IF
         End *IF*
Step 5: *Test the Tanker*
         IF tanker is full **Then**
                   Go *to Step#4*

> *Else*
>> *Return into start point (Xi,Yi)*
> *End IF*
> *Step 6: Integration the user with system through user interface of mobile*
>> *application.*
>> *Do For each new query*
>>> *IF this query as default (i.e., come from responsible side in*
>>> *the hospital) Then*
>> *Being S-Vehicle Service*
> *End S-Vehicle*

Hence, Figures 18.1–18.18 explains our proposed work with simulation results in clear manner.

18.5 APPLICATIONS

This idea can be applied as a new technology in many fields, including:

A. **Industrial Field**
   - Support technological innovation and the spread of the Fourth Industrial Revolution in order to improve productivity and maintain the competitiveness of local sectors and make them a priority.
   - Save time and reduce risk for workers in the fields of sterilization.
   - Allow the delivery of medicines to the intensive care rooms, in which only a very limited number of medical staff are allowed to enter.

B. **Agricultural Field**
   - The system designed to combat pesticide-infected crops can be used if the pesticide is a liquid solution, and it can also be used for remote watering of plants and agricultural crops.

C. **The Field of Chemical Safety and Security**
   - Preventing direct contact between people and sterilized materials, thus achieving the goal of chemical security and safety, which is to protect the human element from injuries caused by the risks of the work environment.
   - Making the machine resemble the S-Vehicle is a way to reduce the contact between the increasing number of patients or virus carriers and their mixing with those who are exposed to infection such as nurses and pharmacists "during the delivery of medicines to patients" or workers in the field of sterilization of rooms, corridors and various facilities of laboratories, hospital halls, and intensive care rooms

D. **The Health Field**
  - Delivering medicines and medical supplies to places that contain people infected with fast-spreading viruses.
  - The integration of technology represented by an S-Vehicle by remote control makes the possibility of the sterilization process last for 24 hours, because the machines can operate continuously without losing efficiency due to fatigue or boredom. All we have to do is enter the target points as a database and make the application work automatically.

18.6 CONCLUSIONS

The sterilization system operated by smart phones is characterized by:

Sterilization of contaminated areas: It works to sterilize areas contaminated with a specific virus using sterilization solutions consisting of highly effective chemicals by specifying the coordinates of the target areas to be sterilized, and all this is done electronically through the managed S-Vehicle that is controlled remotely by a smart phone application. Addressing a real problem and working in real time: our system sterilizes any area whose coordinates are determined in a real way and deals with it simultaneously and answers any inquiry received in an instant through the interaction between the software environment and the electronic circuit that was built using the IoT platform.

The use of modern technology in communication and control: The latest technology has been used in the matter of remote system management in an integrated manner by smart phones in terms of the movement of the S-Vehicle and the opening of the valves of the sprinklers as well as the issue of wireless control, and this saves effort and cost and reduces the need for manpower through programming.

Achieving a major goal: which is to build an integrated system to sterilize and deliver medicines to the affected areas to reduce the rate of infections and the spread of the virus, as this system is considered in one way or another as part of the e-governance that our state seeks.

Economy in financial costs: by reducing the number of personnel used in repeated sterilization operations on a 24/7 basis.

Raising the level of sterilization performance: Preparing new sterilization materials with low toxicity and high effect that are subject to the rules and laws of chemical safety and security, the S-Vehicle will perform the sterilization/fumigation process accurately depending on the appropriate and correct treatment method according to scientific measurements.

Using wireless sensing and control: Through wireless communications and sending control commands from the smart phone application built in the system to the necessary S-Vehicle wirelessly. This service avoids several problems, including the lack of delay in sterilizing large areas continuously and simultaneously.

Strength and durability: The chassis of the designed S-Vehicle has advanced solutions in terms of sterilization and management. It is capable of holding up to 10 kg of sterilizing solutions plus 5 kg of medication and works even in changing conditions.

DECLARATIONS

- **Conflict of interest:** The authors declare that they have no conflict of interest.
- **Ethical approval:** This chapter does not contain any studies with human participants or animals performed by any of the authors.

REFERENCES

1. Yuval Arbel, Chaim FialKoff, and Amichai Kerner, Can reduction in infection and mortality rates from coronavirus be explained by an obesity survival paradox? An analysis at the US state-wide level, *International Journal of Obesity*, 41, 2339–2342, (2020), doi:10.1038/s41366-020-00680-7

2. Akshaya Srikanth Bhagavathula, Jamal Rahmani, and Ashrafi Mahabadi, Novel Coronavirus (COVID-19) knowledge and perceptions: a survey of health care workers, *MedRxiv*, (2019), doi:10.1101/2020.03.09.20033381

3. Hadil Alahdal, Fatema Basingab, and Reem Alotaibi, An analytical study on the awareness, attitude and practice during the COVID-19 pandemic in Riyadh, Saudi Arabia, *Journal of Infection and Public Health*, 13, 1446–1452, (2020), doi:10.1016/j.jiph.2020.06.015

4. J. M. Leipheimer, M. L. Balter, A. I. Chen, E. J. Pantin, A. E. Davidovich, K. S. Labazzo, and M. L. Yarmush, First-in-human evaluation of a hand-held automated venipuncture device for rapid venous blood draws. *Technology* 7, 98–107 (2019).

5. Qian (Chayn) Sun, Robert Odolinski, Jianhong (Cecilia) Xia, Jonathan Foster, Torbjörn Falkmer, and Hoe Lee, Validating the efficacy of GPS tracking vehicle movement for driving behaviour assessment, *Travel Behaviour and Society*, 6, 32–43 (2017), ISSN 2214-367X, doi:10.1016/j.tbs.2016.05.001.

6. A. Baz, P. Yi, and A. Qurashi, Intersection control and delay optimization for autonomous vehicles flows only as well as mixed flows with ordinary vehicles. *Vehicles*, 2, 523–541 (2020), doi:10.3390/vehicles2030029.

7. G.-Z. Yang, B. J. Nelson, R. R. Murphy, H. Choset, H. Christensen, S. H. Collins, P. Dario, K. Goldberg, K. Ikuta, N. Jacobstein, D. Kragic, R. H. Taylor, and M. McNutt, Combating COVID-19—The role of robotics in managing public health and infectious diseases. *Sci. Robot.* 5, eabb5589 (2020).

8. Guang-Zhong Yang and Bradley J. Nelson, Combating COVID-19 The role of robotics in managing public health and infectious diseases, *Science, Robotics* (2020), doi:10.1126/scirobotics.abb5589.

9. Ki Ho Hong, Sang Won Lee, and Hee Jae Huh, Guidelines for laboratory diagnosis of coronavirus disease 2019 (COVID-19) in Korea, *Ann Lab Med*, doi:10.3343/alm.2020.40.5.351.

10. Trung Thien Pham, Manh Ha Nguyen, and Ngoc Sang Nguyen, The disinfectant solution system preventing SARS-COV=2 Epidemic, *International Journal of Scientific Engineering and Science*, ISSN (online), 2456–7361.

11. Waspmote Technical Guide, Document version: v5.9 - 10/2015, Available online at: http://www.libelium.com/development/waspmote/documentation/waspmote-technical-guide/

12. C. R. Kovach, Y. Taneli, T. Neiman, E. M. Dyer, A. J. A. Arzaga, and S. T. Kelber, Evaluation of an ultraviolet room disinfection protocol to decrease nursing home microbial burden, infection and hospitalization rates. *BMC Infect. Dis.* 17, 186 (2017).

13. Hani Al-Dmour, Amer Salman, and Rand Al-Dmour, Influence of social media platforms on public health protection against the COVID-19 pandemic via the mediating effects of public health awareness and behavioural changes: intergrated model, *Journal of Medical Internet Research*, (2020), doi:10.2196/19996.

14. S. N. Zenk, S. A. Matthews, A. N. Kraft, and K. K. Jones, How many days of global positioning system (GPS) monitoring do you need to measure activity space environments in health research? *Health & Place*, 51, 52–60 (2018). doi:10.1016/j.healthplace.2018.02.004, Available online at: https://www.sciencedirect.com/science/article/abs/pii/S1353829217309851?via%3Dihub

15. A. Tubadji, V. Angelis, and P. Nijkamp, Micro-cultural preferences and macropercolation of new ideas: a NetLogo simulation, *J Knowl Econ* 10, 168 (2019), doi:10.1007/s13132-017-0446-4

16. NetLogo: A simple environment for modeling complexity (2019), Available online at: http://citeseerx.ist.psu.edu/viewdoc/summary?doi=10.1.1.117.949.

17. B. Tebrean, S. Crisan, C. Muresan, T.E. Crisan, Low cost command and control system for automated infusion devices, 81–84 (2017). doi:10.1007/978-3-319-52875-5.

18. H. E. Liying, S. U. Yumin, Jiang Lanhong, and S. H. I. Shikao, Recent advances of cerium oxide nanoparticles in synthesis, luminescence and biomedical studies: a review, *Journal of Rare Earths*, 33(8), 791–799, 2015, doi:10.1016/S1002-0721(14)60486-5.

19. S. Rajeshkumar, M.H. Sherif, C. Malarkodi, M. Ponnanikajamideen, Mariadhas Valan Arasu, Naif Abdullah Al-Dhabi, and Selvaraj Mohana Roopan, Cytotoxicity behaviour of response surface model optimized gold nanoparticles by utilizing fucoidan extracted from padina tetrastromatica, *Journal of Molecular Structure*, 2020, 129440, doi:10.1016/j.molstruc.2020.129440.

20. Xiaohui Ju, Anna Fučíková, Břetislav Šmíd, Jaroslava Nováková, Iva Matolínová, Vladimír Matolín, Martin Janata, Tereza Bělinová, and Marie Hubálek Kalbáčová, Colloidal stability and catalytic activity of cerium oxide nanoparticles in cell culture media, *RSC Advance*, 2020, 10, 39373, doi:10.1039/D0RA08063B.

21. Kshitij RB Singh, Vanya Nayak, Tanushri Sarkar, and Ravindra Pratap Singh, Cerium oxide nanoparticles: properties, biosynthesis and biomedical application, *RSC Advance*, 2020, doi:10.1039/D0RA04736H.

19 Comparative Forecasts of Confirmed COVID-19 Cases in Botswana Using Box-Jenkin's ARIMA and Exponential Smoothing State-Space Models

Ofaletse Mphale and V. Lakshmi Narasimhan
University of Botswana, Gaborone, Botswana

CONTENTS

DOI: 10.1201/9781003307822-23

19.1   INTRODUCTION

Coronaviruses are infectious diseases that are closely related to the common cold, Middle East Respiratory Syndrome coronavirus (MERS), and Severe Acute Respiratory Syndrome coronavirus (SARS). These diseases are known to diffuse commonly from animals to human beings. For example, SARS was known to transfuse from civet cats to humans while MERS was transmitted to humans from a type of camel [1]. The coronavirus was officially termed COVID-19 by the World Health Organization (WHO), and its first incident was registered in Wuhan city, Hubei Province, China in December 2019. Since then, the virus had spread rapidly reaching different segments of the world [2–4].

Fatalities from COVID-19 had been presented in amplifying figures worldwide. By August 2021, findings showed that COVID-19 fatalities had surpassed 4.3 million, with confirmed cases exceeding 208 million worldwide [5, 6]. Once developed and manufactured, more than 4.5 billion vaccine doses had been administered globally. As of today, there is no specific treatment for COVID-19 disease. Likewise, studies show that there is limited clinical researche conducted to assess the effectiveness of potential COVID-19 treatments [7–10]. In the absence of specific treatment of COVID-19 disease, health care systems of individual countries remain as the decisive factor when it comes to treatment and management approaches, specifically provision of medications to relieve symptoms, supplemental oxygen administration, fluid therapy, supportive diet, and other factors [11, 12]. Some critical recovery measures have also been delineated by [5]) such as self-isolation, drinking of plenty of water, consumption of paracentamol, personal hygiene, and adequate rests.

COVID-19 disease can affect individuals of all ages and is transmitted through human-to-human contact, specifically through close proximity to an infected individual or by accidentally coming in contact with bodily fluids of such an individual [13]. COVID-19 disease symptoms are similar to those of the flu but with some additional complications in individuals particularly susceptible or those with a compromised immune system. COVID-19 also tends to exacerbate the existing comorbidities, which is why older individuals—who are more likely than younger ones to have such comorbidities—are at a greater risk from the disease. Vaccine immunization strategies practically universally around the world prioritize high-risk population groups such as the elderly, health workers, government employees, police, teachers, and many other front-liners [14, 15]. In addition, there are some safeguard measures, including frequent hand washing, wearing face coverings, and social distancing, aimed at reducing the spread of the disease [5, 16].

Botswana has been working robustly to "flatten the curve" of the COVID-19 pandemic in order to prevent the medical care system capacities from being overwhelmed [17]. The first encounter of COVID-19 diseases in Botswana was on March 30, 2020, following the death of a 78-year-old woman from the village of Ramotswa. Post mortem tests showed that COVID-19 was the cause of death [18, 19]. Since then, the virus spread rapidly. By April 30, 2021, confirmed cases in Botswana had surpassed 50,000, leading to 732 deaths [20]. The government had imposed preventative measures such as banning gatherings of more than 50 people, border closure, quarantine, temporary closing of schools, banning of alcohol sales, curfew, compulsory wearing of face mask, and so on. On March 26, 2021, the government implemented a mass COVID-19 immunization strategy, following the recept of 30,000 vaccine doses from India. These vaccines were secured through the COVID-19 Vaccines Global Access scheme (COVAX). Some days later, the government procured more vaccines through COVAX, including doses made by Sinovac, AstraZeneca, Pfizer, Moderna, nd Johnson & Johnson [21].

Despite the government's efforts to implement strategies to mitigate the effects of COVID-19, evidence showed that the spread of COVID-19 infections in Botswana was on the rise. In August 2021, COVID-19 infections in Botswana had reached its peak with 142,380 confirmed cases and 2,043 COVID-19 related deaths nationally [20, 22]. When examining COVID-19 case notification on a 14-day average, as of August 2021, Botswana had registered the highest COVID-19 daily infections per capita in the world [23] (see Figure 19.1).

Infectious diseases are not only detrimental to human health; they also impose a heavy economic burden on the nation. A report by [24] in August 2021 highlighted that Botswana required an additional amount of 1.13 billion pula (USD100 million) to effectively manage the COVID-19 pandemic. The need to procure these funds have led to undesirable effects on the society, such as higher taxes, reduction in government subsidies, loss of employments, and increased poverty [25]. While most countries are implementing procedures to control the virus such as lockdowns, mobility restrictions, quarantines, and more, the accurate forecasting of infectious diseases remains a global challenge [16, 26], mainly because it is generally very difficult to predict the form(s) future outbreaks are going to take. In addition, because

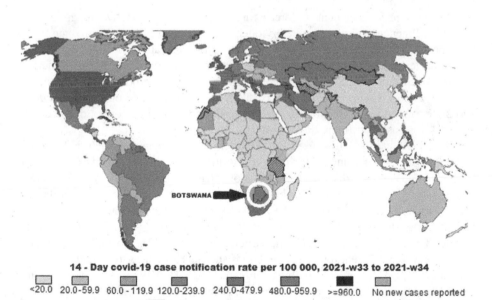

14 - Day covid-19 case notification rate per 100 000, 2021-w33 to 2021-w34

<20.0   20.0-59.9   60.0 - 119.9   120.0-239.9   240.0-479.9   480.0-959.9   >=960.0   No new cases reported

No cases reported by WHO and no cases identified in the public domain

FIGURE 19.1 Fourteen-day COVID-19 case notification rate per 100,000 population as of week 33, August 2021. Source [23].

not all the infectious disease outbreaks turn into a pandemic, anticipating their severity is difficult [27–29].

This study adopts a machine learning–based time series models known as auto regressive integrated moving average (ARIMA) and exponential smoothing state-space to forecast confirmed COVID-19 cases in Botswana in a 60-day period. The ARIMA model follows Box-Jenkins for time series forecasting. The models are critically compared for their forecast accuracy using error metrics such as RMSE, MAE, MAPE, and Lung Box statistical tests. In addition, the execution times of the models are assessed. Then the best-performing model suitable for forecasting the Botswana COVID-19 dataset is determined. Findings of the study are foreseen to raise social awareness at disease-monitoring institutions and the government regulation bodies where they could be utilized to support strategic health decisions and enhance policy improvement procedures for better management of the COVID-19 disease in Botswana.

The rest of the chapter is organized as follows. Section 19.2 presents the literature review regarding the subject being studied. It includes different theoretical and empirical perspectives on application of ARIMA models, ETS algorithms, and other machine learning time series based models used in forecasting of infectious diseases. Section 19.3 presents the methodological framework to be followed by the study analysis process. Section 19.4 presents the results and discussion of the study, while conclusions and future works are discussed in Section 19.5.

19.2 LITERATURE REVIEW

With the recent advancements in forecasting methods such as machine learning, artificial intelligence, and mathematical models, scholars had come to appreciate them and had integrated them in different studies to tackle real-world tasks. Predictive analytics learn from historical data and utilize machine learning approaches to derive future conclusions. The application of machine learning algorithms in technical fields such as engineering, computer science, medicine, statistics, and others had made it possible to recognize infectious disease patterns and accelerate correct diagnosis in order to forecast their future directions.

Infectious diseases are caused by pathogenic microorganisms such as bacteria, viruses, parasites, or fungi, which are transmitted between individuals or from an animal [30]. Zoonotic diseases are groups of infectious diseases that affect animals but can cause diseases when transmitted to humans [5]. Studies had shown that to date, various models and tools had been developed to predict and forecast the plagues of infectious diseases. The most popular are ARIMA models [16, 26, 31, 32], SIR models [28, 31], ETS models [26, 33], artificial intelligence [26, 27], and many others. [33]) compared different forecasting methods such as Holt linear trend method, naive method, single exponential smoothing, simple average, Holt-Winters method, moving average, and ARIMA using root mean square error score. From their findings it was deduced that the naïve model outperformed all other models. However, based on the ARIMA model, the grid search method yielded the best fit model for the series data.

In another study (Atchadé, 2021), a comparison of different COVID-19 forecast models was conducted using the cross-validation technique. In this study MAPE was used to compute forecast accuracy for each model. The findings showed that an ETS model with additive error-trend and no season was the best-fit model. Furthermore, it was determined that to obtain MAPE threshold of 5 percent, the study required at least 100 days of forecasts. A simple time series model was proposed and used to forecast short-time behavior of COVID-19 cases using the global confirmed cases and deaths [34]. The findings indicated that the proposed model produced competitive forecasts and relevant estimates of uncertainties over a 10-day period for 4 months.

A study by [26] employed various time series models to predict the spread of COVID-19 in Italy during the second pandemic wave in the period after October 13, 2020. In this study, time series models such as ARIMA, ETS, neural network auto regression (NNAR) model, the trigonometric exponential smoothing state space model with Box–Cox transformation, ARIMA errors, and trend and seasonal components and their feasible hybrid combinations were utilized to forecast the number of patients hospitalized with mild symptoms and the number of patients hospitalized in the intensive care units. Based on the findings, it was shown that the number of intensive care beds and the necessary attending personnel were expected to double in 10 days and to triple in approximately 20 days. These predictions were also compared with the observed trends and shown to be consistent. Therefore, the study deduced that hybrid models can provide useful insights to support health care decisions, especially in the short term.

A simple multiple linear regression (MLR) model was used to forecast daily confirmed COVID-19 cases using phone call data by [35]. Their findings showed that the proposed MLR model outperformed ETS, ARIMA, Seasonal Naive, Prophet, and a regression model without call data as evaluated by three-point forecast error metrics, specifically one prediction interval and two probabilistic forecast accuracy measures. Based on results it was established that the model could serve as a cornerstone for developing other forecasts methods, which can aid front-line personnel and decision-makers at local level to tackle the pandemic and other similar future challenges.

In Saudi Arabia, [31] applied a classical SIR model to predict the highest number of COVID-19 cases that could be recognized to flatten the curve. Similarly, the ARIMA model was used to predict the prevalence of COVID-19 cases. Their findings led to a conclusion that the SIR model affirmed that the containment technique used by Saudi Arabia to curb the spread of the disease was efficient. By validating the performance of the applied models, ARIMA proved to be a good forecasting method from current data. In another study, [27] optimized deep learning parameters to predict an outbreak of infectious diseases, such as chicken pox. The study made use of social media big data. Predictive models such as ARIMA, deep neural network (DNN), and long short-term memory (LSTM) were investigated. Based on the results, it was established that DNN and LSTM models perform better than ARIMA. However, the LSTM model produced more accurate predictions compared to the DNN model, in particularly modeling a disease outbreak.

19.3   METHODOLOGY

19.3.1   DATASET DESCRIPTION

The dataset used in this study was acquired from the Johns Hopkins University web portal and other relevant sources [6, 20, 22]. These are data repositories that are freely available for public use for academic and nonacademic purposes. The acquired dataset consisted of COVID-19 global registered cases (Confirmed, Recovered, Deaths) from November 31, 2019 to August 30, 2021. Since the study was only interested in investigating confirmed COVID-19 cases in Botswana, some observations and attributes were pruned from the final dataset. The IBM Statistical Package for the Social Sciences (SPSS) and R studio software were used to determine, scrutinize, and execute both ARIMA and ETS models.

The following data preprocessing steps were applied:

  i.   Feature label transformations, replacing missing values (confirmed cases that were left blank were replaced with a '0' value)
 ii.   Removal of outliers (characters and some negative values representing confirmed cases were replaced with an average value derived from the dataset)
iii.   Transformation of the series attributes to appropriate data types (the date attribute in dataset was transformed to date data type, and the confirmed cases attribute data type was set to numeric attributes accordingly).
 iv.   Transformation of the series to proper time series data frame for further analysis.

The final dataset consisted of only confirmed cases in Botswana registered from April 4, 2020 to August 22, 2021. The proposed methodology framework adopted for the study analysis process is illustrated in Figure 19.2.

19.3.2   TIME SERIES ANALYSIS

Time series is simply expressed as a set of data points ordered in time [32]. It is assumed to compose of random walk (nonstationary series) and white noise (zero mean stationary series). In mathematical terms, time series is defined as shown:

$$\mathbf{y_t} = f(t) \tag{19.1}$$

Where $\mathbf{y_t}$ presents the value of the variable under study at time **t**.

If the population is the variable being studies at various time period $t_1, t_2, t_3, \ldots, t_n$, then the time series is briefly elaborated as shown:

$$\mathbf{Time} \rightarrow t : t_1, t_2, t_3, \ldots, t_n \tag{19.2}$$

$$\mathbf{Value}s \rightarrow \mathbf{y_t} : y_{t1}, y_{t2}, y_{t3}, \ldots, y_{tn} \tag{19.3}$$

Time series forecasting approaches could be categorized into two broad classes: univariate time series forecasting and multivariate series forecasting. In univariate

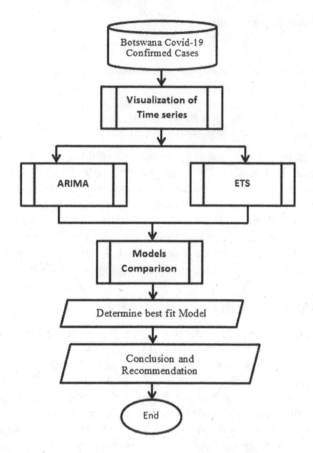

FIGURE 19.2   Proposed methodology framework for the analysis process of the study

series forecasting, predictions of future data points ultimately depend on previous values in the series while in multivariate time series analysis predictors (exogenous variables) other than the series values are taken into account in forecasting. Based on the nature of the dataset that was examined, a univariate time series analysis approach has been deemed appropriate to model forecasts of the study.

The subsequent step is to establish whether the series decomposition is additive or multiplicative in nature. In an additive time series, seasonality and residuals are independent of the trend whereas in multiplicative time series this is reversed. The mathematical description of an additive time series is given as shown in Equation (19.4).

$$O_t = T_t + S_t + R_t \tag{19.4}$$

where

O_t – represents the output
T_t – represents the trend

S_t – represents the seasonality
R_t – represents the output

Similarly, in multiplicative time series, the mathematically description could be given as shown:

$$O_t = T_t * S_t * R_t \tag{19.5}$$

In this study, first, we decompose time series through seasonal and trend decomposition process by Loess (STL). Then, we develop ARIMA and ETS models to generate forecasts. The models are then compared for their forecast accuracy using accuracy metrics, model execution time, and model memory utilization. Furthermore, residual stationarity is analyzed between the models. Finally, conclusions are drawn regarding models' performance and the best model for forecasting of confirmed Botswana COVID-19 cases dataset is determined. A brief discussion of ARIMA and ETS model development and evaluation metrics are given in Sections 19.3–19.6.

19.3.3 ARIMA Algorithm

ARIMA is a statistical machine learning–based algorithm used in time series forecasting. It was discovered by statisticians Box and Jenkins [36] and it is now known as the Box-Jenkins model. The ARIMA model extends auto regressive (AR) and moving average (MA) models by integrating with order of differencing steps and relies on the known historical data to establish future forecast values [37].

To successfully apply the ARIMA model, a nonstationary time series must be transformed from random walk to white noise. Random walk series trends produce unreliable forecasts. Stationary series has a constant mean variance, and its autocorrelation structures are not affected by fluctuations over time. To test for stationarity, an Augmented Duckey Fuller (ADF) test could be used. The ADF test examines the null hypothesis for the presence of a unit root in series. It is described shown in Equation (19.6).

$$y_t = c + \beta_t + \alpha y_{t-1} + \phi_1 \Delta Y_{t-1} + \phi_2 \Delta Y_{t-2} \ldots + \phi_p \Delta Y_{t-p} + e_t \tag{19.6}$$

where

$y(t - p) = \lag p$ of time series
delta $Y(t - p) = p$ difference of the series at time $(t–p)$

The existence of unit root in series makes it nonstationary, which is recognized at value of alpha $(\alpha) = 1$. The criterion used to test the null hypothesis for presence of the unit root is given as shown:

Given alpha is = 1;

H0: The series has a unit root.
H1: The series does not have a unit root. The series is stationary.

To assess the presence of unit a root in series, the p-value obtained should be less than the significance level of 0.05. In that way the null hypothesis is rejected, otherwise it is affirmed that the time series is nonstationary.

Mathematically, the ARIMA model is defined as shown: **ARIMA (p, d, q)** where

p – Represents the order of AR polynomial indicating of the autoregressive model lags
d – Represents the order of the differencing
q – Represents the MA polynomial order of the moving-average process

If the series is already stationary, the ARIMA model can be presented as an ARMA (p, q) with a differencing sequence of d times, where $p, d, q \geq 0$. It is simplified as ARMA model as shown;

$$Yt = \sum_{i=1}^{p} \phi_i Y_{t-i} + a_t - \sum_{j=1}^{q} \theta_j a_{t-j,} \qquad (19.7)$$

Where $\phi_1, \ldots, \phi_p$ are the AR parameters to be estimated, $\theta_1, \ldots, \theta_p$ are the MA parameters to be estimated and are a series residuals that follows a normal distribution. Equation (19.3) could be $a_1, \ldots, a_t$ further simplified by applying the Box-Jenkins backshift operator as shown:

$$\left(1 - \sum_{i-1}^{p} \phi_i B_i\right) Y_t = \left(1 - \sum_{j=1}^{q} \theta_j B_j\right) a_t, \qquad (19.8)$$

Equation (19.7) could be further condensed to Equation (19.8) as shown:

$$\phi_p(B) Y_t = \theta_q(B) a_t, \qquad (19.9)$$

where

$$\phi_p(B) = \left(1 - \sum_{i=1}^{p} \phi_i B_i\right) \text{ and } \theta_t(B) = \left(1 - \sum_{j=1}^{q} \theta_j B_j\right).$$

If the series is nonstationary, the ARIMA model can be further extended by integrating with the order of differencing steps as illustrated as shown:

$$W_t = Y_t - Y_{t-1} = (1-B)Y_t$$
$$W_t - W_{t-1} = Y_t - 2Y_{t-1} + Y_{t-2}$$
$$= (1-B)^2 Y_t$$
$$\vdots$$

$$W_t - \sum_{k=1}^{d} W_{t-k} = (1-B)^d Y_t,$$

(19.10)

where d is the order of differencing steps. Replacing the Yt in the ARMA model with the differences defined in Equation (19.9), the formal definitions **ARIMA** (p, d, q) model can be simplified as shown in Equation (19.10).

$$\phi_p(B) = (1-B)^d Y_t = \theta_q(B) a_t.$$

(19.11)

19.3.4 Exponential Smoothing Algorithm

Exponential smoothing algorithm or error trend season (ETS) models belong to family of time series models known as innovations state space models [26]. There were initially inverted by Robert G. Brown in the late 1950s [38]. Since its inception, it had inspired developments into various forecasting methods in univariate time series analysis [39–41]. Exponential smoothing models are defined using three level components, namely the error (E) component, the trend (T) component, and the seasonal (S) components. These components can be further classified using additive (A), multiplicative (M), or none (N) random errors. The mathematical description of state space is given in Equations (19.12) and (19.13).

$$y_t = w(x_{t-1}) + r(x_{t-1})\varepsilon_t$$

(19.12)

$$x_t = f(x_{t-1}) + g(x_{t-1})\varepsilon_t$$

(19.13)

where

f, w, and g – represents model coefficients.
ε_t – represents the Gaussian white noise of the series

Equation (19.12) is the observation equation, describing the relationship between the observation x_{t-1} and y_t. Equation (19.13) denotes the transition equation, defining the evolution of states over time.

ETS models are flexible in modeling trend and seasonal components of the series in various traits; as such, there are 30 possible permutations of the models that can be generated. These models are classified using the additive random errors and multiplicative random errors. In simple terms, there are 15 models with additive errors and 15 models with multiplicative errors [42]. Table 19.1 illustrates classification of the ETS methods based on its components as shown.

From Table 19.1, ETS 30 possible models can be generated, and each model is examined prior to selecting the best model to represent the dataset. The possible combinations of the ETS models are illustrated in Table 19.2.

For every model it is possible to define it using the ETS (E, T, S) notation [43]. For illustration, we define a simple exponential smoothing model as ETS (A, N, N). This model is described by components of additive errors, no trend, and no seasonal patterns. The model can be expanded by manipulating the trend term and/or the seasonal term to generate other new models. For example, ETS (A, Ad, A), ETS (A, A, M) models, and other models can be generated.

TABLE 19.1

Classification of ETS Methods Using Components

Trend Component	Seasonal Component		
	N (None)	A (Additive)	M (Multiplicative)
N(none)	(N,N)	(N, A)	(N,M)
A (Additive)	(A, N)	(A,A)	(A,M)
A_d (Additive damped)	(A_d, N)	(A_d, A)	(A_d, M)
M(Multiplicative)	(M,N)	(M,A)	(M, M)
M_d (Multiplicative damped)	(M_d, N)	(M_d, A)	(M_d, M)

Source [42].

TABLE 19.2

Possible Combinations of the ETS Models [42]

Model	Model	Model
ETS(M, M, N)	ETS(A, M, A)	ETS(M, N, M)
ETS(M, A, N)	ETS(A, M_d, N)	ETS(M, N, A)
ETS(M, A, M)	ETS(A, M_d, M)	ETS(M, N, N)
ETS(A, M, N)	ETS(A,N, A)	ETS(M, A, A)
ETS(A, N, N)	ETS(M, A_d, M)	ETS(A, A_d, M)
ETS(A, A, M)	ETS(M, A_d, N)	ETS(M, M, A)
ETS(M, M, M)	ETS(M, M_d, M)	ETS(A, A, A)
ETS(A, N, M)	ETS(A, A_d, N)	ETS(A, A_d, A)
ETS(A, A, N)	ETS(M, M_d, A)	ETS (M, A_d, A)
ETS(A, M, M)	ETS(M, M_d, N)	ETS(A, M_d, A)

19.3.5 Testing for Goodness of Fit

Testing for goodness of fit validates whether the models are appropriate fit to the data. In machine learning time series analysis, Akaike information criterion (AIC) and/or Bayesian information criterion (BIC) metrics are commonly employed to assess model fit by using penalized-likelihood criteria [44]. In this study we applied AIC metric over BIC for its flexibility and its ability to detect more complex models while emphasizing on the model performance [45]. In addition, AIC metric has been widely used to assess model fit in various studies that forecast infectious diseases [46–48]. To successfully execute AIC assessment metric, a grid search algorithm (GSA) is implemented using R programming language. The model fit scores were measured for both ARIMA and ETS model using the GSA. The lowest value of AIC was used to denote a good model fit. Mathematically, AIC is given in Equation (19.14) as follows:

$$\mathbf{AIC} = -2\big(\log-\text{likelihood}\big) + 2k \qquad (19.14)$$

where

k is the number of model parameters (the number of variables in the model plus the intercept).
Log-likelihood is a measure of model fit. The higher the number, the better the fit. This is usually obtained from statistical output

19.3.6 Models Prediction Accuracy Measurement

There are various error metrics that could be utilized to assess the prediction accuracy of ARIMA and ETS models. In this paper we implement RMSE, MAE, and MAPE error metrics. The accuracy metrics are:

y' = the predicted value
y = actual value
nd = number of data samples

The formula for computing RMSE is given as follows:

$$\text{RMSE} = \sqrt{\frac{i}{n_d} \sum_{i=1}^{n_d} (y' - y)^2} \qquad (19.15)$$

The lower the values of the RMSE, the better the model fits the data.
Alternatively, MAE measures the average magnitude of the errors in a set of forecasts or prediction, without considering their direction. It is mathematically described as

$$\text{MAE} = \frac{i}{n_d} \sum_{i=1}^{n_d} |y - y'| \qquad (19.16)$$

Similarly, MAPE is given as follows:

$$\text{MAPE} = \frac{i}{n_d} \sum_{i=1}^{n_d} \left| \frac{y - y'}{y} \right| \times 100\% \tag{19.17}$$

MAPE is commonly used metric for assessing model accuracy because it is easy to interpret and easy to explain. It uses percentages to measure accuracy of classifiers and works best when data as zero entries. Therefore, the lower the values of MAPE indicate that the model is a better fit for the dataset.

19.3.7 MODELS FORECAST ACCURACY MEASUREMENT

To examine the behavior of residuals on the generated forecasts, the Ljung-Box test was performed on forecast residuals. If it was learned that the auto correlations of the residues were small, then the model has insignificant lack of good fit. The Ljung-Box test equation is given as shown:

$$Q(m) = N(N+2) \sum_{h=1}^{m} \frac{\hat{\rho}_h^2}{N-h}. \tag{19.18}$$

where

$\hat{\rho}$ is the estimated autocorrelation of the series at lag k,
m is the number of lags being tested.

Alternatively, statistical hypothesis testing of the Ljung-Box test is given as shown:

H0: The model does not exhibit lack of fit.
Ha: The model exhibits lack of fit.

For significance level α, the critical region for rejection of the hypothesis of randomness in Ljung-Box test is given as shown:

$$Q > \chi_{1-\alpha,h}^2 \tag{19.19}$$

where $\chi_{1-\alpha,h}^2$ is the $1 - \alpha$ quantile of the chi-squared distribution with h degree of freedom

19.4 RESULTS AND DISCUSSIONS

The major objective of the study is to model and compare forecasts of confirmed COVID-19 cases in Botswana using ARIMA Box-Jenkin and exponential smoothing state space (ETS) models. Therefore, in order to develop the most suitable ARIMA and ETS models, the study followed the six main stages:

(i) Time series visualization
(ii) ARIMA modeling
(iii) ETS modeling
(iv) Comparison of the models
(v) Recommendation of the best performing model

A brief discussion of the study results of modeling ARIMA and ETS is given in Sections 19.1–19.5.

19.4.1 VISUALIZATION OF TIME SERIES

The series for confirmed COVID-19 cases is plotted and its various components such as seasonality, trends, and noise are analyzed. Plotting the series is an indispensable way to gain preliminary understanding of the series structure and an initial step to determine the most suitable forecasting model for the data [31]. Figure 19.3 presents the graphical illustration of the confirmed COVID-19 cases in Botswana as shown.

Figure 19.3 shows that from April 2020 to early August 2021, confirmed COVID-19 cases in Botswana have been rising steadily with a horizontal trend and some periodic spikes. Furthermore, the series degrades gradually toward the end of August 2021. This series is also described by daily cycles of fluctuations that revert around zero mean, which depicts components of a weak stationarity. In the period from April 2020 to early October 2020, the results showed that there were minimum figures of confirmed COVID-19 cases registered in Botswana. These results could be related to the effectiveness of government policies and precaution measures that are imposed, e.g., national lockdown, quarantine, restriction of movements, compulsory wearing of face coverings in public areas, boarder closure, and more.

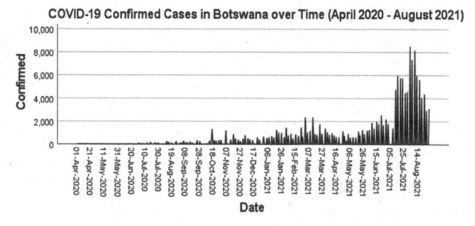

FIGURE 19.3   Confirmed COVID-19 cases in Botswana over time.

In late October 2020, the results show that the series had registered its first sharpest spike. This was during the early period of state of emergency extension in the country. Hence, this could suggest that most precautionary measures are still under consideration or are just implemented. However, the confirmed case figures degrade toward the month of December 2020. Then, toward the month of January 2021, confirmed cases rise steeply. This suggests that the government precaution measures imposed in that period had a slight impact toward controlling COVID-19 daily infections.

Even though mass vaccination of citizens by the government took place from late March 2021, the drastic rise of COVID-19 cases from July to August 2021 could suggest that most citizens are still yet to be fully vaccinated. Furthermore, this could also indicate effects from other COVID-19 variants discovered, such as the ones identified in India, South Africa, and other countries. However, toward late August 2021, the COVID-19 cases decline gradually, suggesting that more citizens are receiving vaccines or are fully vaccinated. In addition, the results could relate to the success of some government interventions at play.

In order to validate whether the series has autocorrelation with its lags, we fitted the auto-correlation function (ACF) and partial auto-correlation function (PACF) with the data. The behavioral patterns of the correlograms are investigated with respect to the upper confidence limits and lower confidence limits. Figure 19.4 presents the graphical illustration of the results of confirmed cases fitted in ACF and PACF plots.

Figure 19.4 shows that both ACF and PACF correlograms follow a similar pattern that depicts significance at lags 3, 4, 5, 7, and 14. This also indicates a series that could be modeled appropriately using ARIMA processes by providing an insight into possible ARIMA candidate models. However, since ARIMA models are determined using AutoARIMA grid search algorithm (GSA), we consider manual computation of ARIMA candidate models to be beyond the scope of this study. Therefore, the next step we decompose the series to separate the trend component and the random component. In this process we decompose the series using seasonal-trend decomposition by Loess (STL) method. STL is a robust decomposition method for obtaining trend, seasonality, and remainder components of the series using an additive model [49]. Figure 19.5 depicts the graphical illustration of series decomposition process in STL, where the trend of confirmed COVID-19 cases in Botswana are increasing constantly

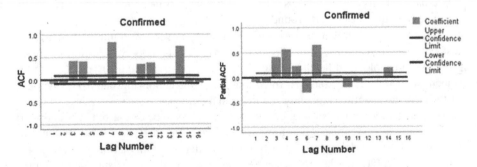

FIGURE 19.4   ACF and partial ACF plots of confirmed COVID-19 cases in Botswana.

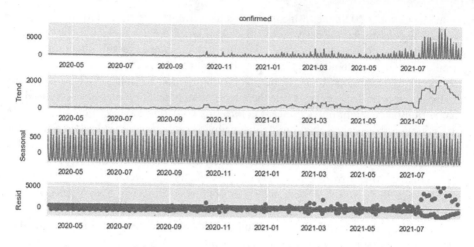

FIGURE 19.5   STL series decomposition of confirmed cases over time.

```
Results of Dickey-Fuller Test:
Test Statistics                         -1.902675
p-value                                  0.330804
#Lags Used                              16.000000
Number of Observations Used            334.000000
Critical value(1%)                      -3.450081
Critical value(5%)                      -2.870233
Critical value(10%)                     -2.571401
dtype: float64
```

FIGURE 19.6   The ADF stationarity test results.

with some random plateaus in late July 2021, and it declines gradually from early to late August 2021. The series does not depict any clear seasonal patterns or cycles. However, in a residual plot, it shows that residues have been constant from April 2020 until September 2020, where started to depict random noise. This also indicates the nonstationarity nature of the series. In a stationary time series, the residual distribution are assumed to revert around zero mean [50].

In order to confirm that the series was stationary or not, we implemented an ADF test on series and the p-value score was determined as 0.330804, which is greater than the threshold significant level of 0.05. In that way the null hypothesis is not rejected. Therefore, the study affirmed that the series is nonstationary. The synopsis of the ADF test results is given in Figure 19.6 as shown;

In ARIMA modeling non-stationary series requires to be converted into stationary series to attain white noise. Therefore, in that case we needed to fit different permutation of ARIMA model parameters (p, d, q) in order to attain stationaries the series. However, with ETS models the series does not require time to be stationary for optimal forecasting. Therefore in that case we fitted the original non-differenced series to the ETS models. Brief discussion on the development of ARIMA and ETS models is given in subsequent Sections 19.2–19.3 as follows.

19.4.2 ARIMA Modeling

In this phase, a grid search algorithm (GSA) known as AutoARIMA is implemented with the help of "forecast" in R platform. The AutoARIMA function is used to compute the goodness of fit for different combinations of ARIMA models. The AIC measure is used to penalize model performance based on maximum likelihood estimation. In this study the lowest score of AIC metric is used to determine the best-fit ARIMA model. An overview of the GSA results from fitting different ARIMA models is shown in Figure 19.7, whereas the best ARIMA model fit is at ARIMA (5, 1, 0). This model shows the AIC measure of 8229.142, which is the lowest AIC score in complete GSA runs for the goodness of fit. The ARIMA model terms such as AR, d, and MA are also determined as 5, 1, and 0 respectively.

After establishing the best-fit ARIMA model, the study also needs to confirm whether the chosen model is appropriate for generating reliable forecasts. ADF test is applied on the chosen ARIMA model to examine behavior of residuals around it. The ADF test results show that the p − value score was 4.193195e-14. This was

```
ARIMA Models    AIC Scores
ARIMA(2,1,2)    : 8296.331
ARIMA(0,1,0)    : 8987.528
ARIMA(1,1,0)    : 8842.266
ARIMA(0,1,1)    : 8517.485
ARIMA(0,1,0)    : 8985.537
ARIMA(1,1,2)    : 8375.252
ARIMA(2,1,1)    : 8310.092
ARIMA(3,1,2)    : 8273.109
ARIMA(3,1,1)    : 8276.579
ARIMA(4,1,2)    : 8258.979
ARIMA(4,1,1)    : 8258.231
ARIMA(4,1,0)    : 8274.495
ARIMA(5,1,1)    : 8254.991
ARIMA(5,1,0)    : 8231.113
ARIMA(5,1,0)    : 8229.142
ARIMA(4,1,0)    : 8272.551
ARIMA(5,1,1)    : 8253.814
ARIMA(4,1,1)    : 8256.762

ARIMA(5,1,0)    : 8229.142

Best model: ARIMA(5,1,0)
```

FIGURE 19.7 AutoARIMA results and their corresponding AIC scores.

extremely small and less than the threshold critical value of 0.05. Therefore, it was inferred that the series is stationary. Furthermore, residuals were purely random with no autocorrelation with the model. Therefore, with this stated assumptions we conclude that the chosen model is an adequate fit to the data.

19.4.2.1 Forecasting with the Best ARIMA Model

In this stage the chosen ARIMA model (5, 1, 0) is used to generate forecasts of confirmed COVID-19 cases forecast in a 60-day period, specifically from August 31, 2021 to October 29, 2021. The actual values (observed) of confirmed cases are plotted against the forecasted values. The 95 percent standard error bond lines (UCL and LCL) are plotted to guide the forecasts error limits. Figure 19.8 depicts the graphical illustration of the observed and forecast values of COVID-19 confirmed cases in Botswana over a 60-day period.

Figure 19.8 shows that given the environmental variables remain constant, i.e., the government precaution measures, policies, medicinal interventions, and other regulation used to control COVID-19 virus are imposed, then the trend of confirmed cases in Botswana is an expected decline with random fluctuations approaching zero mean over the next 60-day period. This could also suggest that with the current government interventions imposed, Botswana may be able to control the spread of COVID-19 infections in the near future.

19.4.3 ETS MODELING

To successfully implement the ETS model, a package "forecast" by [51]) is executed in R platform. AIC assessment metric is used to select an appropriate model automatically using the principle of maximum likelihood estimation. In this phase, the simplest ETS model, ETS (A, Ad, N), described by an Additive error, Additive trends and No seasonal patterns, is chosen among 30 possible state space models. This model depicts the smallest AIC score of 1030642 as shown in Figure 19.9.

In order to validate the model whether the model appropriately fitted the data, we performed residual analysis and tested its stationarity. In that process we apply the

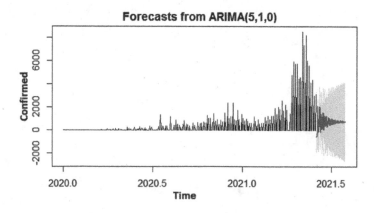

FIGURE 19.8 ARIMA model forecasting over a 60-day period.

```
ETS(A,Ad,N)

call:
 ets(y = chtr.ts, model = "zzz")

   Smoothing parameters:
      alpha = 0.0125
      beta  = 0.0125
      phi   = 0.8713

   Initial states:
      l = 0.7829
      b = 0.4805

   sigma:  931.4632

      AIC      AICC      BIC
 10306.42 10306.58 10331.91
```

FIGURE 19.9   The chosen ETS model based on maximum likelihood criterion (AIC).

```
        Ljung-Box test

data:  Residuals from ETS(A,Ad,N)
Q* = 2317.8, df = 98, p-value < 0.05914

Model df: 5.   Total lags used: 20
```

FIGURE 19.10   The ETS model Ljung-Box test results.

Ljung-Box test, and the p-value score is computed. In Figure 19.10 the ETS residual analysis results shows that residuals are normally distributed with mean close to zero and p-value measure greater than the significant threshold of 0.05. These results also show that the residuals are independent and convey no serial autocorrelations. In a good forecast model, the assumption is that residuals should resemble non-auto-correlated errors [37]. Therefore, with the stated assumptions, we conclude that the model can be trusted to model forecasts of confirmed COVID-19 cases over a 60-day period. The results of performing Ljung-Box test are given in Figure 19.10.

19.4.3.1   Forecasting with the Best ETS Model

In this stage, the chosen exponential smoothing model ETS (Λ, Λd, N) is used to generate forecasts of confirmed COVID-19 cases in Botswana in a 60-day period, specifically from August 31, 2021 to October 29, 2021. The observed values of confirmed cases are plotted against the forecasted values. The 95 percent standard error UCL and LCL are plotted to guide the forecasts error limits. Figure 19.11 depicts the plotting of observed and forecast values of confirmed COVID-19 cases in Botswana over a 60-day period.

Figure 19.11 shows that ETS forecasts of confirmed cases in Botswana are expected to degrade gradually over the next 60 days. These findings are valid given the environmental variables and government interventions to control the virus remain constant. Furthermore, findings also may also suggest that if current environmental variables remain stable, then Botswana may control the spread of COVID-19 infections in the near future.

19.4.4   COMPARISON OF ARIMA AND ETS MODELS

In this phase we critically scrutinized the generated forecasts of both ETS and ARIMA models in 60 days from August 31, 2021 to October 29, 2021. Figure 19.12 shows that

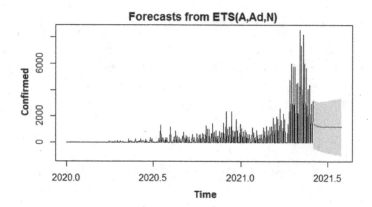

FIGURE 19.11   ETS model forecasts of confirmed COVID-19 cases over a 60-day period.

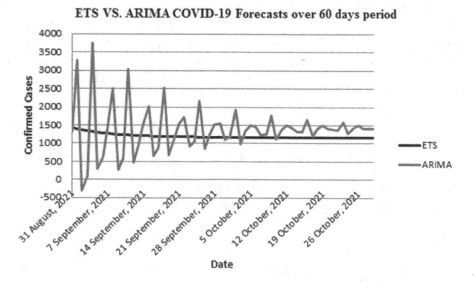

FIGURE 19.12   ETS vs. ARIMA forecasts of confirmed cases over a 60-day period.

confirmed cases in Botswana are expected to decline gradually in the next 60 days. Importantly, ARIMA forecasts show the decline in daily confirmed cases following a linear fluctuating trend. Based on ARIMA forecasts, we expect to witness around 2,300 daily confirmed cases by September 28, 2021 and around 1,500 confirmed cases by October 26, 2021. Similarly, from ETS forecasts, the trend of confirmed COVID-19 cases is toward a decline following a downward-sloping trend. Introspecting from ETS forecasts, we expect to witness around 1,300 confirmed cases by the September 28, 2021 and around 1,100 confirmed cases in Botswana by October 28, 2021.

In the next step we evaluated the models based on metrics of forecast accuracy, execution time and memory usage, and the results are presented in Table 19.3.

Table 19.3 shows that the ARIMA model has a better forecast accuracy that depicts MAE, RMSE, and MAPE of 36.63, 70.03, and 7.36 accuracies, respectively. In contrast, ETS model performs slightly lower with MAE of 41.47, RMSE of 93.80, and MAPE of 7.42 accuracies, respectively. According to [52]), the lesser the forecast error, the more accurate the model is. However, when the models forecast performance is evaluated based on metrics of execution time and memory usage, results show that the ETS model outperformed the ARIMA model. This depicts an execution time of 0.015 seconds and memory usage of 22,176 Bytes. These results also indicate there is no one-size-fits-all forecast model to solve a specific problem case. In other words, no matter how good a forecast is, there will always be variations project its strength and weakness, which could ultimately determine its gain and trade-offs. For instance, an ARIMA model could be the best-performing model if its algorithm could be optimized to execute in short time and utilized less memory. Likewise, an ETS model could be a better-performing model if its forecast accuracy is optimized and improved. In the next step, we analyzed the stationarity of residual on the model's forecast errors at different time lags intervals and the p-value score was computed as shown in Table 19.4.

TABLE 19.3

Comparison of ETS vs. ARIMA Forecast Accuracy, Execution Time, and Memory Usage

MODEL	MAE	RMSE	MAPE	Execution time (s)	Memory Usage (Bytes)
ARIMA	36.63	70.03	7.36	0.051	24224
ETS	41.47	93.80	7.42	0.017	22176

TABLE 19.4

Comparison of ETS vs. ARIMA Forecast Errors Based on Residual Analysis

MODEL	15 Lags Forecast Residuals (Ljung-Box p-value score)	30 Lags Forecast Residuals (Ljung-Box p-value score)	60 Lags Forecast Residuals (Ljung-Box p-value score)
ARIMA	0.9728	0.9995	0.9987
ETS	0.0475	0.0739	0.0735

In Table 19.4, results shows that the behavior of residuals around the ARIMA and ETS forecast errors are purely random, independent, and have no autocorrelation at various time lag intervals. These results depict the Ljung-Box test results with p-value measure greater than significant threshold of 5 percent. However, we also notice that residuals are slightly significant on the ETS model at lag 15 with p-value measure of 0.0475. These results suggest that residuals are nonstationarity and depict serial correlations of coefficients, meaning that there are less volatile at time lag 15. With the stated assumptions, we deduce that ARIMA forecasts are highly reliable and dependable in comparison to ETS forecasts. Furthermore, way we consider ARIMA forecasts as a precise estimate of the truth, which can provide rigor guidance on the direction of the future course of confirmed COVID-19 cases in Botswana over a 60-day period. According to [53]), forecasts of the model are reliable if residual errors are stationary and depicts no serial correlations when tests results depict a p-value score greater than the threshold of 5 percent.

19.4.5 SUMMARY ON THE BEST-PERFORMING MODEL

In this section, a summary is drawn from results of executing various metrics in analyzing the forecasts of the ARIMA and ETS models. The best-performing model is identified by determining the model dominance in performance in different metrics categories. Table 19.5 presents an overview of the analysis results from executing ARIMA and ETS across various performance metrics as shown.

From Table 19.5 it is deduced that the ARIMA model is the best-performing model that can be used to accurately generate short-term forecasts of confirmed COVID-19 cases in Botswana. Based on the results, the ARIMA model dominates the ETS model in most evaluation metrics categories. However, we attain very interesting results when ARIMA and ETS models are compared using metrics of

TABLE 19.5
Summary of the Model Comparison between ETS and ARIMA Results in Various Metrics Categories

			Model Comparison	
Evaluation Metric Category	ARIMA	ETS	ARIMA	ETS
MAE	36.63	41.47	√	
RMSE	70.05	93.80	√	
MAPE	7.36	7.42	√	
Execution time	0.051s	0.017s		√
Memory Usage	24224KB	22176KB		√
15 Lags Forecasts Residuals (Ljung Box – $p\ value$)	0.9728	0.0475	√	
30 Lags Forecasts Residuals (Ljung Box – $p\ value$)	0.9995	0.0739	√	
60 Lags Forecasting Residuals (Ljung Box – $p\ value$)	0.9987	0.0735		√

execution time and memory usage. In this evaluation metric category, the ETS model outperforms ARIMA model. These results suggest that more tuning phases are required with ARIMA to improve its execution time and memory usage in order to improve the model efficiency.

19.5   CONCLUSION AND FUTURE WORKS

The accurate forecasting of infectious diseases had become prevalent for ensuring economic and the humanitarian welfare of every country. Recently, Botswana had implemented various mitigation strategies to curtail the spread of COVID-19 infections in order to "flatten the curve" of the pandemic. This study employs ARIMA and exponential smoothing state space models (ETS) to forecast confirmed cases in Botswana for the next 60-day period. This is critical to better understand COVID-19 disease and provide support for strategic decisions in order to better manage the disease in Botswana. This chapter compares performances of the ARIMA model and the ETS model based on their forecasting using accuracy metrics of root mean squared error (RMSE), mean absolute error (MAE), and mean absolute percentage error (MAPE). In addition, the models are compared using metrics of execution time, memory utilization, and the Ljung-Box test for residual analysis. The study shows that the ARIMA model outperforms the ETS model in generating more reliable and volatile forecasts. This is depicted by the lowest measures of MAE, RMSE, and MAPE. Furthermore, the ARIMA model had depicted more stationary residuals the forecast errors when compared to ETS model forecasts. However, interestingly, the ETS model outperforms the ARIMA model by requiring less execution time and less memory utilization in generating forecasts. In drawing summary of the best-performing model, we conclude that the ARIMA model is such a model, which gives a higher precision across different evaluation metrics in contrast to the ETS model. However, despite the good performance of the ARIMA model, results suggest that reliability and volatility of the ARIMA model can still be improved and optimized to reduce the model execution time and its memory utilization.

In short-term forecasting of confirmed COVID-19 cases in Botswana over the next 60-day period, findings show that given the environmental variables remain constant, i.e., the current government precautionary measures, pharmaceutical interventions, and other strategies used to control the virus, confirmed cases in Botswana are expected to decline in the near future. Therefore, in order to effectively manage the COVID-19 infections, the study recommends that the government should impose stricter precautionary policies and measures, which could involve an execution of phase-level national lockdown, strict curfew regulations, more strictly enforced compulsory wear of face coverings in public areas, strict liquor sale regulations, and strict social distancing regulations. In addition, the government should encourage citizen participation and confidence toward COVID-19 immunization initiatives, and the public should abide by the COVID-19 precaution measures at all the times. This study is currently one of the groundbreaking studies that employ time series models to forecasts confirmed COVID-19 cases in context of a whole country. Therefore, in future research, the study intends to acquire more empirical data that covers longer periods for more reliable forecasts in order to generate long-term forecasts. A multivariate time series model with exogenous regressors can be employed, to investigate effects of other independent variables in forecast accuracy. Finally, machine learning techniques such as artificial neural networks and data science forecast algorithms like Facebook prophet and Amazon Deep AR+ could be adopted to provide different perspectives to correlate forecasts of confirmed COVID-19 cases in Botswana.

REFERENCES

1 Singla, R., Mishra, A., and Joshi, R. e. (2020). *Human Animal Interface of SARS-CoV-2 (COVID-19) Transmission: A Critical Appraisal of Scientific Evidence.* Springer Nature Switzerland, 119–130. doi:10.1007/s11259-020-09781-0

2 BBC News. (2020, December 28). *BBC News.* Retrieved February 12, 2021, from Covid-19 pandemic: Tracking the global coronavirus outbreak: https://www.bbc.com/news/world-51235105

3 Our World in Data. (2020, January 7). *Statistics and Research.* Retrieved March 3, 2021, from Coronavirus Pandemic (COVID-19): https://ourworldindata.org/coronavirus

4 Vara, V. (2020, April 16). *Pharmaceutical technology.* Retrieved March 12, 2021, from Latest Analysis: https://www.pharmaceutical-technology.com/features/coronavirus-outbreak-the-countries-affected/

5 World Health Organization. (2021, January 10). *WHO Health Topic Page: Zoonoses.* Retrieved January 12, 2021, from https://www.who.int/topics/zoonoses/en/

6 Worldometer. (2021, September 2). *Covid-19 Coronavirus Pandemic.* Retrieved September 17, 2021, from Worldometer: https://www.worldometers.info/coronavirus/

7 Hodgson, S. H., Mansatta, K., and Mallet, G. et al. (2020). What defines an efficacious COVID-19 vaccine? A review of the challenges assessing the clinical efficacy of vaccines against SARS-CoV-2. *The Lancert.* doi:10.1016/S1473-3099(20)30773-8

8 IWK Health Center. (2021, 7 January). *COVID-19 Research.* Retrieved March 16, 2021, from Library Services: https://library.nshealth.ca/COVID19Research/Publications

9 Jia, L., Li, K., Jiang, Y., Guo, X., and Zhao, T. (2020). Prediction and analysis of Coronavirus Disease 2019. *NASA Astrophysics Data System.* Retrieved January 23, 2021, from https://arxiv.org/ftp/arxiv/papers/2003/2003.05447.pdf

10 Stieg, C. (2020, March 3). *Health and Wellness.* Retrieved May 25, 2021, from How this Canadian start-up spotted coronavirus before everyone else knew about it: https://www.cnbc.com/2020/03/03/bluedot-used-artificial-intelligence-to-predict-coronavirus-spread.html

11 Barlow, A., Landolf, K. M., Barlow, B., Yeung, S. Y., Heavner, J. J., Claassen, C. W., and Heavner, M. S. (2020). Review of emerging pharmacotherapy for the treatment of coronavirus disease 2019. *Pharmacotherapy*, *40*(5), 416–437. doi:10.1002/PHAR.2398

12 Hajjar, L., Costa, I., and Rizk, S.E. (2021). Intensive care management of patients with COVID-19: A practical approach. *Ann. Intensive Care*, *11*(36). Retrieved from doi:10.1186/s13613-021-00820-w

13 Stadnytskyi, V., Bax, C. E., Bax, A., and Anfinrud, P. (2020). The airborne lifetime of small speech droplets and their potential importance in SARS-CoV-2 transmission. *Proceedings of the National Academy of Sciences of the United States of America. 117.* Centers for Disease Control and Prevention. doi:10.1073/PNAS.2006874117

14 ECDC. (2021b). *Overview of the implementation of COVID-19 vaccination strategies and deployment plans in the EU/EEA.* Retrieved August 26, 2021, from https://www.ecdc.europa.eu/sites/default/files/documents/covid-19-overview-vaccination-strategies-deployment-plans-6-may-2021.pdf

15 Modern Healthcare. (2020, December 26). *Coronavirus outbreak: 'Chaotic': Oregon braces as COVID vaccine opens for elderly*. Retrieved September 9, 2021, from Safety and Quality: https://www.modernhealthcare.com/safety-quality/coronavirus-outbreak-live-updates-covid-19

16 Ceylan, Z. (2020). Estimation of COVID-19 prevalence in Italy, Spain, and France. *PMC US National Library of Medicine National Institute of Health*, doi:10.1016/j.scitotenv.2020.138817.

17 Ministry of Health. (2021, 8, 26). *COVID-19 Update*. Retrieved September 12, 2021, from Ministry Of Health & Wellness, Botswana: https://www.moh.gov.bw/coronavirus.html

18 IOL. (2020, March 31). *Woman, 79, first person to die of Covid-19 in Botswana*. Retrieved September 10, 2021, from News: https://www.iol.co.za/news/woman-79-first-person-to-die-of-covid-19-in-botswana-45855994

19 Wikipedia. (2021, August 26). *COVID-19 pandemic in Botswana*. Retrieved September 7, 2021, from Wikipedia The Free Encyclopedia: https://en.wikipedia.org/wiki/COVID-19_pandemic_in_Botswana#cite_note-9

20 AccuWeather. (2021, September 16). *Coronavirus (COVID-19) Tracker*. Retrieved September 17, 2021, from Botswana Weather: https://www.accuweather.com/en/bw/national/covid-19

21 WHO. (2021, March 30). *New dawn for Botswana's COVID-19 response*. Retrieved from Health Topics: https://www.afro.who.int/news/new-dawn-botswanas-covid-19-response

22 Johns Hopkins University of Medicine. (2021, September 16). *Corona virus resource center*. Retrieved September 16, 2021, from COVID-19 Dashboards by the Centerfor System Science and Engineering (CSSE) at Johns Hopkisn University: https://coronavirus.jhu.edu/map.html

23 ECDC. (2021a, August 26). *COVID-19 situation update worldwide, as of week 33, updated 26 August 2021*. Retrieved September 5, 2021, from European Centre for Disease Prevention and Control: https://www.ecdc.europa.eu/en/geographical-distribution-2019-ncov-cases

24 Benza, B. (2021). *Botswana's COVID-19 budget balloons as it battles for vaccines*. Retrieved August 20, 2021, from REUTERS: https://www.reuters.com/world/africa/botswanas-covid-19-budget-balloons-it-battles-vaccines-2021-08-17/

25 Xinhua. (2021, January 31). *Botswana Anticipates tough Financial Budget due to COVID-19*. Retrieved September 17, 2021, from XINHUANET: http://www.xinhuanet.com/english/2021-01/31/c_139711407.html

26 Perone, G. (2021). Comparison of ARIMA, ETS, NNAR, TBATS and hybrid models to forecast the second wave of COVID-19 hospitalizations in Italy. *Eur J Health Econ*, 1–24. doi:10.1007/s10198-021-01347-4.

27 Chae, S., Kwon, S., and Lee, D. (2018). Predicting infectious disease using deep learning and big data. *International Journal of Environmental Research and Public Health*. doi: 10.3390/ijerph15081596.

28 Malavika, B., Marimuthu, S., Melvin, J., Nadaraj, A., Asirvatham, E. S., and Jeyaseelan, L. (2021). Forecasting COVID-19 epidemic in India and high incidence states using SIR and logistic growth models. *Clinical Epidemiology and Global Health*, 9, 26–33.

29 WHO. (2021, September 7). *World Health Organisation*. Retrieved September 12, 2021, from WHO Coronavirus Disease (COVID-19) Dashboard: https://covid19.who.int/

30 Steptoe, A. and Poole, L. (2015). *Infectious Diseases: Psychosocial Aspects*. International Encyclopedia of the Social & Behavioral Sciences (Second Edition).

31 Abuhasel, K. A., Khadr, M., and Alquraish, M. M. (2020). Analyzing and forecasting COVID-19 pandemic in the Kingdom of Saudi Arabia using ARIMA SIR models. *Wiley – Computational Intelligence*. doi:10.1111/coin.12407.

32 Fanoodi, B., Malmir, B., and Jahantigh, F. F. (2019). Reducing demand uncertainty in platelet supply chain through artificial neural networks and ARIMA models. *Elsevier Computers in Biology and Medicine*. doi:10.1016/j.compbiomed.2019.103415.

33 Chaurasia, V. and Pal, S. (2020). *Application of Machine Learning Time Series Analysis for Prediction COVID-19 Pandemic*. Berlin: Springer. doi:10.1007/s42600-020-00105-4

34 Petropoulos, F., Makridakis, S., and Stylianou, N. (2020). COVID-19: Forecasting confirmed cases and deaths with a simple time series model. *International Journal of Forecasting*. doi:10.1016/J.IJFORECAST.2020.11.010

35 Rostami-Tabar, B. and Rendon-Sanchez, J. F. (2021). Forecasting COVID-19 daily cases using phone call data. *Applied Soft Computing - ELSEVIER*, *100*, 106932.

36 Box, G. and Jenkins, G. (1976). *Time Series Analysis: Forecasting and Control, Revised Edition*. San Francisco: Holden Day.

37 Fattah, J., Ezzine, L., and Aman, Z. (2018). Forecasting of demand using ARIMA model. *International Journal of Business Management*. doi:10.1177/1847979018808673

38 Brown, R. G. (1956). *Exponential Smoothing for Predicting Demand*. Brussels: Arthur D. Little Inc., p. 15.

39 Brown, R. G. (1959). *Statistical Forecasting for Inventory Control*. New York: McGraw/ Hill.

40 Holt, C. E. (1957). *Forecasting Seasonals and Trends by Exponentially Weighted Averages (O.N.R. Memorandum No. 52)*. Pittsburgh US: Carnegie Institute of Technology. doi:10.1016/j.ijforecast.2003.09.015

41 Winters, P. R. (1960). Forecasting sales by exponentially weighted moving averages. *Management Science*, *6*(3), 324–342. doi:10.1287/mnsc.6.3.324

42 Jofipasi, C., Miftahuddin, M., and Sofyan, H. (2018). Selection for the best ETS (error, trend, seasonal) model to forecast weather in the Aceh Besar District. *IOP Conference Series:Materials Science and Engineering*, 352. doi:10.1088/1757-899X/352/1/012055

43 Sindhanuru, H. (2021, 8, 19). *Exponential Smoothing (ETS) Framework*. Retrieved July 26, 2021, from Latent View: https://www.latentview.com/idealab/ exponential-smoothing-ets-framework/

44 Kuha, J. (2004). AIC and BIC: Comparisons of assumptions and performance. *Sociological Methods & Research*, *33*(2), 188–229. doi:10.1177/0049124103262065

45 Brownlee, J. (2020, August 28). *Machine Learning Mastery – Making Developers Awesome of Machine Learning*. Retrieved September 9, 2021, from Probabilistic Model Selection with AIC, BIC, and MDL: https://machinelearningmastery.com/ probabilistic-model-selection-measures/

46 Portet, S. (2020). A primer on model selection using the Akaike Information Criterion. *Infectious Disease Modelling*. doi:10.1016/j.idm.2019.12.010

47 Stocks, T., Britton, T., and Höhle, M. (2020). Model selection and parameter estimation for dynamic epidemic models via iterated filtering: Application to rotavirus in Germany. *Biostatistics*, *21*(3), 400–416. doi:10.1093/biostatistics/kxy057

48 Wendi, L., Sanyi, T., and Yanni, X. (2015). Model selection and evaluation based on emerging infectious disease data sets including A/H1N1 and Ebola. *Computational and Mathematical Methods in Medicine*, *2015*, 14. doi:10.1155/2015/207105

49 Cleveland, R. B., Cleveland, W. S., McRae, J. E., and Terpenning, I. (1990). STL: A seasona-trend decomposition procedure based on loess. *Journal of Official Statistics*, 6, pp. 3–373.

50 Koopmans, L. H. (1995). *Multivariate Spectral Models and Their Applications*. Amsterdam: Science Direct-Elsevier.

51 Hyndman, R. J. and Khandakar, Y. (2008). Automatic time series forecasting: The Forecast Package for R. *Journal of Statistical Software*, *27*.

52 Analytics Vidhya. (2020, July 12). *Analytics Vidhya.* Retrieved September 13, 2021, from Basics of Forecast Accuracy: https://medium.com/analytics-vidhya/basics-of-forecast-accuracy-db704b0b001b

53 Ljung, G. M. and Box, G. E. (1978). On a measure of a lack of fit in time series models. *Biometrika, 65*(2), 297–303. doi:10.1093/biomet/65.2.297

20 Recent Advancement in Deep Learning
Open Issues, Challenges, and a Way Forward

Sakshi Purwar and Amit Kumar Tyagi
Vellore Institute of Technology, Chennai, India

CONTENTS

20.1 INTRODUCTION

Profound learning is a next degree of AI: with the assistance of AI, the PC or machine "gains" from the given information. For example, a developer can "encourage" a PC to picture canines by giving it a set of images only some of which contain canines (they would have to be labeled "canine"), while the other part contains something else—felines, for example (labeled "not a canine"). Along with the images, a set of calculation factors is introduced to distinguish between canines and felines. The PC then "gains" from the guidance and uses it to analyze other images, improving over the long run as it effectively recognizes more pictures of canines and felines and adds to its instructing set. If the machine gives incorrect outcomes, a developer would assist with changing the code. It is a strategy that reenacts the construction of the human mind [1]. This strategy is a progression of calculation for tracking down various leveled portrayals of the information [2]. This automation prerequisite empowered the production of insightful frameworks and created a favorable climate for the utilization of the frameworks called human-made brainpower and AI [3]. The framework can check on its own if its pointer is correct or wrong. In this it is completed by consistently evaluating information by means of layers of fake organizations that impersonate the dynamic cycles in our human minds. To function effectively, profound learning calculations require much bigger informational collections than conventional AI applications. Later on, machines will be utilized to do ordinary assignment, what humans are doing on a regular basis. At the moment, however, machines are not capable of recognizing certain sounds and dialects, showing that their capabilities are still below those of humans in this regard. The aim of this chapter is to discuss ways in which this issue can be rectified.

This chapter is organized as follows. Section 20.2 examines advancement and history of profound learning. Inspiration driving this work is examined in Section 20.3. Section 20.4 examines well-known applications utilizing normal language preparing or profound learning neural organization. Advantages and traps/shortcoming of profound learning apparatuses/calculations are discussed in Section 20.5. Existing research related to this work is examined in Section 20.6. Section 20.7 sums up the chapter and offers a few suggestions for future improvements.

20.2   EVOLUTION

Profound learning history traces its roots all the way back to 1943 [4], when Warren McCulloch and Walter Pitts fostered a PC model dependent on the human cerebrum neural organizations. Continuing this concept, Warren McCulloch and Walter Pitts utilized a combination of arithmetic and calculations that they called edge rationale. Profound learning has developed bit by bit from that point forward, with two major breaks in its development throughout the long term. In 1960, Henry J. Kelley is credited for the advancement of the essentials of a constant back propagation model. In 1962, Stuart Dreyfus created a less difficult adaptation dependent on the chain rule. The hypothesis of back engendering existed since the mid-1960s, but its value hadn't been realized until 1985. The most punctual endeavors to foster profound learning calculation date back to 1965, when models of polynomial (confounded condition) initiation work were utilized by Alexey Grigoryevich Ivakhneko and Valentin Grigoryevich Lapa, which were then examined statically. A short pause in the creation followed, until Kunihiko Fukushima, who fostered the neural organizations with various pooling and developmental layers, first utilized traditional neural organizations (see Figure 20.1). In 1979, Fukushima made a fake neural organization, called acknowledgment, utilizing multifaceted, various-leveled engineering.

In 1950, Alan Turing published an article titled "Machine and Intelligence," which advertised what today is called the Turing test as a subfield of intelligence. Among the beneficial and successful natural language systems developed in the 1960s was SHRDLU, a natural language system that worked in bounded "blocks of words" with restricted vocabularies; it was written between 1964 and 1966.

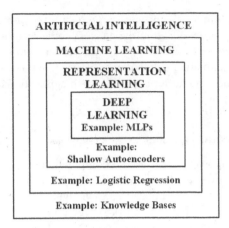

FIGURE 20.1 Evolution of deep learning [4].

20.3 MOTIVATION

Identification of natural language or handwritten language is a vital task and requires attention from computer science (deep learning) researchers to make humans' life easier and longer. Deep learning (DL) can be used in such areas as computer vision, sentiment-based news aggregation, bots, autonomous vehicles, coloring illustrations, image analysis and caption generation, text generation, and language identification [5]. Today's DL is used to provide efficient services without making any hurdle using Artificial Intelligence/Robotics to users, which is also our main task (via designing an algorithm for natural language processing).

20.4 POPULAR APPLICATIONS USING NATURAL LANGUAGE PROCESSING (NLP)

There exist various applications where natural language processing is used, such as handwriting, speech, and text recognition. Some of the popular applications are listed here:

- Finding a certain topic in a database.
- Drawing out facts from a large record.
- Dialogue-based application.
- Solution arrangement.
- Utility hand over a telephone.
- Text-based application

Finding appropriate documents on certain topics from a database of text (for example, finding relevant books in a library) involves drawing out facts from a message. It can also involve finding articles on certain topics (for example building a database of all stock transaction described in news on a given day). Another application is translating documents or publications (e.g., books, training manuals) from one language to another. There are numerous instances in which a solution arrangement system will need to correctly process natural languages; some of those include: (i) search engines, (ii) advanced text editors, (iii) commercial machine translation systems, (iv) information extraction, (v) collaborative filtering, and (f) translation memories. Some DL libraries and popular tools used in such applications will be discussed in the following subsections.

20.4.1 Deep Learning Libraries and Framework

Profound learning empowers multifaceted computational models to learn information portrayals with various deliberation levels. The two techniques have significantly worked on the cutting edge in discourse acknowledgment, visual item ID, and article recognition. At the point where framework is prepared with a lot of information, its reaction can basically match that of a human mind. Indeed, when a circumstance challenges the human mind, it assumes a significant part in filling the hole. We presently have open-source, profound learning systems that are not difficult to utilize and that point toward working on the execution of mind-bogglingly enormous-scope profound learning models. We can present complex models, such as convolution neural organizations utilizing these mind-boggling systems. A profound learning system is a library, interface, or apparatus that makes it simpler and quicker for us to construct profound learning models without going into the hidden calculation particulars. By utilizing an assortment of preconstructed and streamlined segments, they give an unmistakable and succinct approach to characterize models. The greater part of the DL systems is developed with the guide of the field's greatest programming organizations the likes of—and including—Google, Facebook, and Microsoft. These companies own immense volumes of data, high execution foundations, human knowledge, and subsidizing assets. Such apparatuses incorporate Tensor Flow, Microsoft CNTK, Caffe, Caffe2, Torch, PyTorch, and MX Net (alluded in Table A.20.A2). Other DL systems and libraries including Chainer, Theano, Deeplearning4J, and H2O from various gatherings and examination foundations are likewise exciting and fitting for business use. The central issues for a decent profound learning system [6]: Performance upgraded, Good help to the local area, Comprehensible and speedy to code, Calculate slopes naturally, decreased calculations, and parallelized measures. Some of the profound learning systems and libraries are examined in [7].

20.4.1.1 Tensor Flow

Tensor Flow was introduced by engineers and researchers of Google Brain team. It is the popular software library used in the DL field. It is open-source software that supports multiple languages (such as C++, R, Python) to create DL models. Already code is written for most of complex DL models. This framework is issued by Gmail, Uber, Nvidia, and many others. It is considered a registering assortment, yet it also has the capacity to run applications on versatile stages, for example, iOS and Android. It is valuable to fabricate and try different things with designs of profound learning, and its plan is useful for the combination of information, for example, input charts SQL tables and pictures together.

20.4.1.2 PyTorch

Like Tensor Flow, the essential instrument for profound learning applications is PyTorch. This structure is intended for Facebook administrations, utilized by Twitter, and deals power. It is most adaptable edge work. PyTorch is a port to the profound learning outline work of Torch that can be utilized to foster profound neural organizations and figure tensors. Light is a system dependent on Lua, while PyTorch runs on Python. In contrast to Tensor Flow, a progressively refreshed diagram is utilized in the PyTorch library. It implies you can make changes in the process to the engineering. Information parallelism and disseminated learning model are upheld by PyTorch and it has numerous previously prepared models. It is appropriate for momentary tasks and proto-composing. PyTorch programming develops computational charts from tensors and registers. Utilizing PyTorch, we can chip away at a wide range of profound learning difficulties, including pictures (detection, classification, etc.), NLP, and reinforcement learning.

20.4.1.3 Keras

Keras is a Python covering library associated with other DL devices, for example, Tensor Flow, CNTK, Theano, Monet beta, and deep learning 4j reported (Keras2018). Keras is an open-source, quickly advancing, with back-end programming from predominant innovation organizations like Google and Microsoft. It has famous Deep Learning APIi 0 with incredible documentation. It runs on Python 2.7 adaptation to 3.6 variants. It was created and overseen by Francois Chollet. Keras model is used in serialization/deserialization, APIs, call-backs, and information stream utilizing Python generators.

20.4.1.4 Sonnet

Based on top of Tensor Flow, Sonnet is a profound learning stage. It is planned by the world-popular organization Deep Mind to make neural organizations with a perplexing engineering. Undeniable level item situated libraries trigger intricacy when planning calculations for the production of neural networks (NN) or other forms of machine learning (ML). Sonnet's fundamental benefit is that we can utilize it to reproduce easily the examination displayed in Deep Mind's papers than Keras, as Deep Mind will utilize Sonnet itself.

20.4.1.5 MXnet

MXnet is a profound learning device that is exceptionally versatile and can be utilized on a wide scope of gadgets. This system upholds an enormous number of dialects, including C++, Python, R, Julia, Javascript, Scala, and Perl. It works equally well on different GPUs (with enhanced calculations and quick setting exchanges). It has a capacity to tackle any issue quickly.

20.4.1.6 DL4j (Deep Learning for Java)

Profound taking in 4j or DL4J contrasts with various ML/DL structures in its API dialects, reasoning, and reconciliations. It is a current open-supply, designated, DL library created in Java (JVM), expected in the business Java advancement environment and Big Data preparation. DL4J structure accompanies worked-in GPU help, that is, a significant capacity for the schooling technique and supports Hadoop and Spark (DL4J 2018; Sky mind 2017). The library consists of various subdrives along with uncooked records changed into work vectors (DataVec), hardware for NN design (DeepLearning4j), and third model import (Python and Keras styles). Deeplearning4j has Java, Scala, and Python APIs. It serves for different sorts and configurations of info data without issues extendable by other specific sorts and codecs. The DataVec toolbox acknowledges uncooked data comprehensive of pictures, video, sound, text, or time assortment on entering and permits its ingestion, standardization, and change into included vectors. It likewise can stack insights into Spark RDDs. DL4J incorporates some of the significant NLP gear along with Sentence Iterator (for taking care of literary substance piece by utilizing piece solidly into a natural language processor), Tokenizer (for fragmenting the printed content at the degree of single words or n-grams), and Vocab (reserve for putting away metadata). Particular codecs might be brought through upholding custom entering organizes correspondingly as in Hadoop through Input Format. We present numerous profound neural organization executions with different programming bundles in Table A.20.A2.

20.5   BENEFITS AND PITFALLS OF EXISTING ALGORITHMS

Deep learning and neural network are used in many applications today. For applications like image, text, audio, video, etc., recognition DL is used. Deep learning solves some recognized characters (printed or handwritten) very efficiently. We do face several challenges and disadvantages with DL and variants of neural networks. Overall, we also get several benefits with DL and its tools with solving real-world problems.

Advantages: Deep mastering is an application that previously required imaginative and prescient knowledge into engineering challenges solvable by way of non-vision professionals. Deep mastering transfers the logical burden from a software developer, who develops and scripts a regulations-based algorithm, to an engineer training the gadget. It additionally opens a brand-new variety of possibilities to remedy packages that have in no way been tried without a human inspector. In this manner, DL makes device vision less difficult to work with, while expanding the bounds of what a computer and digital can and should be inspecting. On other hand, there is no need to design the features; they are automatically learned to be suitable for the task at hand, and robustness to natural data variability is automatically learned. The same neural network path can be used for many different applications and data types. Performance improves with more data; the method is massively parallelizable.

Disadvantage: Deep learning studying requires a huge dataset and, subsequently, a lengthy practice period in terms of cost. Device mastering methods like SVMs and other habits are effortlessly deployed even by relative gadget mastering beginners. Deep learning studying approach generally tends to study the entirety of the dataset. It is harder to encode prior information approximately, as the structure of deep learning techniques generally tends to examine everything. It is better to encode earlier expertise about structure of photo (or audio or text), as the discovered characteristics are often difficult to understand. Many imaginative and prescient capabilities are also now not simply human-understandable, for instance, concatenations and combos of different capabilities.

We discuss several deep learning models (including key features, as benefits and weaknesses) in Table A.20.A1. The next section discusses some work related to DL and its open issues.

20.6 RELATED WORK

As per advances applied, in particular PC vision and reach sensor innovation, electronic travel help (ETA) can be isolated into two gatherings. The sense of sight can be compensated by utilizing PC vision (CV) innovation. In [8], new methods are applied to PC vision (CV) to identify static deterrents and moving items while strolling in transit for outwardly disabled. The framework breaks down picture pixels from a camera introduced on the client's chest to decide the line of way and deterrents within the boundary. In [9], a camera utilized edge recognition and planar movement following techniques to recognize steps in the scene. In [10], creators fostered an EYE Cane, a camera-inserted white stick gadget to assist with recognizing the bearing of walk utilizing CV and neural organization calculation. Not many ETAs utilize sound system vision innovation to distinguish hindrances inside and out of the scene [11, 12]. Specialists have utilized smart phones to foster ETAs [13]. A smart phone–based framework was created, and a catadioptric sound system was created and introduced on the smart phone to secure sound system picture sets from the smart phone camera. In [14], creators proposed on-floor CV-based obstruction location calculation that was carried out utilizing a Nokia smart phone.

In ETA, range sensors—for instance, ultra-sensors—are broadly applied to inform the clients about distinguished snags. In [15], utilizing ultrasonic repeating innovation, the researcher introduced a gadget called Shrewd Aide, which is utilized to advise about the obstacles in the way, allowing the client to adjust their path of movement. A Bluetooth correspondence module is incorporated in a Smart Guide gadget and utilized to send messages to any Bluetooth-empowered cell phone. In [16], creators proposed a model of an Electronic Long Cane (ELC) for detecting boundaries over the knee. Vibration actuators and ultrasonic sensors are fixed in the handle of the ELC. In [17], researchers created a gadget with ultrasonic sensors associated with a white stick to find limits. Those sensors are set at inordinate level and espresso level with exceptional heading directions as an approach to find impediments. To acquire 3D pictures from climate machines utilizes a period of-flight camera with infrared (IR) brightening. In 3D photographs the hole data is changed over and delivered to the client utilizing a cluster of 10 self-retractable pins. Ultrasonic sensors are recognizably helpless against apparition echoes.

As a result, obstacles are frequently viewed as shorter than they really are, accordingly decreasing the ultrasonic sensor's incredible reach. In this way the broad ultrasonic pillar projection mentality further mixes the issue of apparition echoes. In ETAs, laser assortment locaters are mounted. For instance, one such gadget was created in [18]. Numerous sensors, including infrared and ultrasonic sensors and spinner, had been installed in [19] to find the apex level and a head level execute. To separate the broad mode and the pointing method of the white stick, whirligig is utilized. The client gets the measurements with the help of two haptic criticism frameworks, explicitly a motivation to emulate the thump of a real stick so a far-off obstruction might be analyzed and a vibrating material figure out how to give a vibe of distance by means of the individual's conspicuous movement. The client can produce a portrayal of climate and accomplish a setting comment with the guide of the utilization of CV-based ETAs. There are downsides to utilizing cameras. These issues might be settled via advanced cells. However, present-day smart phones have reserved space for see cameras, which can likewise allow the individual to painstakingly keep the smart phone inside the course wherein obstacles can emerge [14]. Contrasted with CV-based ETAs, ETAs used for reach sensor age, along with IR and ultrasonic sensors, are especially modest. Such ETAs can be intended to act naturally contained within microcontroller frameworks. However, the realities provided via those ETAs are obliged as best in terms of how the presence and surmised area of the obstructions are expressed to the client. Specialists suppose that criticism delivering systems are used in ETAs. Criticism data that should be familiar to the individual are changed over through activating vibration vehicles into haptic signs in greatest recorded ETAs. So as not to overburden the individual's hearable channels that are regularly needed to discern moving toward danger, pay attention to the surrounding sounds, and keep a conversation, among other things, hearable data is filtered out or transformed into something else. To incite the material sensation, vibration vehicles are utilized even if they interfere with other detecting channels. ETAs convey the vibration vehicles on clothes [12] or gloves [20] with wearable criticism-delivering devices. Hardly any ETAs fixed the criticism devices at the white stick to permit the shopper to encounter the input records while getting the stick [12, 19, 21].

20.7   CONCLUSION

The use of DL or neural networks comes with various shortcomings, as well as some advantages. A lot of research in the previous decades has addressed several issues, including inability to handle large volumes of data, lack of availability of efficient analytic tools, and others. Improvements such as medical algorithm, self-driving cars, investing financial assets, and deep neural networks (DNN) can be used to reduce complexity in these applications (for more applications, refer Table A3). It is important for researchers to add some security features (in DL algorithms) to avoid many serious issues like security, privacy, etc. Hence, this chapter has detailed developments in DL and neural networks (including popular tools). For future work, we can extend our work in solving several real-world problems through new DL techniques/tools, which have not been solved yet (like black box problem, data is too hungry and being produced at very large scale, etc.).

APPENDIX A

TABLE 20.A1
Deep Learning Models and Their Variants (Including Key Features)

Description of Models	Key Features
Deep Neural Network a) General deep framework usually used for classification or regression b) Made of many hidden layers (more than 2) c) Allows complex (nonlinear) hypotheses to expressed	**Benefits** a) Widely used with successes in many areas **Weaknesses** a) Training is not trivial because once the error is back-propagated to the first few layers, they become minuscule b) The learning process can be very slow
Deep Autoencoder a) Aim to recreate the input vector b) It has same number of input and output nodes c) It is an unsupervised learning method	**Benefits** a) Does not require labeled data for training b) Many variations have been proposed to make the representation more robust; Sparser autEnc.[6], DenoisingAutEnc.[7], Contractive AutEnc.[8], Convolutional AutEnc.[9] **Weaknesses** a) Require a pre-training stage b) Training can also suffer from vanishing of the error
Deep Belief Network a) In this composition of RBM where each subnetwork's hidden layer serves as the visible b) Layer for the next c) Has undirected connection just at the top two layers d) Allows unsupervised and supervised training of the network	**Benefits** a) Proposed a layer-by-layer greedy learning strategy to initialize the network b) Inference tractable maximizing the likelihood directly **Weaknesses** a) Training procedure is computationally expensive due to the initialization process and sampling
Convolutional Neural Networks a) It is well suited for 2D data such as images b) Every hidden convolutional filter transforms its input to a 3D output volume of neuron activations c) It is inspired by the neurobiological model of the visual cortex	**Benefits** a) Few neuron connections required with respect to typical NN **Weaknesses** a) It may require many layers to find an entire hierarchy of features b) It usually requires a large dataset of labeled images
Recurrent Neural Networks a) It is capable of analyzing streams of data b) Useful in application where the output depends on the previous computations c) Share the same weights across all steps	**Benefits** a) Can memorize sequential events b) Can model time dependencies c) It shows great success in natural language processing applications **Weaknesses** a) Learning issues are frequent due to vanishing gradient problem

TABLE 20.A2
Deep Neutral Network Implementation (Software-Wise) [22–28]

Name of Tools	License	Platform	Interface	OpenMP Support	Supported Techniques			Cloud Computing
Caffe	Free BSD	Linux, Win, OSX, Andr	C++, Python, MATLAB	NO	YES	YES	NO	NO
CNTK	MIT	Linux, Win	Command Line	YES	YES	YES	NO	NO
Deep learning 4Jk	Apache 2.0	Linux, Win, OSX, Andr	Java, Scala, clojure	YES	YES	YES	YES	NO
Wolfurm Muth	Proprietary	Linux, Win, OSX, Cloud	Java, C++	NO	NO	YES	YES	YES
Tensor flow	Apache2.0	Linux, OSX	Python	NO	YES	YES	YES	NO
Thenno	BSD	Cross-Platform	Python	YES	YES	YES	YES	NO
TORCH	BSD	Linux, Win, OSX, Andr, iOS	Lua, LuaJIT, C	YES	YES	YES	YES	NO

TABLE 20.A3
Application of Deep Learning

Author	Applications	Method/Algorithm	Year
Tai Sing Lee, David Mumford	Hierarchical Bayesian inference in the visual cortex	Particle filtering and Bayesian- belief Propagation	2003
Hinton,Geoffrey, E.Simon Osindero, Yee-Whyeteh.	Digit classification	Complementary priors on belief networks	2006
Mohammed, Abdel-Aramean, George Dahl, Geoffrey Hinton	Deep belief networks for phone recognition	Back-propagation and associative memory architecture	2009
Abdel-Hamid Ossama, Mohamed Abdel-rahman, Jiang Hui,Penn Gerald	Multi-speaker speech recognition	Local filtering and max pooling infrequency domain	2012
Kiran B. Raja, R. Raghavendra, Vinay Krishna Vemuri, Christoph Busch	Iris recognition by using smart phone cameras	Deep sparse filtering	2015

REFERENCES

1. R. Wason, "Deep learning: evolution and expansion," *Cognitive System Research*, 2018, 52, 701–708.
2. E. Bati, "Deep convolution neural networks with an application towards geospatial object recognition," *Diss. Middle East Technical University Ankara*, 2014.
3. S. H. Tajmir, and T. K. Alkasab, "Toward augmented radial changes in radiology education in the era of machine learning and artificial intelligence," *Academic Radiology*, 2018, 25, 747–750.
4. Kamalika Some, "The history evolution and growth of deep learning", October 2018, https://www.analyticsinsight.net/the-history-Evolution-and-growth-of-deep-learning.
5. https://www.cleanpng.com/png-machine-learning-deep-learning-artificial-intellig-3386961/download-png.html.
6. Pulkit Sharma, "5 Amazing Deep Learning Frameworks Every Data Scientist Must Know!", March 2019, https://towardsdatascience.com/top-10-best-deep-learning-frameworks-in-2019-5ccb90ea6de.
7. Oleksii Kharkovyna, "Top 10 Best Deep Learning Frameworks in 2019", June 3, 2019, https://towardsdatascience.com/top-10-best-deep-learning-frameworks-in-2019-5ccb90ea6de.
8. J. Jose, M. Farrajota, J. M. Rodrigue, iand J. M. H. du Buf, "The smart vision local navigation aid for blind and visually impaired persons", *International Journal of Digital Content Technology and its Applications*, 2011, 5, 362–375.
9. D. C. Hernandez, T. Kim and K.H. Jo, "Stairway detection-based ion single camera by motion stereo", *24th International Conference on Industrial Engineering and Other Application of applied Intelligent Systems*, 2011, Syracuse.
10. J. S. Ju, EKo, and E. Y. Kim, "EYE Cane: navigating with camera embedded whitecane for visually impaired person", *11th ACM Conference on Computers and Accessibility*, 2009, Pittsburgh.
11. L. Chen, B. L. Guo, and W. Sun, "Obstacle detection system for visually impaired people based on stereo vision", *2010 4th International Conference on Genetic and Evolutionary Computing*, 2010.
12. V. Pradeep, G. Medioni, and J. Weiland, "Awearable system for the visually impaired", *32nd annual International Conference of the IEEE Engineering in Medicine and Biology Society*, 2010, Buenos Aires.
13. S. Akhter, J. Mir Salahuddin, F. B. Marquina, et al., "A smartphone-based haptic vision substitution system for the blind", *IEEE 37th Annual Northeast Bio Engineering Conference*, 2011, Troy.
14. E. Peng, P. Peursum, L. Li, and S. Venkatesh, "A smartphone-based obstacle sensor for the visually impaired", *7th International Conference on Ubiquitous Intelligenceand Computing*, 2010, Xi'an.
15. D. Abdul Rasool and S. Sabra, "Mobile-embedded smart guide for the blind", *2011 International Conference on Digital Information and Communication Technology and Its Applications*, 2011, Bourgogne.
16. A. R. García, R. Fonseca, and A. Dura´n, "Electronic long cane for locomotion improving on visual impaired people: a case study", *2011 Pan American Health Care Exchanges*, 2011, Brazil.
17. M. Okayasu, "Newly developed walking apparatus for identification of obstructions by visually impaired people," *Journal of Mechanical Science and Technologya*, i 2010, 24, 1261–1264.

18. Kurata, M. Kourogi, T. Ishkawa, et al., "Indoor-outdoor navigation system for visually-impaired pedestrians: preliminary evaluation of position measurement and obstacle display", *15th Annual International Symposium on Wearable Computers*, 2011, San Francisco.

19. S. Gallo, D. Chapais, L. Santos-Carreras, et al., "Augmented white cane with multimodal haptic feedback", *3rd IEEE RAS & EMBS International Conference on Biomedical Robotics and Biomechatronics*, 2010, Tokyo.

20. S. Krishna, S. Bala, T. McDaniel, et al., "VibroGlove: an assistive technology aid for conveying facial expressions", *28th ACM Conference on Human Factors in Computing Systems*, 2010, Atlanta.

21. T. Ando, M. Yamamoto, M. Seki, and M. G. Fujie, "Development of a cane with a haptic interface using IC tags for the visually impaired", *2009 IEEE/RSJ International Conference on Intelligent Robots and Systems*, 2009, St. Louis.

22. Center Berkeley, "Caffe," 2016 [Onlinc]. Available: http://caffe.berkeleyvision.org/

23. Microsoft, "Cntk," 2016 [Online]. Available: https://github.com/Microsoft/CNTK

24. Skymind, "Deeplearning4j," 2016 [Online]. Available: http://deeplearning4j.org/

25. Wolfram Research, "Wolfram math," 2016. [Online]. Available: https://www.wolfram.com/mathematica/

26. Google, "Tensorflow," 2016 [Online]. Available: https://www.tensorflow.org/

27. THEANO=Universite de Montreal, "Theano," 2016 [Online]. Available: http://deep-learning.net/software/theano/

28. R. Collobert, K. Kavukcuoglu, and C. Farabet, "Torch," 2016 [Online]. Available: http://torch.ch/

Index